FROM THE LIBRARY OF
ROBERT LORAN FORD

W9-BUE-056

A BAPTIST
SOURCE BOOK

*With Particular Reference
to Southern Baptists*

Robert A. Baker

BROADMAN PRESS

Nashville, Tennessee

© 1966 • BROADMAN PRESS
All rights reserved
4265-19
ISBN: 0-8054-6519-7

DEWEY DECIMAL CLASSIFICATION NUMBER: 286.09
Library of Congress Catalog Card Number: 66-22076
Printed in the United States of America

FROM THE LIBRARY OF
ROBERT LORAN FORD

Preface

During nearly twenty-five years of teaching Baptist history I have carried books by the armload to class in order to give the students a firsthand glimpse of the materials from which history is constructed. The 241 documents selected for this book are the ones most often used. They provide source materials for much of Southern Baptist life. As a means of including as many documents as possible in the wordage allotted, the introductory sections have been kept brief. Many fine documents had to be eliminated. Those referring to the organizational structure of the Southern Baptist Convention have been published by the Executive Committee under the title, *The Southern Baptist Convention Organization Manual* (Nashville, 1964), making it possible to bypass those documents here.

The title given this work was chosen as the best description of the material. The collection includes documents on Negro Baptist history, several on Landmark and English Baptists, and over seventy-five which relate immediately to Baptists in the North. All of these are relevant to Southern Baptist history.

In the reproduction of the documents, both the source and a standard work which quotes the material are sometimes shown. This does not necessarily mean reliance on a secondary work, for I have either personally copied or examined most of the documents quoted herein. It is often difficult to know which text to use when there are variations in the several copies of a source such as Morgan Edwards, for example. In such cases the version used by an authoritative state scholar helps standardize the text. There are a few instances where the secondary work has been the only text available to me. Every effort has been made to insure accuracy in locating and transcribing the materials. Occasionally, some liberty is taken in the use of titles in documentation. For example, rather than follow the wavering between "Proceedings" and "Annual" relative to the Southern Baptist Convention, the uniform title "Annual" is used. "Minute" is chosen for the annual reports of the Home Mission Society.

Many people have contributed to this work. Baptist writers, North and South, have preserved these and many other valuable documents; and even though the material is in the public domain, indebtedness is acknowledged to men like Edwards, Backus, Benedict, Semple, Foss and Mathews, Ryland, and Paschal. I would also express appreciation for my distinguished teacher, W. W. Barnes, who introduced me to this field of investigation many years ago. My thanks to Mrs. Sue Rainey, my secretary, who has spent many hours in copying and verifying texts and has caught many of my errors before they were put into print. I hasten to add, however, that the errors which still remain are my own and not hers. My companion at home has made her usual valuable contribution.

ROBERT A. BAKER

FROM THE LIBRARY OF
ROBERT LORAN FORD

Contents

PART FOUR. SEPARATION AND WAR (1845-1865)

PART FIVE. GROWTH OF DENOMINATIONAL CONSCIOUSNESS (1865-1917)

PART SIX. THE MODERN PERIOD (1917-1966)

Part One
Beginnings of Southern Baptist Life
1682-1740

Section One

Background of Southern Baptist Churches

The first Southern Baptists were the Particular and General Baptist immigrants from England, some of them by way of New England.

Particular Baptists from New England

The first Baptist church in the South was located in Charleston, South Carolina. Its first pastor, William Screven, and some of its members came from Kittery, Maine, bringing a Particular Baptist church already in existence. At Charleston this group united with other Baptists from England, mainly Particular Baptists. The following documents describe the ordination of William Screven in Maine, the organization of the church at Kittery in 1682, the church covenant adopted at that time, and an excerpt from the Assembly Confession of English Baptists of 1689 which illustrates the distinctive doctrine of the atonement held by Particular Baptists.

1. William Screven set apart

A Coppy of A writing given to Brother Screeven in answer to A Request by letter from A Brother and others. Agreed upon att A Church meeting the 11th of 11 mo 1681. From the Church of Christ in Boston the 11th of 11 mo 1681. To all whome itt may concerne these are to Certify that our beloved Brother William Screeven is A member in Comunion with us and haveing had tryall of his gifts Amongst us and finding him to be A man whome god hath quallifyed & furnished with the gift of his holy spiritt and grace, enabling him to open and Apply the word of god which may be through the blessing of the lord Jesus usefull in his hand for the begitting and building up soules in the knowledg of god, doe therefore Appoint & Approve & alsoe encourage him to Exercise his gift in ye place where he lives or else where as the providence of god may cast him & soe the lord help him to Ey his glory in all things and to walk humbly in ye fear of his name.

signed by us in the behalf
of ye rest   ISAACK HULL
JOHN FARNUM.

(Church Record of First Baptist Church, Boston, Massachusetts.)

2. The Kittery church organized

Upon serious & Solemn Consideration of the Church About A motion or Request made by severall members that lived att Kittery, y^t they might become A Church & that they might p-ceed therein provided they were such as should be Approved for such A Foundacon work, the Church gave there grant and att ye time Appointed did send severall messengers to make y^t strict Inquiry & Examinason as they ought in such A case who att there Returne brought ye Coppys here Inserted 26th of 7 mo 1682.

The Church of Christ att Boston y^t is baptized upon profession of faith haveing taken into serious consideration ye Request of our Brethren att Kittery Relateing to there being A Church by themselves y^t soe they might Injoy the precious ordinances of Christ which by reson of distance of habitason they butt seldome could injoy have therefore thought meet to make Choice of us whose names are und'written as Messengers to Assist them in ye same and coming up to them we have found them A Competent Number and in ye same faith with us for upon carefull examination of them in matters of Doctrine & practise & soe finding one with us by there (we hope) Conshiencous Acknowledgm^{tt} of ye Confession of faith putt forth by ye Elders & Brethren of ye Churches in London and ye Contry in England dated in ye year 1682.

And they haveing given themselves up to ye lord & too one Another in A Solemn Covenant to walk as said Covenant may Express & alsoe haveing Chosen theire officers whome they with us have Appointed & ordained, we doe therefore in ye name of ye lord Jesus & by the Appointm^{tt} of his Church deliver them to be A Church of Christ in ye faith and order of ye Gospel.

signed by us in ye name of ye Church the 25 of 7 mo 1682.

ISAACK HULL
THOMAS SKINNER
PHILLIPP SQUIRE.

(Ibid.)

3. *The covenant of the church*

Wee whose names are here und'written doe solemnly & on good Consideration god Assisting us by his grace give up our selves to ye lord & to one another in Solem Covenant, wherein wee doe Covenant & promise to walk with god & one with another In A dew and faithfull observance of all his most holy & blessed Commandm.^{tts} Ordinances Institutions or Appointments, Revealed to us in his sacred word of ye ould & new Testament and according to ye grace of god & light att present through his grace given us, or here after he shall please to discover & make knowne to us thro his holy Spiritt according to ye same blessed word all ye Dayes of our lives and this will wee doe, If ye lord graciously please to Assist us by his grace and Spiritt & to give us Divine wisdome, strength, knowl-

edg, & understanding from Above to p-forme ye same without which we cann doe nothing John 15:4 2 Corinthians 3:5.

Signed by
WM SCREEVEN, Elder
HUMPHRY CHURCHWOOD, Deacon·
ROBERT WILLIAMS
JOHN MORGRADYE
RICHARD CUTT
TIMOTHY DAVIS
LEONARD DROWN
WM ADDAMS
HUMPHRY AXILL
GEORG LITTEN

This is A true Coppy compared with ye origenall & owned by all our Brethren and seven sisters as Attest
WM SCREEVEN in
behalf of ye rest.

(Ibid.)

4. *Distinctive doctrine of Particular Baptists*

CHAP. III.
Of Gods Decree.

3. By the *decree* of God, for the manifestation of his glory some men and Angels are predestinated, or fore-ordained to Eternal Life, through Jesus Christ, to the praise of his glorious grace; others being left to act in their sin to their just condemnation, to the praise of his glorious justice.

4. These Angels and Men thus predestinated, and fore-ordained, are particularly, and unchangeably designed, and their number so certain, and definite, that it cannot be either increased, or diminished.

5. Those of mankind that are predestinated to life, God, before the foundation of the world was laid, according to his eternal and immutable purpose, and the secret Councel and good pleasure of his will, hath chosen in Christ unto everlasting glory, out of his meer free grace and love; without any other thing in the creature as a condition or cause moving him thereunto.

6. As God hath appointed the Elect unto glory, so he hath by the eternal and most free purpose of his will, fore-ordained all

the means thereunto, wherefore they who are elected, being faln in Adam, are redeemed by Christ, are effectually called unto faith in Christ, by his spirit working in due season, are justifyed, adopted, sanctified, and kept by his power through faith unto salvation; neither are any other redeemed by Christ, or effectually called, justified, adopted, sanctified, and saved, but the Elect only.

(From W. J. McGlothlin, *Baptist Confessions of Faith* [Philadelphia, 1911], pp. 233-34.)

General Baptists from England

Some of the members of the first Baptist church in the South were General Baptists from England. The following documents record a call from Carolina to English General Baptists in 1702 and two articles from the General Baptist Confession of 1679 illustrating their doctrine of the atonement and their centralized organizational viewpoint.

1. Call from Carolina in 1702

Whereas our Brethren of the Baptist perswation and of the Generall Faith who haue their aboad in Caralina haue desierd us to Supply them with a Ministry or with books, we being not able at present to doe the former haue collected ye Sum of Seuen pounds twelve Shillings wch wth wt can be farther obtain'd we haue put into the hands of our Bror S Keeling to Supply ym wth ye latter. & yt ye sd Bror Keeling doe wright a letter to them in the name of this Assembly.

(From W. T. Whitley, ed., *Minutes of the General Assembly of the General Baptist Churches in England* [London, 1909], I, 75.)

2. Distinctive doctrines of General Baptists

(1) Universal atonement

XVIII. ARTICLE
Of Christ dying for all mankind.
God the father, out of his royal bounty,

and fountain of love, when all mankind was fallen by sin, in breaking of the first covenant of works made with them in Adam, did chuse Jesus Christ, and sent him into the world to die for Adam, or fallen man. And God's love is manifest to all mankind, in that he is not willing, as himself hath sworn, and abundantly declared in his word, that mankind should perish eternally, but would have all to be saved, and come to the knowledge of the truth. And Christ died for all men, and there is a sufficiency in his death and merits for the sins of the whole world, and hath appointed the gospel to be preached unto all, and hath sent forth his spirit to accompany the word in order to beget repentance and faith: so that if any do perish, it's not for want of the means of grace manifested by Christ to them, but for the non-improvement of the grace of God, offered freely to them through Christ in the gospel.

(From W. J. McGlothlin, *op. cit.*, pp. 137-38.)

(2) Centralized ecclesiology

XXXIX. ARTICLE.
Of general Councils, or Assemblies.

General councils, or assemblies, consisting of Bishops, Elders, and Brethren, of the several churches of Christ, and being legally convened, and met together out of all the churches, and the churches appearing there by their representatives, make but one church, and have lawful right, and suffrage in this general meeting, or assembly, to act in the name of Christ; it being of divine authority, and is the best means under heaven to preserve unity, to prevent heresy, and superintendency among, or in any congregation whatsoever within its own limits, or jurisdiction. And to such a meeting or assembly, appeals ought to be made, in case any injustice be done, or heresy, and schism countenanced, in any particular congregation of Christ, and the decisive voice in such general assemblies is the major part, and such general assemblies have lawful power to hear, and determine, as also to excommunicate.

(*Ibid.*, p. 154.)

Section Two

Earliest Baptist Churches in the South

South Carolina

1. Charleston

(1) *Letters of William Screven while pastor*

a. *To the Boston Church on June 2, 1707*

Dearly beloved, this may inform you, that I have many thoughts of heart about you, and am much concerned for you; and hope I may say, my prayers are to God for you, though I am not with you; nor can I come as I was inclined to do, our help being taken from us; for our minister who came from England is dead, and I can by no means be spared. I must say it is a great loss, and to me a great disappointment, but the will of the Lord is done. I have longed to hear that you was supplied with an able minister, who might break the bread of life among you; but if the Lord do not please to supply you in the way you expected, your way will be to improve the gifts you have in the church. Brother Callender and Joseph Russell, I know, have gifts that may tend to edification, if improved. I think you should call one or both of them to it.

(From Isaac Backus, *A History of New England* [Newton, Mass., 1871], 2d ed., I, 467-68.)

b. *To Ellis Callender of Boston on August 6, 1708*

I rejoice that you are inclined to, and employed in, the blessed work of the Lord for the support of his cause, and the comfort of his saints left to a poor, languishing church with you; as it must and will, with the blessing of God, be if you have the blessed ordinances of the holy Jesus among

you again. . . . I pray God to be with your spirit and strengthen you to the great work to which you are called; and that the little vine may be flourishing under your hand. . . . I have been brought very low by sickness; but I bless God I was helped to preach and administer the communion last Lord's day, but am still weak. Our society are for the most part in health, and I hope thriving in grace. We are about ninety in all. I rest your affectionate brother and fellow-laborer, in the best of services, for the best reward,

WILLIAM SCREVEN.

(*Ibid.*)

(2) *Letters to church from England in 1711*

The church at Charleston almost had a schism over the severe treatment of a Negro slave by one of its members. Evidently William Fry and William Sadler had written for advice to the South Moulton Baptist Church in Devonshire, since the replies were addressed to them. The South Moulton church took the side of the slaveholder, but said it would refer the matter to the association. The Western Baptist Association took the same position as the church.

a. *From the South Moulton Baptist Church, Devonshire*

Bretherin and belov'd for Jesus Sake

Your [letter] rec'ed and the 7 of the 11th month 1710, was read, which Occassioned much Sorrow, and heaviness in our hearts, upon information of the low condition of your Sion, and the difference which, as a root of bitterness, is Sprung up among you, and trouble you. And whereas you have Sent to us by letter, to Crave our assistance, for composing the Said difference; you may assure your Selves, we have done our utmost, both by our prayers, and Studys, to Effect the Same; reckoning our Selves bound in gospell bonds to Endeavor yours, as well as our own Welfare.

We must not pretend to an Infallable Judgment and therefore in your case, it being dubious, wee give not a finall determination; but our Opinion. The mater of difference, and what hath been occasion of Offence, we apprehend, to bee a Brother's dealing with his transgressing Slave, after Such manner, (as thought by Some of you) not becomming a Church.

. . . .

Take nothing amiss at our hands Brethren, but receive this as from your cordiall friend, And we beg leave to acknowledge as before, that we, knowing but in part, and practising but in part, do Suspend our determination, designing on your behalf to represent it to our next Association, where we hop to have the concurrent Judgment of many able Ministers, designing, by the will of God to Communicate it to you when oppertunity may offer, and till then we commite you to the care, guidances, and protection of the great Shepheard of the Sheep, who thro, the Eternall Spirite offered him Self without Spot for his Church, and is assended up on high, having received guifts for men, and is able to furnish man with, numerous guifts, graces, and comforts, that you may be built up, beautified and made meett to be partakers of the Inheritance with the Saints in light, which is the hearty prayer of us your poor Sympathizing Bretheren in the bonds of the blessed gospell of Chr.

b. *From the Western Baptist Association in England*

The opinion of the major part of the members of Association (Some few Excepted who Submitted)

As to that case you represent to us, for our Judgment Concerning the punishment of a Male Negro Slave. We apprehend, the Master, Acting according to the Law of your Province, in gelding his Slave, hath not Commited any Crime, to give any Offence to Any Member to break Communion with him in the Church; because we finde by Scripture, that 'tis lawfull to buy them, Gen: 17. 13,23,27. And if lawfull to buy them 'tis lawfill to keep them in order, and under government; and for Self preservation, punish them to prevent farther Mischief that may Ensue by their running

away and [?] rebelling against their Masters, Exodus 21. 21,21. But we advyse [?] the members of the Church, that they all Endeavour to keep the Unity of the Spirite in the bond of peace. To Avoyd giveing, or takeing Offence on light or Indifferent Causes; but in all things, to walk in love one with another To Show their Charity, And to be mercifull, and Compassionate to all men, to Slaves, and beast, as becomes those that profess the doctrine of a merciful Saviour.

(Originals of these letters in Backus Collection, Andover-Newton Seminary, Newton, Mass.)

(3) An Ornament for Church Members, *by William Screven*

Screven evidently prepared an exhortation to his church under this title, but it is not now extant. Morgan Edwards preserved a section of it.

And now for a close of all, (my dear brethren and sisters, whom God hath made me, poor unworthy me, an instrument of gathering and settling in the faith and order of the gospel) my request is, that you, as speedily as possible, supply yourselves with an able and faithful minister. Be sure you take care that the person be orthodox in faith, and of blameless life, and does own the confession of faith put forth by our brethren in London in 1689, etc.

(From David Benedict, *A General History of the Baptist Denomination in America* [Boston, 1813], II, 123.)

2. Welsh Neck Church

The second center of Baptist infiltration into South Carolina took place in the vicinity of what is now Society Hill. The story begins in Wales. Several Baptists in the counties of Penbroke and Caermarthen in Wales organized themselves into a Baptist church in 1701, and in June of that year embarked for America, landing in Philadelphia on September 8, 1701. For about a year and a half they settled in the area of

Pennepek, near Philadelphia. In 1703 they removed to what is known as the Welsh Tract in Delaware. In 1736 a number of them came to South Carolina and accepted land under the generous policy of the English crown which was designed to encourage settlers. In January, 1738, thirty of these Welsh Baptists organized a Baptist church, at first called Peedee, but later termed the Welsh Neck Church.

(1) Excerpts from minutes of Welsh Tract church dismissing their members to form a new church

Our brothron and sisters whos names are as followeth Abel Morgan teaching Elder (Abel Morgan is returned) James James, Ruling Elder Thomas Evan, Deacon Daniel James Samuel Miles [Wilds] John Harry John Harry Junior Thomas Harry Jeremiah Rowel Richard Barrow Thomas Money Nathaniel Evan Mary James Annie Evan Sarah James Mary Wilds Elizabeth Harry Eleanor Jenkin Sarah Harry Margaret William Mary Rowel Sarah Barrow, are removed to Carolina and was recommended by a letter to ye church of Christ in Charles Town or elsewhere in South Carolina, or they might constitute themselves into a church from [sic] us Nov 1735.

Our brother Samuel Evan and his wife Mary Ann Evan was recommended unto our christian friends on pedee in South Carolina April 30, 1737.

Our brethren and sisters whose names are here set down, were recommended unto the care of our christian friends on pedee in South Carolina Daniel Devonald Thomas James David Harry Philip James David James Abol James Simon Persons Mary Boulton Catherine Harry Elizabeth James Elizabeth Jones Elimor James Mary Hugh November 4, 1737.

Our brother John Jones and his wife Ann Jones who were members of our communion are removed and recommended to our christian friends on Pedee in South Carolina by a letter March 11, 1738.

Our sisters Ales Thomas and Jane David

and Mary Dovenald are recommended by letter to our christian friends on Peedee in South Carolina November 3, 1739.

Our brothron and sisters whos names are as followeth Abel Morgan, son and Walter Down Elizabeth Jones Lettis Douglas Rachel Alison Rachel Downs was recommended and dismissed by a letter to our sister church on Pee Dee river in South Carolina Nov ye 1st, 1741.

(From *Records of the Welsh Tract Baptist Meeting . . . 1716 to 1828* [Wilmington, Del., 1904]. Quoted in Leah Townsend, *South Carolina Baptists 1670-1805* [Florence, S. C., 1935], p. 62.)

(2) Founding of church described by Benedict

This church originated in the following manner: In the year 1737, the following Baptist members of the Welsh-Tract church, which was then in the province of Pennsylvania, but now in the State of Delaware, arrived here; viz. James James, Esq. and wife, and three sons, Philip, who was their minister, Abel, Daniel, and their wives; Daniel Devonald and wife, Thomas Evans and wife, one other of the same name and his wife; John Jones and wife, three of the Harrys, Thomas, David, and John and his wife; Samuel Wilds and wife, Samuel Evans and wife, Griffith Jones and wife, and David and Thomas Jones and their wives. These thirty members, with their children and households, settled at a place called Catfish, on Pedee-river, but they soon removed about fifty miles higher up the same river, where they made a permanent settlement, and where they all, except James James, Esq. who died at Catfish, were embodied into a church, Jan. 1738.

(From David Benedict, *op. cit.*, II, 130.)

Virginia

The first Baptist church on record in Virginia was founded by General Baptists from England under the leadership of Robert Norden. It was planted in Prince George County in 1714. The following excerpts in-

clude the pertinent English Baptist records and the American material.

1. An Act of the Virginia Assembly in 1661-62

Whereas, many schismatical persons, out of their averseness to the orthodox established religion, or out of the new fangled conceit of their own heretical inventions, do refuse to have their children baptized; Be it therefore enacted by the authority aforesaid, that all persons who in contempt of the divine sacrament of Baptism, shall refuse when he may carry their child to a lawful minister of that county to have them baptized, shall be amerced two thousand pounds of tobacco; half to the informer; half to the public.

(From Henning's Statutes, quoted in George W. Paschal, *History of North Carolina Baptists* [Raleigh, 1930], I, 55-56.)

2. Excerpts from minutes of General Assembly of the General Baptists of England in their meeting of May 19, 1714

To Stir them Up for Some Assistance for Robt. Norden and Thos. White who are Appointed & Approved by this Assembly to go to Virginia to propogate the Gospell of truth.

. . . .

Agreed the persons Appointed to go to Virginia go with all Conveniant Speed.

(From W. T. Whitley, *op. cit.*, I, 125.)

3. Oath and Subscription by Robert Norden in Virginia in 1715

1715, June 14. Robert Norden an Annabaptist preacher appears in Court and takes the Oaths and Subscribes the Declarations mentioned in the Act of Parliament of the 1st of William & Mary & Entitled an Act for Exempting their Majestys Protest Subjects Dissenting from the Church of England from the penaltys of Certain Laws. Ordered the sd Declarations be recorded.

I Robert Norden do Sincerely promise and Solemnly Declare before God and the World that I will be true and faithful to his Majesty King George, and I do Solemnly promise and Declare that I do from my heart abhor, detest and renounce, as Impious and Hereticall that Damnable Doctrine and Position that Princes Excommunicated or Deprived by the Pope or any Authority of the See of Rome may be Deposed or Murthered by their Subjects or any other whatsoever, and I do Declare that no foreign Prince, Person, Prelate, State Superiority, Preheminence or Authority, Ecclesiastical or Spiritual within this Realm [sic]

ROBERT NORDEN.

I, Robert Norden Profess faith in God the Father and in Jesus Christ his Eternall Sonn the true God and in the Holy Spiritt, One God Blessed for ever more, and I do acknowledge the Holy Scriptures of the Old and New Testament to be given by Divine Inspiration. Robert Norden.

(From *Deed Book of Prince George County, 1714-1720*, No. 1, p. 58.)

4. House of Matthew Marks made public meetinghouse in 1715

Matthew Markes having petitioned this court that his house be entered a publick meeting house for those persons called Annabaptists, its Ordered the same be done accordingly.

1715, July 12. On Motion of Nicholas Robertson its Ordered that his house be recorded a publick meeting house for the Sext of Annabaptists.

(From *Order Book of Prince George County, 1714-20*, p. 20.)

5. References to Isle of Wight and Surrey churches in 1729

There is a comely little church in the Isle of Wight county, of about thirty or forty members, the Elder of which is one Richard Jones, a very sensible old gentleman, whom I have great love for. We see each other at every Yearly Meeting, and sometimes more often. There is another church in Surry county, where my brother Jones lives, I suppose of about thirty more.

(From David Benedict, *op. cit.*, II, 24.)

North Carolina

The earliest North Carolina Baptist churches were at Chowan, Shiloh, Meherrin, and Sandy Run (Bertie), all evidently stemming from the work of General Baptists Paul Palmer and Joseph Parker. As early as 1714 a Church of England minister, John Urmstone, complained that two of his vestrymen in the Chowan Precinct were professed Anabaptists. In 1718 he met similar problems, as seen in the following excerpt.

1. Letter of May 2, 1718, by Urmstone

I have been in Currituck where I baptized 35 children and the mother of one of them: she hath three sisters and two brethren, all adults, the sons and daughters of an Anabaptist, who pretends to be a physician, fortune-teller, and conjuror; always chosen Burgess for that precinct and a leading man in our Assemblies, a fit man you will say for a vestryman, but we have too many such in other vestries, whence it is we find so little favor among them.

(From *Colonial Records*, II, 304. Quoted in Paschal, *op. cit.*, I, 131.)

2. Church in Chowan

This day I received a letter from ye Baptist church in North Carolina, settled about two years (in ye year 1727) since, by Mr. Paul Palmer, signed by John Parker, John Jordan, Benjamin Evans, John Parker, John Brinkley, Michael Brinkley, Thomas Darker, James Copland, John Welch, Joseph Parke, William Copland, Joseph Parker.

This church consists of 32 members, it meets at Chowan.

(From C. E. Barrows [ed.], *The Diary*

of *John Comer* [Philadelphia, 1892], pp. 84-85.)

3. Shiloh church in Camden County

(1) Petition of 1729

To the Worshipful Court of Pascquotank Precinct now setting:

The Honorable Petition of the subscribers, humbly sheweth, That whereas there is a Congregation of the People call[d] Baptis gather[d] In this Precinct, meeting togther for Religious Worship In ye Dwelling House of William Burges, on the north side of Pascotanc, on the head of Raymond's Creek, he, ye said Burges, having granted same for ye use of ye said meeting, we Pray ye same may be recorded and we ye humble Petitioners in duty bound should pray.

W. Burges	William Jones
Paul Palmer	Philip Torksey
Francis Brockett	Robert Wasson
Thomas Herenton	Charles Leutrough

(From J. R. B. Hathaway, *North Carolina Historical and Genealogical Register*, I, 283.)

(2) License of Paul Palmer

North Carolina.

Permission is hereby granted to Paul Palmer, of Edenton, a Protestant Minister to teach or Preach the word of God in any part of the said Province (he having qualified himself as such) pursuant to an Act of Parliament made in the first year of King William and Queen Mary Intitled an "Act for Tolerating Protestant Dissenters."

Given under my hand at Edenton for the 4th day of October Anno Dom., 1738.

(From G. W. Paschal, *op. cit.*, I, 159.)

Part Two
Rapid Expansion in the South
1740-1814

Section One

Organization and Expansion

Development of associations in the South

The first Baptist association in America was the Philadelphia Association founded in 1707. It evidently grew out of the work of Elias Keach at Pennepek, Pennsylvania, and seems to have been a reproduction of the English Baptist associations which had developed there during the civil war under Charles I (1625-49). There is no record of any influence by the Philadelphia Association upon the South during the first period (before 1740). This is not entirely unexpected, for most of the Baptists in Virginia and North Carolina were General Baptists, while the Particular Baptist church at Charleston, South Carolina, had considerable controversy during the first half of the eighteenth century, partly over disagreement between General and Particular Baptists in the church. The Philadelphia Association did influence the South after 1740, however, through their Confession of Faith, through affiliation with southern churches, through the reorganization of many General Baptist churches into Calvinistic churches, and through assistance in organizing new associations in South Carolina and Virginia.

1. Relation of the Philadelphia Association to the South

(1) Their Confession of Faith adopted in 1742

The major part of the Philadelphia Con-

fession of Faith came from England. Before 1660 in England, Baptists had been popularly associated with the violent and heretical radicals of Münster. However, noble Baptist writings were beginning to convince many that Baptists were not anarchists and violent heretics. Furthermore, with the restoration of Charles Stuart in 1660, the Presbyterians, who for a brief season had enjoyed a place in the sun, were transformed into Dissenters by the Episcopal Church. The Presbyterians had published in 1648 the Westminster Confession of Faith, and this became the doctrinal standard of Presbyterians and Congregationalists. In 1677, at a meeting of Particular Baptist leaders in London, a Baptist Confession of Faith was prepared following rather closely the Westminster Confession, probably in an effort to show that Baptists were in many doctrines in complete agreement with other Dissenters in England. After the Act of Toleration of 1689, another meeting of Baptist leaders took place in London in 1689. This 1677 Confession of Faith was approved as a statement of their beliefs, and for that reason is called the Assembly or Second London Confession.

In 1742, the Philadelphia Association in America adopted this Confession of Faith, adding two articles on singing of psalms in worship and laying of hands upon baptized believers. Some of the distinctive parts of this Assembly Confession have been quoted hitherto. The following two articles were added.

CHAPTER XXIII.
OF SINGING PSALMS, &C.

We believe that 'acts 16 25 eph 5 19 col

3 16' singing the praises of God, is a holy Ordinance of Christ, and not a part of natural religion, or a moral duty only; but that it is brought under divine institution, it being injoined on the churches of Christ to sing psalms, hymns, and spiritual songs; and that the whole church in their public assemblies, as well as private christians, ought to 'heb 2 12 jam 5 13' sing God's praises according to the best light they have received. Moreover, it was practiced in the great representative church, by 'matt 26 30 mat 14 26' our Lord Jesus Christ with his disciples, after he had instituted and celebrated the sacred ordinance of his Holy Supper, as a commemorative token of redeeming love.

CHAPTER XXXI.
OF LAYING ON OF HANDS.

We believe that (Heb 5 12 and 6 1 2 Acts 8 17 18 and 19 6) laying on of hands (with prayer) upon baptized believers, as such, is an ordinance of Christ, and ought to be submitted unto by all such persons that are admitted to partake of the Lord's Supper; and that the end of this ordinance is not for the extraordinary gifts of the Spirit, but for (Eph 1 13 14) a farther reception of the Holy Spirit of promise, or for the addition of the graces of the Spirit, and the influences thereof; to confirm, strengthen, and comfort them in Christ Jesus; it being ratified and established by the (Acts 8 and 19 6) extraordinary gifts of the Spirit in the primitive times, to abide in the Church, as meeting together on the first Day of the week was, Acts 2 1 that being the day of worship, or Christian Sabbath, under the gospel; and as preaching the word was, Acts 10 44 and as Baptism was, Mat 3 16 and prayer was, Acts 4 31 and singing Psalms, &c was Acts 16 25 26 so this of laying on of hands was, Acts 8 & ch 19 for as the whole gospel was confirmed by (Heb 2 3 4) signs and wonders, and divers miracles and gifts of the Holy Ghost in general, so was every ordinance in like manner confirmed in particular.

(From W. J. McGlothlin, *op. cit.,* pp. 297-98.)

(2) An Essay on the Authority of Associations adopted by the Philadelphia Association in 1749

The first statement among American Baptists relative to the power of an association was prepared by the Philadelphia Association.

At our annual Association, met September the 19th, 1749, an essay on the power and duty of an Association of churches, was proposed, as above hinted, to the consideration of the Association; and the same, upon mature deliberation, was approved and subscribed by the whole house; and the contents of the same was ordered to be transcribed as the judgment of the Association, in order to be inserted in the Association book, to the end and purpose that it may appear what power an Association of churches hath, and what duty is incumbent on an Association; and prevent the contempt with which some are ready to treat such an assembly, and also to prevent any future generation from claiming more power than they ought—lording over the churches.

ESSAY

That an Association is not a superior judicature, having such superior power over the churches concerned; but that each particular church hath a complete power and authority from Jesus Christ, to administer all gospel ordinances, provided they have a sufficiency of officers duly qualified, or that they be supplied by the officers of another sister church or churches, as baptism, and the Lord's supper, &c.; and to receive in and cast out, and also to try and ordain their own officers, and to exercise every part of gospel discipline and church government, independent of any other church or assembly whatever.

And that several such independent churches, where Providence gives them their situation convenient, may, and ought, for their mutual strength, counsel, and other valuable advantages, by their voluntary and free consent, to enter into an agreement and confederation, as is hinted in our printed Narrative of discipline . . .

Such churches there must be agreeing in doctrine and practice, and independent in their authority and church power, before they can enter into a confederation, as aforesaid, and choose delegates or representatives, to associate together; and thus the several independent churches being the constituents, the association, council or assembly of their delegates, when assembled, is not to be deemed a superior judicature, as having a superintendency over the churches, but subservient to the churches, in what may concern all the churches in general, or any one church in particular; and, though no power can regularly arise above its fountain from where it rises, yet we are of opinion, that an Association of the delegates of associate churches have a very considerable power in their hands, respecting those churches in their confederation; for if the agreement of several distinct churches, in sound doctrine and regular practice, be the first motive, ground, and foundation or basis of their confederation, then it must naturally follow, that a defection in doctrine or practice in any church, in such confederation, or any party in any such church, is ground sufficient for an Association to withdraw from such a church or party so deviating or making defection, and to exclude such from them in some formal manner, and to advertise all the churches in confederation thereof, in order that every church in confederation may withdraw from such in all acts of church communion, to the end they may by ashamed, and that all the churches may discontenance such, and bear testimony against the defection.

. . . .

And further, that an Association of the delegates of confederate church may doctrinally declare any person or party in a church, who are defective in principles or disorderly in practice, to be censurable, when the affair comes under their cognizance, and without exceeding the bounds of their power and duty, to advise the

church that such belong unto, how to deal with such, according to the rule of gospel discipline; and also to strengthen such a church, and assist her, if need be, by sending able men of their own number to help the church in executing the power vested in her by the ordinance of Jesus Christ, and to stand by her, and to defend her against the insults of such offending persons or parties.

(From A. D. Gillette [ed.], *Minutes of the Philadelphia Baptist Association from A.D. 1707, to A.D. 1807* [Philadelphia, 1851], pp. 60-63.)

(3) Sensitivity of Philadelphia Association to church autonomy

The association was quite sensitive to the prerogatives of churches during all this early period. A few examples will illustrate.

a. *Requests for ministerial assistance*

As to a request from the Great Valley, we would have them encourage the gifts they have among them, and send to their nearest neighbors' churches for helps and supplies as often as they and them can agree.

As to the request from Piscataqua, for the help of our ministering brethren at their general meeting, we judge it necessary that our ministering brethren do supply such general meetings; nevertheless, we not knowing who, nor how to bind any of them, we think it necessary that the church, where such are held, send them, that, if possible, they may be certain of some help.

(Ibid., p. 31.)

b. *Appeals to the association*

The following query was left on the book last year for consideration: Whether an appeal from any member of the associated churches, or from one excommunicated from any of said churches, may be made to the Association?

Resolved: That in some cases they may, as every church may sometimes suspend their prerogatives, of which every church is to judge for itself.

. . . .
Some jealousy arising on account of an appeal to the Association, mentioned pages 100 and 101, it was agreed that the word *appeal* was not quite proper, as the Association claims no jurisdiction, nor a power to repeal any thing settled by any church; but if, before settlement, parties agree to refer matters to the Association, then to give their advice.

(*Ibid.*, pp. 101-2, 105.)

c. *Ordination of ministers*

3. The church of Newton desired the Association to appoint time and ministers to ordain Mr. Nicholas Cox; the Association reply, that the appointment of both properly belongs to his church.

(*Ibid.*, p. 119).

2. *Work of Philadelphia Association in the South*

(1) *Virginia*

Philadelphia Association minutes make reference to three churches in Virginia as a part of their body (p. 95): Opekon (Mill Creek), Ketocton, and Smith's Creek. Opekon was "Calvinized" from the remains of a General Baptist group which had come from Maryland (see Semple, p. 375n.). Ketocton was constituted by John Thomas, a Philadelphia Association minister (see Minutes, pp. 65, 95). Smith's Creek was formed by Baptist immigrants from Pennsylvania (see Ryland, pp. 12, 14).

a. *Opekon "Calvinized" in 1752: Report of John Gano*

We examined them, and found that they were not a regular church. We then examined those who offered themselves for the purpose, and those who gave us satisfaction we received, and constituted a new church. Out of the whole who offered themselves, there were only three received. Some openly declared they knew they could not give an account of experiencing a work of grace, and therefore need not offer themselves. Others stood ready to offer if the church was formed. The three before mentioned were constituted, and six more were baptized and joined with them. After the meeting ended, a number of old members went aside and sent for me. They expressed their deplorable state, and asked me if I would meet with them that evening, and try to instruct them. They were afraid the ministers blamed them. They had been misled, but it was not their fault, and they hoped I would pity them. I told them I would with all my heart, and endeavored to remove their suspicion of the ministers. They met, and I spoke to them from these words: *"They being ignorant of God's righteousness, and going about to establish their own righteousness, have not submitted themselves unto the righteousness of God."* I hope I was assisted to speak to them in an impressive manner, and they to hear, at least some of them, so as to live. They afterwards professed and became zealous members, and remained so, I believe, until their death.

(From David Benedict, *op. cit.*, [1860], p. 643.)

b. *Ketocton and Opekon received*

In 1752 the Philadelphia Association received an application from a church at Ketocton, Virginia, which had been constituted in 1751 by John Thomas, a minister of the Philadelphia Association. This is the reference in the Philadelphia minutes to the people in Fairfax County, Virginia.

Appointed Brethren Owen Thomas and Benjamin Griffith to write a letter to some people in Fairfax county, Virginia, in behalf of the Association.

(From A. D. Gillette, *op. cit.*, p. 65.)

Concluded, to receive the church of Ketockton, and the church of Opekon, in Virginia, into fellowship with this Association.

(*Ibid.*, p. 71.)

c. *Ordination of John Garrard*

In connection with a visit of Peter P. VanHorn of New Jersey and Benjamin Miller of Pennsylvania, John Garrard was ordained in Opekon (Mill Creek) in 1755.

This is the reference made in the minutes of the Philadelphia Association in 1755.

Appointed, that one ministering brother from the Jerseys, and one from Pennsylvania, visit North Carolina: the several churches to contribute to bear their expense.

. . . .

Concluded, that it be left to the discretion of the ministering brethren that travel to Carolina, to ordain Mr. Jaret [Garrard], in Virginia.

(Ibid., pp. 72-73.)

d. *Smith's Creek church organized in 1756*

In 1744 several Baptist families moved from Pennsylvania and settled on Smith's Creek (a tributary of the North Fork of the Shenandoah) in Virginia. Various Philadelphia Association ministers visited them, and in the spring of 1756 John Alderson and his wife moved there from New Britain, Pennsylvania. In August, Alderson organized the Smith's Creek Church. Samuel Newman, one of the first settlers in the area, became deacon and clerk, Alderson became pastor.

Smith's Creek, Frederick county, Virginia. John Alderson, pastor, constituted August 16, 1756, joined association October 12, 1762, eleven charter members.

(Ibid., p. 93.)

(2) *In North Carolina*

The first congregations in North Carolina were of the General Baptist order. However, between 1750 and 1760, through the work of ministers from the Philadelphia Association, the General Baptist churches of North Carolina, with the exception of two or three feeble bodies, turned to the Calvinism of the Philadelphia Association. It appears likely that this Calvinizing movement began with the work of Robert Williams of Northampton County, who had learned the Calvinistic doctrines in the Welsh Neck Baptist Church in 1745 and returned to North Carolina about 1750 to preach his views. (See Paschal, op. cit., I, 204 ff.)

Evidently Williams sent word to the Philadelphia Association concerning the needs of North Carolina Baptist churches. This association had already been active in this very kind of work. In 1752 four of its ministers (Benjamin Miller, Isaac Sutton, John Thomas, and John Gano) had traveled southward together to the Potomac at the instruction of the association; then Miller and Sutton had gone to Opekon church at its request to give advice and assistance, while Thomas and Gano went to the Ketocton church, which had requested that some ministers come to observe the ordinances there. Evidently the four met again at Opekon where they reorganized the old General Baptist church into a Calvinistic body. (See the document under Virginia.)

Probably in response to the request of Williams, Gano visited the Carolinas, leaving Philadelphia after the associational meeting in October, 1754. After preaching in Charleston, he made several stops in North Carolina, including one at Fishing Creek (Reedy Creek) in May, 1755, where he had an interesting meeting with the General Baptist leaders (referred to in the quotation from Morgan Edwards). In response to his story, the Philadelphia Association appointed Peter P. VanHorn and Benjamin Miller to visit the Carolina churches. Leaving Philadelphia on Tuesday, October 28, 1755, they visited first the Kehukee church and reorganized it on a Calvinistic basis. Quickly, most of the other General Baptist churches were reorganized into Particular Baptist churches.

Paschal believes that not more than 5 percent of the members of these General Baptist churches were in the newly constituted Particular Baptist churches, and these probably from the solicitation of the ministers who had first been won over. Only elders Joseph Parker, William Parker, and John Winfield remained in their General Baptist convictions. (See Paschal, op. cit., I, 222.)

a. *"Calvinizing" the North Carolina General Baptist churches*

As a typical example of this movement, the account of Morgan Edwards relative to the Fishing Creek (Reedy Creek) church is given.

The [church] began Dec. 6, 1755, when the following pursons were constituted into a church by means of Rev. mess. Benjamin Miller and P. P. Vanhorn: Samuel Davis, Samuel Mangum, James Petty and wife Sarah Davis, Richard Acock and wife, Richard Rennett, Martha Acock. The most remarkable things: (1) This is a church by a kind of transformation from general to particular Baptists, this transformation happened at Quehuky by means of Robert Williams who sowed the seeds of Calvinism, after him a private man, (whose name was William Wallis) conversed with them and made some impression; then Edward Brown preached it, then Thomas Pope; then William Walker; afterwards Gano clenched it in 1753; afterwards by said Miller and Vanhorn. (2) Mother of John McGlamery, Ledbetter and Smart, Thomson, Wm. Washington, Walker. The present minister

REV. WILLIAM WALKER.

Born January 24, 1717, at Newkent county, Virginia. Bred a churchman, embraced the sentiments of the Baptists August 9, 1746, and had the ordinance administered by Wm. Surgenor at Quehooky. Ordained in 1748 by Josiah Hart and Deacon; embraced Calvinism in the year 1752. Took care of the church about 1755. Married Jane Bays, by whom he has children: Peter, Sarah, William, Mary, Martha, James, John, Joel, Lydia, Mercy Hope.

(From Morgan Edwards, *Materials for a History of Baptists in North Carolina.* Quoted in Paschal, *op. cit.,* I, 233-34.)

b. *Reference in Minutes of Philadelphia Association*

Appointed, that one ministering brother from the Jerseys, and one from Pennsylvania, visit North Carolina: the several churches to contribute to bear their expense.

(From A. D. Gillette, *op. cit.,* p. 72.)

c. *The significance of this Calvinizing movement*

Paschal suggests that significant changes resulted from the movement in North Carolina: (1) more emphasis on regeneration rather than baptism; (2) a closely organized and disciplined body celebrating the Lord's Supper regularly; (3) the extensive use of the rigid church covenant, with its strict disciplinary emphasis. Because of its doctrinal and historical interest, as well as its scarcity, one such church covenant is included here as typical of those used in the reconstituted Calvinistic North Carolina Baptist churches.

For as much as God has been graciously pleased to make known unto us by his revealed will, his word of truth, the great privileges of the blessed Gospel of our dear Lord and Saviour Jesus Christ, and hath made us experience his love and favour in that he hath called us from our state of nature in which state we were enemies to God by wicked works, and has revealed Christ in us the hope of glory, therefore, for the better carrying on to our mutual comfort and the advancement of the great privileges of the true religion of the glory of God and praise of his glorious Gospel grace, we whose names are hereunto subscribed, inhabitants of Franklin, Wake and Nash Counties and State of North Carolina, being all of us baptized on a profession of faith and belief of our ever living and only true God, and of a Trinity of Persons in unity of Essence, the Father, the Son and the Holy Ghost, subsisting in the unity of the Godhead, the eternally begotten Son of God, and [one] with the Father in Essence, and equal in Person, in the fulness of time, did take human nature into that inseparable union with his Divine person, and in the same did fulfill the Law, died on the cross, thereby making atonement for sin, satisfied divine justice and purchased peace for sinners, that all mankind fell from the estate of created innocency in, with and by Adam's first sin, and became liable to the wrath of God's holy law, convinced of their estate and condition, consequently have no hope of eternal life, until by the same law convinced of this, and the damning nature of all sin in us from the root, and so made to fly for eternal life by faith in the Lord Jesus Christ who alone is the mediator of the New Covenant, and the redeemer of God's elect without any merit in us, or moving cause of Good in us foreseen to merit his mercy, was delivered to death for our offences, and that we might be truly justified by his free and sovereign grace was raised again for our justification, and in whom only we have redemption through his precious blood, even the forgiveness of our sins, we believe that he ascended into heaven and there sitteth at the right hand of God the Father; from thence he will come to judge the quick and the dead at the last great day, and believing also the doctrine of the Scriptures in all orthodox points, the doctrine of baptism, laying on of hands peculiar to the ministerial function, final perseverance in grace, the resurrection of the dead bodies of men and the eternal judgment, together with all those principles and articles of doctrine and practice contained in the confession of faith adopted by the Baptist Association at Philadelphia anno Dom 1742 and reprinted in 1743, having unanimously appointed the 7th day of September 1793 to join together in a Gospel Church relation and fellowship at Poplar Springs Meeting-House, under the pastoral care of the Reverend William Lancaster, and having spent part of the day in prayer we gave ourselves to the Lord, and unto one another by the will of God according to 2 Corinthians, 8th Chapter and 15th verse; as a church of Christ we do solemnly and voluntarily and mutually covenant with one another to meet together every Lord's day, as many as can conveniently, to celebrate the worship of the Almighty God, to edify one another in his service, in the best manner we can, and do promise to each other to keep the day holy and watch over each of our families and children under our

care, that they may do the same; at all [times] behaving ourselves as becometh the Gospel of our dear Redeemer Jesus Christ whom we now take for our head and king, our prophet and our priest, and according to our ability to promote the glory of God, our own benefit and the good of others so as not to break the order of the Gospel Church by taking upon ourselves any office or dignity of the same of the ministry or other until thereunto called by the voice of the church according to God's ordinances—he that exalteth himself shall be abased, and he that humbleth himself shall be exalted—and that no man taketh the office unto himself unless he is thereunto called; and jointly to maintain the worship of God and to edify one another in love, and as God shall enable us by his grace to maintain the doctrine of the blessed Gospel and to regulate our practices by the word of God, and to watch over one another therein in the Lord, Philippians 2 chapter and 4th verse, and admonish, encourage, and reprove each other if need be according to Gospel rules in love, and to be admonished and reproved by each other as the word of God directs, as far as God shall enable us; to perform all mutual duties towards each other and to those that shall hereafter join with us, and to keep our appointed meetings and to keep our secrets, being taught of God's word that the church of Christ is a garden enclosed, a spring shut up, a fountain sealed; and not to depart from one another illegally or without regular dismission; and that we shall, as God gives us means, ability, conveniency and opportunity, attend on the means of grace, the institution of the ordinances of the Gospel, hoping and relying upon Almighty God for grace, wisdom and spiritual understanding, guidance and ability to adorn this our profession and to perform our duties, hoping that he will bless us with grace suitable to our privileges; which he in his goodness and mercy hath bestowed upon us in his house through Jesus Christ our Lord to whom be glory in the church throughout all ages, world without end, Amen.

To the Church of Christ at Poplar Springs Meeting-House.

A true copy, this 28th November, 1793. Isaac Pippin, C.C.

(From the Church Book of Poplar Springs, copied from the Church Book of Sandy Creek Church in Franklin County, North Carolina. Found in Paschal, *op. cit.*, I, 220-22.)

3. Associations organized in southern states

During this period Baptists in nine southern states formed their first associations, as follows: Charleston, South Carolina (1751); Sandy Creek, North Carolina (1758); Ketocton, Virginia (1766); Salisbury, Maryland (1782); Georgia, Georgia (1784); Elkhorn, South Kentucky, and Salem (all three organized in 1785 in Kentucky); Holston, Tennessee (1786); Mississippi, Mississippi (1807); Illinois, Illinois (1807); and Missouri, Missouri (1809). In addition to these first associations in the several states, additional associations were organized in the South to make a total of sixty-three before 1814. The following excerpts are from the organization of the first association in the South (Charleston) as a typical example.

(1) Organization of the Charleston Association (1751)

Oliver Hart, who had been active in the Philadelphia Association, became pastor of the First Baptist Church, Charleston, South Carolina, in 1749, and through his instrumentality, the first association in the South was organized.

Mr. Hart had seen, in the Philadelphia Association, the happy consequences of union and stated intercourse among Churches maintaining the same faith and order. To accomplish similar purposes, an union of the four Churches before mentioned was contemplated and agreed on. Accordingly on the 21st of Oct. 1751 Delegates from Ashley River and Welch Neck met those of Charleston in the said City.

The Messengers from Euhaw were prevented from attending. It was agreed that an annual meeting thenceforward be holden on Saturday preceding the 2d Sabbath of Nov. to consist of the Ministers and messengers of the several Churches: that the two first days should be employed in public worship, and a Sermon introductory to business preached on the Monday following at 10 o'clock.

The object of the Union was declared to be the promotion of the Redeemer's kingdom, by the maintenance of love and fellowship, and by mutual consultations for the peace and welfare of the churches. The independency of the churches was asserted, and the powers of the Association restricted to those of a Council of Advice. It was agreed to meet again in Charleston, Nov. 1752. At that time the delegates from Euhaw attended, and the proceedings of the first meeting were ratified. The instrument of Union bears the following signatures: John Stephens, Oliver Hart, Francis Pelot, John Brown, (f) Joshua Edwards, (g) Ministers: James Fowler, William Screven, Richard Bedon, Charles Barker, Benjamin Parmenter, Thomas Harrison, Philip Douglas, and John Mikell, Messengers.

(From Wood Furman, comp., *A History of the Charleston Association of Baptist churches in the State of South Carolina* [Charleston, 1811], pp. 8-9.)

The First Great Awakening and Separate Baptists

In 1739 George Whitfield brought the First Great Awakening into the South through his preaching. The earlier Baptists, known as the Regular Baptists, benefited from his ministry, but the effect of the Awakening on Southern Baptists occurred principally in the Separate Baptist movement. In 1739 there were three or four Regular Baptist churches in South Carolina, probably two in Virginia, and one in North Carolina, making a total of six or seven Baptist churches in the South, with about two hundred to three hundred members. *The effect of the Awakening can be glimpsed by the statistics of 1790.*

1. Expansion by 1790

By 1790 Baptist churches had been planted in many states other than the three in which they were found in 1739. Churches were organized in Maryland (1742), Georgia (1772), Tennessee (1779), and Kentucky (1781), and Baptists were swarming elsewhere toward the West.

(1) South Carolina
   70 churches
   48 ordained and 29 licensed preachers
   4,167 members in the churches
(2) Virginia
   204 churches
   150 ordained and 112 licensed preachers
   20,443 members
(3) North Carolina
   94 churches
   77 ordained and 77 licensed preachers
   7,503 members
   Deceded Territory of North Carolina
   18 churches
   15 ordained and 6 licensed preachers
   889 members
(4) Maryland
   12 churches
   8 ordained and 3 licensed preachers
   776 members
(5) Georgia
   42 churches
   33 ordained and 39 licensed preachers
   3,211 members
(6) Kentucky
   42 churches
   40 ordained and 21 licensed preachers
   3,105 members

(From *The Annual Register of the Baptist Denomination in North America:* to the first of November, 190, by John Asplund, *passim.*)

2. Leaders of the Separate Baptist movement

During the Great Awakening in New England in the 1740s, members and ministers separated from the state-established churches, in which religion was at a low ebb, and insisted on vital faith as a prerequisite to church membership. They were popularly called "Separates." When some of them began to require personal faith prior to baptism by immersion, they were called "Separate Baptists." One of these, Shubal Stearns (1706-1771), left his pastorate at Tolland, Connecticut, in August, 1754, "filled with missionary zeal to carry light into dark places," and joined his brother-in-law, Daniel Marshall, at Opekon, Virginia (Mill Creek). Here Stearns was restless, and after receiving a letter from friends in North Carolina telling of the spiritual needs of the people there, he and fifteen others (including Daniel Marshall, Joseph Breed, and their wives) traveled two hundred miles to what is now Randolph County in North Carolina and established the Sandy Creek church in the summer of 1755.

(1) Shubal Stearns

a. A description

Mr. Stearns was but a little man, but of good natural parts, and sound judgment. Of learning he had but a small share, yet was pretty well acquainted with books. His voice was musical and strong, which he managed in such a manner, as one while to make soft impressions on the heart, and fetch tears from the eyes in a mechanical way; and anon to shake the nerves, and to throw the animal system into tumults and perturbations. All the Separate ministers copy after him in tones of voice and actions of body; and some few exceed him. His character was indisputably good, both as a man, a Christian, and a preacher. In his eyes was something very penetrating, which seemed to have a meaning in every glance, of which I will give one example; and the rather because it was given me by a man of good sense, I mean Tidence Lane.

"When the fame of Mr. Stearns' preaching (said Mr. Lane) had reached the Yadkin, where I lived, I felt a curiosity to go and hear him. Upon my arrival, I saw a venerable old man sitting under a peach tree with a book in his hand, and the people gathering about him. He fixed his eyes upon me immediately, which made me feel in such a manner as I had never felt before. I turned to quit the place, but could not proceed far. I walked about, sometimes catching his eyes as I walked. My uneasiness increased and became intolerable. I went up to him, thinking that a salutation and shaking hands would relieve me; but it happened otherwise. I began to think that he had an evil eye, and ought to be shunned; but shunning I could no more effect, than a bird can shun the rattlesnake when it fixes its eyes upon it. When he began to preach, my perturbations increased, so that nature could no longer support them, and I sunk to the ground."

(From Morgan Edwards, *Materials*. Quoted in Paschal, *op. cit.*, I, 286-87.)

b. *One of his letters*

The Lord carries on his work gloriously in sundry places in this province, and in Virginia and in South Carolina. There has been no addition of churches since I wrote last year but many members have been added in many places. Not long since I attended a meeting in Hoy [Haw] river, about thirty miles from hence. About seven hundred souls attended the meeting, which held six days. We received twenty-four persons by a satisfactory declaration of grace, and eighteen of them were baptized. The power of the Lord was wonderful.

(From Isaac Backus, *Abridgement of History of Baptists in New England*, p. 251.)

c. *Covenant assigned to Stearns (1757)*

Paschal thinks that the preamble and concluding paragraph may not reflect the views of Stearns, particularly those phrases which are italicized. Although the Separates were generally very mild Calvinists or leaned toward Arminianism at first, the majority of them became Calvinists before 1810. (See Benedict, op cit., II, 107.)

Holding believers' baptism; laying on of hands; *particular election of grace by predestination of God in Christ;* effectual calling by the Holy Ghost; free justification through the imputed righteousness of Christ; progressive sanctification through God's grace and truth; the final perseverance, or continuance of the saints in grace; the resurrection of these bodies after death, at that day which God has appointed to judge the quick and the dead by Jesus Christ, by the power of God, and by the resurrection of Christ; and life everlasting. Amen.

1st. We do, in the presence of the great and everlasting God who knows the secrets of all hearts, and in the presence of angels and men, acknowledge ourselves to be under the most solemn covenant with the Lord to live for him and no other. We take the only living and true God to be our God, one God in three persons, Father, Son and Holy Ghost.

2d. We receive the Holy Scriptures of the Old and New Testament to be the revealed mind and will of God, believing them to contain a perfect rule for our faith and practice, and promise through the assistance of the Holy Spirit, to make them the rule of our life and practice in all church discipline, acknowledging ourselves by nature children of wrath, and our hope of mercy with God to be only through the righteousness of Jesus Christ, apprehended by faith.

3rdly. We do promise to bear with one another's infirmities and weaknesses, with much tenderness, not discovering them to any in the church, but by gospel rule and order, which is laid down in Matthew 18:15, 16, 17.

4th. We do believe that God has ordained that they who preach the gospel shall live of the gospel; and we call heaven and earth to witness that we without the least reserve, give up ourselves through the help and aiding grace of God's Spirit, our souls and bodies and all that we have to this one God, to be entirely at his disposal, both ourselves, our names and estates, as God shall see best in his own glory; and that we will faithfully do by the help of God's Spirit, whatsoever our consciences, influenced by the word and spirit of God shall direct to be our duty both to God and man; and we do by the assistance of Divine grace, unitedly give ourselves to one another in covenant, promising by the grace of God to act towards one another as brethren in Christ, watching over one another in the love of God, especially to watch against all jesting, light and foolish talking which are not convenient, (Eph. 5:4)—everything that does not become the followers of the holy Lamb of God; and that we will seek the good of each other and the church universal for God's glory; and hold communion together in the worship of God, in the ordinance and discipline of this church of God, according to Christ's visible kingdom, so far as the providence of God admits of the same: "Not forsaking the assembling of ourselves together, as the manner of some is," but submitting ourselves unto the discipline of the church, as a part of Christ's mystical body, according as we shall be guided by the word and Spirit of God, and by the help of Divine grace, still looking for more light from God, as contained in the Holy Scriptures, believing there are greater mysteries to be unfolded and shine in the church beyond what she has ever enjoyed: looking and waiting for the glorious day when the Lord Jesus shall take to Himself his great power, and "have dominion also from sea to sea, and from the river unto the ends of the earth."

This covenant we make with full and free consent of our minds, believing that through his *free and boundless grace* it is owned of God and ratified in heaven, before the throne of God and the Lamb. Amen. Even so, come, Lord Jesus. Amen, and amen.

(From Devin, *Grassy Creek Church*, pp. 43 ff. Quoted in Paschal, *op. cit.*, I, 401-2.)

(2) Daniel Marshall

While Daniel Marshall was not as gifted as Stearns, he was indefatigable in his zeal and activity. In 1754 he came to Opekon, or Mill Creek, Virginia, and with his wife was baptized by Samuel Heaton and licensed "to the unrestrained exercise of his gifts." He began to exercise them at Mill Creek with impressive results.

They were very zealous, had much preaching, and were remarkably warm in their religious exercises, and more particularly so after Mr. Daniel Marshall came among them. They went to such lengths that some of the more cold-hearted lodged a complaint in the Philadelphia Association. Mr. Miller was sent to see what was the matter. When he came he was highly delighted with the exercises, joined them cordially, and said if he had such warm-hearted Christians in his church he would not take gold for them. He charged those who had complained, rather to nourish than complain of such gifts. The work of God revived among them, and considerable additions were made to the church.

(From Robert B. Semple, *A History of the Rise and Progress of the Baptists in Virginia*, rev. by G. W. Beale [Richmond, 1894], p. 376.)

3. Growth and work of the Sandy Creek Baptist Church

The fall after Braddock's Defeat, Nov. 22, 1755, the following persons came from Opekon in Virginia and settled in the neighborhood of Sandy Creek, viz.: Rev. Shubal Stearns and wife, Daniel Marshall and wife, Joseph Breed and wife, Shubal Stearns, Senr. and his wife, Ebenezer Stearns and wife, Enis Stinson and wife, Peter Stearns and wife, Jonathan Polk and wife: the same year they built a little meeting house near the present, where they administered the Lord's Supper. Soon after the neighborhood was alarmed and the Spirit of God listed to blow as a mighty rushing wind in so much that in three years' time they had increased to three churches and upwards of 900 communicants, viz: Sandy Creek, Abbot's Creek, Deep River. The most remarkable events are these: (1) It is a mother church, nay a grandmother and a great grandmother. All the Separate Baptists sprang hence: not only eastward towards the sea, but westward towards the great river Mississippi, but northward to Virginia and southward to South Carolina and Georgia. The word went forth from this Sion, and great was the company of them who published it, in so much that her converts were as drops of morning dew. The first church that sprang hence was Abbot's Creek, then Deep River, Little River, New River, (Ezekiel Hunter), Southwest (Charles Marklin), Trent (James McDaniel), Staunton River, Virginia, (William Murphy), Fall Creek, Virginia, (Samuel Harris), Dan River, Virginia, (Dutton Lane), Grassy Creek (James Reed), John Waller's Church, Virginia, Amelia, Virginia, (Jeremiah Walker), Fair Forest, South Carolina, (Phil. Mulkey), Congaree, South Carolina, (Joseph Rees), Stephen's Creek, South Carolina, (Joseph Murphy), &c. The ministers, Daniel Marshall, Philip Mulkey, John Newton, Joseph Murphy, William Murphy, Dutton Lane, Ezekiel Hunter, Charles Marklin, James McDaniel, Joseph Rees, James Reed, Samuel Harris, John Waller, Jeremiah Walker-Ireland, Elijah Creague, Elnathan Davis.

(From Morgan Edwards, *Materials.* Quoted in Paschal, *op. cit.*, I, 271-72.)

Sandy Creek church is the mother of all the Separate Baptists. From this Zion went forth the word, and great was the company of them who published it: it, in 17 years, has spread branches westward as far as the great river Mississippi; southward as far as Georgia; eastward to the sea and Chesapeake Bay; and northward to the waters of

the Potomac; it, in 17 years, is become the mother, grandmother, and great-grandmother to 42 churches, from which sprang 125 ministers. . . . I believe a preternatural and invisible hand works in the assemblies of the Separate Baptists bearing down the human mind, as was the case in the primitive churches, I Cor. xiv:25.

(*Ibid.*, p. 329.)

4. Organization of the Sandy Creek Association in 1758

The minutes of this first Separate Baptist Association are not extant, and the story must be pieced together from the notes of Morgan Edwards, R. B. Semple, and David Benedict. It will be observed that Morgan Edwards is correct as to the date of the organization of this association, but that Semple has more detailed information from an independent source.

It began in 1758, in June 2nd Monday, at Sandy Creek, and therefore called the Sandy Creek Association. The constituents were the church of Sandy Creek, of Abbott's Creek, and of Deep River.

(*Ibid.*, p. 395.)

Having now constituted several churches, and there being some other that exercised the rights of churches, tho' not formally organized, Mr. Stearns conceived that an association composed of delegates from all these would have a tendency to impart stability, regularity, and uniformity to the whole. For this prudent purpose he visited each church and congregation and explaining the contemplated plan induced them all to send delegates to his meeting house in the ensuing January, which was in the year 1760.

We have already noticed (page 6th) that through the counsel of Mr. Stearns an association was formed and organized January 1760, and who met again in July of the same year. Including both these meetings, the list of the churches stood thus:

Sandy Creek. Elder Shubal Stearns.

Deep River. Nathaniel Powell (a brother).

Abbott's Creek. Elder Daniel Marshall.
Little River. Joseph Breed (a Brother).
Neus River. Ezekiel Hunter.
Black River. John Newton.
Dan River.
Pittsylvania C'ty, Va. Elder Samuel Harris.
Lunenburg C'ty, Va. William Murphy.

(From Semple, *op. cit.*, p. 6.)

5. Division of the Sandy Creek Association in 1770

(1) The separation

In 1770 the Sandy Creek Association divided and became three associations, the one in North Carolina retaining the name of Sandy Creek, the one in South Carolina taking the name of the Congaree Association, and the one in Virginia being called the General Association of Separate Baptists.

At the meeting of this body in 1770, their harmony was interrupted and their assembly assumed a new and unpleasant appearance, and the division of the Association, which convenience would have dictated, was now effected from painful necessity. It had been usual with them to do nothing in Associations, but by unanimity. If in any measure proposed, there was a single dissentient, they laboured first by arguments to come to unanimous agreement; when arguments failed, they resorted to frequent prayer, in which all joined. When both these failed, they sometimes appointed the next day for fasting and prayer, and to strive to bring all to be of one mind. At this session they split in their first business; nothing could be done on the first day. They appointed the next for fasting and prayer. They met and laboured the whole day, and could do nothing, not even appoint a Moderator. The third day was appointed for the same purpose, and to be observed in the same way. They met early, and continued together until three o'clock in the afternoon, without having accomplished any thing. A proposal was then made, that the Association should be

divided into three districts, that is, one in each State. To this there was an unanimous consent at once.

(From Benedict, *op. cit.* [1813], II, 52.)

(2) The cause of the division

The cause was partly convenience, but chiefly a mistake which this association fell into relative to their power and jurisdiction; they had carried matters so high as to leave hardly any power in particular churches, unfellowshipping ordinations, ministers and churches that acted independent of them; and pleading "That though complete power be in every church yet every church can transfer it to an Association"; which is as much as to say that a man may take out his eyes, ears, etc., and give them to another to see, hear etc. for him; for if power be fixed by Christ in a particular church they can not transfer it; nay, should they formally give it away yet it is not gone away.

(From Morgan Edwards, *Materials*. Quoted in Paschal, *op. cit.*, I, 404.)

The good old Mr. Stearns, who was not wholly divested of those maxims which he had imbibed from the traditions of his fathers, is said to have been the principal promoter of this improper stretch of associational power, which, however, was soon abandoned by those, who, for a time, tampered with it, to their embarrassment and injury.

(From Benedict, *op. cit.* [1813], II, 53.)

6. Union of Separate and Regular Baptists

When the Separate Baptists moved into central North Carolina in 1754, and as they spread throughout Virginia, South Carolina, and Georgia in the years immediately following, their enthusiasm and religious habits provoked considerable opposition from the Baptist churches already established in these states, which took the name Regular Baptists in contrast with the Separate Baptists. Before the American Revolution there were efforts in some of these states to unite the two types of Baptists in associational organizations, but without success. The organization of the General Committee and the struggle for religious liberty in Virginia during the post-Revolutionary period provided the foundation for a formal union of Separate and Regulars in 1787, and the influence of this union brought formal action by important groups of North Carolina and Kentucky Baptists shortly thereafter. In South Carolina and Georgia there came the gradual elimination of distinctions between Regular and Separate Baptists without formal action (see Leah Townsend, History of South Carolina Baptists, p. 181, and David Benedict, op. cit., II, p. 157). The documents on Virginia, North Carolina, and Kentucky are given.

(1) Union in Virginia in 1787

In 1786, when the General Committee (of Separate Baptists) met, it was recommended to the various associations that they "appoint delegates to attend the next General Committee for the purpose of forming an union with the Regular Baptists." Although Separate Baptists had been dubious about accepting any confession of faith, they finally adopted the Philadelphia Confession, which actually cleared the way for a formal union with the Regular Baptists.

To prevent the confession of faith from usurping a tyrannical power over the conscience of any, we do not mean that every person is bound to the strict observance of everything therein contained; yet that it holds forth the essential truths of the Gospel, and that the doctrine of salvation by Christ and free, unmerited grace alone ought to be believed by every Christian and maintained by every minister of the Gospel. Upon these terms we are united; and desire hereafter that the names Regular and Separate be buried in oblivion, and that, from henceforth, we shall be known by the name of the United Baptist Churches of Christ in Virginia.

(From Semple, op. cit., p. 101.)

(2) Union in North Carolina in 1788

North Carolina Baptists had divided over the problem of some members who had been baptized before they had been converted. This question had arisen during the first efforts of the Regular Baptists in North Carolina to unite with the Separate Baptists in 1772, as will be seen from the following excerpt. The Revolutionary War intervened, but in 1785 the reformed Kehukee Regular Baptist Association, under the leadership of Lemuel Burkitt, endeavored to promote the union. The report of the committee in 1776 and the formal action in 1788, when two Separate Baptist churches were received into the association, are described in excerpts.

a. First efforts to unite Regular and Separate Baptists in North Carolina in 1772, resulting in division of the Kehukee Association

The Kehukee Association, desirous of fellowship and a general communion between these two parties, sent Elders Jonathan Thomas and John Meglamre to the Separate Baptist Association, which was holden in one of the northern counties in Virginia, to endeavour to effect an union. Accordingly their Association delegated Elders Elijah Craig and David Thompson to the Kehukee Association, which was holden at Kehukee meeting house, in Halifax county, N. Carolina, August, 1772, and rendered their reasons why they could not commune with the Regulars. Their reasons were as follows, viz. 1. They complained of the Regulars not being strict enough in receiving experiences, when persons made application to their churches for baptism, in order to become church members. 2. They refused to communion with Regular Baptist churches, because they believed that faith in Christ Jesus was essential to qualify a person for baptism, yet many of the Regular churches had members in them who acknowledged they were baptized before they believed. 3. The Separates found fault with the Regulars for their *manner of dress*, supposing they indulged their members in superfluity of apparel. These, with a few other non-essentials, weie the reasons they refused communion with us: but the most weighty reason was, "the Regulars holding persons in fellowship in their churches, who were baptized in unbelief;" which was a matter of some consequence, and operated strongly on the minds of many belonging to the Kehukee Association.

(From Lemuel Burkitt and Jesse Read, *A Concise History of the Kehukee Baptist Association* [Halifax, N. C., 1803], 38-40.)

b. *Formal union of Regular and Separate Baptists in 1788*

It was the opinion of this Association, that those *bars*, which heretofore subsisted between the Baptists amongst us, formerly called *Regulars* and *Separates*, be taken down; and a general union and communion take place according to the terms proposed at brother Joshua Freeman's, in Bertie county, May, 1786; and that the names *Regular* and *Separate* be buried in oblivion, and that we should be henceforth known to the world by the name of the *United Baptists*.

(*Ibid.*, p. 94.)

(3) *Union of Separate and Regular Baptists in Kentucky*

The union was ardently desired by many individuals of both parties, and the bodies at large appeared favourably disposed towards the attempt; but they knew not by what means to accomplish it, nor could they agree on the terms on which they should unite. The Separates were afraid of being bound and hampered by Articles and Confessions, and the Regulars were unwilling to unite with them, without something of the kind. A general convention of delegates met on the business, and overtures were made on both sides; but both parties being too tenacious of their favourite maxims to make sufficient abatements, their endeavours at that time proved unsuccessful.

A similar attempt was made in 1793, which, like the other, terminated without accomplishing the desirable object. In this year, five churches being dissatisfied with the Separate Association, respecting their proceedings in this affair, and also in some other matters, withdrew, and formed the Tate's Creek Association.

But in the time of the great revival, the out-pourings of the Divine Spirit, and its softening influence on the minds of the saints, prepared the way for that reconciliation and union, which all their weighty arguments and assiduous endeavours had not been able to accomplish. This astonishing work, in the year 1800 and following, prevailed most powerfully amongst the Separates as well as the Regulars. The churches and members were now much intermixed. All were visited and refreshed by the copious and abundant rain of righteousness which was poured upon the land; and, regardless of names, they unitedly engaged in enjoying and forwarding the precious and powerful work. By this means, those little party asperities, which had unhappily prevailed, were much mollified and diminished; their cold and indifferent charity for each other was inflamed; and with most of them their notions of doctrine were found to be not so different as they had supposed. An union was now proposed in earnest, and soon effected with ease. Both Associations had become large, containing together between seven and eight thousand members. Committees were appointed by both bodies to confer on the subject of an union, who, after mature deliberation, agreed to the following terms: *"Terms of Union between the Elkhorn and South Kentucky or Separate Associations.*

"We the committees of the Elkhorn and South Kentucky Associations, do agree to unite on the following plan.

"1st. That the Scriptures of the Old and New Testament are the infallible word of God, and the only rule of faith and practice. 2d. That there is one only true God, and in the Godhead or divine essence, there are Father, Son, and Holy Ghost. 3d. That by nature we are fallen and depraved creatures. 4th. That salvation, regeneration, sanctification, and justification, are by the life, death, resurrection, and ascension of Jesus Christ. 5th. That the saints will finally persevere through grace to glory. 6th. That believers' baptism by immersion is necessary to receiving the Lord's supper. 7th. That the salvation of the righteous, and punishment of the wicked will be eternal. 8th. That it is our duty to be tender and affectionate to each other, and study the happiness of the children of God in general; to be engaged singly to promote the honour of God. 9th. And that the preaching *Christ tasted death for every man*, shall be no bar to communion. 10th. And that each may keep up their associational and church government as to them may seem best. 11th That a free correspondence and communion be kept up between the churches thus united.

"Unanimously agreed to by the joint committee.

"AMBROSE DUDLEY,
JOHN PRICE,
JOSEPH REDDING,
DAVID BARROW,
ROBERT ELKIN,
DANIEL RAMEY,
THOMAS J. CHILTON,
MOSES BLEDSOE,
SAMUEL JOHNSON."

Matters being thus prepared, a general convention, composed of delegates from all the churches in both Associations, met October, 1801, at Howard's Creek meeting-house, in the county of Clark, when they unanimously acceded to the terms of union, which their committees had prepared, and agreed to lay aside the names of Regular and Separate, and to travel together in future in communion and fellowship as united brethren.

This was the last body of the Separate Baptists which relinquished the appellation by which they had been distinguished for almost fifty years.

(From Benedict, *op. cit.* [1813], II, 237-40.)

Section Two

Development of Patterns for Benevolent Activity

These were the years when American Baptists were seeking the best method of doing benevolent work. During this period two methods were utilized. One was the associational method, in which missions or other benevolences were carried on by a committee of the association. This was begun by the Philadelphia Association in 1755 and adopted by other associations as they organized. An excerpt is included from the minutes of the Shaftsbury Association of Vermont, which developed a missionary committee that functioned about the same way as modern mission boards.

The other method was adopted in 1802, influenced by William Carey's missionary society in London and similar organizations. An excerpt will be given from the records of the first of these societies, the Massachusetts Baptist Missionary Society. It is significant that Baptists in the North followed the society method until 1907, while Southern Baptists organized under the associational or convention method in 1845.

The Shaftsbury Association missionary plan in 1802

The *Elders* and *Brethren*, met in Association at Pittstown, June 2d and 3d, 1802. To the churches which they represent, send Greeting:

Beloved Brethren,

In our last years' minutes, we recommended to you a proposition for raising money by annual contribution, for the support of the Gospel in destitute parts of the wilderness; and whereas, some of the churches have manifested their approbation, and sent forward their liberality, while others seem in suspense, and call for further information as to the *design* of such contribution, and the *rules* by which it is to be conducted; we therefore, think it our duty, at this time, to give you a particular statement of the design of said contribution, and the rules by which the application of it, is to be regulated. And,

1st. The *design* of the proposition is to place things in such a situation as to enable the Association to send able and faithful ministers to preach the gospel, and endeavor to build up the visible cause of the Redeemer in such parts of the United States, or the Canadas, as are destitute of gospel privileges; and, as far as they can have access, among the natives of the wilderness.

2d. The design is to prevent, as far as possible, the prevalence of imposture in those parts of the world; and for the better accomplishing of these purposes, the business is to be regulated by the following

PLAN.

"I. A committee of Twelve Brethren, *six ministers and six other Brethren*, shall be annually chosen, so long as the Association, shall judge it expedient, to send out missionaries; which committee shall have a chairman, clerk and treasurer of their number, who shall be chosen at their first meeting after their election. A majority of said committee shall be a quorum to transact business.

"II. The duty of the committee shall be as follows:

"1. To take charge of the contributions made by the churches for the assistance of the missionaries.

"2. They shall faithfully examine all candidates for the mission, and recommend *such*, and only *such*, as they judge to be pious, able, judicious and experienced ministers of the gospel.

"3. When the committee recommend a missionary, they shall determine the *time* of his mission; and the *places* where the duties thereof shall be performed; which shall be in such *new* settlements of the United States, or the Canadas, where the inhabitants are destitute of a preached gospel, and cannot obtain it. And the mis-

sionaries shall keep a fair account of their expenses during their mission, and make due returns to the committee of the same, together with a journal of their travels. And if more money has been furnished to them, than they have found necessity for, they shall return the same to the Treasurer of the committee; but if the sum advanced, has not been sufficient to defray their necessary expenses, such deficiency shall be made up to them, if the state of the fund will admit of it.

"4. The committee shall furnish each missionary with such sum, out of the Treasury, as they shall judge sufficient to bear his expenses during his mission, and no more; unless the special circumstances of the missionary require some extra consideration; in which case they shall have a right to act discretionary.

"5. The Treasurer shall keep a particular account of all the sums contributed, and of all monies disbursed; and the clerk shall keep fair records of the proceedings of the committee, both of which shall be annually exhibited to the association, and published in their minutes for the satisfaction of the churches.

"6. The committee shall have no fee nor reward for their services.

"7. This association shall have a right to alter any of these articles, or *make such new ones*, at any of their annual meetings, as time, and experience shall point out, to be for the better. And any church, disposed to contribute, shall have a right to discontinue their contributions at any time when they think proper, upon giving their reasons for so doing."

Thus, Dear Brethren, we have laid before you, our *design*, and the *rules* we mean to observe in prosecuting the same; and we must use the freedom to beseech you, with united hearts and hands, to step forward in support of the glorious kingdom of the blessed Immanuel. We beseech you, brethren, "Ye know the grace of our Lord Jesus Christ, that though he was rich, yet for your sakes he became poor, that ye, through his poverty, might be rich." Oh!

let it never be said that those who have been made partakers of the infinite benevolence of the dear Redeemer, should have so little regard for him, as to grudge to part with a little of their property in the support of his cause. Oh, criminal covetousness! may the Lord deliver us from it!

Finally, let us all unite our efforts, both at home and abroad, with our gifts and property, to propagate the truth and build up the visible cause of religion in a sinning world. And may the great author of all true benevolence so instruct and influence our hearts, that we may be willing to spend and be spent in His cause. And may His Holy Spirit crown our feeble efforts with abundant success, to the *praise and glory of his grace, through* JESUS CHRIST *our* LORD.

(From Stephen Wright, *History of the Shaftsbury Baptist Association* [Troy, N. Y., 1853], pp. 87-89.)

The missionary society organized in Massachusetts in 1802

"*Article I.* This Society shall be distinguished and known by the name of the MASSACHUSETTS BAPTIST MISSIONARY SOCIETY.

"*Article II.* This Society shall be composed of such members only as shall subscribe and pay at least *one dollar* annually to its funds.

"*Article III.* The members, at their first meeting, and at their annual meeting ever after, shall by ballot appoint Twelve Trustees, eight whereof shall be ministers, or professing brethren of the Baptist denomination; the other four may be chosen from the members at large; who shall conduct the business of the Society in the manner hereafter described.

"*Article IV.* The object of this Society shall be to furnish occasional preaching, and to promote the knowledge of evangelistic truth in the new settlements within these United States; or . further if circumstances should render it proper.

"*Article V.* The Trustees shall have power to apply the funds of the Society, according to their discretion, in all cases in which they shall not be limited by special direction of the Society.

"*Article VI.* They shall have power to appoint and dismiss missionaries, to pay them, and generally to transact all the business necessary for the accomplishment of the important object of the Society.

· · · · · · · · · · · · · · ·

"*Article XIII.* In order more effectually to aid the intentions of the Society, it is proposed to have a sermon delivered at one of the Baptist meeting-houses in Boston at such time as the Society shall determine; and a public contribution by the people.

"*Article XIV.* It shall be in the power of the Society, at their annual meeting, from time to time, to make such amendments and alterations as experience shall dictate, or to dissolve the same when the purposes of its institutions shall render its existence no longer necessary."

(From W. H. Eaton, *Historical Sketch of the Massachusetts Baptist Missionary Society and Convention* [Boston, 1903], pp. 9-11.)

Section Three

Organized Benevolent Activity

Evidently encouraged by the example of the Philadelphia Association, the Charleston Association in 1755 began a missionary program. This association also made active efforts to advance ministerial education and to institute missions among the Indians. The Sandy Creek and Kehukee Associations also carried on missionary activity during this period.

Charleston Association

1. A missionary secured

In 1775, the Association taking into consideration the destitute condition of many places in the interior settlements of this and the neighboring States [then provinces] recommended to the churches to make contributions for the support of a missionary to itinerate in those parts. Mr.

Hart was authorized and requested, provided a sufficient sum should be raised, to procure if possible a suitable person for the purpose. With this view he visited Pennsylvania and New Jersey in the following year, and prevailed with Rev. John Gano to undertake the service; who attended the annual meeting and was cordially received. The Association requested Mr. Gano to visit the Yadkin first and afterwards to bestow his labours wherever Providence should appear to direct. He devoted himself to the work: it afforded ample scope for his distinguished piety, eloquence and fortitude; and his ministrations were crowned with remarkable success. Many embraced and professed the Gospel. The following year he received from the Association a letter of thanks for his faithfulness and industry in the mission.

(From Wood Furman, *op. cit.*, pp. 10-11.)

2. Mission to Catawba Indians

In 1800 the Charleston church inquired about the duty of the association to preach to the Catawba Indians. As a result, in 1802 John Rooker began work with the Indians. This work continued intermittently until 1817, when it was abandoned.

In 1802, provision was made for the employment of a missionary to travel and preach in destitute places. The object failed of accomplishment for the want of a suitable person to undertake it. A mission however to the Catawba Indians, which had for some time been contemplated, was now commenced. Rev. John Rooker was engaged for a year to preach to them, at least once a month, and to consult the chiefs and other persons of influence, on their disposition to have a school founded among them. Mr. Rooker at the next meeting reported, that "The Indians had given him a very favorable reception; were much pleased with the attention the Association had shown by appointing a missionary to them; had attended very seriously to his preaching, and from the first expressed an earnest desire that a school might be established among them for the instruction of their youth: also, that there appeared the beginning of a work of grace among the white people, who attended on his preaching when ministering to the Indians; and that he was in hopes the Indians would share in the blessing." It was in consequence determined to continue the mission, and Mr. Rooker was authorized to employ a teacher to instruct the youth in the common branches of education, and the principles of Christianity. A school was accordingly established, and has been continued. Samples of writing done by the Indian youth, have been exhibited from year to year, evincing considerable proficiency. Letters also have been repeatedly received from the chiefs of the nation, requesting a continuance of the mission and school. At the meeting of 1806, Robert Mursh, an Indian of the Pomunky tribe, living with the Catawbas, and a licensed preacher, was present, and preached with acceptance to a large and affected audience.

(*Ibid.*, pp. 30-31.)

3. Theological education

Both as individuals and as a body, the Charleston Association assisted northern efforts to provide ministerial training by help given to Isaac Eaton's school and Brown University. In 1755, however, the association began a fund to assist candidates for the ministry and drew up plans for a permanent organization to carry on this work. Perhaps because of opposition to this plan, Richard Furman, pastor of the First Baptist Church of Charleston, wrote the circular letter of the association in 1797 on the subject of ministerial education.

(1) The beginning of ministerial aid in the Charleston Association

At the same time [1755] the expediency of raising a fund to furnish suitable candidates for the ministry with a competent share of learning, was taken into consideration; and it was recommended to the churches generally to collect money for the purpose. The members present engaged in behalf of their constituents to furnish £133 to begin the Fund: and Messrs. Stephens, Hart, and Pelot were chosen trustees. . . .

The general contribution from the Churches was not so great as was wished. But a society instituted in Charleston in 1755 which was called "the Religious Society" and flourished many years, was highly useful in aiding the Association in its benevolent design. Several young men were furnished by it with the means of pursuing studies preparatory to the ministry. Of this number were Messrs. Samuel Stillman and Edmund Botsford, both from the Church in Charleston. The former was ordained there Feb. 26, 1759; and in 1807 finished at Boston a long life distinguished by fervent piety, shining talents; and eminent usefulness. The latter survives as the venerable Pastor of the Church at George-Town.

(*Ibid.*, pp. 11-12.)

(2) *Charleston Association Education Fund*

The association appointed a committee in 1789 to recommend a plan for assisting in the education of pious young men for the ministry. Richard Furman was its chairman. He submitted a system of rules for the Education Fund which, after amendment and some discussion, were adopted in 1792, and incorporation was secured. Furman acted as president of the General Committee from its beginning, and by 1810 (when Wood Furman's History went to press) contributions of every sort totaled over nine thousand dollars.

A SUMMARY OF THE RULES.

"This committee shall be known and distinguished by the name of the General Committee for the Charleston Baptist Association Fund."

"Once a year a Charity Sermon shall be preached in each church; at which time and place, collections shall be made from the congregation, and the money so col-

lected, together with any donations or bequests received for the purpose, shall be applied towards forming and supporting a fund to assist pious young men, designed for the work of the ministry, and destitute of other assistance, in obtaining education; together with such other religious and public uses, as may be approved by the churches, should the Fund finally prove sufficient."

A committee consisting of a delegate from each church chosen for the purpose, shall convene at the same time and place with the Association. They may be members of that body, but invested with distinct powers as members of the committee. They shall receive the collections, determine on the manner of applying the fund according to the foregoing Rule, and examine candidates for the churches' bounty. The management of the fund is exclusively invested in those churches who contribute to it. The committee thus formed is to continue one year, or till a new election. A President, Treasurer, Secretary, and two Assistants, shall be annually chosen, and form a select committee to transact, when the General Committee is not in session, such business as the General Committee shall judge necessary. The President shall contract for the education of such persons as are taken on the churches' bounty, and the expenses consequent thereon shall be paid by the Treasurer, on the President's written order. The Treasurer shall give bond to the President in double the value of all monies or specialties in his hands. No person shall be admitted on the bounty but such as come well recommended, and appear on examination to be truly pious, of evangelical principles, of good natural abilities, and desirous of devoting themselves to the work of the ministry. Each person so admitted shall be under the direction of the committee while pursuing a course of studies, and be liable to refund the money expended on his education, within 4 years after the completion of it, if he does not within that time enter on the ministry to the satisfaction of the committee. When there are more candidates than can be received on the bounty, preference shall be given to those who are members of churches in this Association: secondly, to those who are most promising. If any person while obtaining education under the patronage and direction of this body, shall embrace principles subversive of the great truths of the Gospel, or abandon himself to an irreligious course of life, he shall, on proper evidence of the fact, and after suitable endeavors to reclaim him, if ineffectual, be dismissed.

(Ibid., pp. 46-48.)

(3) Richard Furman's circular letter of 1797

For forty years Richard Furman was the leader in the cause of ministerial education, not only in the Charleston Association, but in his state and beyond. Both Columbian College and the university bearing his name developed to some extent from his influence. His circular letter of 1797 is an important landmark in the history of theological education in the South.

Beloved Brethren,

The answer we are about to give to the query inserted for discussion in our Minutes of the last year, respecting the obligations of churches, to make provision for the instruction and improvement of the persons they call to the ministry, will be in the affirmative. But under such limitations and explanations as you will find in the following view of the subject; which, with all plainness and christian candour, we submit to your serious consideration.

The question evidently respects those persons who have received no education, or so small a proportion of it, that they remain ignorant of important subjects of knowledge; such as are either comprehended in the nature and evidence of religion, or intimately connected with them; and who, of course, are unacquainted with some of the best means of attaining divine knowledge, and of communicating it with advantage to others. To those who are already acquainted with these subjects, the question will not apply.

. . . .

The education, or improvement, contemplated in the query, does not consist in a gingle, or pomp or words; in idle speculations; trifling criticisms; or a vain philosophy: but in solid, rational, and useful knowledge. In knowledge which comprehends an acquaintance with the construction, force, and beauty of language; the right exercise of reason and judgment; and with the laws and powers of nature, of the material world, as established by the Great Creator; to which it adds, just views of God himself, his perfections and government; the nature, properties, and powers of created spiritual beings; their relation to God, and to each other; their dependence, duties, and obligations; the history of events, in which the providence of God, the interest of the church, and the truth of religion, have been, and are deeply concerned; and which, especially, brings us into a clear and well digested acquaintance with the doctrines of revelation, concerning our gracious Redeemer and his glorious salvation.

The duty of the church, in respect of such improvement, according to our ideas, consists in an attentive, conscientious regard to the subject; in a prudent faithful use of the best means in their power for obtaining the benefit; and in contributing freely of their substance to defray necessary expences, in the case of poor candidates. To which may be added, the exertion of talents by those who are able to give instruction.

. . . .

Another reason in proof of the obligation of churches, is the practicability of the measure. We do not mean that it is universally practicable, or necessary, to bestow on all who are admitted to the ministry, what is commonly called a liberal education. The age, matrimonial connection, and other circumstances of some candidates may obstruct it: the poverty of the churches they are connected with, and the want of learned men among them, may also greatly prevent it on their part: and these circumstances must be considered as affording providential direction. But in every case, where the duty is faithfully attended to, some useful improvement may be arrived at, by the help of proper books, which may be obtained without great expense; and by the occasional assistance of those who have themselves obtained some advantages. A good acquaintance with the language in which a person is to perform his ministrations, and the study of divinity, are certainly, with a little exertion, practicable to all. In other cases, and especially with respect to young men, it would not be difficult to go much farther. The greatest difficulties may be expected in the first exertions; and particularly among churches who have been in the habit of neglecting this duty. For when learned ministers are procured in some churches, and, from the encouragement given to education, seminaries of learning begin to be generally formed among them, the difficulties are chiefly surmounted. But the greatest obstacles to the execution, or adoption, of such a plan, are low contracted sentiments, and an avaricious disposition. For where there is really a willing mind, and just sentiments, much can, and will be done. It is obvious that the same sentiments and disposition which obstruct a measure of this nature, operate likewise to the neglect of that necessary and important duty of supporting gospel ministers, actually employed in the church; and this is common in some places, notwithstanding God hath positively appointed "That those who preach the gospel, should live of the gospel." This neglect frequently extends also, to houses erected for the worship of God, which are in many instances found to be mean and contemptible, while those who worship in them, and are guilty of all these neglects, dwell at ease, in affluence, and convenience, pleasure or vanity. O! how long shall it be said in truth, of churches as well as individuals, "All seek their own; not the things which are Jesus Christ's?" How long

shall that solemn interrogation remain in its full force: "Is it time for you, O! ye, to dwell in your ceiled houses, and my house to lie waste?" In primitive times it was otherwise, when the "Deep poverty of a church, contributed to the riches of their liberality." But we are not to estimate our ability in such a case as this, by what an individual church can do. As subject of such vast importance should be the object of united efforts: churches should combine their contributions to a point of common interest and usefulness. In this case we may not only hope, soon to see, many persons furnished with useful education for the ministry, where the cause of God now languishes for want of them; but also seminaries of learning erected for this purpose, and libraries stored with the most valuable productions, of genius, learning and piety, formed for the diffusion of necessary and useful knowledge.

. . . .

But that no mistakes may take place in your minds, we add, that it is far from being our intention to represent human learning, as a sufficient, or the principal qualification for the gospel ministry. We only consider it as an handmaiden to grace. We acknowledge also, with pleasure, and with gratitude to God, that some have been raised up, and still exist in the church, who, though they had but small advantage from education, are not only men of piety and zeal; but able ministers of the New Testament. Learning has by some been idolized; and it is no wonder that when thus put, in our estimation, into the place of gracious qualifications and the Spirit's influence, it should be rendered impotent, and be as dry breasts. But this furnishes no just reason for its being despised or neglected, in respect of its right use and application.

. . . .

We need not inform you, dear brethren, that a plan, of a public nature, founded on this principle has been already established among us; that when under consideration, it had the general approbation of your delegates in Association; and that it has already begun to produce good effects. Some churches are entitled to much commendation for the support they have given it. Happy should we be, could we say as much of all!

(*Ibid.*, pp. 114-24.)

Activity of the Sandy Creek Association

For twelve years, all the Separate Baptists in Virginia, and the two Carolinas, continued in connection with this Association, which was generally held at no great distance from the place where it originated. All who could, traveled from its remote extremities, to attend its yearly sessions, which were conducted with great harmony, and afforded sufficient edification to induce them to undertake with cheerfulness these long and laborious journeys. By the means of these meetings, the gospel was carried into many new places, where the fame of the Baptists had previously spread; for great crowds attending from distant parts, mostly through curiosity, many became enamored with these extraordinary people, and petitioned the Association to send preachers into their neighborhoods. These petitions were readily granted, and the preachers as readily complied with the appointments. These people were so much engaged in their evangelical pursuits, that they had no time to spend in theological debates, nor were they very scrupulous about their mode of conducting their meetings. When assembled, their chief employment was preaching, exhortation, singing, and conversation about their various exertions in the Redeemer's service, the success which had attended them, and the new and prosperous scenes which were opening before them. These things so inflamed the hearts of the ministers, that they would leave the Association with a zeal and courage which no common obstacles could impede.

(From Benedict, *op. cit.* [1860], p. 685.)

North Carolina Society's mission to the Indians

There were several attempts to evangelize the Indians in Georgia and North Carolina in the opening years of the nineteenth century. The Georgia Association considered the matter from 1801 to 1806, evidently without taking specific action. In North Carolina, the Baptist Philanthropic Missionary Society was organized to reach the Indians with the gospel. Their Address to the Public in 1808 is quoted below. The work of this society and its later history are not known, but probably it prepared the way for the state convention of North Carolina.

The missionary spirit first made its appearance in the Kehukee Association in October, 1803, and the following May it was introduced into the Portsmouth in such a feeling manner that not only the Conference, but many of the spectators, were flooded in tears. The cooperation of the brethren composing the Neuse Association was easily obtained and a suitable number appointed to commence the all-interesting work. A directory was formed, a constitution adopted, and subscriptions exhibited to the public, soliciting means of support. But hitherto we have been just able to meet and concert measures, without either suitable persons or means to effect our philanthropic designs.

(From *Address to the Public.* Quoted in A. L. Vail, *The Morning Hour of American Baptist Missions* [Philadelphia, 1907], p. 190.)

Section Four
Southern Baptists and the American Revolution

Practically all American Baptists were patriots during the Revolutionary War. A substantial price was put on the head of Dr. Richard Furman by the English because of his great aid to the colonial cause. Dr. Oliver Hart, pastor of the First Baptist

Church of Charleston, South Carolina, was forced to flee from the Briitsh army. In North Carolina the Baptists had a severe struggle for their liberties under the administration of Governor Tryon, who had taken his office in March, 1765. The Regulator movement was a struggle against injustice and governmental extortion; some have called the Battle of Alamance the beginning of the American Revolution. Eminent southern historians have judged that Baptists were very active in this movement for liberty (see Paschal, op. cit., I, chaps. xiv-xvi). The reprisals by Tryon after Alamance evidently drove Baptists both southward and westward, resulting in the establishment of many new Baptist churches in other areas. Morgan Edwards, the Baptist historian, visited this area very shortly after the Battle of Alamance took place, and his statements are significant.

Morgan Edwards on the Battle of Alamance

It [*the Sandy Creek church*] began with sixteen souls, and in a short time increased to six hundred and six, spreading its branches to Deep River and Abbot's Creek, which branches are gone to other provinces, and most of the members of this church have followed them; in so much that in seventeen years it is reduced from six hundred and six to fourteen souls. The cause of this dispersion is the abuse of power which too much prevailed in the province, and caused the inhabitants at last to rise up in arms, and fight for their privileges; but being routed, May 16, 1771, they despaired of seeing better times, and therefore quitted the province. It is said 1,500 families departed since the battle of Alamance, and to my knowledge a great many more are only waiting to dispose of their plantations in order to follow them. This is to me an argument that their grievances were real, and their oppressions great, notwithstanding all that has been said to the contrary.

The church at Little River was no less remarkable than the one already mentioned; for this was constituted in 1760, five years after the Sandy Creek, and in three years increased from five to five hundred, and built five meeting houses; but this church was also reduced by the provincial troubles and consequent dispersion of the inhabitants mentioned above.

(From Morgan Edwards, *Materials.* Quoted in Paschal, *op. cit.*, I, 381.)

Permission requested to preach to the troops during the Revolutionary War

The right to preach to the soldiers was secured through a petition by the General Baptist Association in 1775.

To the Honourable Peyton Randolph, Esq., and the several delegated Gentlemen, convened at Richmond, to concert Measures conducive to the Good and Well-being of this Colony and Dominion, the humble Address of the Virginia Baptists, now Associated in Cumberland, by Delegates from their several Churches: GENTLEMEN OF THE CONVENTION,—While you are (pursuant to the important Trust reposed in you) acting as the Guardians of the Rights of your Constituents, and pointing out to them the Road to Freedom, it must needs afford you an exalted satisfaction to find your Determinations not only applauded, but cheerfully complied with by a brave and spirited people. We, however distinguished from the Body of our Countrymen by appellatives and sentiments of a religious nature, do nevertheless look upon ourselves as Members of the same Commonwealth, and, therefore, with respect to matters of a civil nature, embarked in the same common Cause.

Alarmed at the shocking Oppression which in a British Cloud hangs over our American Continent, we, as a Society and part of the distressed State, have in our Association consider'd what part might be most prudent for the Baptists to act in the present unhappy Contest. After we had determined "that in some Cases it was lawful to go to War, and also for us to make a Military resistance against Great Britain, in regard of their unjust Invasion, and tyrannical Oppression of, and repeated Hostilities against America," our people were all left to act at Discretion with respect to inlisting, without falling under the Censure of our Community. And as some have inlisted, and many more likely so to do, who will have earnest Desires for their Ministers to preach to them during the Campaign, we therefore deligate and appoint our well-beloved Brethren in the Ministry, Elijah Craig, Lewis Craig, Jeremiah Walker and John Williams to present this address and to petition you that they may have free Liberty to preach to the Troops at convenient Times without molestation or abuse; and as we are conscious of their strong attachment to American Liberty, as well as their soundness in the principles of the Christian Religion, and great usefulness in the Work of the Ministry, we are willing they may come under your Examination in any Matters you may think requisite.

We conclude with our earnest prayers to Almighty God for His Divine Blessing on your patriotic and laudable Resolves, for the good of Mankind and American Freedom, and for the success of our Armies in Defence of our Lives, Liberties and Properties. Amen.

Sign'd by order and in behalf of the Association the 14th August, 1775.

SAM'L HARRISS, *Moderator.*

JOHN WALLER, *Clerk.*

Agreeably with the objects of the above petition, the Convention, as appears from the Journal, under date of "Wednesday, August 16, 1775,"

"Resolved, That it be an instruction to the commanding officers of the regiments or troops to be raised that they permit dissenting clergymen to celebrate divine worship, and to preach to the soldiers, or exhort, from time to time, as the various operations of the military service may permit, for the ease of such scrupulous consciences as may not choose to attend divine service as celebrated by the chaplain."

(From Semple, *op. cit.*, pp. 492-94.)

Section Five

The Struggle for Religious Liberty

In Virginia

1. *Imprisonment and persecution of Virginia Baptist preachers*

In Virginia there was a head-on collision between the established Church of England and the Baptists, who felt that they must obey God rather than man. Between 1768 and 1777 at least thirty Baptist preachers were imprisoned, whipped, or stoned. Typical of the persecution was that endured by John Waller and his companions.

Urbanna Prison, Middlesex County, August 12, 1771.

Dear Brother in the Lord,

At a meeting which was held at brother McCain's, in this county, last Saturday, whilst brother William Webber was addressing the congregation from James II; 18, there came running towards him, in a furious rage, Captain James Montague, a magistrate of the county, followed by the parson of the parish, and several others, who seemed greatly exasperated. The magistrate, and another, took hold of brother Webber, and dragging him from the stage, delivered him, with brethren Wafford, Robert Ware, Richard Falkner, James Greenwood and myself, into custody, and commanded that we should be brought before him for trial. Brother Wafford was severely scourged, and brother Henry Street received one lash, from one of the persecutors, who was prevented from proceeding to farther violence by his companions; to be short, I may inform you that we were carried before the above magistrate, who, with the parson and some others, carried us, one by one, into a room, and examined our pockets and wallets for fire-arms, &c., charging us with carrying on a mutiny against the authority of the land. Finding none, we were asked if we had license to preach in that county; and learning we had not, it was required of us to give bond and security not to preach any more in the county, which we modestly refused to do, whereupon, after dismissing brother Wafford, with a charge to make his escape out of the county by twelve o'clock the next day on pain of imprisonment, and dismissing brother Falkner, the rest of us were delivered to the sheriff, and sent to close jail, with a charge not to allow us to walk in the air until court day. Blessed be God, the sheriff and jailor have treated us with as much kindness as could have been expected from strangers. May the Lord reward them for it! Yesterday we had a large number of people to hear us preach; and among others, many of the great ones of the land, who behaved well, while one of us discoursed on the new birth. We find the Lord gracious and kind to us beyond expression in our afflictions. We cannot tell how long we shall be kept in bonds; we therefore beseech, dear brother, that you and the church supplicate night and day for us, our benefactors and our persecutors.

I have also to inform you that six of our brethren are confined in Caroline jail, viz., brethren Lewis Craig, John Burrus, John Young, Edward Herndon, James Goodrick and Bartholomew Cheming. The most dreadful threatenings are raised in the neighboring counties against the Lord's faithful and humble followers. Excuse haste. Adieu.

JOHN WALLER.

(From *Religious Herald* [Virginia], January 18, 1828.)

2. Petitions for relief during the Revolutionary War

When the revolt against England began, Baptists used the opportunity to smite the establishment of the Church of England in Virginia; and in the meeting of the General Baptist Association in August, 1775, petitions protesting the religious establishment were circulated for signatures. The receipt of these petitions is noted in the Journal of the Virginia Convention of 1776.

"Thursday, *June 20, 1776.*

"A petition of sundry persons of the Baptist Church, in the county of Prince William, whose names are thereunto subscribed, was presented to the Convention and read, setting forth that at a time when this Colony, with the others, is contending for the civil rights of mankind against the enslaving schemes of a powerful enemy, they are persuaded the strictest unanimity is necessary among ourselves; and, that every remaining cause of division may, if possible, be removed, they think it their duty to petition for the following religious privileges, which they have not yet been indulged with in this part of the world, towit: That they be allowed to worship God in their own way, without interruption; that they be permitted to maintain their own ministers, and none others; that they may be married, buried and the like without paying the clergy of other denominations; that, these things granted, they will gladly unite with their brethren and to the utmost of their ability promote the common cause.

"*Ordered,* That the said petition be referred to the Committee of Propositions and Grievances; that they inquire into the allegations thereof and report the same, with their opinion thereupon, to the Convention."

(From the *Journal* of the Virginia Convention for 1776, p. 58. Quoted in Semple, *op. cit.*, pp. 494-95.)

3. Bill of Rights, Virginia Constitution

Before the Virginia Convention considered the petitions by the Baptists, they adopted their constitution in 1776, and the sixteenth section of the Bill of Rights, originally written by George Mason, was amended by James Madison to substitute free exercise of religion for toleration.

That religion, or the duty which we owe to our Creator, and the manner of discharging it, can be directed only by reason and conviction, not by force or violence, and therefore all men are equally entitled to the free exercise of religion according to the dictates of conscience; and that it is the mutual duty of all to practice Christian forbearance, love and charity towards each other.

(From *A Declaration of Rights* adopted by the Virginia Convention of 1776, section sixteen. Quoted in Semple, *op. cit.*, p. 495.)

4. Preamble to an act adopted October, 1776

The Bill of Rights just quoted probably was the cause for an act which exempted dissenters from contributing to the support and maintenance of the established church.

I. Whereas several oppressive acts of Parliament respecting religion have been formerly enacted, and doubts have arisen, and may hereafter arise, whether the same are in force in this Commonwealth or not: For prevention whereof, *Be it enacted by the General Assembly of the Commonwealth of Virginia, and it is hereby enacted by the authority of the same,* That all and every act of Parliament, by whatever title known or distinguished, which renders criminal the maintaining any opinions in matters of religion, forbearing to repair to church or the exercising any mode of worship whatsoever, or which prescribes punishments for the same, shall henceforth be of no force or validity within this Commonwealth.

II. And whereas there are within this Commonwealth great numbers of dissenters from the Church Establishment by law who have been heretofore taxed for its support, and it is contrary to the principles of reason and justice that any should be compelled to contribute to the maintenance of a Church with which their consciences will not permit them to join, and from which they can therefore receive no benefit: For remedy whereof, and that equal liberty, as well religious as civil, may be universally extended to all the good people of this Commonwealth, *Be it enacted by the General Assembly of the Commonwealth of Virginia, and it is hereby enacted by the authority of the same,* That all dissenters of whatever denomination from the said Church shall, from and after the passing of this act, be totally free and exempt from all levies, taxes and impositions whatever towards supporting and maintaining the said Church as it now is or hereafter may be established, and its ministers.

(From Semple, *op. cit.*, pp. 495-96.)

5. Development of a General Committee

The General Baptist Association in Virginia was one of four Baptist associations in the state in 1783, and it was felt that a single body representing all of these associations could throw the united strength of Baptists in Virginia into the struggle for religious liberty better than the separate bodies. Consequently, in October, 1783, the General Association dissolved, with the recommendation that a General Committee be organized. This was of great consequence in the development of Virginia Baptists, particularly in a uniting of all in the struggle for religious liberty.

(1) Organization of the General Committee

The General Committee accordingly met for the first time on Saturday, October 9, 1784. Delegates from four Associations assembled. William Webber was appointed moderator, and Reuben Ford clerk.

Of the plan of government the following are the only articles proper to be noticed:

1. The General Committee shall be composed of delegates sent from all the District Associations that desire to correspond with each other.

2. No Association shall be represented in the committee by more than four delegates.

3. The committee thus composed shall consider all the political grievances of the whole Baptist Society in Virginia, and all references from the District Associations respecting matters which concern the Baptist Society at large.

4. No petition, memorial or remonstrance shall be presented to the General

Assembly from any Association in connection with the General Committee; all things of that kind shall originate with the General Committee.

(From Semple, *op. cit.*, pp. 94-95.)

(2) Petition by General Committee on marriage laws and religious discrimination

The memorial of the Committee of Several Baptist Associations, Assembled at Dover Meeting-House, the 9th day of October, 1784, humbly sheweth:

That your Memorialists still complain of a part of the Marriage Act and Vestry Law, as grievous to Dissenters; for in the former, they are forbid going out of their Counties to Solemnize the Rights of Matrimony, even among Members of their Own Societies and Congregations, whereby the good purpose, which the Wisdom of your Honourable House intended by that Act, is Disappointed. And in the latter, the property of Dissenters is taken from them by those who are not their Representatives.

Your Memorialists therefore humbly pray that all Distinctions in your Laws may be done away, and that no order or Denomination of Christians in this Commonwealth have any Separate Privileges allowed them, more than their Brethren of other Religious Societies, distinguished by other Names: lest they Tyrannize over them.

Your Memorialists have hoped for a removal of their Complaints and the enjoyment of equal liberty; since it hath pleased your Honourable House to declare that their Complaints are just and their Petitions Reasonable; to you, therefore, they look up, that every grievous Yoke be broken, and that the oppressed go free; and that in every Act the bright beams of equal Liberty and Impartial Justice may shine. Your Memorialists shall ever pray.

WILLIAM WEBBER, Chairman

(Original in Virginia State Library. Quoted in Garnett Ryland, *The Baptists of Virginia* [Richmond, 1955], p. 123.)

(3) Resolution against general assessment

A bill had been introduced into the Virginia Assembly which would levy a tax for supporting ministers and providing places of worship, and each taxpayer could designate which society of Christians should receive his tax. Other denominations supported this bill. Baptists were the only organized group to oppose it. It called forth the famous Memorial and Remonstrance by James Madison and the resolution of the General Committee.

a. *James Madison's A Memorial and Remonstrance*

A MEMORIAL AND REMONSTRANCE.

To the Honorable the General Assembly of Commonwealth of Virginia:

We, the subscribers, citizens of the said Commonwealth, having taken into serious consideration a bill, printed by order of the last session of General Assembly, entitled "A bill establishing a provision for teachers of the Christian religion"; and conceiving that the same, if finally armed with the sanctions of a law, will be a dangerous abuse of power, are bound, as faithful members of a free State, to remonstrate against it, and to declare the reasons by which we are determined. We remonstrate against the said bill:

Because we hold it for a fundamental and unalienable truth, "that religion, or the duty which we owe to the Creator, and the manner of discharging it, can be directed only by reason and conviction, not by force or violence." The religion, then, of every man must be left to the conviction and consciences of every man; and it is the right of every man to exercise it as these may dictate. . . .

Because, if religion be exempt from the authority of the society at large, still less can it be subject to that of the legislative body. . . .

Because it is proper to take alarm at the first experiment on our liberties. We hold this prudent jealousy to be the first duty of citizens and one of the noblest characteristics of the late revolution. The freemen of America did not wait until usurped power had strengthened itself by exercise and entangled the question in precedents. They saw all the consequences in the principle, and they avoided the consequences by denying the principle. We revere this lesson too much soon to forget it. Who does not see that the same authority which can establish Christianity in exclusion of all other religions may establish with the same ease any particular sect of Christians in exclusion of all other sects? That the same authority which can force a citizen to contribute three pence only of his property for the support of any one establishment may force him to conform to any other establishment in all cases whatsoever.

Because the bill violates that equality which ought to be the basis of every law, and which is more indispensable in proportion as the validity or expediency of any law is more liable to be impeached. "If all men are by nature equally free and independent," all men are to be considered as entering into society on equal conditions, as relinquishing no more, and therefore retaining no less, one than another of their natural rights; above all are they to be considered as retaining an *equal* title to the free exercise of religion according to the dictates of conscience." . . .

As the bill violates equality by subjecting some to peculiar burdens, so it violates the same principle by granting to others peculiar exemptions. Are the Quakers and Menonists the only sects who think a compulsive support of their religions unnecessary and unwarrantable? . . .

Because the bill implies either that the civil magistrate is a competent judge of religious truths, or that he may employ religion as an engine of civil policy. The first is an arrogant pretention, falsified by the extraordinary opinion of rulers, in all ages and throughout the world; the second, an unhallowed perversion of the means of salvation.

Because the Establishment proposed by the bill is not requisite for the support of the Christian religion. . . .

Because experience witnesses that ecclesiastical establishments, instead of maintaining the purity and efficacy of religion, have had a contrary operation. . . .

Because the Establishment in question is not necessary for the support of civil government. . . .

Because the proposed Establishment is a departure from that generous policy which, offering an asylum to the persecuted and oppressed of every nation and religion, promised a lustre to our country and an accession to the number of its citizens. . . .

Because it will have a like tendency to banish our citizens. The allurements presented by other situations are every day thinning their number. To superadd a fresh motive to emigration, by revoking the liberty which they now enjoy, would be the same species of folly which has dishonored and depopulated flourishing kingdoms.

Because it will destroy that moderation and harmony which the forbearance of our laws to intermeddle with religion has produced among its several sects. . . .

Because the policy of the bill is adverse to the diffusion of the light of Christianity. . . .

Because attempts to enforce by legal sanctions acts obnoxious to so great a proportion of citizens tend to enervate the laws in general and to slacken the bands of society. . . .

Because a measure of such singular magnitude and delicacy ought not to be imposed without the clearest evidence that it is called for by a majority of citizens; and no satisfactory method is yet proposed by which the voice of the majority in this case may be determined or its influence secured. . . .

Because, finally, "the equal right of every citizen to the free exercise of his religion according to the dictates of conscience" is held by the same tenure with all our other rights. If we recur to its origin it is equally the gift of nature; if we weigh its importance it cannot be less dear to us; if we consult the "Declaration of those rights which pertain to the good people of Virginia as the basis and foundation of government," it is enumerated with equal solemnity, or rather with studied emphasis. Either, then, we must say that the will of the Legislature is the only measure of their authority, and that in the plenitude of this authority they may sweep away all our fundamental rights, or that they are bound to leave this particular right untouched and sacred; either we must say that they may control the freedom of the press; may abolish the trial by jury; may swallow up the executive and judiciary powers of the State; nay, that they may annihilate our very right of suffrage and erect themselves into an independent and hereditary assembly; or we must say that they have no authority to enact into a law the bill under consideration. We, the subscribers, say that the General Assembly of this Commonwealth have no such authority; and that no effort may be omitted on our part against so dangerous a usurpation, we oppose to it this remonstrance, earnestly praying, as we are in duty bound, that the Supreme Lawgiver of the universe, by illuminating those to whom it is addressed, may, on one hand, turn their councils from every act which would affront His holy prerogative or violate the trust committed to them, and on the other guide them into every measure which may be worthy of His blessing; may redound to their own praise, and may establish most firmly the liberties, the property, and the happiness of this Commonwealth.

(From Semple, *op. cit.*, pp. 500-509.)

b. *Resolution of General Committee against general assessment, dated August, 1785*

Resolved, That it be recommended to those counties which have not yet prepared petitions to be presented to the General Assembly against the engrossed bill for a general assessment for the support of the teachers of the Christian religion, to

proceed thereon as soon as possible; that it is believed to be repugnant to the spirit of the Gospel for the Legislature thus to proceed in matters of religion; that no human laws ought to be established for this purpose; but that every person ought to be left entirely free in respect to matters of religion; that the holy Author of our religion needs no such compulsive measures for the promotion of His cause; that the Gospel wants not the feeble arm of man for its support; that it has made, and will again, through divine power, make its way against all opposition; and that should the Legislature assume the right of taxing the people for the support of the Gospel, it will be destructive to religious liberty.

Therefore, This committee agrees unanimously that it will be expedient to appoint a delegate to wait on the General Assembly with a remonstrance and petition against such assessment.

(From Semple, *op. cit.*, p. 96.)

6. *Passage of the "Act for Establishing Religious Freedom," prepared by Thomas Jefferson*

Instead of a bill for general assessment, the Virginia Assembly considered an act which had been introduced into the Virginia Assembly in 1779 by Thomas Jefferson and endorsed by the General Baptist Association in that same year. It became a law in January, 1786, and was a victory for the principles of the Baptists.

Be it enacted by the General Assembly, That no man shall be compelled to frequent or support any religious worship, place or ministry whatsoever, nor shall he be enforced, restrained, molested, or burthened in his body or goods, nor shall he otherwise suffer on account of his religious opinions or belief; but that all men shall be free to profess, and by argument to maintain, their opinion in matters of religion, and that the same shall in no wise diminish, enlarge or affect their civil capacities.

And though we well know that this assembly elected by the people for the ordinary purposes of legislation only, have no power to restrain the acts of succeeding assemblies, constituted with powers equal to our own, and that therefore to declare this act to be irrevocable would be of no effect in law; yet we are free to declare, and do declare, that the rights hereby asserted are of the natural rights of mankind, and that if any act shall be hereafter passed to repeal the present, or to narrow its operation such act will be an infringement of natural right.

(From Hening, *Statutes*, XIX, 84.)

7. *Memorial against incorporation of the Protestant Episcopal Church and possession of the glebe lands*

In December, 1784, an act was passed by the General Assembly, giving the new Protestant Episcopal Church the privilege of incorporation and confirming to their use the glebe land which had formerly been possessed by the Church of England. The General Committee of Baptists presented a resolution to the Assembly on this matter.

The Representatives of Several Baptist Associations in Virginia Assembled in Committee, August 5, 1786, Beg leave Respectfully to address your Honorable House:

When Britain, with her cruel Usurpation over her Colonies in America, reduced them to the necessity of taking up Arms to vindicate their Natural Claims, A declaration of Rights was made by the good People of Virginia, Assembled in full and free Convention, as the Basis and foundation of Government and A Constitution, so Liberal in Civil and free in religious concerns, that we readily took the Oath of Fidelity to the State. From this principle we expatiated! for this free government we advanced our property and exposed our lives on the field of battle with our fellow Citizens; being often Stimulated with the harmonious Proclamation of equal Liberty of conscience and equal claim of property.

. . . .

But, to our great Surprize, in the Session of 1784, at the request of a few Clergymen, the members of the late established Church of England were incorporated into a Society, called the "Protestant Episcopal Church," as a body Corporate and politic. To the ministers and members of that Church and their Successors were given all and every Tract, or Tracts, of Glebe Land already purchased, and every other thing the property of the late established Church of England, to the Sole and only use of the Protestant Episcopal Church. If Religion or the duty which we owe to our Creator, and the manner of discharging it, can be directed only by reason and conviction, not by force and violence (so fully expressed in the XVI Art. of the Bill of Rights, and the late Act for establishing Religious Liberty) we cannot see with what propriety the General Assembly could incorporate the Protestant Episcopal Church, give her a name, Describe the character of her members, modulate the forms of her government & appoint the Time and place of her meeting. If this is not done by force, what force can there be in law? and to what lengths this may lead and what violence it may produce, time only can discover, but we fear the awful consequences. The act appears a Bitumen to Cement Church and State together: the foundation for Ecclesiastical Tyranny and the first steps towards an Inquisition.

New Testament Churches, we humbly conceive, are, or should be, established by the Legislature of Heaven and not earthly power; by the Law of God and not the Law of the State; by the acts of the Apostles and not by the Acts of an Assembly. The Incorporating Act, then, in the first place, appears to cast great contempt upon the divine Author of our Religion, whose Kingdom is not of this world. Secondly, to give all the property of the State established church to one Society, not more virtuous or deserving than other Societies in the Commonwealth, appears contrary to justice and the express words of the IV Art. of the Bill of Rights, which prohibits rewards or emoluments to any

Man, or set of men, except for services rendered the State; and what services that Church has rendered the State, either by her Clergy or Laity, more than other Churches have done, we know not.

. . . .

If the members of the Protestant Episcopal Church prefer Episcopacy to any other form of Government, they have an undoubted Right as free Citizens of the State to enjoy it. But to call in the aid of Legislature to Establish it threatens the freedom of Religious Liberty in its Consequences. And, whereas, the Incorporating Act appears to be pregnant with evil and dangerous to religious Liberty, your Petitioners humbly remonstrate against it; and trust that the wisdom of your Hon. House will repeal the exceptionable parts of the said Act and apply the property to the use of the community in such a manner as to you shall seem just.

WILLIAM WEBBER, Clk.

(From Garnett Ryland, *op. cit.*, pp. 127-30.)

8. *John Leland*, The Rights of Conscience . . .

One of the outstanding leaders in the Virginia struggle for religious liberty was John Leland, who moved to Virginia from Massachusetts in 1775 and served for about fifteen years before returning to New England. His vigorous style is illustrated in one of his famous writings.

The question is, "*Are the rights of conscience alienable, or inalienable?*"

The word *conscience*, signifies *common science*, a court of judicature which the Almighty has erected in every human breast: a *censor morum* over all his conduct. Conscience will ever judge right, when it is rightly informed, and speak the truth when it understands it. But to advert to the question—"Does a man upon entering into social compact surrender his conscience to that society to be controlled by the laws thereof, or can he in justice assist in making laws to bind his children's consciences

before they are born?" I judge not, for the following reasons:

1. Every man must give an account of himself to God, and therefore every man ought to be at liberty to serve God in that way that he can best reconcile it to his conscience. If government can answer for individuals at the day of judgment, let men be controled by it in religious matters; otherwise let men be free.

2. It would be sinful for a man to surrender that to man, which is to be kept sacred for God. . . .

3. But supposing it was right for a man to bind his own conscience, yet surely it is very iniquitous to bind the consciences of his children; to make fetters for them before they are born is very cruel. . . .

4. Finally, religion is a matter between God and individuals, religious opinions of men not being the objects of civil government nor in any way under its control.

It has often been observed by the friends of religious establishment by human laws, that no state can long continue without it; that religion will perish, and nothing but infidelity and atheism prevail.

Are these things facts? Did not the Christian religion prevail during the first three centuries, in a more glorious manner than ever it has since, not only without the aid of law, but in opposition to all the laws of haughty monarchs? And did not religion receive a deadly wound by being fostered in the arms of civil power and regulated by law? These things are so.

From that day to this we have but a few instances of religious liberty to judge by; for in almost all states civil rulers (by the instigation of covetous priests) have undertaken to steady the ark of religion by human laws; but yet we have a few of them without leaving our own land.

The state of Rhode-Island has stood above 160 years without any religious establishment. The state of New-York never had any. New-Jersey claims the same. Pennsylvania has also stood from its first settlement until now upon a liberal foundation; and if agriculture, the mechanical arts and commerce, have not flourished in these states equal to any of the states I judge wrong.

It may further be observed, that all the states now in union, saving two or three in New-England, have no legal force used about religion, in directing its course or supporting its preachers. And moreover the federal government is forbidden by the constitution to make any laws establishing any kind of religion. If religion cannot stand, therefore, without the aid of law, it is likely to fall soon in our nation, except in Connecticut and Massachusetts.

To say that "religion cannot stand without a state establishment" is not only contrary to fact (as has been proved already) but is a contradiction in phrase. Religion must have stood a time before any law could have been made about it; and if it did stand almost three hundred years without law it can still stand without it.

The evils of such an establishment are many.

1. Uninspired fallible men make their own opinions tests of orthodoxy, and use their own systems, as Procrustes used his iron bedstead, to stretch and measure the consciences of all others by. . . .

2. Such establishments not only wean and alienate the affections of one from another on account of the different usages they receive in their religious sentiments, but are also very impolitic, especially in new countries; for what encouragement can strangers have to migrate with their arts and wealth into a state, where they cannot enjoy their religious sentiments without exposing themselves to the law? . . .

3. These establishments metamorphose the church into a creature, and religion into a principle of state, which has a natural tendency to make men conclude that *bible religion* is nothing but a *trick of state.* . . .

4. There are no two kingdoms and states that establish the same creed or formularies of faith (which alone proves their debility). In one kingdom a man is condemned for not believing a doctrine that he would be condemned for believing in another kingdom. Both of these establishments cannot be right—but both of them can be, and surely are, wrong.

5. The nature of such establishments, further, is to keep from civil office the best of men. . . .

If these and many more evils attend such establishments—What were and still are the causes that ever there should be a state establishment of religion?

The causes are many—some of them follow.

1. The love of importance is a general evil. . . .

2. An over-fondness for a particular system or sect. . . .

3. To produce uniformity in religion. Rulers often fear that if they leave every man to think, speak and worship as he pleases, that the whole cause will be wrecked in diversity; to prevent which they establish some standard of orthodoxy to effect uniformity. But is uniformity attainable? Millions of men, women and children, have been tortured to death to produce uniformity, and yet the world has not advanced one inch towards it. And as long as men live in different parts of the world, have different habits, education and interests, they will be different in judgment, humanly speaking.

Is conformity of sentiments in matters of religion essential to the happiness of civil government? Not at all. Government has no more to do with the religious opinions of men than it has with the principles of the mathematics. Let every man speak freely without fear—maintain the principles that he believes—worship according to his own faith, either one God, three Gods, no God, or twenty Gods; and let government protect him in so doing, i.e., see that he meets with no personal abuse or loss of property for his religious opinions. Instead of discouraging him with proscriptions, fines, confiscation or death; let him be encouraged, as a free man, to bring forth his arguments and maintain his points with all boldness; then if his doctrine is false it will be confuted, and if it is true (though ever so novel) let others credit it. When every man has this liberty what can he wish for more? A liberal man asks for nothing more of government.

. . . .

It is not supposable that any established creed contains the whole truth and nothing but the truth; but supposing it did, which established church has got it? . . .

Truth disdains the aid of law for its defence—it will stand upon its own merits. . . .

4. The common objection "that the ignorant part of the community are not capacitated to judge for themselves" supports the popish hierarchy, and all protestant as well as Turkish and pagan establishments, in idea.

But is this idea just? Has God chosen many of the wise and learned? Has he not hid the mystery of gospel truth from them and revealed it unto babes? Does the world by wisdom know God? Did many of the rulers believe in Christ when he was upon earth? Were not the learned clergy (the scribes) his most inveterate enemies? Do not great men differ as much as little men in judgment? . . .

5. The groundwork of these establishments of religion is *clerical influence.* . . .

(From Leland, *The Rights of Conscience inalienable, and, therefore Religious Opinions not cognizable by Law: Or, The high-flying Churchman, stripped of his legal Robe, appears a Yaho [New London, Conn., 1791],* reprinted in *The Connecticut Dissenters Strong Box: No. I* [New London, Conn., 1802], 5-13.)

In North Carolina

The legislation in North Carolina that freed Baptists from the religious restrictions imposed upon them was the achievement of Henry Abbott, pastor of Pasquatank. He was elected to the State Congresses which met at Halifax in April and November, 1776. Here he was appointed a member of the committee to draft a Bill of Rights and Constitution. He had a large part in

the adoption of Article XXXIV of the Constitution and Article XIX of the Bill of Rights, which are quoted below. In addition, on December 22, 1776, he introduced a resolution concerning the right of all ministers to perform the marriage ceremony, which had been a matter of controversy. These documents make it clear that North Carolina Baptists were active in the matter of religious liberty in that state.

1. *Article XXXIV of the North Carolina Constitution concerning religious liberty adopted in 1776*

There shall be no establishment of any one religious church or Denomination in this State in Preference to any other, neither shall any person, on any pretence whatsoever, be compelled to attend any place of worship contrary to his own Faith or Judgment, or be obliged to pay for the purchase of any Glebe, or the building of any House of Worship, or for the maintenance of any Minister or Ministry, contrary to what he believes right, or has voluntarily and personally engaged to perform, but all persons shall be at liberty to exercise their own mode of worship. Provided, that nothing herein contained shall be considered to exempt preachers of treasonable and seditious Discourses, from legal trial and punishment.

(Quoted in Paschal, *op. cit.,* I, 459.)

2. *Article XIX of the Bill of Rights of North Carolina adopted in 1776*

That all men have a natural and inalienable right to worship Almighty God, according to the dictates of their own consciences.

(*Ibid.,* p. 458.)

3. *The right to perform marriage ceremonies in North Carolina adopted in 1776*

All regular ministers of the Gospel of every Denomination shall be empowered to celebrate matrimony, according to the rights and ceremonies of their respective churches.

(*Ibid.,* p. 356.)

Religious liberty in the national Constitution

At the time of the adoption of the Constitution, it was asserted that all powers not specifically given to the central Government were reserved to the states. Consequently, the authors of the Constitution felt that separation of church and state and religious liberty had sufficient safeguards, since no specific powers in that sphere were granted to the federal body. The only mention of religion referred to holding public office and asserted that no religious test should ever be required as a qualification to any office or public trust under the United States. The General Committee in March, 1788, voted unanimously that the Constitution did not make sufficient provision for safeguarding religious liberty. John Leland, a member of the committee, offered himself as a candidate from Orange County for the Virginia Convention, opposing the ratification of the Constitution. James Madison, who favored it, conferred with Leland, who disclosed the fears of the Baptists at this point. Madison agreed to introduce amendments to the Constitution to safeguard religious liberty; Leland then threw his influence to Madison, who was elected. Virginia ratified the Constitution, and in June, 1789, Madison introduced his promised amendments, the first of which provided the safeguard requested by Baptists.

Congress shall make no law respecting an establishment of religion, or prohibiting the free exercise thereof.

(From the United States Constitution, First Amendment.)

Correspondence with George Washington concerning religious liberty

1. The letter of the General Committee of Virginia Baptists

The General Committee addressed President George Washington on August 8, 1789, relative to the newly adopted national Constitution, and Washington made his historic reply.

To the President of the United States of America:

Sir,

Among the many shouts of congratulation that you receive from cities, societies, states, and the whole world, we wish to take an active part in the universal chorus, by expressing our great satisfaction in your appointment to the first office in the nation. When America, on a former occasion, was reduced to the necessity of appealing to arms to defend her natural and civil rights, a WASHINGTON was found fully adequate to the exigencies of the dangerous attempt; who, by the philanthropy of his heart, and prudence of his head, led forth her untutored troops into the field of battle, and by the skilfulness of his hands, baffled the projects of the insulting foe, and pointed out the road to independence, even at a time when the energy of the Cabinet was not sufficient to bring into action the natural aid of the confederation from its respective sources.

The grand object being obtained, the independence of the states acknowledged, free from ambition, and devoid of a thirst for blood, our HERO returned with those he commanded, and laid down his sword at the feet of those who gave it to him: Such an example to the world is new. Like other nations we experience that it requires as great valour and wisdom to make an advantage of a conquest as to gain one.

The want of efficacy in the confederation, the redundancy of laws, and their partial administration in the states, called aloud for a new arrangement of our system. The wisdom of the states for that purpose was collected in a grand convention, over which you, Sir, had the honour to preside. A national government, in all its parts, was recommended as the only preservative of the union; which plan of government is now actually in operation. When the Constitution first made its appearance in Virginia, we, as a society, had unusual strugglings of mind, fearing that the liberty of conscience (dearer to us than property and life) was not sufficiently secured; perhaps our jealousies were heightened on account of the usage we received in Virginia under the British government; when mobs, bonds, fines and prisons were our frequent repast.

Convinced on the one hand, that without an effective national government the states would fall into disunion and all the consequent evils; on the other hand, it was feared that we might be accessory to some religious oppression, *should any one society in the Union preponderate all the rest.* But amidst all the inquietudes of mind, our consolation arose from this consideration, the plan must be good, for it bears the signature of a *tried, trusty friend;* and if religious liberty is rather insecure in the Constitution "the administration will certainly prevent all oppression, for a WASHINGTON will preside." According to our wishes, the unanimous voice of the Union has called you, Sir, from your beloved retreat, to launch forth again into the faithless seas of human affairs, to guide the helm of the States. May that Divine munificence which covered your head in battle, make you yet a greater blessing to your admiring country in time of peace. Should the horrid evils that have been so pestiferous in Asia and Europe, faction, ambition, war, perfidy, fraud, and persecution for conscience sake, ever approach the borders of our happy nation; may the name and administration of our beloved President, like the radiant source of day, scatter all those dark clouds from the American hemisphere.

And while we speak freely the language of our own hearts, we are satisfied that we express the sentiments of our brethren whom we represent. The very name of WASHINGTON is music in our ears; and although the great evil in the States is the want of mutual confidence between rulers and the people, yet we all have the utmost confidence in the President of the States; and it is our fervent prayer to Almighty God, that the federal government, and the government of the respective states, without rivalship, may so cooperate together, as to make the numerous people, over whom you preside, the happiest nation on earth; and you, Sir, the happiest man, in seeing the people whom, by the smiles of Providence, you saved from vassalage by your martial valour and made wise by your maxims, sitting securely under their vines and fig-trees, enjoying the perfection of human felicity. May God long preserve your life and health for a blessing to the world in general, and the United States in particular; and when, like the Sun, you have finished your course of great and unparalleled services, and you go the way of all the earth, may the Divine Being, who will reward every man according to his works, grant unto you a glorious admission into his everlasting kingdom, through Jesus Christ. This, great Sir, is the prayer of your happy admirers.

By order of the Committee.
SAMUEL HARRIS, Chairman.
REUBEN FORD, Clerk.

2. Washington's reply

To the General Committee representing the United Baptist Churches in Virginia.
Gentlemen,

I request that you will accept my best acknowledgments for your congratulation on my appointment to the first office in the nation. The kind manner in which you mentioned my past conduct equally claims the expression of my gratitude. After we had, by the smiles of Divine Providence on our exertions, obtained the object for which we contended, I retired, at the conclusion of the war, with an idea that my country could have no farther occasion for my services, and with the intention of never entering again into public life. But when the exigencies of my country seemed to require me once more to engage in public affairs, an honest conviction of duty superseded my former resolution, and became my apology for deviating from the happy plan which I had adopted.

If I could have entertained the slightest apprehension that the constitution framed in the convention where I had the honour to preside, might possibly endanger the religious rights of any ecclesiastical society, certainly I would never have placed my signature to it; and if I could now conceive that the general government might ever be so administered as to render the liberty of conscience insecure, I beg you will be persuaded, that *no one would be more zealous than myself to establish effectual barriers against the horrors of spiritual tyrany, and every species of religious persecution.*

For, you doubtless remember, I have often expressed my sentiments, that every man, conducting himself as a good citizen, and being accountable to God alone for his religious opinions, ought to be protected in worshipping the Deity according to the dictates of his own conscience.

While I recollect with satisfaction, that the religious society of which you are members, have been throughout America, uniformly, and almost unanimously the firm friends to civil liberty, and the persevering promoters of our glorious revolution, I cannot hesitate to believe, that they will be faithful supporters of a free, yet efficient, general government. Under this pleasing expectation, I rejoice to assure them, that they may rely upon my best wishes and endeavours to advance their prosperity.

In the meantime, be assured, gentlemen, that I entertain a proper sense of your fervent supplication to God for my temporal and eternal happiness.

I am, gentlemen, your most obedient servant,

GEORGE WASHINGTON.

(From Semple, *op. cit.,* pp. 484-89.)

Section Six

The Second Great Awakening

The extraordinary revival west of the Alleghenies in the opening decade of the nineteenth century was not an isolated phenomenon. Virginia had experienced many revival seasons since the middle of the eighteenth century, which continued intermittently until the close of this period (see Ryland, op. cit., pp. 141-42, 177-78). But the unusual character of the Second Great Awakening gives it significance.

Baptists and the revival in Kentucky and Tennessee

From 1799 to 1803, there were, in most parts of the United States, remarkable outpourings of the Divine Spirit, among different denominations; multitudes became the subjects of religious concern, and were made to rejoice in the salvation of God. The revival among the Baptists in the southern and western States, has already been frequently referred to, and accounts of the astonishing additions to their churches have been given. This great revival in Kentucky began in Boone county on the Ohio River, and in its progress extended up the Ohio, Licking, and Kentucky Rivers, branching out into the settlements adjoining them. It spread fast in different directions, and in a short time almost every part of the State was affected by its influence. It was computed that about ten thousand were baptized and added to the Baptist churches in the course of two or three years. This great work progressed among the Baptists in a much more regular manner than people abroad have generally supposed. They were indeed zealously affected, and much engaged. Many of their ministers baptized in a number of neighbouring churches from two to four hundred each. And two of them baptized about five hundred a-piece in the course of the work. But throughout the whole, they preserved a good degree of decorum and order. Those camp-meetings, those great parades, and sacramental seasons, those extraordinary exercises of falling down, rolling, shouting, jerking, dancing, barking, &c. were but little known among the Baptists in Kentucky, nor encouraged by them. . . .

(From Benedict, *op. cit.* [1813], II, 251-52.)

These accounts were taken from people of unquestionable veracity, and no doubt can be entertained of their correctness. These jerking exercises were rather a curse than a blessing. None were benefited by them. They left sinners without reformation, and Christians without advantage. Some had periodical fits of them seven or eight years after they were first taken; and I know not as they have got over jerking yet.

There was among these enthusiastick people one more exercise of a most degrading nature, called the *barks*, which frequently accompanied the jerks. Many persons of considerable distinction, in spite of all the efforts of nature, as it was said, were "forced to personate that animal, whose name, appropriated to a human creature is counted the most vulgar stigma. These people would take the position of a canine beast, move about on all-fours, growl, snap the teeth, and bark in so personating a manner, as to set the eyes and ears of the spectator at variance." Some might be forced to these degrading exercises, but it is certain that many turned dogs in a voluntary manner. A minister in the lower parts of Kentucky informed me, that it was common to hear people barking like a flock of spaniels on their way to meeting. There they would start up suddenly in a fit of barking, rush out, roam around, and in a short time come barking and foaming back. But enough has been said of these frantick scenes. The above accounts are not fabulous tales, but they are real and melancholy facts.

In the upper counties in Kentucky, where the revival was the greatest among the Baptists, they were not at all affected with these delirious exercises. In the Green River country and in East-Tennessee, they prevailed considerably amongst them. With the Methodists they prevailed generally. The Presbyterians were divided respecting them; some opposed, while others encouraged them. Some of these exercises seemed really forced upon the subjects of them by some invisible power, whether good or bad the reader must judge for himself; but dancing, barking, rolling, shouting, and so on, were undoubtedly, for the most part, works of choice and imitation, which were hypocritically played off by a set of deluded, mistaken people. Where these fantastick exercises were opposed, they were the least prevalent. Those ministers who encouraged them, had enough of them to attend to.

In West-Tennessee the Baptists were not troubled with these works of delusion, but they prevailed here among the Presbyterians and Methodists; and some, who came from other parts, attempted to introduce them in the Baptist meetings. A Baptist minister by the name of Mr. Connico, was once preaching where one of the jerkers began his motions. The preacher made a pause, and with a loud and solemn tone, said, "In the name of the Lord, I command all unclean spirits to leave this place." The jerker immediately became still, and the report was spread abroad, that Mr. Connico cast out devils.

(Ibid., pp. 255-56.)

The revival in North Carolina

Both the Sandy Creek Association and the Kehukee Association (formerly Separate and Regular Baptists, respectively) were affected by the revival. An excerpt from Benedict describes the Sandy Creek situation, while Lemuel Burkitt describes the Kehukee.

1. Sandy Creek Association

Two very comfortable and extensive revivals had been experienced in this association, since the death of Mr. Stearns, before the one about to be mentioned. But by deaths and removals it was, at the close of the eighteenth century, in every respect much reduced. The ministers had become few in number, and the churches small and languid; iniquity greatly abounded in the land, and the love of many had waxen cold. But towards the close of the year 1800, that astonishing work which had been prevailing a short time in Kentucky and other parts, made a sudden and unexpected entrance amongst them, and was attended

with most of the new and unusual appearances, which in many places it assumed.
This work was not confined to the Baptists,
but prevailed, at the same time, amongst
the Methodists and Presbyterians, both of
which denominations were considerably
numerous in the parts. These two last
denominations, soon after the commencement of the revival, united in their communion and camp-meetings. The Baptists
were strongly solicited to embark in the
general communion scheme; but they, pursuant to their consistent (many call them
rigid) principles, declined a compliance.
But they had camp or field-meetings
amongst themselves, and many individuals
of them united with the Methodists and
Presbyterians in theirs. The Baptists established camp-meetings from motives of convenience and necessity, and relinquished
them as soon as they were no longer
needful.

. . . .

In the progress of the revival among the
Baptists, and, especially, at their camp-
meetings, there were exhibited scenes of the
most solemn and affecting nature; and in
many instances there was heard at the same
time, throughout the vast congregation, a
mingled sound of prayer, exhortation,
groans, and praise. The fantastick exercise
of jerking, dancing, &c. in a religious way,
prevailed much with the united body of
Methodists and Presbyterians, towards the
close of the revival; but they were not
introduced at all among the Baptists in
these parts. But falling down under religious
impressions was frequent among them.
Many were taken with these religious
epilepsies, if we may so call them, not only
at the great meetings, where those scenes
were exhibited, which were calculated to
move the sympathetick affections; but also
about their daily employments, some in the
fields, some in their houses, and some when
hunting their cattle in the woods. And in
some cases, people were thus strangely
affected when alone; so that if some played
the hypocrite, with others the exercise must
have been involuntary and unaffected. And

besides falling down, there were many
other expressions of zeal, which in more
moderate people would be considered
enthusiastick and wild.

The above relation was given me by
Rev. George Pope, the pastor of the church
at Abbot's Creek, who is a man of sense
and moderation, and who, with many of
his brethren, was much tried in his mind,
and stood aloof from the work at its
commencement; but it spread so rapidly
and powerfully, that they soon discovered
such evident marks of its being a genuine
work of grace, notwithstanding its new
and unusual appearances, that their doubts
subsided, and they cordially and zealously
engaged in forwarding and promoting it.
Mr. Pope, in the course of the revival,
baptized about 500 persons. Large numbers
were also baptized by John Culpepper,
William McGregore, and many others.

(*Ibid.*, pp. 108-11.)

2. Kehukee Association

*When Lemuel Burkitt in North Carolina
heard of the great revival in Kentucky, he
made a personal visit to that state and
returned home on fire for revival. The
following is his account.*

There was a small appearance of the
beginning of the work in Camden, and the
Flat Swamp, and Connoho church, But at
the Association at Great Swamp, in 1801,
Elder Burkitt just returning from Tennessee
and Kentucky, brought the news to this
Association, and proclaimed it from the
stage, that in about eight months six thousand had given a rational account of a
work of grace on their souls, and had been
baptized in the State of Kentucky, and
that a general stir had taken place
amongst all ranks and societies of people,
and that the work was still going on. The
desirable news seemed to take such an
uncommon effect on the people, that numbers were crying out for mercy, and many
praising and glorifying God. Such a Kehukee Association we had never before seen.
The ministers all seemed alive in the work
of the Lord, and every Christian present in

rapturous desire, was ready to cry, *Thy kingdom come*. The ministers and delegates carried the sacred flame home to their churches, and the fire began to kindle in the greatest part of the churches, and the work increased. The first appearance that was discovered was, *great numbers of people* attended the ministry of the word, and the congregations kept increasing. It was observed in some places, that as many people would now meet at a meeting on a common day, as used to meet on a Sunday, and as many would come on Sundays as used to attend at great meetings. And it was also observed that the audience was more *solemn* and *serious* than usual. This was the first beginning. Thus the work began to revive in many places within the bounds of the Association. The word preached was attended with such divine power, that at some meetings two or three hundred would be in floods of tears, and many crying out loudly, *What shall we do to be saved?* Another thing was observed, *old Christians* were so revived they were all on fire to see their neighbors, their neighbors' children and their own families so much engaged. Their souls seemed melted down in love, and their *strength renewed like the eagle's.* Many *backsliders* who had been runaway for many years, returned weeping home. The ministers seemed all united in love, and no strife nor contention amongst them, and all appeared to be engaged to carry on the work, and did not seem to care whose labors were most blessed so the work went on; and none of them seemed desirous to take the glory of it to themselves, which ought carefully to be observed. God is a jealous God, and will not suffer any of his creatures to take the glory of his work to themselves. We hope that no person will ascribe the glory of the work to any person or persons whatever, but to the Lord alone; for true religion is a *work of God*. The work increasing, many were converted, and they began to join the churches. In some churches where they had not received a member by baptism for a

year or two, would now frequently receive, at almost every conference meeting, several members. Sometimes twelve, fourteen, eighteen, twenty, and twenty-four at several times in one day. Twenty-two and twenty-four were baptized several times at Flat Swamp, Cashie, Parker's meeting-house, Fishing Creek, Falls of Tar River, &c. Some of the churches in the revival received nearly two hundred members each. In four churches lying between Roanoke and Meherrin Rivers, in Bertie, Northampton, and Hertford counties, were baptized in two years about six hundred members; and blessed be God the work seems yet progressing. The work has engaged the attention of all sorts of people—rich and poor, and all ranks. Many very respectable persons in character and office have been called in in this revival. There are a few churches within the bounds of the Association that have not as yet experienced a revival, but we hope for them. According to the accounts returned to the two last Associations fifteen hundred have been added to the churches by baptism in the Kehukee Association.

(From Burkitt and Read, *op. cit.*, pp. 144-47.)

The revival in South Carolina

Details of the camp meetings in South Carolina, particularly in what is known as the back country, are few. Benedict gives a brief summary, which is included herein, and two letters provide vivid descriptions of these revivals.

1. Benedict's summary

The great revival in this country, soon after the commencement of the present century, has often been referred to in the preceding narrative. We should be pleased to give a more particular account of it than we have hitherto done, or than we, for the want of materials, are able to do. The most we can say is, that between the years 1800 and 1803, there were most surprising movements of a religious nature on the minds of the people in South-

Carolina; and notwithstanding the manifest enthusiasm of many, the great Shepherd of the sheep gathered into his fold a large and precious number of Adam's ruined family. Of these, between three and four thousand joined the churches belonging to the Bethel and Broad River Associations. Large numbers were, at the same time, added to the Methodist and Presbyterian churches.

Camp meetings, during these refreshing seasons, were often held in the middle and upper regions of the State, which were promoted mostly by the Methodists and Presbyterians. Many of the Baptists, however, attended them, and united with their brethren of other denominations, so far as they could consistently with their principles. They also held meetings of a similar nature among themselves, so long as the necessity for them continued; and when that ceased, they returned to their usual places of worship.

(From Benedict, *op. cit.* [1813], II, 164.)

2. *Letter of David Lilly dated August 23, 1802*

I take my pen in hand to transmit to you good tidings. A great work of God is going on in the upper parts of this State. Multitudes are made to cry out, "What shall we do to be saved?" A few days ago, I returned from our Association. We have had a truly refreshing season. A vast concourse of people assembled on Saturday, and considerable appearances of solemnity soon took place; but no uncommon effect till Sunday late in the evening. Then the Lord was pleased to manifest his power to many hearts. Numbers were powerfully exercised through the whole night, and some were thrown to the ground.

On Monday the work increased. The hearts of many were made to melt; and several men, noted for their impiety, were stricken and lay among the prostrate. I must acknowledge it was a memorable time with my soul; the like I had not felt for many years before. In general, the people

were much engaged through the greater part of Monday night. Before sun-rise, on Tuesday morning, the sacred flame began to burn afresh; several, who had been before unaffected, came to the earth. The Association rose about 3 o'clock in the afternoon; and such a degree of brotherly affection as appeared among the ministers and messengers of the churches, I scarcely ever saw. It was enough to melt the heart of the greatest infidel living. So very intent were the people to hear, that they petitioned for preaching, after business was finished; and some of the ministers continued with them, in constant exercise, till midnight. During this time, the work appeared to increase. About twenty persons came to the ground, several of whom were lusty strong men; and many more were made to pray heartily to God. Among the number very deeply affected, were several officers of considerable rank, and others of equal respectability. Be assured, my brother, the Lord is doing great things for his people in this country.

. . . .

Yours, &c.

D. L.

(From *Georgia Analytical Repository*, Vol. I, number 3.)

3. *Letter of Richard Furman dated August 11, 1802*

Rev. and dear Sir,

Having promised you some imformation [sic] respecting the extraordinary meeting at the Waxhaws, to which I purposed going at the time I wrote in May, and having accordingly attended it, I now sit down to perform my promise.

It was appointed by the Presbyterian clergy in that part of the country, but clergymen of other denominations were invited to it; and it was proposed to be conducted on the same principles and plan with those held in Kentucky. The place of meeting is about 170 miles from Charleston, in the midst of a large settlement of Presbyterians, but not far distant from some congregations of Baptists and Methodists.

This Presbyterian congregation is one of the first which were formed in the upper parts of this State; has for its pastor a Mr. Brown, who is a respectable character; and is furnished with a commodious place of worship. But as the place of worship would not be in any wise equal to the numbers expected, a place was chosen in the forest for an encampment. The numbers which assembled from various parts of the country, formed a very large congregation, the amount of which has been variously estimated; to me there appeared to be 3000, or perhaps 4000 persons; but some supposed there were 7000 or 8000. My information respecting the number of ministers who attended, was probably not correct; but from what I observed, and collected from others, there were 11 Presbyterians, 4 Baptists, and 3 Methodists. The encampment was laid out in an oblong form, extending from the top of a hill down the south side of it, toward a stream of water, which ran at the bottom in an eastern direction, including a vacant space of about 300 yards in length and 150 in breadth. Lines of tents were erected on every side of this space; and between them, and behind, were the waggons and riding carriages placed; the space itself being reserved for the assembling of the congregation, or congregations rather, to attend publick worship. Two stands were fixed on for this purpose: at the one, a stage was erected under some lofty trees, which afforded an ample shade; at the other, which was not so well provided with shade, a waggon was placed for the rostrum.

The publick service began on Friday afternoon, the 21st of May, with a sermon by the Rev. Dr. M'Corkel, of the Presbyterian church; after which, the congregation was dismissed: but at the same time the hearers were informed, that they would be visited at their tents, and exhorted by the ministers, during the course of the evening. To this information an exhortation was added, that they would improve the time in religious conversation, earnest prayer, and singing the praises of God. This mode

of improving the time, both by the ministers and a large proportion of the hearers, was strictly adhered to: not only were exhortations given, but many sermons also were preached along the lines in the evening; and the exercises continued, by the ministers in general, till midnight; and by the Methodist ministers, among their adherents, nearly or quite all the night.

On Saturday morning, the ministers assembled, after an early breakfast, and appointed a committee to arrange the services for that day and the two following. The committee consisted wholly of Presbyterian ministers. They soon performed the work of their appointment, and assigned the several ministers present their respective parts of the service. By this arrangement, two publick services were appointed at each stand for that day; three for the Sabbath, together with the administration of the communion, at a place a little distant from the encampment; and two at each stand again for Monday. The intervals, and evenings in particular, to be improved in the same manner as on the former day. Necessary business calling me away on Sunday evening, I did not see the conclusion of the meeting. This, however, I can say, it was conducted with much solemnity, while I was at it; and the engagedness of the people appeared to be great. Many seemed to be seriously concerned for the salvation of their souls; and the preaching and exhortations of the ministers in general were well calculated to inspire right sentiments, and make right impressions. In the intervals of publick worship, the voice of praise was heard among the tents in every direction, and frequently that of prayer by private Christians. The communion service was performed with much apparent devotion, while I attended, which was at the serving of the first table. The Presbyterians and Methodists sat down together; but the Baptists, on the principle which has generally governed them on this subject, abstained. Several persons suffered at this meeting those bodily affections, which have been before experienced at Kentucky, North-

Carolina, and at other places, where the extraordinary revivals in religion within this year or two have taken place. Some of them fell instantaneously, as though struck with lightning, and continued insensible for a length of time; others were more mildly affected, and soon recovered their bodily strength, with a proper command of their mental powers. Deep conviction for sin, and apprehension of the wrath of God, was professed by the chief of them at first; and several of them afterwards appeared to have a joyful sense of pardoning mercy through a Redeemer. Others continued under a sense of condemnation, after those extraordinary bodily affections ceased; and some from the first, appeared to be more affected with the greatness and goodness of God, and with the love of Christ, than with apprehensions of divine wrath. In a few cases there were indications, as I conceived, of enthusiasm, and even affection; but in others a strong evidence of supernatural power and gracious influence. Several received the impression in their tents; others in a still more retired situation, quite withdrawn from company; some, who had been to that moment in opposition to what was thus going on, under the character of the work of God; and others, who had been till then careless. The number of persons thus affected, while I was present, was not great in proportion to the multitude attending. I have, indeed, been informed several more were affected the evening after I came away. . . .

I am, reverend and dear Sir, your friend and servant in the gospel,

RICHARD FURMAN.

(From Benedict, *op. cit.* [1813], II, 167-71.)

The revival in Georgia

Some account of the share which Georgia had in the great revival in 1800 and onward, has already been given. Many thousands, during the progress of this revival, were added to the Baptist churches. Mr. Jesse Mercer, of the Georgia Association, in the course of two years baptized about three hundred persons. In 1809, another revival began in the upper part of the State, in the bounds of the Georgia and Sarepta Associations, and many hundreds were hopefully born into the kingdom of God, and united with the churches of his saints.

In 1812, there was a very extensive revival in many different parts of the State. By the four Associations of Oakmulgee, Sarepta, Georgia, and Savannah, it appears that three thousand and eight hundred were added to them all, in the course of the year. To the Savannah were added about fifteen hundred, and to the Sarepta over twelve hundred and fifty.

(From Benedict, *op. cit.* [1813], II, 188.)

Summary of statistics in 1814 after the Second Great Awakening

Benedict provides an extensive table on pp. 497-553 of Vol. II of his 1813 edition. The figures evidently were collected for 1812 for most Baptists in America. Since these are reasonably accurate for the close of this period (1814), these figures are given to indicate the growth of Baptists in the period from 1740 to 1814.

State	Associations	Ministers	Churches	Members
Maryland	2	15	32	1,326
Virginia	16	283	283	35,164
North Carolina	11	110	194	12,083
South Carolina	5	96	157	10,794
Georgia	5	115	171	16,299
Tennessee	6	141	162	12,294
Kentucky	13	142	263	21,660
Missouri	1	13	20	894

Section Seven

A Baptist Publication

Beginning of The Georgia Analytical Repository

One of the first papers published by a Baptist in America was The Georgia Analytical Repository *of Henry Holcombe, pastor of the Baptist church in Savannah, Georgia. This paper ran through six issues from May and June, 1802, to March and April, 1803. The pages continued numbering from issue to issue, and a total of 288 pages is found in this publication. While the paper declared itself to be nonsectarian, most of the material in these six issues concerns Baptist life.*

Urged by, what we still conceive to be, the *necessity* of the measure, we again, respectfully enquire, if we may not, though *infants* in learning and religion, rationally indulge the pleasing hope of contributing, with effect, towards the maturity of both literature and piety, by combining and properly directing our efforts, in the encouragement and support of a *periodical piece*, for that *important*, because *all-comprehending purpose?* . . .

Among Georgians, *especially*, to whom it will probably, with a few exceptions, be eventually confined, it promises admission, and security, to *whatever sketches* may be considered interesting in a religious, or moral view. . . . It is ready to receive, and may be expected to contain, *analized* intelligence from every part of the christian world, a *brief* view of the rise, and present circumstances of all religious bodies in the state, *succinct* accounts of the contribution and incorporation of churches, minutes of their associations, or conferences, the ordination of ministers, opening places of worship, remarkable conversions, revivals in religion, *short* judicious essays on *any* subject of importance, the outlines, or an *analysis*, of good sermons, interesting deaths, of persons of all descriptions, well authenticated anecdotes, select sentences, poetry, and such remarks on the works and ways of God, in creation, Providence, and Grace, as may excite attention to the footsteps of divine intelligence and goodness, and thereby illustrate, and confirm the holy scriptures.

On the pages enriched with these materials, the public may be assured, the spirit of a *party* shall *never breathe*. Controversy will be carefully avoided, and the strictest impartiality observed toward all denominations.

(From *Preface*, I, 1, for May and June, 1802.)

Part Three
The United Period
1814-1845

Section One

Development of National Bodies

In the period from 1814 to 1845 American Baptists North and South united in organizing national bodies for benevolent work. Before 1814, many efforts had been made to develop national bodies without success, principally because Baptists were unwilling to organize simply for the sake of organization. However, with the conversion to Baptist views of Adoniram and Ann Hasseltine Judson and Luther Rice in 1812, American Baptists recognized the need for a national body to support the new foreign mission program. National Baptist societies were organized in 1814 for foreign missions (although for a brief period this body also supported home missions and education), in 1824 for tract or publication work, and in 1832 for home missions.

Background

1. The Judsons become Baptists in September, 1812

The Judsons and Rice sailed on separate ships for India as missionaries for the Congregationalists. En route they made separate investigations concerning what the New Testament teaches about baptism, knowing they would be forced to answer the English Baptist missionaries in India. All three became Baptists and were baptized by immersion in India. Rice returned to America to secure support for the foreign mission work from the Baptists.

(1) Ann Hasseltine Judson's account

Isle of France, Port Louis, February 14, 1813.

I will now, my dear parents and sisters, give you some account of our change of sentiment, relative to the subject of baptism. Mr. Judson's doubts commenced on our passage from America. While translating the New Testament, in which he was engaged, he used frequently to say that the Baptists were right in their mode of administering the ordinance. Knowing he should meet the Baptists at Serampore, he felt it important to attend to it more closely, to be able to defend his sentiments. After our arrival at Serampore, his mind for two or three weeks was so much taken up with missionary inquiries and our difficulties with government, as to prevent his attending to the subject of baptism. But as we were waiting the arrival of our brethren, and having nothing in particular to attend to, he again took up the subject. I tried to have him give it up, and rest satisfied in his old sentiments, and frequently told him, if he became a Baptist, *I would not.* He, however, said he felt it his duty to examine closely a subject on which he had so many doubts. After we removed to Calcutta, he found in the library in our chamber many books on both sides, which he determined to read candidly and prayerfully, and to hold fast, or embrace the truth, however mortifying, however great the sacrifice. I now commenced reading on the subject, with all my prejudices on the Pedobaptist side. We had with us Dr. Worcester's, Dr. Austin's, Peter Edwards's, and other Pedobaptist writings. But after closely examining the subject for several weeks, we were constrained to acknowledge that the truth appeared to lie on the Baptists' side. It was extremely trying to reflect on the consequences of our becoming Baptists. We knew it would wound and grieve our dear Christian friends in America—that we should lose their approbation and esteem. We thought it probable the commissioners would refuse to support us; and, what was more distressing than any thing, we knew we must be separated from our missionary associates, and go alone to some heathen land. These things were very trying to us, and caused our hearts to bleed for anguish. We felt we had no home in this world, and no friend but each other. Our friends at Serampore were extremely surprised when we wrote them a letter requesting baptism, as they had known nothing of our having had any doubts on the subject. We were baptized on the 6th of September, in the Baptist chapel in Calcutta. Mr. J. preached a sermon at Calcutta, on this subject, soon after we were baptized, which, in compliance with the request of a number who heard it, he has been preparing for the press. Brother Rice was baptized several weeks after we were. It was a very great relief to our minds to have him join us, as we expected to be entirely alone in a mission.

(Quoted in Francis Wayland, *A Memoir of the Life and Labors of the Rev. Adoniram Judson, D.D.* [Boston, 1853], I, 106-8.)

(2) Judson requests baptism

Calcutta, August 27, 1812.
To the REV. MESSRS. CAREY, MARSHMAN, and WARD.

As you have been ignorant of the late exercises of my mind on the subject of baptism, the communication which I am about to make may occasion you some surprise.

It is now about four months since I took the subject into serious and prayerful consideration. My inquiries commenced during my passage from America, and after much laborious research and painful trial,

which I shall not now detail, have issued in entire conviction, that *the immersion of a professing believer is the only Christian baptism.*

In these exercises I have not been alone. Mrs. Judson has been engaged in a similar examination, and has come to the same conclusion. Feeling, therefore, that we are in an unbaptized state, we wish to profess our faith in Christ by being baptized in obedience to his sacred commands.

ADONIRAM JUDSON, JR.

(*Ibid.,* p. 109.)

(3) Judson resigns from the Congregational Board

Calcutta, September 1, 1812.
Rev. and dear Sir: My change of sentiments on the subject of baptism is considered by my missionary brethren as incompatible with my continuing their fellow-laborer in the mission which they contemplate on the Island of Madagascar; and it will, I presume, be considered by the Board of Commissioners as equally incompatible with my continuing their missionary. The board will, undoubtedly, feel as unwilling to support a Baptist missionary as I feel to comply with their instructions, which particularly direct us to baptize *"credible believers with their households."*

The dissolution of my connection with the Board of Commissioners, and a separation from my dear missionary brethren, I consider most distressing consequences of my late change of sentiments, and indeed, the most distressing events which have ever befallen me. I have now the prospect before me of going alone to some distant island, unconnected with any society at present existing, from which I might be furnished with assistant laborers or pecuniary support. Whether the Baptist churches in America will compassionate my situation, I know not. I hope, therefore, that while my friends condemn what they deem a departure from the truth, they will at least pity me and pray for me. . . .

I am, sir, your friend and servant,

ADONIRAM JUDSON, JR.

Rev. Dr. Worcester, Corresponding Secretary of the American Board of Commissioners for Foreign Missions.

(Ibid., p. 110.)

(4) Judson appeals to American leaders for support: his letter to Lucius Bolles

Calcutta, September 1, 1812.
REV. SIR: I recollect that, during a short interview I had with you in Salem, I suggested the formation of a society among the Baptists in America for the support of foreign missions, in imitation of the exertions of your English brethren. Little did I then expect to be personally concerned in such an attempt.

Within a few months, I have experienced an entire change of sentiments on the subject of baptism. My doubts concerning the correctness of my former system of belief commenced during my passage from America to this country; and after many painful trials, which none can know but those who are taught to relinquish a system in which they had been educated, I settled down in the full persuasion that the immersion of a professing believer in Christ is the only Christian baptism.

Mrs. Judson is united with me in this persuasion. We have signified our views and wishes to the Baptist missionaries at Serampore, and expect to be baptized in this city next Lord's day.

A separation from my missionary brethren, and a dissolution of my connection with the Board of Commissioners, seem to be necessary consequences. The missionaries at Serampore are exerted to the utmost of their ability in managing and supporting their extensive and complicated mission.

Under these circumstances I look to you. Alone, in this foreign heathen land, I make my appeal to those whom, with their permission, I will call *my Baptist brethren* in the United States.

With the advice of the brethren at Serampore, I am contemplating a mission on one of the eastern islands. They have lately sent their brother Chater to Ceylon,

and their brother Robinson to Java. At present Amboyna seems to present the most favorable opening. Fifty thousand souls are there perishing without the means of life; and the situation of the island is such that a mission there established might, with the blessing of God, be extended to the neighboring islands in those seas.

But should I go thither, it is a most painful reflection that I must go alone, and also uncertain of the means of support. But I will trust in God. He has frequently enabled me to praise his divine goodness, and will never forsake those who put their trust in him. I am, dear sir,

Yours, in the Lord Jesus,
ADONIRAM JUDSON, JR.

(Ibid., pp. 111-12.)

2. Luther Rice becomes a Baptist in November, 1812

(1) Rice tells of his baptism

November 1st, 1812, was this day baptised in the name of the Holy Trinity. The Lord grant that I may ever find his name to be a strong tower, to which I may continually resort and find safety.

(Quoted in James B. Taylor, *Memoir of Rev. Luther Rice* [Baltimore, 1841], p. 106.)

(2) Rice writes Thomas Baldwin

Calcutta, Oct. 23, 1812.
Rev. and dear Sir,

ALTHOUGH I have not the happiness of your personal acquaintance, my peculiar situation will, I trust, be a sufficient apology for writing. Little indeed did I think, when leaving America as a Missionary, under direction of the Board of Commissioners, that I should so soon make a communication of such a nature as the present to Dr. Baldwin. It is probably inexpedient to detail the considerations which have recently issued in a change of sentiment respecting the important rite of Christian baptism. For your satisfaction, however, permit me to transcribe a part of my letter to Dr. Worcester, as Secretary of the Board of Commissioners, relative to this interesting event.—"The subject respecting the solemn and important ordinance of Christian baptism, presented itself to my mind in such an attitude, that I could not conscientiously refrain from examining it. With very considerable means at command, I have endeavoured, I trust, with prayerfulness, in the fear of God, and with no small impression of the delicacy and high responsibility of my situation, to give it a careful and very serious examination. But it is with emotions peculiarly afflicting, that I proceed to inform you, that in the result of this examination, I am compelled to relinquish a view of that sacred ordinance which I have formerly apprehended to be highly important. I am now satisfactorily convinced that those only who give credible evidence of piety, are proper subjects, and that immersion is the proper mode of baptism. This being the case, we think it expedient and proper that I should unite with brother Judson in a mission, rather than with the other brethren."

For my views respecting the plan of the mission which we wish to establish under the patronage of a Baptist Missionary Society, which we cannot but hope and expect will be soon formed in America, I must beg leave to refer to the letter of brother Judson upon the subject. Indeed, time will only allow me to add, without farther particulars, my affectionate and respectful salutations.

LUTHER RICE.

(From *The Massachusetts Baptist Missionary Magazine*, Vol. III, No. 10, May, 1813.)

3. Boston Baptists organize in October, 1812

When news of the conversion of the Judsons and Rice reached America, there was an immediate enthusiastic response from various parts of the country. Several societies were organized for the purpose of contributing to the foreign mission work. The principal body was that of Boston Baptists, and the following excerpt describes their organization.

FOREIGN MISSION SOCIETY.

REALIZING the vast importance of Truth, in advancing the best interests of man; and conceiving that in late events the finger of Providence has pointed out to us our immediate duty, in forming a Foreign Mission Society;—we, whose names are hereunto annexed, do cordially unite as a Society, for the purpose of propagating the gospel in India and other foreign parts; and mutually agree to be governed by the following

CONSTITUTION.

1. This Society shall be known by the name of "The Baptist Society for propagating the Gospel in India and other foreign Parts."

2. Its avowed and determinate object is, to send forth and support Missionaries in preaching the gospel, or in translating the Word of Life.

3. The immediate management of the concerns of this Society shall be vested in a Board, consisting of a President, Vice-President, Recording Secretary, Corresponding Secretary, Treasurer, and seven Trustees, to be elected by ballot at the first meeting of the Society, by a majority of the members present.

4. The officers of this Institution shall be chosen triennially at the stated annual meeting, which shall be holden in Boston on the second Wednesday in October. Provided however, That if at any annual meeting seven members shall express their desire for a re-election of officers, a new choice shall be made. Any vacancies which may occur, shall be filled at the next annual meeting.

5. The President shall have power to convene the Board whenever he shall judge the interests of the Society require it, or when requested thereto by three of the Trustees.

6. Seven members of the Board shall constitute a quorum to do business.

. . . .

9. The Corresponding Secretary shall open a correspondence with such Societies, Churches, or individuals, as the Board

shall direct, with a view to promote the great objects of this Institution.

10. The Treasurer shall faithfully keep the money paid into the treasury, and be ready at all times to deliver the whole or any part thereof, to the order of the Board of Trustees. His book shall be ever open to the inspection of any of the Trustees or members. Competent security shall be required by the Trustees for the stock that shall be entrusted to his care. It shall also be his duty annually at the meeting of the Society to present a specific account of the state of the funds.

11. This Society shall consist of all such persons as subscribe and pay two dollars or more into its treasury annually. Any subscriber may withdraw his name at pleasure.

12. Should Societies be formed in other places, having the same objects in view, the Board will appoint one or more persons to unite with Delegates from such other Societies in forming a General Committee, in order more effectually to accomplish the important objects contemplated by the Institution.

13. All donations to this Society, specifically designated for the translations of the Scriptures in India, shall be faithfully appropriated to that particular object.

(From *The Massachusetts Baptist Missionary Magazine*, Vol. III, No. 9, March, 1813.)

4. *English missionaries urge American Baptists to support the Judsons and Rice*

(1) *Letter from Joshua Marshman to Thomas Baldwin*

Serampore, September 1, 1812.

A note which brother Judson sent to brother Carey last Saturday has occasioned much reflection among us. In it he declares his belief that believers' baptism alone is the doctrine of the Scriptures, and requests to be baptized in the name of the Lord Jesus.

This unexpected circumstance seems to suggest many ideas. The change in the young man's mind, respecting this ordinance of Christ, seems quite the effect of divine truth operating on the mind. It began when no Baptist was near, (on board ship,) and when he, in the conscientious discharge of his duty, was examining the subject in order to maintain what he then deemed truth on his arrival in Bengal. And so carefully did he conceal the workings of his mind from us, on his arrival, that he scarcely gave us a hint respecting them before he sent this note to brother Carey. This was not indeed very difficult for him to do, as we make it a point to guard against obtruding on missionary brethren of different sentiments any conversation relative to baptism.

This change then, which I believe few who knew brother Judson will impute to whim, or to any thing besides sincere conviction, seems to point out something relative to the duty of our Baptist brethren with you, as it relates to the cause of missions. It can scarcely be expected that the Board of Commissioners will support a Baptist missionary, who cannot, of course, comply with their instructions, and baptize *whole households* on the parents' faith; and it is certain that the young man ought not to be left to perish for want, merely because he loved the truth more than father or mother; nor be compelled to give up missionary work for want of support therein. Now, though we should certainly interfere to prevent a circumstance like this happening, particularly as we have given our Pedobaptist brother Newell, gone to the Isle of France, an order to draw there upon us should he be in distress, yet, to say nothing of the missionary concerns already lying on us, and constantly enlarging, it seems as though Providence itself were raising up this young man, that you might at least partake of the zeal of our Congregational missionary brethren around you. I would wish, then, that you should share in the glorious work, by supporting him. Let us do whatsoever things are *becoming*, and whatsoever things are *lovely*, and leave the reverse of these for others.

After God has thus given you a missionary of your own nation, faith, and order, without the help or knowledge of man, let me entreat you, and Dr. Messer, and brethren Bolles and Moriarty, humbly to accept the gift.

To you I am sure I need add no more than to beg you to give my cordial love to all our brethren around you.

I may probably write you again soon, and in the meantime remain yours, in the Lord,

JOSHUA MARSHMAN.

(Quoted in Francis Wayland, *op. cit.*, I, 112-13.)

(2) Letter from William Carey, October 20, 1812

Letter from the Rev. Dr. Carey, to Rev. Dr. Staughton, dated Calcutta, October 20, 1812.

My dear brother Staughton,

IT was only this morning that I was informed of a ship's going so soon as tomorrow to America; I intended to have written you a long letter, but now the time is so short, that you must take the will for the deed.

Our brethren and sisters arrived safe and well, as did also our American brethren; and brother and sister May, Miss Green, &c. Since their arrival in Bengal, brother and sister Judson have been baptized; Judson has since that preached the best sermon upon baptism that I ever heard on the subject, which we intend to print. I yesterday heard that brother Rice had also fully made up his mind upon baptism.

As none of us had conversed with brother Judson before he shewed strong symptoms of a tendency towards believers' baptism, I inquired of him what had occasioned the change. He told me that on the voyage he had thought much about the circumstances that he was coming to Serampore where all were Baptists, that he should in all probability have occasion to defend infant sprinkling among us, and that in consequence he set himself to examine into the grounds of Pedo-baptism. This

ended in a conviction that it had no foundation in the Word of God, and occasioned a revolution in his sentiments which was nearly complete before he arrived in India. He mentioned his doubts, and convictions to Mrs. J. which operated to her conviction also, and they were both of them publickly baptized at Calcutta. I expect, however, that he will give the account of this change in an appendix to his sermon, which will, of course, be more correct than my statement.

Brother Rice was, on the voyage, thought by our brethren to be the most obstinate friend of Pedobaptism of any of the Missionaries. I cannot tell what has led to his change of sentiment, nor had I any suspicion of it till one morning when he came before I was up, to examine my Greek Testament; from some questions which he asked that morning, I began to suspect that he was inquiring: but I yesterday heard that he was decidedly on the side of believers' baptism. I expect therefore that he will soon be baptized.

What must be done with these men? Should the board of commissioners which sent them out discard them? We shall stretch out a helping hand to men who have forsaken their all to preserve a good conscience; but we are servants of our society, and do not consider ourselves at liberty to appropriate their funds to any specific purpose without their consent. We shall write immediately to them upon this subject. But is it impossible to form a Baptist Mission Society in America, either as an auxiliary society of ours in England, or as a sister, yet independent society? We will do all we can to give advice to the American Missionaries; and, if desired, will be the medium of communication to them just the same, as to our own brethren. Do stir in this business; this is a providence which gives a new turn to American relation to Oriental Missions. Brethren Judson and Rice intend to go to Java, either directly or circuitously, for you must know that they are not permitted to continue in any place belonging to the king of G.

Britain or his allies, Manritius excepted.

I hope none of our Baptist brethren in America will glory over their Congregational brethren on account of this circumstance. The fact is important, but let us improve it as christians.

I have filled my paper. Accept my thanks for the *Picture of Philadelphia*, and the other pamphlets. I am much pleased with your Greek Dictionary. The work of the Lord still prospers among us; but as I have filled my paper with other things, I shall write particulars of the progress of the gospel to Dr. Rogers, and refer him to you for an account of Judson and Rice.

I am,
very affectionately yours,
W. CAREY.

(From *The Massachusetts Baptist Missionary Magazine*, Vol. III, No. 11, September, 1813.)

(3) Letter from Carey, of Dec. 20, 1812

From Dr. Carey to the same.
Without date, written probably about the 20th of Dec. 1812.

MY DEAR BROTHER,

I AM not certain that Capt. Brown is returning to America, nor that he will take my letter; I however write that I may be ready if he should go. And the more so as I fear the intercourse between us will be far more difficult than it has been, should war take place between England and America.

I informed you in my last, of the baptism of brother and sister Judson, and have now to say that brother Rice was also baptized two months ago. I consider their baptism as a glorious triumph of truth over prejudice, and bless the Lord for it. . . . I hope our Baptist friends in America will take these two brethren under their protection, and consider them as their missionaries. We shall not desert them, nor their companions, should they be in want.

. . . .

Very affectionately yours,
W. CAREY.

(Ibid.)

(4) Letter from Ward

My dear brother Staughton,

. . . .

Could you not form a Society in the United States to receive contributions for the mission and translations, and promote annual collections all over the United States; I mean by annual sermons? Put your shoulder to this, my dear Staughton. You have now two countrymen Baptist Missionaries in India; brethren, Judson and Rice. I had the pleasure of baptizing these two brethren as well as sister Judson.

I am,
My dear brother Staughton,
ever yours,
Serampore, Dec. 23, 1812.   W. WARD.
(Ibid.)

5. American Baptists suggest that English Baptists employ the Judsons and Rice

(1) Letter from Sharp to Fuller.

Boston, March 5, 1813.

MY DEAR BROTHER: We have lately heard with peculiar pleasure of the arrival of your missionary brethren at Serampore. The same vessel brought us the intelligence that Rev. Adoniram Judson, one of the American missionaries, together with his wife, had experienced a change of views on the subject of baptism, and had expressed a desire to be immersed in the name of the Lord Jesus.

This intelligence has made a deep impression on our minds. We cannot bear that our brother should be neglected, or left to suffer because of his attachment to the truth. He looks to us for aid, and we stand ready to support him. We have formed a society, as you will perceive by the accompanying circular, named "The Baptist Society for Propagating the Gospel in India and other Foreign Parts."

The brethren here, however, suppose that it would much more advance the cause of Christ, and that brother Judson would be much more useful and happy in the missionary service, if he were intimately connected with, and under the direction of, our beloved brethren at Serampore. Their acquaintance with the county, the manners, prejudices, and superstitions of the people, their knowledge of the missionary efforts, likely, with the blessing of God, to be most efficient, a knowledge the result of twenty years' experience, their weight of years, their unshaken fortitude, intense zeal, and unquestionable integrity, and their disinterested course in so glorious a cause, render it very desirable that our brother should be considered as one of the mission family. I am therefore requested, in behalf of the newly-formed society in Boston, to solicit that Mr. Judson may be taken into the society of the Baptist brethren in India, and be under the direction of Messrs. Carey, Marshman, and Ward, and also be entitled to such privileges as would naturally arise from such a coalition.

We shall esteem it an honor and a pleasure to render him the pecuniary aid which from time to time he may need. Indeed, we expect that our exertions will not be limited to the support of our American brethren, but that we shall be able to forward to Serampore a willing tribute for the general cause.

Wishing you every blessing, I remain,
Dear sir, yours, very affectionately,
DANIEL SHARP.
Rev. Andrew Fuller, Sec. Baptist Mission in England.

(Quoted in Francis Wayland, *op. cit.*, I, 124-25.)

(2) *Letter of Daniel Sharp to Adoniram Judson*

May 6, 1813.
DEAR BROTHER: By the arrival of the Tartar, in January last, we received the intelligence of your change of views on the subject of Christian baptism, and also intimations of your readiness to embark in a mission under our patronage, should a society be formed among the Baptists in America for that purpose.

Your letters excited peculiar emotions. We considered it as the voice of God calling us to the formation of a missionary society. That we might not, however, be charged with acting prematurely, or be considered as interfering with the Board of Commissioners, we ascertained whether they intended to continue you in their service before we formally decided to engage you in ours.

Satisfied on inquiry what was our path of duty, we formed ourselves into a society for propagating the gospel in India and other foreign parts. At a meeting of the trustees, we unanimously agreed to employ you as our missionary, and to stand prepared to support you with all the pecuniary aid we can command.

By the arrival of another vessel, we have heard that the Rev. Mr. Rice entertains the same sentiments as yourself on the subject of baptism. This event gives us joy, because it must add much to your comfort in a foreign land to have a fellow-laborer in the gospel. The board have not met since Mr. Rice's letter was received, but I am confident that he will be taken under their care. We have not had time to mature our thoughts so as to say with decision whether it would be best for you to be connected with, or independent of, our brethren at Serampore.

At present it appears to us that a connection with them would most subserve the interests of the Redeemer's kingdom in India, and be most productive of happiness to yourselves. All the benefits which can be derived from union with men of integrity, disinterested benevolence, and a knowledge of the country, growing out of a twenty years' experience, would accrue to you from a relation with them. These considerations induced us in March last to write to Mr. Fuller, of Kettering, on the subject, expressing our wishes that you might be considered as belonging to the mission family at Serampore. Should it appear, from future events, more desirable that you should act alone, or as American missionaries, separately from the English brethren, then, no doubt, we shall be pleased to have it so; but our present sentiments are, that you had better act with and by their advice.

In behalf of the society,
Yours, affectionately,
DANIEL SHARP.

(Ibid., pp. 122-24.)

6. *Luther Rice's idea for a national organization of Baptists*

While passing from Richmond to Petersburg in the stage, an enlarged view of the business opened upon my contemplations. The plan which suggested itself to my mind, that of forming one principal society in each state, bearing the name of the state, and others in the same state, auxiliary to that; and by these large, or state societies, delegates be appointed to form one general society.

(Quoted in James B. Taylor, *op. cit.*, p. 146.)

7. *Preparation for a national organizational meeting*

REMARKS ON THE FOREIGN MISSION.

WE have the pleasure of stating to our readers, that under the smiles of Providence, we have now a fair prospect of sending the gospel to some of the benighted heathen.

Our esteemed brother Rice, mentioned in our last, has returned from India, and is now visiting our brethren of the south, for the purpose of uniting them with us in this great object. By letters received from him, it appears, that the proposed Mission is every where received with the utmost cordiality.

Mr. Rice is probably now in Charleston or Savannah. Letters have been received from him, from Philadelphia and Petersburg, of a pleasing nature.

. . . .

Mr. Rice has suggested the propriety of immediately fixing on the time and place of meeting, so that delegates may be duly appointed for that purpose. He has suggested Philadelphia as the most central place, and the early part of June as the most eligible time, (taking all circumstances into view) for the meeting. The writer of this, would not wish to dictate to his brethren, but at present perceives no very formidable objections to the proposal. The expense of such a Convention would be trifling compared with the magnitude of the object: Our success, under God, in providing funds for the foreign mission, depends on union among ourselves. It is believed that this union would be greatly promoted by such a meeting. It might also be productive of much good in other respects, as it would bring a number of ministering brethren together, who are now strangers by face to each other; by this means they would become acquainted with each other's sentiments and views, and would be able to encourage and strengthen each other's hands. It is to be hoped, that a blessing would also attend their labours while met, causing the hearts of many to rejoice.

(From *The Massachusetts Baptist Missionary Magazine*, Vol. III, No. 12, December, 1813.)

Organization of the General Missionary Convention, May 18-21, 1814

Through the work of Luther Rice and by general agreement of the leaders, a convention of thirty-three men met on May 18, 1814, at the First Baptist Church, Philadelphia, to discuss organizing a Baptist foreign mission body. The members were Richard Furman, Thomas Baldwin, William Rogers, William Staughton, Lucius Bolles, Henry Holcombe, William Bullein Johnson, Robert B. Semple, John Williams, Horatio Gates Jones, Stephen Gano, Burgiss Allison, Joseph Mathias, William White, James A. Ranaldson, Henry Smalley, Daniel Dodge, Jacob Grigg, John P. Peckworth, Silas Hough, Lewis Richards, Richard Proudfoot, William Boswell, Isaiah Stratton, Thomas Brooks, Luther Rice, John Sisty, Matthias B. Tallmadge, Matthew Randall, Stephen C. Ustick, Thomas

Hewitt, Edward Probyn, and Nathanael Smith, all but the last seven being ministers. (See Albert L. Vail, The Morning Hour of American Baptist Missions [Philadelphia, 1907], pp. 310-75, for a brief biography of each of these men.)

1. A constitution adopted

After a committee of fifteen had been unable to suggest a satisfactory constitution, a new committee of five was appointed, consisting of Messrs. Furman, Baldwin, Gano, Semple, and White. Although he was not on the committee, the distinguished jurist, Matthias B. Tallmadge, evidently had a large part in the preparation of the constitution. After the proposed constitution was considered seriatim and some amendments adopted, unanimous approval was given to the following document.

BAPTIST MISSION TO THE HEATHEN.

PERHAPS no event has ever taken place among the Baptist denomination in America, which has excited more lively interest, than the late missionary Convention held in the city of Philadelphia.

It was indeed a sight no less novel than interesting, to behold brethren who had hitherto been unknown to each other by face, collecting from north to south, from nearly all the States, from Massachusetts to Georgia, (a distance of more than 1000 miles) for the important purpose of forming a General Convention, in order to concentrate the energies, and direct the efforts of the whole denomination throughout the United States, in sending the gospel to the Heathen.

It was foreseen, that in order to accomplish this great object, much labour and toil would be required, and that nothing short of a patient unshaken perseverance, could furnish a reasonable ground to hope for success. The great distance, to some of the brethren, presented a very discouraging aspect; but the thought of meeting such a number of the dear servants of Christ, upon such an important occasion, inspired them with resolution, "and fired their zeal along the road."

Through the kind providence of a gracious God, nearly all the Delegates which had been appointed, were permitted to meet. Extracts from the proceedings of this interesting meeting, will now be given; but for a full and perfect account, we must refer our readers to the Minutes of the Convention.

On the 18th of May last, the Delegates from the different States, assembled in the meeting house of the first Baptist church in the city of Philadelphia, when

"The Rev. Dr. Furman of Charleston, S. C. was called to the Chair, who opened the meeting with an appropriate prayer, in which the feelings of all present appeared to be solemnly united.

Rev. Dr. Baldwin of Boston, was requested to officiate as Secretary."

After much prayerful deliberation, in which a candid and liberal interchange of sentiments and feelings relative to the great object of the meeting were developed, the following Constitution was unanimously adopted.

CONSTITUTION.

WE the delegates from Missionary Societies, and other religious Bodies of the Baptist denomination, in various parts of the United States, met in Convention, in the City of Philadelphia, for the purpose of carrying into effect the benevolent Intentions of our Constituents, by organizing a plan for eliciting, combining, and directing the energies of the whole denomination in one sacred effort, for sending the glad tidings of Salvation to the Heathen, and to nations destitute of pure Gospel-light, DO AGREE to the following Rules or fundamental Principles, viz.

I. That this body shall be styled "The General Missionary Convention of the Baptist Denomination in the United States of America, for Foreign Missions."

II. That a triennial Convention shall, hereafter, be held, consisting of Delegates, not exceeding two in number, from each of the several Missionary Societies, and other religious bodies of the Baptist Denomination, now existing, or which may hereafter be formed in the United States, and which shall each regularly contribute to the general Missionary Fund, a sum, amounting, at least, to one hundred Dollars, per annum.

III. That for the necessary transaction and dispatch of business, during the recess of the said Convention, there shall be a Board of twenty-one Commissioners, who shall be members of the said Societies, Churches, or other religious bodies aforesaid, triennially appointed, by the said Convention, by ballot, to be called the "Baptist Board of Foreign Missions for the United States:" seven of whom shall be a quorum for the transaction of all business; and which Board shall continue in office until successors be duly appointed; and shall have power to make and adopt by-laws for the government of the said Board, and for the furtherance of the general objects of the Institution.

IV. That it shall be the duty of this Board, to employ Missionaries, and, if necessary, to take measures for the improvement of their qualifications; to fix on the field of their labours, and the compensation to be allowed them for their services; to superintend their conduct, and dismiss them, should their services be disapproved; to publish accounts, from time to time, of the Board's Transactions, and an annual Address to the public; to call a special meeting of the Convention on any extraordinary occasion; and, in general, to conduct the executive part of the missionary concern.

V. That such persons only, as are in full communion with some regular Church of our Denomination, and who furnish satisfactory evidence of genuine Piety, good Talents, and fervent Zeal for the Redeemer's Cause, are to be employed as Missionaries.

. . . .

XII. That the said Convention shall have power, and in the interval of their meeting, the Board of Commissioners on the recommendation of any one of the constituent bodies belonging to the Convention, shall also have power, to elect honorary members of piety and distinguished liberality, who, on their election, shall be entitled to a seat, and to take part in the debates of the Convention: but it shall be understood that the right of voting shall be confined to the delegates.

XIII. That in case any of the constituent bodies shall be unable to send representatives to the said Convention, they shall be permitted to vote by proxy, which proxy shall be appointed by writing.

XIV. That any alterations which experience may dictate from time to time, may be made in these Articles, at the regular meeting of the Convention, by two thirds of the members present.

RICHARD FURMAN, Pres.
THOMAS BALDWIN, Sec'ry.

(From *The Massachusetts Baptist Missionary Magazine*, Vol. IV, No. 3, September, 1814.)

2. Organization and first meeting

After the adoption of the Constitution, the Convention preceeded agreeably to the 3d Article, to elect the board of Commissioners, when the following persons were returned as duly chosen: viz. Richard Furman, Wm. Rogers, Henry Holcombe, Wm. Staughton, Thomas Baldwin, Burgiss Allison, James A. Ranaldson, Daniel Dodge, Obadiah Brown, John Williams, William White, John P. Peckworth, Wm. B. Johnson, Robert B. Semple, Stephen Gano, Lucius Bolles, Lewis Richards, Matthias B. Tallmadge, Jeremiah Vardeman, H. G. Jones, and William Moulder.

And also in conformity to the 12th Article, the following gentlemen were elected honorary members, viz. Robert Ralston, Esq. and Capt. Benjamin Wickes of Philadelphia, Hon. Jonas Galusha of Shaftsbury, Vermont, John Bolton, Esq. of Savannah, Georgia, and Rev. Thomas B. Montanye, Pennsylvania.

Tuesday, May 24, the members of the board present, (15 in number) met at the First Baptist Meeting-House, Philadelphia, and after addressing the throne of grace, proceeded agreeably to the 6th Article, to organize the board.

1. Dr. Baldwin was called to the chair, and Rev. Mr. Johnson was requested to act as secretary.

2. Proceeded to the election of officers. Dr. Furman was chosen President, but (notwithstanding the earnest solicitations of his brethren,) he declined the office, on the account of his great distance from the seat of the board. Dr. Baldwin was then elected to the Presidency. Dr. Holcombe was chosen first, and Dr. Rogers, second Vice-President. Hon. Judge Tallmage was elected Treasurer, but declined, on account of the delicate state of his health: Mr. John Caldwell of New-York, was then chosen to that office. Dr. Staughton was chosen Corresponding Secretary, and Rev. Mr. White, Recording Secretary.

Wednesday, May 25th. The board met agreeably to adjournment, at the Meeting-House in Sansom-Street. Dr. Holcombe opened the meeting by prayer, after which the following business was transacted:

1. Certain communications were made to the board by the Rev. Mr. Rice, containing remarks on fields for Missionary labour; together with a statement of the monies he had received, and expended on his journey to the southern States: on which resolved—That the Board possess a high sense of the zealous, disinterested and faithful services of their beloved brother, and feel a lively emotion of gratitude to the Lord, for the success with which his labours have been crowned. Ordered that the communication be published. (See the Minutes of the Convention.)

2. Resolved, That Mr. Rice be appointed, under the patronage of this board, as their Missionary, to continue his itinerant services, in these United States, for a reasonable time; with a view to excite the public mind more generally, to engage in Missionary exertions: and to assist in orig-

inating Societies, or Institutions, for carrying the Missionary design into execution.

3. On motion, Resolved, That the Rev. Adoniram Judson, Jun. now in India, be considered as a Missionary, under the care and direction of this Board; of which he shall be informed without delay: That provision be made for the support of him and his family accordingly: and that one thousand dollars be transmitted to him by the first safe opportunity: That the Secretary of the Particular Baptist Society, for Missions in England, be informed of this transaction; and that this Board has assumed the pledge given by the Boston Mission Society, to pay any bills which may be drawn on them, in consequence of advances they may have made in favour of Mr. and Mrs. Judson.

4. Resolved, That our brother Judson be requested, for the present, to pursue his pious labours in such places, as, in his judgment, may appear most promising: and that he communicate his views of future permanent stations to this board, as early as he conveniently can.

5. Resolved, That the proceedings of the late Convention, and of this board be communicated to the Baptist Missionary Society in England, and to their Missionaries at Serampore, assuring them that it is the desire of this board to hold an affectionate intercourse with them, in the work of the Lord: that they will ever be grateful for any information which the extensive experience of their brethren may enable them to impart on the subject of fields for Missionary action, &c. &c. and will derive joy from the reflection, that though in these transactions their respective seats of council be remote from each other, their hearts and aims are harmonious.

6. Resolved, That a suitable compensation be made to our brother Rice for his labours in originating Mission Societies, and that brethren Rogers, Holcombe and Staughton, be a committee to confer with him, and decide on the subject.

(Ibid.)

3. *Address of the body to the public*

ADDRESS.

The General Convention of the Baptist delegates for Missionary purposes, assembled in the Meeting-House of the First Baptist Church in Philadelphia, on Wednesday, the 18th May, 1814; to their constituents, the churches of Jesus Christ, the Ministers of the Gospel, and the friends of religion in general, present their christian love and cordial wishes.

BELOVED BRETHREN AND FRIENDS,

. . . .

But, while we call your attention to the spread of evangelic truth, we would impress on your minds that many other and most important advantages may arise to the interests of Christ among us from our acting as societies and on the more extended scale of a Convention, in delightful union. The independence of the churches, we trust will ever, among us, be steadfastly maintained; but with this, as they are entirely voluntary, the holy combinations we wish for, can never interfere. Is it not a fact that our churches are ignorant of each other to a lamentable degree? But for the labours of one or two individuals, it is probable that whole Associations might have assembled in different parts of our Union without being known or knowing that others existed. We have "one Lord, one faith, one baptism," why should our ignorance of each other continue? why prevent us from uniting in one common effort for the glory of the Son of God? At the present Convention the sight of brethren who had never met each other before, and who a few months ago had never expected to meet on earth, afforded mutual and unutterable pleasure. It was as if the first interviews of heaven had been anticipated.

The efforts of the present Convention have been directed chiefly to the establishment of a foreign Mission; but, it is expected that when the general concert of their brethren, and sufficient contributions to a common fund shall furnish them with proper instruction and adequate means,

the promotion of the interests of the churches at home, will enter into the deliberations of future meetings.

It is deeply to be regretted that no more attention is paid to the improvement of the minds of pious youth who are called to the gospel ministry. While this is neglected, the cause of God must suffer. Within the last fifty years, by the diffusion of knowledge and attention to liberal science the state of society has become considerably elevated. It is certainly desirable the information of the minister of the sanctuary should increase in an equal proportion. Other denominations are directing their attention with signal ardour to the instruction of their youth for this purpose. They are assisting them to peruse the sacred writings in their original languages, and supplying other aids for pulpit services, which, through the grace of the Holy Spirit, may become eminently sanctified for the general good. While we avow our belief that a refined or liberal education is not an indispensable qualification for ministerial service, let us never lose sight of its real importance, but labour to help our young men by our contributions, by the origination of education Societies, and if possible, by a general theological seminary, where some, at least, may obtain all the advantage, which learning and mature studies can afford, to qualify for acting the part of men who are set for the defence of the gospel. Improvement of this nature will contribute to roll away from the churches the reproach of neglecting to support the ministry of the word. They will be unwilling to receive for nothing that which has cost their ministers much.

Finally, brethren, "be ye steadfast, immovable, always abounding in the work of the Lord, forasmuch as ye know that your labour is not in vain in the Lord."

RICHARD FURMAN, President.

Attest,

THOMAS BALDWIN, Secretary.

(Ibid.)

4. The work of Luther Rice in the homeland

66

Luther Rice was appointed agent to secure collections and arouse interest in missions in the homeland. He and others expected that this activity would be brief, and that he would thereafter be appointed to the foreign mission field. Circumstances made it impossible, however, for him ever to return to India. This excerpt shows his indefatigable activity.

The 25th of July, I left Philadelphia, and arrived in Warrenton, N. C. on the evening of Friday, 2d August, at least 370 miles. After attending the North Carolina general meeting of correspondence, near that place, I took stage on the night of Monday, about midnight, having been occupied after meeting, till that hour, in writing, without going to bed, and about 2 o'clock, on Wednesday morning, arrived again in Richmond, Va. more than 100 miles from Warrenton. In the evening of the same day, preached in Richmond, wrote twenty-one letters on Thursday, besides doing some other necessary business, and at 3 o'clock, on Friday morning, left that city, and preached in the evening of the same day, in Goochland county, forty miles from Richmond. At a yearly meeting, same place, preached again on Saturday at 12 o'clock, and on the Sabbath, that is, the next day, was with the Appomattox Association; preaching in Prince Edward county, about sixty miles from where I was in Goochland county.

The following Sabbath, 18th of August, I was with the County Line Association, in Caswell county, N. C., having had but an easy week's ride of about 166 miles; and was with the Mountain Association, in Burke county, N. C. the next Sabbath, having gone that week, 214 miles. The following Saturday, was with the Shiloh Association, in Culpepper county, Va., having been under the necessity of riding *more than four hundred miles in less than six days.* Was at the Green Briar Association the next Sabbath, in Monroe county, Va., having gone in the week, the latter part of which was rainy, about 222 miles.

The next Sabbath, at the North District Association, Montgomery county, Kentucky, 290 miles; raining all the week, excessively bad roads, mountains, rivers, creeks, and mud—my health began to be impaired. The following Sabbath, with the Franklin Association, near Frankfort, Ky., only about 100 miles riding for me the whole week, nearly three days of which were spent in Lexington, preaching, hearing preaching, visiting, and necessary business, &c. &c.

The Friday following, I was at the Union Association, in Knox county, Ky., and left it the same evening, intending to be with the Caney Fork Association, in Warren county, Tennessee, on the Sabbath; but after very severe riding, failed, finding the distance too great, and unable to procure a fresh horse by the way; but the next Sabbath, 6th of October, was with the Flint River Association, Bedford county, Tennessee, having gone about 300 miles in the week. The next Sabbath, was with the Tennessee Association, in Blount county, Tennessee, 226 miles the week's ride. The Friday following was at the opening of the Broad River Association, in Rutherford county, N. C. Left that on the same afternoon, and on Sabbath morning, by meeting-time, was with the Pee Dee Association, in Montgomery county, N. C.; riding between the two, about 120 miles.

Being obliged to ride in the night, on Friday night I got lost. The roads in this part of our country are none of them fenced, and are mostly through woods; I had to go that night in by roads, but little traveled—missed the way, got out of roads, at length, into mere paths, and ultimately, lost the path—found myself alone in a dreary wilderness, unable to discover the point of compass; totally ignorant which way to direct my course, to find any road or habitation of men. I stopped, and besought the Lord to lead me out—rose from my supplications, and attempted to advance. In less perhaps, than two minutes, certainly, in less than five, fell into the road which conducted me to the place that I calculated to reach that night, at which I arrived about 1 o'clock. Have now just come from attending the Sandy Creek Association, and am on my way to the Charleston. Such is the outline of my course since leaving Philadelphia. Frequently, after completing a day's ride, instead of indulging in the repose which nature solicits, it is necessary for me to employ my pen; however, fatigues too often overcome me, or perhaps I too easily yield to the inclination for rest.

(Quoted in James B. Taylor, *op. cit.*, pp. 168-71.)

5. Enlargement of sphere in 1817

The structure of the General Missionary Convention was a compromise between the associational and the society methods. A reflection of the associational structure is seen in the addition of two benevolences for its attention in 1817: home missions and education.

(1) Scope of General Mission Convention enlarged in 1817 to include home missions and education

Suggestions which have been offered relative to the propriety of altering, in some points, the Constitution of the Convention, the Board have taken into serious consideration. They apprehend that instruments of this description ought to be held as sacred as possible, so that changes occur only when imperious necessity, or a conviction of solid advantages shall require them. They have reason to believe that bequests have been made to the Convention, which a variation of the title might render precarious. But from the experience of three years, and the best light they have been able to obtain, they are of opinion that the following alterations will be beneficial, and are expedient, *viz.* That the powers of this Convention be extended so as to embrace home missions and plans for the encouragement of education; and that henceforward the quorum of the Board for the transaction of business be five.

(From *The American Baptist Magazine*

and *Missionary Intelligencer*, Vol. I, No. 5, September, 1817, p. 170.)

(2) Peck and Welch set apart for the home mission task

Application was made on the part of the Rev. Messrs. John M. Peck, and James E. Welch, for an appointment to a Western mission, having reference ultimately to the Western Indians. This application was accompanied with a statement by their tutor, the Rev. Dr. Staughton, much in favour of their religious character and deportment while members of his family, and of their talents and acquirements for the sacred ministry, which was highly satisfactory to the Board.

Resolved, unanimously, That the said brethren, James E. Welch and John M. Peck, be accepted as Missionaries of this Board; that they be instructed to proceed, as soon as convenient, to the westward, with a view to commence their labours at St. Louis, or its vicinity, in the Missouri Territory; that 1000 dollars be placed in their hands, to assist them in going with their families to St. Louis, and to support them in the commencement of their missionary exertions; that they be authorized and requested to make collections of money, and of books, as opportunities offer, with a view of aiding the Western mission, and give account of the same to the Board; that they be instructed also to make inquiries, after arriving in the missionary field, relative to the native tribes in that quarter; and that, on the ensuing Sabbath, they be solemnly *set apart* to the service of the said Western mission.

(Ibid., pp. 174-75.)

At five, P.M. the people assembled again, to witness the setting apart of Messrs. Peck and Welch for the Western Mission. Dr. Furman preached from Acts xiii. 2. The usual questions were proposed by the pastor, and answered by the brethren. Prayer was then offered up, by Rev. Dr. Baldwin. The Rev. Mr. Mercer addressed a solemn charge to the missionaries, (then standing in the aisle,) and Dr. Staughton

A BAPTIST SOURCE BOOK

very affectionately tendered the right hand. All the ministering brethren present united in the same apostolic ceremony, expressing their devout wishes, that the good-will of Him who dwelt in the bush, might accompany them in all their journeyings and labours.

(From *The American Baptist Magazine and Missionary Intelligencer*, Vol. I, No. 4, July, 1817, p. 134.)

6. Criticism of organizational form

Between November, 1823, and May, 1824, a writer using the pseudonym "Backus" wrote a series of six letters printed in the principal American Baptist magazine of the day, in which he discussed the nature, advantages, and defects of the Baptist associational structure. In Letters V and VI, enlarging upon the defects in the associational system, he makes some significant observations about the contemporary Baptist organizational forms and suggests ways of improvement. These views are important because this "Backus" was Francis Wayland, the most influential voice in New England for a generation. Other pseudonymous letters later appeared, in general favoring Wayland's point of view.

(1) Part of Letter V

To the Editor of the Am. Bap. Magazine
Dear Sir,

In some former letters I submitted to your consideration, some remarks on the subject of Baptist Associations. I then noticed the advantages and defects of the system as it now exists among us. The present communication will terminate the series of observations which I propose to submit to your readers.

I shall now proceed to consider the most striking defect with which, in my opinion, our system is chargeable. It is, that at present, our whole plan is unfinished. We have the *basis* of a system of perfect representation throughout the whole United States, and here the thing has remained for half a century at a stand. To me it resembles the foundation of a house which had been accurately planned, and judiciously located, for which the materials had been all procured, and brought to the place of building, and then the whole business suspended. I will illustrate my meaning by an appeal to facts. Our system evidently proceeds upon the principal of universal representation. Every church belongs to some Association. Each sends its delegates to sit in council. It is supposed that they are to devise measures for the good of the whole, in any manner not inconsistent with the principles of the gospel, and those views of church government which are deemed essential. Thus far has our system been carried, and here it has stopped. And stopping here, a great part of the benefit which might be derived from the plan is utterly lost. We have no concert of action. We have never agreed upon any general plan of union. We have no means of general information. Each Association is an insulated body, destitute of any regular connexion with any other part of the denomination. Each church knows its own Association, but it knows not, nor can it know, definitely and accurately, any thing beyond it. We resemble an army, of which the companies have never been united into brigades. No means exists for bringing the whole force to bear upon a single point. Every part is weak because all are divided.

. . . .

Now it is evident that the same principles apply to us as a denomination. It is the duty of each of us as individuals, to do all in our power to promote the interests of the Redeemer's kingdom. It is also our duty to do it collectively as a branch of the general church of Christ. But to do this, we must act in concert. We do not wish to bind the consciences of our brethren. We do not want to abridge the liberties of any individual church. These we hold sacred, and we always shall so hold them; but we want them to assist us, and want to assist them, in all the plans that they or we may devise for promoting the salvation of our fellow men. The fact is, there are many thousands of us in the United States, whose belief of the gospel is the same. We have one Lord, one fatih, one baptism. Why should we not unite all efforts together, and thus do our utmost to promote the cause of Christ in the United States, and throughout the world? Why should we be divided into a thousand little departments, almost ignorant of each other, and, in consequence of this ignorance, unable to assist each other in our plans for doing good? We all in substance have the same articles of belief. Why should we not compare them together and publish them to the world? In no other way can we escape the reproach which justly falls upon many who call themselves Baptists, and at the same time hold articles of belief the very reverse of our own. We have all the same mode of church government. But it is no where to be found with any authentic acknowledgement as that of the Baptist church in the United States. Our rules, forms of proceeding, articles of belief, and many other matters of importance to us, are only kept by oral tradition. We would see them embodied in a visible shape, so that innovations in doctrine and practice may be hereafter prevented.

. . . .

I am yours, most sincerely,

BACKUS

(From *The American Baptist Magazine and Missionary Intelligencer*, May, 1824, pp. 324-25.)

(2) *Part of Letter VI*

Dear Sir,

My last letter closed with the question, How may a general union of our churches throughout the United States be accomplished? I shall now suggest the answer to it. Here I confess I distrust myself. I know it is much easier to point out a difficulty, than administer a remedy. And I know that it is much easier to theorize on these subjects, than to bring any theory into practice. What I shall suggest therefore will be with diffidence, and will be rather intended to draw the attention of my brethren to this subject, than to point

out to them a plan of operation. My only inducement, if I know my own heart, is the hope of suggesting something which may be of utility to our denomination. If any thing can be suggested with more probability of usefulness, I shall with great readiness commit my plans to the flames.

First, then, it should be distinctly recognized that each church is distinct and independent. No body which ever can be created, should have any power to control its belief or its practice. The only object of combination should be the good of the whole, and the promotion of the general interests of the cause of Christ amongst us.

Let us begin with Associations. An Association is a meeting of ministers and messengers from all the churches within a certain district. All the Associations together, therefore, comprise the whole of our church. Any plan of representation which may be devised for combining them all together, would give us the voice of every man in our connexion. And moreover, every Association is well acquainted with the state of all the churches in its own limits. The information of all our Associations then, yearly collected, would give us the regular information concerning our whole church, the number of ministers, of churches, of members, their increase or diminution, and every thing which relates to them. Again, our churches are all willing to do something for the cause of missions and of education. Many churches cannot do much, but most can do something. But they are not regularly called upon. There are no regular channels through which their liberality can flow to the general treasury. They need to have a duty assigned, and a part allotted to them. As it is now, each one stands alone, and all feel weak from the fact of that loneliness. And besides, in some parts of our country, our churches are poor, they stand in need of assistance, but they know not where to go to seek it, nor in what manner to ask for it. There is really no provision made by which their wants may be relieved.

In other parts of our country, our churches are liberal, and would willingly assist those districts which are in need, but they are ignorant of their necessities, and moreover, there is no channel through which their liberality can be conveyed.—But to return. We see then that the Associations are in possession of all the information we could desire, if it could only be regularly collected. We see they are representative bodies, and could declare the faith and practice of their churches. And moreover, they are representative deliberative bodies, and are empowered to devise means for the promotion of the cause of Christ, not inconsistent with their received rules of faith and practice. The question then returns, in what manner can they be so combined as to effect these valuable purposes?

The model of our system of general and state governments will at once suggest itself to every American. The Associations in one state could easily send delegates to a state convention. This would embody all the information, and concentrate the energies of a state. These state conventions could send delegates to a general convention, and thus the whole denomination might be brought into concentrated and united action.

But it will be asked, perhaps, when these conventions are formed, what is there for them to do? We will answer. It would be the duty of a state convention to ascertain correctly the condition of the churches within its own limits. For instance, how many had been added, dismissed, or had died, since its last meeting; what ministers had been licensed, or ordained; what ministers had been dismissed, or deposed; what was the general state of their churches; where was assistance wanted; where it could be most judiciously afforded, and in general, to present as accurate an account as possible of the state of the churches within its own limits. Another part of their duty would be to encourage the churches to systematic exertion in the cause of Christ. This might easily be done

through the means of the Associations whom they represent. Each Association should therefore appoint a treasurer, who should receive the missionary and education contributions of the churches. These contributions the treasurer might pay over to the delegate to the state convention. And the money thus collected, might be appropriated as the convention might advise. A part of it would be doubtless retained for missionary labour within the state, and the rest sent on to the general convention for the foreign missions.

Again, to carry forward this object, it would be proper that every state convention should appoint a Board of domestic missions for conducting missionary exertion within their own boundaries. The special object of this board would be to assist destitute churches, and supply places with the preaching of the gospel, whenever a promising door was opened for usefulness. And in general, the duty of a state convention would be to devise and carry into effect measures for the promotion of personal piety, and for the advancement of the cause of Christ within its own boundaries.

The state conventions might send delegates, who, when assembled, would form the general convention. Under this body might be placed the general missionary and education concerns of the denomination. These objects are dear to us all; and they have become so important as to deserve and require the general superintendence of all our churches. I am aware that they are in a measure under that general superintendence at present. But it is evident that the system of representation is very imperfect, and is far from being so constituted, as to combine the general sentiment of our whole church. The convention at present is composed of delegates from missionary societies, and of course must, in its very nature, be mostly composed of persons elected from the vicinity of its place of meeting. And besides, were the meeting ever so universally attended, its foundation is radically defective. A missionary society is not a representative body, nor can any number of them speak the language of a whole denomination. Most of them are female societies, which have no influence beyond their own members. But it is needless to pursue this subject. Every one sees at a glance the difference between the representative of a state convention, which comprised two or three hundred churches within its limits, and thus the bearer of their opinions, and him who is only the delegate from a missionary society which contributes fifty or one hundred dollars to the treasury.

Thus, then, the superintendence of the missionary and education concerns of our denomination, would be one important business of the general convention. And it cannot but be observed, that whatever was conducted under the direction of such an assembly, would gain the fullest confidence of all our churches. The convention would appoint and locate the different boards, hear their reports, credit their accounts, and censure or approve of their proceedings, as their wisdom should direct. Another of their duties might be, by delegates, to correspond with our brethren in England, who, we believe, would themselves see the benefit of such an association; and thus the Baptists on both sides of the Atlantic, would be united together in a solid phalanx. Another of their duties might be to originate and superintend a general book system, by which a vastly greater mass of intelligence might be circulated among our brethren, and a very considerable sum be raised for the propagation of the gospel. Another might be the devising of some plan for collecting and publishing our articles of faith and order, as they are held in our churches, and thus bringing us to more conformity of practice. Besides these, and many more which might be named, it will at once be seen, how great an opportunity would be presented to such an assembly, for exciting all our churches to every laudable exertion for the extension of religion. Whatever they recommended, would, by their minutes and by the delegates, be carried home to each state con-

vention, and from thence, by their delegates to each Association, and by the messengers of each Association, to every church; and thus an impulse would be communicated in a few months to every individual of our communion in the United States. The additional means which would thus be afforded for doing good, are absolutely incalculable. We should all be as the heart of one man, and should abundantly exemplify the truth of the maxim, that united action is powerful action.

Let it not be said that this is impossible. What denomination in our country except our own is without it? And what others do, we can do. Let it not be considered visionary. At least, if it be so esteemed, let each one seriously reflect, and be able to give his reasons why he so considers it. Let each of our associations take this subject into serious consideration during their meetings in the ensuing summer, and at least, give it a serious investigation. At any rate, let us not say nothing can be done. Let us recollect it is the cause of our Redeemer that calls for our exertions; and if it shall seem that this can be promoted by such an arrangement as has been proposed, or by any other of a similar nature, let us lose no time in striving to effect it.

I am truly yours,

BACKUS

(*Ibid.*, pp. 325-28.)

7. Return to a single benevolence

After several years of this threefold operation, the General Missionary Convention turned away from education and home missions and returned to the original function of the body—foreign missions only. This action fixed the character of the society method—one benevolence for one society.

(1) Report of the decision

The most important acts, which have passed during the present session, are, first, the removal of the seat of the Foreign Missions from Washington to Boston. This arrangement has for several years been somewhat in contemplation on account of the peculiar facilities for such operation, which Boston presents. It has now been completed with entire harmony and perfect unanimity.

Another measure of equal importance which has been effected is the entire separation of the Missionary and Education concerns of the convention.—They had formerly been under the direction of the same body, but experience has for several years indicated that both would flourish much better apart. In pursuance of this conviction, the Trustees of the Columbian College, who were originally nominated by the Convention, were requested to vest the right of nomination in some other corporation, and the constitution of the Convention was so amended as to restrict its operations wholly to missionary exertion.

These alterations, after full discussion, were adopted without dissent, and entirely to the satisfaction of every party concerned. Resolutions were also passed expressive of the interest of the Convention in the success of the College, and various measures were with much promptness adopted, with the design of improving the state of its financial concerns.

(From *The American Baptist Magazine,* New Series, Vol. VI, No. 6, June, 1826.)

(2) Reasons for this action

BAPTIST GENERAL CONVENTION.
In our last number we took occasion hastily to state the fact that the Constitution of the Convention had been so amended as to restrict its operations exclusively to Missionary business. The reasons for this amendment were then of necessity omitted, and this omission it is now our intention very briefly to supply. Some of the considerations which seemed to justify this measure at the meeting of the Convention, were, if we mistake not, the following.

1. There is no necessary connexion between the Missionary and Education concerns of our denomination. Both are important, both are necessary; but this is no reason why both should be managed

by the same men, or their funds cast into one common treasury.

2. It is difficult to conceive of any substantial benefit which could result to either from this connexion. . . .

3. Some reasons might easily be suggested why they had better be disunited. The feelings of our brethren in different portions of the United States in relation to these two objects are not entirely coincident. Some are more particularly favorable to missionary, and others to education exertions. This blending of these two concerns together must evidently injure the success of both of them in respect to all persons in both these classes. Either party would give more liberally towards his favorite object if it stood alone, and totally disconnected with the other.

And again it is evident that complication of object in any case diminishes the prospect of success. A benevolent purpose is better sustained when it is managed by men who are singly devoted to its promotion. In the present imperfect state it is not to be expected that any number of men could be found who would devote equal attention to both education and missions, and at the same time give to each the full attention that it deserved. One or the other will almost of necessity be neglected, as the claims of its rival are more urgent, and being neglected by its constituted guardians, will lose its interest in the feelings of the publick.

4. The history of this connexion in the present case has abundantly demonstrated the evil of connecting these charities together. It has proved that each has been of very serious injury to the other.

The Convention was originally, as it is at present exclusively, a missionary Association. After some time, we believe at its third triennial meeting, education objects were amalgamated with it. Before this amalgamation, and with a single object of pursuit, its proceedings were harmonious, and its exertions singularly blessed. A missionary spirit was awakened throughout our country, and the receipts into the treasury were such as to gladden the friends of Zion. From the moment of this union, however, a reverse may be dated. The spirit of missions flagged. The receipts into the treasury were diminished. The college at each succeeding meeting demanded more attention from the Convention, and the mission received less. The missionary cause lost its place in the hearts of Christians, until the souls of the heathen were almost forgotten, and every paper and every report seemed exclusively devoted to the praises and the successes of the Columbian college.

Such has been the effect of this arrangement upon the missionary cause. But if we look a little further, we shall see that they have not been less deleterious to the very cause of education. The college and the business of education commenced under flattering auspices. Their friends were numerous and liberal, and their receipts encouraging. Soon, however, its prospects became less flattering, until the whole concern is now, as is well known, considerably in debt. Such a result, indeed, might have been almost anticipated. The education cause takes a less firm hold upon the feelings of the benevolent, than the missionary cause. It must always succeed, and be secondary to it. So soon as these two causes interfere, and if blended under one management, they will interfere, the one weakens the energies of the other, and then ruins itself.

. . . .

We shall mention but one more out of many reasons which have led to this division of benevolent labour. An impression had gone abroad that the Convention was responsible for the pecuniary transactions of the college. The fact was directly the reverse. When this impression had become known to the Convention it seemed due to the publick not only to show that this responsibility did not exist, but to prevent the recurrence of such a misapprehension in future. The proper course seemed to be to render these two corporations entirely independent of each other.

(From *The American Baptist Magazine*, New Series, Vol. VI, No. 7, July, 1826.)

Organization of the American Baptist Publication Society

In this united period Southern Baptists assisted in the founding of the General Tract Society in 1824, which subsequently became the American Baptist Publication Society.

On Wednesday evening, Feb. 25, a meeting was held, pursuant to notice, for the purpose of forming a Baptist Tract Society. After prayer, by the Rev. Luther Rice, the Rev. Dr. Staughton was appointed Chairman, and Mr. James D. Knowles, Secretary.

It was then resolved, That a Tract Society be formed. A Constitution was proposed, and after some amendments, was adopted, as follows:

CONSTITUTION.

Art. 1. The name of this Society shall be, *"The Baptist General Tract Society."* Its sole object shall be to disseminate evangelical truth, and to inculcate sound morals, by the distribution of tracts.

Art. 2. Any person may become a member of this Society, by paying the sum of one dollar annually. The payment of ten dollars at one time, shall constitute a person a member for life.

Art. 3. There shall be an annual meeting of the Society, on the last Wednesday in February, when the following officers shall be chosen, by ballot, viz.: A President, Vice-President, Agent, Recording Secretary, Treasurer, and a Board of Directors, consisting of the President, Vice-President, Agent, Recording Secretary, and Treasurer, who shall be Directors in consequence of their office, and seven members of the Society. Five Directors shall constitute a quorum for business. The Board shall have power to supply any vacancy that may occur in its own body.

Art. 4. The Directors shall superintend the publication and distribution of such tracts, as they shall approve; the appointment of subordinate agents; the establishment of depositories, the formation of auxiliary societies, &c. They shall hold frequent meetings, under such regulations as they may adopt, in conformity with the general provisions of this Constitution. They shall appoint the place and the hour, for the annual meeting of the Society; and may, if they think proper, make arrangements for an annual sermon, or public addresses, and a collection for the benefit of the Society. The Directors and the Treasurer shall make an annual report of their proceedings.

.   .   .   .

Art. 7. Every member shall be entitled to receive three-fourths of the amount of his subscription in tracts at cost. Auxiliary Societies shall be entitled to the same privilege.

Art. 8. Any person, by paying twenty-five dollars, at one time, shall be a Director for life. The Presidents of Auxiliary Societies shall be, ex officio, members of the Board of Directors.

(From *The Columbian Star* [Philadelphia], March 6, 1824.)

Organization of the American Baptist Home Mission Society

The third great benevolent society developed jointly by Southern Baptists and others was the American Baptist Home Mission Society organized in 1832. John Mason Peck had been quite active in the Mississippi Valley, and many voices urged the formation of a national society for home mission work. After Peck and Jonathan Going of Massachusetts had visited the needy western fields in 1831, an official call was made to organize a national home mission society. On April 27, 1832, in New York City, the American Baptist Home Mission Society was born.

CONSTITUTION
of the
American Baptist Home Mission Society.

Article I. This Society shall be called the American Baptist Home Mission Society.

Article II. The great object of the Society shall be to promote the preaching of the gospel in North America.

Article III. Any person may become a member of this Society by contributing annually to its funds; thirty dollars paid at one time shall constitute a member for life; one hundred dollars paid at one time shall constitute a director for life; and any person on paying a sum which, in addition to any previous contribution, shall amount to one hundred dollars, shall be a director for life; and any Baptist Church, or Association, or State Convention, or Missionary Society, that contributes annually to the objects of this Society, shall be entitled to be represented by one or more delegates, in its annual meetings.

Article IV. The officers of this Society shall be a President, Vice Presidents, a Treasurer, an Auditor, a Corresponding Secretary, a Recording Secretary, and fifty Directors, who shall be annually appointed by the Society.

Article V. The Officers and Life Directors shall appoint an Executive Committee of thirteen persons, including the Treasurer, the Corresponding Secretary, and the Recording Secretary, residing in the city of New-York and its vicinity, five of whom shall be a quorum at any meeting regularly convened. This Committee shall have power to appoint its own meetings, form its own rules of business, and fill any vacancies which may occur during the year, and convene special meetings of the Board and of the Society; shall appoint missionaries, and instruct them as to the field and manner of their labours; shall dispose of the funds for the objects of the Society, provided that all moneys contributed for any specific purpose shall be faithfully applied only to that particular object; shall create such agency or agencies for the appointment of missionaries and for other purposes as the interests of the Society may require; and shall make an annual report of their proceedings to the Society. All the Officers, Executive Committee, Agents and Missionaries of the Society shall be members of some regular Baptist Church, in general union with the body of that denomination.

Article VI. The Treasurer shall give bonds to such amount as the Executive Committee shall think proper.

Article VII. Any Baptist Missionary Society may become auxiliary, by agreeing to pay into the treasury of this Society the whole of its surplus funds, and sending to the Corresponding Secretary a copy of its constitution and annual reports, mentioning the names of its missionaries, and the fields of their operations.

Article VIII. Every Auxiliary Society which shall agree to pay the whole of its funds to this Society, shall be entitled to a missionary, or missionaries to labour in such field as it may designate, to an amount at least equal to that of its contributions: provided such designation be made at the time of payment.

Article IX. The officers of Auxiliary Societies shall be ex-officio Directors of this Society, and their members shall be members of this Society.

Article X. The annual meeting of the Society shall be held at such time and place, as the Society shall determine at a previous annual meeting.

Article XI. No alteration of this Constitution shall be made without an affirmative vote of two thirds of the members present at an annual meeting; nor, unless the same shall have been proposed at a previous annual meeting, or recommended by the Executive Committee.

(From Home Mission Society *Minute* for 1833, p. 2.)

Section Two

Development of State Bodies

Constitution of the first state convention

It is a curious fact that Baptists in America developed a national body (in

1814) before organizing state conventions. The first state body was formed in 1821 by South Carolina Baptists. Many other states, southern and northern, quickly followed this pattern.

Whereas, by an address to the Baptist Associations of this State, which was circulated among the churches of their connexion during the present and past year, it was made to appear, that it would be of great advantage to the denomination to form themselves into a State Convention, which should be a bond of union, a centre of intelligence, and a means of vigorous, united exertion in the cause of God, for the promotion of truth and righteousness; that so those energies, intellectual, moral and pecuniary, which God has bestowed upon the denomination in this State, might be concentrated, and brought into vigorous, useful operation: And whereas, Delegates from the Charleston, Edgefield, and Savannah River Associations, are, in consequence of said representation, convened at Columbia at this time, to whom the proposed measure appears to be proper, interesting and important—Therefore, we the said Delegates, (regretting indeed the failure of present co-operation on the part of the other Baptist Associations of the State, in the benevolent coalition we are forming, but indulging the hope, as well from communications received from some of them, as from the vast importance and interesting nature of the design, that, in future, such co-operation will be afforded,) do now agree upon the following outline of a plan for such union and exertion; but do designedly delay the definitive adjustment, until another meeting shall be held; that we may not be wanting in respect to our brethren, who are not represented in this body; and that we may improve the opportunity now afforded for affectionately inviting them to join in the benevolent, pious concert whose blessed object it is to strengthen the bonds of spiritual union and intercourse, and thus to promote the glory of God our Saviour. But in prospect of this co-operation, we now agree upon the following general principles as the basis of union, and affectionately present them to the consideration of our brethren throughout the State.

1. This coalition of Associations shall be styled, *"The State Convention of the Baptist Denomination in South Carolina."*

2. The grand objects of this Convention shall be the promotion of evangelical and useful knowledge, by means of religious education; the support of missionary service among the destitute; and the cultivation of measures promotive of the true interest of the churches of Christ in general, and of their union, love and harmony in particular.

3. This Convention shall consist of Delegates from the Associations in this State; to whom may be added representatives from other religious bodies of the Baptist connexion.

4. The Convention shall have proper officers for conducting its business.

5. The Convention shall recognize the independence and liberty of the Churches of Christ, and consequently shall not in any case arbitrarily interfere with their spiritual or secular interests. But, when requested, will be considered as under obligations to afford them any assistance which may be in their power.

6. In regard to funds which may at any time be contributed for the promotion of the general objects here contemplated, discretion in their appropriation shall be exercised by the Convention, or by a board that they may appoint for the transaction of business; but no application of monies, given for a specific object, shall be made by them or their board to any other use.

7. In what relates to education, the organization and support of a seminary of learning in this State, for the gratuitous education of indigent, pious young men for the gospel ministry, on a plan in accordance with the interests of that established by the denomination at large, in the United States, shall be considered by this body as an object of primary importance. Not but

that other youth, whose education shall be paid for, may be admitted as pupils: it being distinctly understood, that the course of education and government, shall be conducted with a sacred regard to the interests of morality and religion, on principles of Christian liberality.

8. With regard to missionary service, the Convention will feel it their duty to have a special regard to its promotion, and to use their vigorous efforts to engage the most able, pious and suitable ministers of their denomination in the prosecution of this important design.

9. As duty and obligation unite to prove that religious education of children is a matter of primary importance, this Convention will feel it their duty to encourage the establishment of Sunday Schools, as well as the religious instruction of children in families.

10. This Convention proposes to embrace in its definitive plan, measures for collecting funds by means of charity sermons, societies, donations and bequests, for the purpose of carrying into effect the objects of its attention, upon those principles of liberality, zeal for God, and love to immortal souls, which the gospel inculcates.

11. The whole plan here exhibited, has been formed under a consciousness of entire dependence upon Divine Grace for success, in reference to the truth inculcated in that solemn declaration of Holy Writ, "Not by might, nor by power, but by my Spirit, saith the Lord of Hosts."

Signed by order of the Convention, this sixth day of December, A.D. 1821.

RICHARD FURMAN, Pres.
ABNER BLOCKER, Sec.

(From *The American Baptist Magazine,* New Series, Vol. III, No. 11, September, 1822, pp. 435-36.)

Evaluation of this move by a Boston editor

On the 4th of December, 1821, delegates from the Charleston, Edgefield and Savannah River Associations, met in Columbia for the purpose of organizing a Baptist State Convention for South Carolina. The meeting was deeply interesting, and the constitutional principles which we subjoin were adopted with great cordiality.

We cannot but remark, that our brethren in the South have in this as in many other cases, presented us an example most worthy of imitation. We have long been sensible of the want of some such organization as this for every state in the Union. That our denomination may have all the influence which we could desire, all that is needed is, a cordial co-operation with each other. Our Associations unite our churches; why should not a Convention unite our associations? Our Presbyterian, Congregational, Episcopalian and Methodist brethren have a central point in each state, to which their exertions may be directed. They all experience the benefit of such an arrangement. Might we not do well to imitate their example? It is well remarked in the address of the Convention to their constituents—"It takes some time for the individual workman to build a house, or the single labourer to clear a field; certain parts of the work likewise are such, that each one is more than the individual can perform unaided. But many hands united, give success and speedy execution to the enterprise. If to an invading enemy, a state should oppose in battle only a small number of companies, or regiments at a time, keeping its force divided; a few thousand of these invaders, acting together, might soon subdue that state, however strong in numbers. While on its united forces, ten times the number of enemies, could make no impression, and might be beheld by them with contempt—These considerations direct us to united, as well as vigorous exertions in the cause of God.

We here publish the constitutional principles of the body to which we have alluded. We intreat our ministering brethren especially, to give them a thoughtful perusal. Let each one, wherever he may reside, ask himself, why might not a general convention be established in *this* state as well

as South Carolina? It may cost us some labor to arrange its first organization. But would not the beneficial effects upon the churches of Christ in ten years, amply recompense a whole life of labor. We do hope that this subject may be agitated at all our Associations, that the collective wisdom of our teachers and brethren may be brought to bear upon so important a subject.

(*Ibid.*, p. 435.)

Section Three

Controversial and Schismatic Movements

Alexander Campbell

Campbell and his father, Thomas, were baptized by Matthew Luce in 1812 and organized the Brush Run Church in Brooke County, Virginia. This church affiliated with the Redstone Baptist Association. In 1823 Alexander Campbell began the publication of The Christian Baptist *and started an incessant attack on Baptist practices in missions, on payment of regular salaries to ministers, on organizational methods, confessions of faith, and so on. In 1825 Alexander Campbell preached at the Dover Association of Virginia and at the church of Robert Semple. Semple's letter to Campbell is prophetic. The first formal action taken against Campbell in Virginia spells out the typical Baptist response, although large numbers of Baptist churches in the Southeast followed Campbell out of Baptist affiliation.*

1. Letter of Robert B. Semple to Alexander Campbell in December, 1825

Your opinions on some other points are, I think, dangerous, unless you are misunderstood, such as casting off the Old Testament, exploding experimental religion in its common acceptation, denying the existence of gifts in the present day commonly believed to exist among all spiritual christians, such as preaching, &c. Some other of your opinions, though true, are pushed to extremes, such as those upon the use of creeds, confessions, &c., &c. Your views of ministerial support, directed against abuses on that head, would be useful, but leveled against all support to ministers (unless by way of alms) is so palpably contrary to scripture and common justice, that I persuade myself that there must be some misunderstanding. In short your views are generally so contrary to those of the Baptists in general, that if a party was to go fully into the practice of your principles I should say a new sect had sprung up, radically different from the Baptists, as they now are.

(From Garnett Ryland, *op. cit.*, p. 232.)

2. Summary of Campbell's views in first formal action by Virginia Baptists

In 1830 the Appomattox Association condemned the views of Alexander Campbell, approving the action of other associations in withdrawing from his fellowship and warning against his writings.

Whereas, there is satisfactory evidence, that the writings of Alexander Campbell have exerted a very mischievous influence upon members of Baptist Churches, stirring up envy and strife, and fomenting divisions among those who had before lived in fellowship and peace. *And whereas,* it appears from the Minutes of the Beaver Association that Mahoning Association has been cut off from the fellowship of the neighboring Associations for maintaining or countenancing the following sentiments, or creed, deducible from the writings of the said A. Campbell:

1. They maintain that there is no promise of salvation without baptism.
2. That baptism should be administered to all who say they believe that Jesus Christ is the Son of God, without examination on any other point.
3. That there is no direct operation of the Holy Spirit on the mind prior to baptism.

4. That baptism produces the remission of sins and the gifts of the Holy Spirit.
5. That the Scriptures are the only evidence of interest in Christ.
6. That obedience places it in God's power to elect to salvation.
7. That no creed is necessary for the Church, but the Scriptures as they stand.
8. That all baptized persons have a right to administer the ordinance of baptism.

Therefore Resolved, That this Association most cordially approves the course adopted by the Beaver and her sister Associations, in withdrawing from the Mahoning.

Resolved, That it be earnestly recommended to all the churches who compose this Association to discountenance the writings of the said Alexander Campbell.

And whereas, we regard the common translation of the Bible sufficiently plain as respects doctrine and ordinances and, as we believe, that a translation suited to the sentiments or creed exposed by the Beaver Association eminently calculated to mislead the feeble minded—spread the leaven of heresy—sow the seeds of discord, debate and strife among brethren, and thus mar the peace of the churches; and as the abettors of these sentiments, or this creed, profess to derive them from a true and proper interpretation of the New Testament by Dr. Geo. Campbell, McNight and Doddridge, and edited by Alexander Campbell;

Therefore Resolved, That it be earnestly recommended to our churches not to countenance this new translation of the New Testament.

Resolved, That it be recommended to the ministers and churches composing this Association, not to invite into their pulpits any minister who holds the sentiments or creed named above.

(*Ibid.,* pp. 234-35.)

The Hard-Shell or Primitive movement

Alexander Campbell was Arminian in his theology but opposed missions on exegetical and practical grounds. The Hard-Shell group, on the other hand, opposed missions on theological grounds. They felt that human effort to win men was sacrilegious because God had reserved this work to himself. If men were elected, they would be saved without human agency; if they were not elected, human agency would do no good. The following excerpts illustrate the principal names and events in the development of this movement.

1. John Taylor on missions

But great as this evil may be in religious society, there is another in my belief much greater, though bearing the semblance, and innocence of a lamb, by which advantage is taken of many of our greatest men, and which has made a general sweep among Baptist associations, bearing all down before it. The deadly evil I have in view, is under the epithets or appellations of *Missionary Boards, Conventions, Societies,* and *Theological Schools,* all bearing the appearance of great, though affected sanctity, as the mystery of iniquity did in the days of Paul, when the man of sin was in embryo. Ten or twelve years ago, I obtained the use of two large octavo volumes of about a thousand pages, on the subject of Papal missions, in the great country of Paraguay, in the new settlements of the great river of Paraguay in South America. . . . Most of the Protestant societies, since the days of Luther and Calvin, have had propensities to send out missionaries, as stated in a large work of Adam Clark, lately published in America by Mr. Coles. . . . This work I have had patience to read through, and though there are some things interesting in the work, the greater part is so romantic, that except the reader has more of faith than is needful to make a christian, he sickens at the imposition or insult offered to his understanding. . . . But the most respectable, and perhaps the most useful that Coles has published, is the English Baptist Mission to Calcutta; for there England has many subjects, and though the natives are but sparingly benefited as yet, their other subjects, and especially their soldiery, have been.

But, to be sure, nothing ever could be more preposterous than an American Mission to that part of the world, of which the American Baptists never would have thought, but for Luther Rice; and as this man is in a manner the life and soul of the American Missionary operations, it will not be improper to give some little history of him and his old colleague, Judson. About eight or ten years past, (and previous to any Baptist Missionary Society in Kentucky) two young men by the names of Mills and Schermorhorn, who emanated from the same school with Judson and Rice, being on a missionary tour, from the Presbyterian Board of Missions in the East, by their direction, were to travel through the states of Ohio, Kentucky, Tennessee, the Natchez settlement and to New Orleans; and then return to the board who sent them, make a report by a faithful journal, of all the Missionary and Bible Societies they had formed, all the money they had collected, their success in preaching, &c. . . . By an acquaintance of mine in Cincinnati, they were induced to travel sixty miles out of their way to see me, then living in the lower end of Gallatin county. The object of an interview with me, was to know the state of the Baptist society in Kentucky, and shape their course accordingly. They were at my house about one day and night. They were respectable looking young men, well informed, and zealous in the cause in which they were employed. They gave me a full history of the ordination and mission of Messrs. Judson and Rice, and the mighty effect it had on the people of New England; and particularly this good effect, that many poor ministers could scarcely get their bread before, but by stirring up the people in the mission cause, and getting them in the habit of giving their money, it was now cheerfully communicated by thousands, so that ministers who staid at home, were now richly supplied. Was all this Priestly art? Those young visitants of mine were very sociable, and among other freedoms asked me how I had got through the world, as they saw me then well settled and now old; which led to another question, what amount of supplies I had generally received from the people for preaching? After having considered it very puny indeed, and in a friendly way blamed the badness of my policy; after finding that the Baptists in Kentucky were a great people (from the copies of Minutes I presented them of different associations,) now about fifteen associations in the state, and about that number of churches in an adjacent county (Shelby) they became quite impatient with my indolence, assuring me if I would only stir up the people to Missions and Bible Society matters, I should find a great change in money affairs in favor of the preachers; urging by questions like this, do you not know when the sponges are once opened they will always run? Only said they, get the people in the habit of giving their money for any religious use, and they will continue to appropriate for all sacred purposes. . . . Being in my own house, and these respectable young men being strangers, as also not of my own society, common modesty forbade my making as free as I should have done at another place and time. But surely it will not be thought uncharitable to say, that I did begin strongly to smell the *New England Rat*. It may be well remembered, that this Mills and Schermorhorn, were educated in the same school, sent on a mission from the same Board that Judson and Rice were, though to different parts of the world. Their being baptized at Calcutta is no evidence of their religious or political principles being changed, only in the use of much water. We do not know so much of Mr. Judson as we do of Mr. Rice. The most we know of the former, is from the letters of him and his wife. If we attend to the long, celebrated letter of Mrs. Judson, in the first report of the Board of Foreign Missions, in page 34 it would look as if her husband had the same taste for money that the horse-leech has for blood. . . .

The first piece of policy with Luther and his board, (for I call them his board,) was to enlist all the Baptist associations in the United States, upwards of a hundred as they since boast. Their means for so doing was a Circular published, a copy of which was sent by the trusty hand of their agent, Luther himself, or some understrapper of his; but much better executed when delivered by himself. The purport of this circular letter was, among other fine tales, craving a correspondence with all the associations. . . . With the circular, was sent by the board, their first report on Missionary matters, a pamphlet of near sixty pages, all of which was chiefly dictated by Luther. Their first number was in the year 1815. This same year with all the above named lumber, Mr. Rice made his first appearance in Kentucky, at Elkhorn association, near Lexington. He got to the place on Saturday evening after meeting had adjourned, and though a year before, the association had decided that there should be no collections made on the Lord's day, a few leading men encouraged Luther in the prime part of the day, to preach a Missionary sermon, and make a collection. When Luther rose up, the assembly of thousands, seemed strickened with his appearance. A tall, pale looking, well dressed young man, with all the solemn appearance of one who was engaged in the work of the Lord, and perhaps he thought he was. He also being a stranger, every eye and ear was open; his text was "thy kingdom come." He spoke some handsome things about the kingdom of Christ; but every stroke he gave seemed to mean *MONEY*. For my own part I was more amused with his ingenuity than edified by his discourse, and more astonished at his art in the close, than at any other time. He had the more pathos the nearer he came getting the money, and raising his arms as if he had some awfully pleasing vision, express without a hesitating doubt, that the angels were hovering over the assembly, and participating in our heavenly exercise, and just ready to take their leave, and bear the good tidings to heaven of what we were then about, in giving our money for the instruction and conversion of the poor heathens; and as if he had power to stop Gabriel's flight, in the most pathetic strain cried, stop angels, til you have witnessed the generosity of this assembly. About this time, perhaps twenty men, previously appointed, moved through the assembly with their hats, and near two hundred dollars were collected. Though I admire the art of this well taught Yankee, yet I considered him a modern Tetzel, and that the Pope's old orator of that name was equally innocent with Luther Rice, and his motive about the same. He was to get money by the sale of indulgences for the use of the Pope and Church. Luther's motive was thro' sophistry and Yankee art, to get money for the Mission, of which himself was to have a part. . . . Money and power were the signs of the times, when the mystery of iniquity began to work in the days of Paul. The same principle is plainly seen in the great Board of Missions in America, and Rice their chief cook, as also in their mighty convention. Witness their resolves in their first triennial meeting; their hateful flattery of each other; their fulsome public thanks to their officers while in session; as also no quantum of money can be too much to answer their purposes—3d Report, 1st page.

. . . .

The very many modes and artful measures of those great men to get money, are disgustful to common modesty. They begin with missionary societies; then they create a great board of different officers, and then select the most vigorous and artful agent they can find, to create more societies of different grades, as Female Societies, Cent Societies, Mite Societies, Children Societies, and even Negro Societies, both free and bond; besides the sale of books of various kinds, and in some instances the sale of images. Every Missionary to a foreign country is authorised to follow all these arts, as well as common begging to get money; so that no set of men ever yet seen on the earth, manifest a greater thirst

by these various modes of peddling to get money. . . .

But it seems as if these men would die if they did not get plenty of money. What a striking contrast! Are not these gentlemen on the side of Satan and his ministers, though striving to transform themselves as the ministers of Christ? How bold the Devil is! And what but modern missionary brass, could ever induce these men to such shameful presumption?

. . . .

My object is, if possible, to drive these presuming men out of Baptist associations; for there they crept in unawares, with no more right there than the false brethren of whom Paul speaks; for they are a motly tribe at best.

(From the pamphlet by John Taylor, *Thoughts on Missions,* 1820.)

2. Daniel Parker

Elders Robt. Hurt from Virginia, Luther Rice from Burmah, were invited and took seats. Rice, as Agent for the Baptist Board of Foreign Missions, came forward and laid some copies of their third Report on the table. The churches, who wanted, received them; and at his request, Bro. R. C. Foster was directed to transmit a copy of the minutes of the Association to the Board. Hurt, Rice and Burns were requested to preach on Lord's day. At the close of Rice's sermon, (according to a resolution passed on Saturday), a collection was taken up for Foreign Missions. I do not recollect the amount, but think it was a fair one for the times. Some of the brethren asked Elder Parker if he contributed any thing. His reply was—No; he had no counterfeit half dollars; if he had he would have thrown in, but as he had none he would not throw away good money for such an object. About this time clouds of suspicion and distrust began to gather around him, respecting his *two-seed* doctrine, which was generally regarded heresy. I will here narrate two anecdotes, to show the eccentricity and want of refinement which characterized the man: He was a poor man, and had settled in Sumner county, with an increasing family—worked hard and preached much. He once had an appointment at night, some four or five miles from home. The day being very warm, while hoeing corn, he had rolled up his pants nearly to his knees. The sweat and dust had made mortar on his feet and legs, while he worked on watching the sun so as to start just early enough to meet his appointment. Laying aside his hoe, he hastened off without shifting clothes or even washing. He reached the place in due time—commenced preaching, and continued some time before he looked down and discovered his ridiculous figure. He afterwards said that it made him feel a little bad at first, but his subject was so absorbing, he had no time to look at his legs and feet. At another time, he was invited by his Brother Foster (who at that time was regarded a very prominent Baptist) to preach in Nashville. The appointment was accepted, and the time came. Parson Blackburn, an Old School Presbyterian, a very learned man and said to be the greatest orator in the State, sat side by side with Bro. Foster. The house was soon crowded, and Parker commenced preaching. In a little time his neck-tie became too burdensome, as it was an article he was not much addicted to wearing, drawing it off he laid it aside, continuing his discourse in the meantime. He soon finds it necessary to relieve himself of his coat; and his vest is next laid aside. At this stage of the stripping process, Blackburn whispers to Foster, in an ironical way, "Will he pull his shirt off?" After preaching was over, Foster, who was highly insulted at Blackburn's question, asked him, "What do you think of Bro. Parker now?" He replied, "It is a pity that man has not a good education, and some refinement. He might have made a right good preacher." Foster replied with a snarl, "He is the best preacher in the State as he is." So they parted, one at least highly incensed, Parker sowed two seeds plentifully in Sumner, and the adjacent counties in Kentucky, and scattering some on the south side of the Cumberland

river, left them to germinate, for others to cultivate and reap. He moved up to Illinois, and there published his pamphlet entitled, "Two Seed in Broken Doses."

(From John Bond, *History of the Baptist Concord Association from 1796-1859* [Nashville, 1860], pp. 27-29.)

3. *The Kehukee Association declares itself antimissions*

A paper purporting to be a declaration of the Reformed Baptists in North Carolina, dated 26th August, 1826, which was presented at last Association and referred to the churches to express in their letters to this Association their views with regard to it, came up for deliberation. Upon examination it was found that most of the churches had given their opinions, and after an interchange of sentiments among the members of this body, it was agreed that we discard all Missionary Societies, Bible Societies, and Theological Seminaries, and the practices heretofore resorted to for their support, in begging money from the public: and if any persons should be among us as agents of any such societies, we hereafter discountenance them in those practices, and if under the character of a minister of the Gospel, we will not invite them into our pulpits, believing these societies and institutions to be the inventions of men and not warranted from the word of God. We further do unanimously agree, that should any of the members of our churches join the fraternity of Masons, or being members thereof continue to visit the Lodges and parades, we will not invite them to preach in our pulpits, believing them to be guilty of such practices; and we declare non fellowship with them and such practices altogether.

(From Mark Bennett, *Review of the History of the Kehukee Baptist Association* [Raleigh, 1854], p. 19.)

4. *The Black Rock Declaration*

On September 28-29, 1832, *a group of Particular (Predestinarian) Baptists met at the Black Rock Baptist Church, Baltimore,*

Maryland, and set forth a strong antimission, antitract, anti-Sunday School, antitheological education, and anti-Bible society declaration. A portion of their lengthy address illustrates their approach.

To the Particular Baptist Churches of the "Old School" in the United States.

BRETHREN:—It constitutes a new era in the history of the Baptists, when those who would *follow the Lord fully,* and who therefore manifest a solicitude to be, in all things pertaining to religion, conformed to the *Pattern showed in the mount,* are by Baptists charged with *antinomianism, inertness, stupidity, &c.,* for refusing to go beyond the word of God; but such is the case with us.

Brethren, we would not shun reproach, nor seek an exemption from persecution; but we would affectionately entreat those Baptists who revile us themselves, or who side with such as do, to pause and consider how far they · have departed from the ancient principles of the Baptists, and how that in reproaching us they stigmatize the memory of those whom they have been used to honor as eminent and useful servants of Christ, and of those who have bourne the brunt of the persecutions leveled against the Baptists in former ages. For it is a well-known fact that it was in ages past a uniform and distinguishing trait in the character of the Baptists, that they required a *"Thus saith the Lord,"* that is, direct authority from the word of God for the order and practices, as well as the doctrine, they received in religion.

It is true that many things to which we object as departures from the order established by the great Head of the church, through the ministry of his apostles, are by others considered to be connected with the very essence of religion, and absolutely necessary to the prosperity of Christ's kingdom. They attach great value to them, because human wisdom suggests their importance. We allow the Head of the church alone to judge for us; we therefore esteem those things to be of no use to

the cause of Christ, which he has not himself instituted.

We will notice severally the claims of the principal of these modern inventions, and state some of our objections to them for your candid consideration.

We commence with the Tract Societies. These claim to be extensively useful. Tracts claim their thousands converted. They claim the prerogative of carrying the news of salvation into holes and corners, where the gospel would otherwise never come; of going as on the wings of the wind, carrying salvation in their train; and they claim each to contain gospel enough, should it go where the Bible has never come, to lead a soul to the knowledge of Christ. The nature and extent of these and the like claims, made in favor of tracts by their advocates, constitute a good reason why we should reject them. These claims represent tracts as possessing in these respects a superiority over the Bible, and over the institution of the gospel ministry, which is charging the great I Am with a deficiency of wisdom. Yea, they charge God with folly; for why has he given us the extensive revelation contained in the Bible, and given the Holy Spirit *to take of the things of Christ and show them to us,* if a little tract of four pages can lead a soul to the knowledge of Christ? But let us consider the more rational claims presented by others in favor of tracts, as that they constitute a convenient way of disseminating religious instruction among the more indigent and thoughtless classes of society. Admitting the propriety of this claim, could it be kept separated from other pretensions, still can we submit to the *distribution of tracts* becoming an order of our churches or our associations, without countenancing the prevalent idea that tracts have become an instituted means approved of God for the conversion of sinners, and hence that the distribution of them is a religious act, and on a footing with supporting the gospel ministry?

If we were to admit that tracts may have occasionally been made instrumental by the Holy Ghost for imparting instruction or comfort to inquiring minds, it would by no means imply that tracts are an instituted *means of salvation,* to speak after the manner of the popular religionists, nor that they should be placed on a footing with the Bible, and the preached gospel, in respect to imparting the knowledge of salvation.

Again, we readily admit the propriety of an individual's publishing and distributing, or of several individuals uniting to publish and distribute what they wish circulated, whether in the form of tracts, or otherwise; but still we cannot admit the propriety of uniting with or upon the plans of the existing Tract Societies, even laying aside the idea of their being attempted to be palmed upon us as religious institutions. Because that upon the plan of these societies, those who unite with them pay their money for publishing and distributing they know not what, under the name of religious truth; and what is worse, they submit to have sent into their families weekly or monthly, and to circulate among their neighbors, anything and everything for religious reading, which the agent or publishing committee may see fit to publish. They thus become accustomed to receive everything as good which comes under the name of religion, whether it be according to the word of God or not; and are trained to the habit of letting others judge for them in matters of religion, and are therefore fast preparing to become the dupes of priestcraft. Can any conscientious follower of the Lamb submit to such plans? If others can, we cannot.

. . . .

Brethren, we have thus laid before you some of our objections to the popular schemes in religion, and the reasons why we cannot fellowship them. Ponder these well. Weigh them in the balances of the sanctuary; and then say if they are not such as justify us in standing aloof from those plans of men, and those would-be *religious societies,* which are bound together, not by the fellowship of the gospel,

but by certain money payments. If you cannot for yourselves meet the reproach by separating yourselves from those things which the word of God does not warrant, still allow us the privilege to *obey God rather than man.*

(From *Minutes of the Proceedings, and Resolutions Drafted, by the Particular Baptists, convened at Black Rock, Md., September 28th, 1832* [Middletown, N.Y.], pp. 5ff.)

Sectional wrangling over home missions

The unity of Northern and Southern Baptists was threatened by two divisive factors, both sectional in nature. One of these was the widespread feeling in the South that the Home Mission Society was neglecting the needs of the southern section while answering the calls of the northwestern area. Although the charge was unfounded over a long period, some of the annual reports of the Society gave grounds for this belief. Almost simultaneously plans were made to organize home mission bodies in the deep Southwest and in the Mississippi Valley. On May 16, 1839, Robert T. Daniel led in the organization of a Southern Baptist society for home missions, with headquarters at Columbus, Mississippi, asserting that the mission needs of the area were the only motivation for forming the body. This society did not prosper and died with Daniel in 1842. (See Baptist Banner and Western Pioneer [Kentucky], February 24, 1842, for a summary of the life and death of this society.) The separate body for the Mississippi Valley did not materialize.

1. Complaints of neglect

(1) From Kentucky in 1837

It appears from the "last report of the Executive Committee of the American Baptist Home Mission Society" that they have not a single missionary in all Kentucky, Alabama, Louisiana and Florida, and that they partially or entirely sustain one missionary in Mississippi, three in Tennessee and three in Arkansas, making in all seven missionaries for these six states and one Territory . . . only one missionary to every 428,581 souls, while in the state of Michigan, . . . they have sixteen missionaries . . . one missionary to every 4,000 souls. . . . Why are these states (Illinois and Indiana) so liberally supplied? Are they more needy? Are they more destitute? They are more liberally supplied because of Northern contributions, and because Northern preachers refuse to come to the south. . . . It is, therefore, apparent, that the only way to produce effort in the south must be brought about by the formation of a Southern Baptist Home Mission Society.

(From *Baptist Banner* [Kentucky], September 12, 1837, p. 3, cols. 2-4.)

(2) In 1844 from Georgia

Hitherto our contributions have been generally expended in the free States of the West, Michigan, Ohio, Indiana, Illinois and the territories of Iowa and Wisconsin. A few missionaries have been sent to Missouri, a still smaller number to Arkansas and Texas, Florida and Louisiana have been overlooked . . . equally destitute with Iowa and Wisconsin, and where probably a greater amount of good could be effected, with the same expense and labour. . . . The American Home Mission Society have made it (Mississippi Valley) the chief scene of their operation. . . . Meanwhile the South and Southwestern new states, equally destitute, have been measurably overlooked.

The emigrants to the West have been chiefly from the New England and Middle States. . . . In Florida, in Louisiana, in Arkansas, is an extensive field, more destitute, as far as Baptists are concerned, than any other in the United States. Indiana has an equal number of ministers with Alabama, Illinois and Mississippi, yet scores of missionaries have been sent to those two western states, and none to the latter. . . .

This feeling (of hostility to the south) is the strongest in Maine, New Hampshire, Vermont, and Michigan; yet these states,

while supplying thousands of emigrants to the West, have never collectively given half as much in one year to the Home Mission Society, as has been contributed by Virginia in the same space of time.

(From *Christian Index* [Georgia], July 19, 1844, p. 3.)

(3) In 1845 from Kentucky

The South is sustaining missions in the Eastern and Northern States instead of the contrary, as many of our Eastern friends suppose. . . . Those nine southern states have not only supported all the domestic missions of this Board in the entire south, but those of Canada and Texas also, and furnished the liberal sum of $554.97½ to support domestic missions in northern states. . . . The south will not only lose nothing by being thrust out from the Northern Society; but it also proves that the domestic missions of the south can be better sustained in our separate existence. . . . We once before (about two years ago) made a similar expose from a monthly report.

(From *The Baptist Banner and Western Pioneer* [Kentucky], June 26, 1845, p. 2.)

2. Robert T. Daniel and the Southern Baptist Home Mission Society

Circular of Robert T. Daniel
Calling for Organization of
Southern Baptist Home Mission Society

To all the friends of Christian effort among Baptists of the south and southwestern States.

The preaching of the gospel is still God's appointed method of saving men. To call and qualify preachers is exclusively his own prerogative; yet that call and those qualifications are to be recognized and authenticated to men, by the church, who are presumed to have the mind of Christ; and to the church are also committed interesting responsibilities in regard to the encouragement and support needed by ministers in their work.

The Baptist denomination in the southern and western States has been greatly increased. Churches and ministers are numerous, and are placed in circumstances eminently favorable, under a proper guidance, to extension and usefulness. One great obstacle to the utmost success is, that their ministers are too much *secularized*. Engaged in worldly vocations for temporal support, they do far less ministerial labor than if wholly given to the work, and the little they attempt carries less force than if sustained by the frequent repetition, the increasing strength, the regularity and ardor attendant on exclusive engagement in the service of Christ. That ministers are now devoted to worldly business is not attributed to them as a fault. In most cases necessity, a hard necessity, is laid upon them. Still the obstacle to usefulness is not the less on that account. To remove this obstacle societies have been instituted for the purpose of relieving ministers from the necessity of laboring in worldly business; and these societies have sustained the charge of their families, while they have been running to-and-fro proclaiming the everlasting gospel. In the instance of the American Baptist Home Mission Society, this effort has been attended with most encouraging success. With the same means, much more labor has been done, and more good accomplished, in a short time, than could have been expected in many years, without the efforts of the society. The plan seems suited to general and permanent success; and it is believed that an institution of this kind, operating in harmony with the American Baptist Home Mission Society, would be peculiarly suited to the wants and interests in the south and southwestern States, at the present juncture. It would not interfere with the rights and peculiarities of churches; but in a harmless, yet effectual manner, would concentrate the energies of the good, the intelligent and liberal of all churches, unincumbered by conflicting views, in God's own method of promoting the objects most dear to Zion's glorious King.

For the purpose of framing an organization of this kind in the south so consonant both with reason and scripture, a meeting of those friendly to the object is to be held at Columbus, Miss., on Thursday before the 3d Lord's-day in May, 1839.

All that love our Lord Jesus Christ, and desire to unite in promoting his cause, are earnestly invited to attend at the time and place above written. By the request of many.

ROBERT T. DANIEL.

(From *Baptist Banner and Western Pioneer* [Kentucky], March 21, 1839.)

3. The Mississippi Valley proposal

Western Baptist Home Mission Society

At a meeting of a number of Baptist brethren, held in Louisville, May 11th, 1839, at the house of Elder W. C. Buck, to consult upon principles of mutual action and co-operation in home missions throughout the valley of the Mississippi, Elder W. C. Buck was called to the Chair, and J. M. Peck, of Illinois, appointed Secretary.

After a mutual exchange of views in reference to the late Convention held at Lexington, and the resolutions and speeches made upon the subject, the following resolutions, with the principles appended, was taken up for discussion, and a unanimous expression of opinion in their favor was made. . . .

RESOLUTION.

Resolved, That a general organization for home missionary operations throughout the western valley be effected on the following principles, so soon as a sufficient number of the denomination can be induced to co-operate.

PRINCIPLES.

1. Such an organization should have the general supervision of home missions in this field, but should co-operate in entire concert and harmonious action with the American Baptist Home Mission Society.

2. The organization should be formed by delegates from State conventions and associations, and other Baptist bodies, in each State where such general organizations have been formed, and by delegates from

Baptist associations, churches, and missionary societies under Baptist management, where such State organizations do not exist.

3. The State conventions and State associations, or their respective boards or committees, still to superintend and manage missionary operations within their sphere of action, but to become auxiliary to the general organization, furnish such surplus funds as can be obtained to supply other destitute fields in the west, and a summary of their labors to be included in the general report, and thus union and mutual co-operation throughout the whole field be promoted.

4. To create and give influence, and produce efficient co-operation throughout the western States, a Board of Directors shall be chosen, proportionable to each State. These directors to have privilege of a seat and vote to the Executive Committee, when present, and to give advice by correspondence.

5. At some central and commercial point in the great valley there should be an executive committee to manage and direct all necessary operations, appoint missionaries, (except such as may be under the immediate supervision of State or local organizations,) designate the fields of their labors, and appropriate funds.

6. A Corresponding Secretary and a General Agency, to be wholly devoted to the interests of home missions; visit the principal towns; attend the conventions and general associations in each State, and local associations wherever convenient; bring the subject and urge its importance before the churches and brethren; conduct the correspondence; ascertain and bring to the notice of the Executive Committee every destitute field that needs aid; arrange to provide for attaining funds, and keep the whole concern in operation.

7. An office to be opened at the centre of operations, and the committee to meet semi-monthly.

8. The Banner and Pioneer to be employed as an efficient organ to carry into effect this system of mutual co-operation, and to awaken the churches to benevolent action in home missions.

Signed,

W. C. Buck, Chairman.

J. M. Peck, Secretary.

(From *Baptist Banner and Western Pioneer* [Kentucky], September 19, 1839.)

Slavery-abolition controversy

The slavery-abolition controversy among American Baptists had deep roots. Protests of the Virginia colonial government were disregarded by the English crown when slavery was introduced in 1619. For a period the South took the lead in trying to abolish this evil practice. Finally, they learned to embrace it. The practical reviving of the issue came in the 1830s when English Baptists, having been instrumental in procuring legislation to eliminate slavery from the British West Indies, urged American Baptists to take similar action against slavery in America.

1. English agitation

(1) Letter from ministers in London

FROM THE BOARD OF BAPTIST MINISTERS IN AND NEAR LONDON TO THE PASTORS AND MINISTERS OF THE BAPTIST DENOMINATION THROUGHOUT THE UNITED STATES OF AMERICA.

Dear Brethren:—We, the members of the Board of Baptist Ministers in and near London, desire affectionately and with much earnestness, to commend ourselves to your candid and Christian attention. Partakers of the same faith as yourselves, we have long been solicited to cultivate a more intimate and influential intercourse with you, in the hope that we might mutually benefit each other, and extend the kingdom of our common Lord.

. . . .

We understand that the number of slaves in the United States is considerably above two millions, while the system under which they are held is said to be characterized by some features peculiarly revolting and oppressive. But it is not our purpose to enter into details; we wish rather to fix your attention on the system as a whole—its unchristian character, its degrating tendency, the misery it generates, the injustice, cruelty and wretchedness it involves. Is it not an awful breach of the Divine law, a manifest infraction of that social compact which is always and everywhere binding? And if it be so, are you not, as Christians, and especially as Christian ministers, bound to protest against it, and to seek, by all legitimate means, its speedy and entire destruction? You have a high and holy part, dear brethren, to act; and future generations will bless your name, and the God whom you serve will approve your conduct, if you are prompt and diligent in its performance. An opportunity is now offered you of extending the happiness of your species; of raising a degraded class of your population to freedom, intelligence, and virtue; of redeeming yourselves from reproach; and of vindicating the character of your most holy faith.

(Signed in behalf of the Board,)
W. H. MURCH, Chairman,
Theological Tutor, Stepney College. London, Dec. 31, 1833.

(From the *Free Missionary* [Boston, Mass.], June, 1845. Quoted in *Facts for Baptist Churches*, A. T. Foss and E. Mathews, eds. [American Baptist Free Mission Society, 1850], pp. 17-20.)

(2) Two replies

a. From the Boston Board

A LETTER FROM THE BAPTIST BOARD OF FOREIGN MISSIONS IN AMERICA IN ANSWER TO ONE FROM THE BOARD OF BAPTIST MINISTERS IN AND NEAR LONDON, DATED DECEMBER 31, 1833.

BAPTIST MISSIONARY ROOMS, BOSTON, Sept. 1, 1834.

Dear Brethren:—Your communication, dated London, Dec. 31, 1833, was received some time since, by one of the officers of the Baptist General Convention; but as the Convention to which it was chiefly addressed, will not convene til April, 1835, the communication was, after some delay, presented to the Baptist Board of Foreign Missions, as the executive organ of the Convention. The Board referred it to a Committee, and we now communicate to you a copy of their report, and of the resolutions adopted by the Board. We commend them to your candor, with a confident belief that you will do justice to the views and feelings of the Board, encompassed as they are by difficulties which cannot be fully understood by persons in other countries.

It may assist you to form a more correct opinion of the whole subject, if we allude to a few of the circumstances which make slavery in this country a matter of peculiar difficulty, and which, consequently require those who would promote the real welfare of the colored race, to act with great caution.

In the first place, the political organization of the United States is widely different from that of England; and this difference makes it impossible to adopt here a course similar to that which the British Parliament have adopted in reference to slavery in the West Indies. This country is not one of a state with an unrestricted legislature, but a confederacy of States, united by a Constitution, in which certain powers are granted to the National Government, and all other powers are reserved by the States. Among these reserved powers is the regulation of slavery. Congress have no power to interfere with the slaves in the respective States; and an act of Congress to emancipate the slaves, in those States, would be as wholly null and void, as an act of the British Parliament for the same purpose. The Legislatures of respective States cannot interfere with the legislation of each other. In some of the States, where laws forbidding emancipation exist, the minority cannot, if disposed, give freedom to their slaves. You perceive, then, that the National Government, and the people of the Northern States, have no power nor right, to adopt any direct measures in reference to the emancipation of the slaves in the Southern States. The slaveholders themselves are the only men who can act definitely on this subject, and the only proper and useful influence which the friends of emancipation in other States can use, consists in argument and entreaty. The existence of our union, and its manifold blessings, depend on a faithful adherence to the principles and spirit of our Constitution, on this, and all other points.

This view of the case exonerates the nation, as such, and the States in which no slaves are found, from the charge of upholding slavery. It is due, moreover, to the Republic, to remember that slavery was introduced into this country long before the colonies became independent States. The slave trade was encouraged by the Government of Great Britain, and slaves were brought into the colonies against the wishes of the colonists, and the repeated acts of some of the colonial Legislatures. These acts were negatived by the King of England; and, in the Declaration of Independence, as originally drawn by Mr. Jefferson, it was stated among the grievances which produced the Revolution, that the King of England had steadily resisted the efforts of the colonies to prevent the introduction of slaves. Soon after the Revolution, several of the States took measures to free themselves from slavery. In 1787, Congress adopted an act, by which it was provided, that slavery should never be permitted in any of the States to be formed in the immense territory northwest of the Ohio; in which territory the great States of Ohio, Indiana and Illinois have since been formed. There are now thirteen out of the twenty-four States, in which slavery may be said to be extinct. Maryland is taking measures to free herself from slavery. Kentucky and Virginia will, it is believed, follow the example. We state these facts to show, that the Republic did not originate slavery here, and that she has done much to remove it altogether from her bosom. She took measures earlier than any other country for the suppression of the slave trade, and she is now zealously laboring to accomplish the entire extinction of that abominable traffic.

. . . .

Besides these general considerations, there is one which affects the duty of the Baptist General Convention. *There is now a pleasing degree of union among the multiplying thousands of Baptists throughout the land.* Brethren from all parts of the country unite in our General Convention, and co-operate in sending the gospel to the heathen. Our Southern brethren are liberal and zealous in the promotion of every holy enterprise for the extension of the gospel. They are, generally, both ministers and people, slaveholders; not because they all think slavery right, but because it was firmly rooted long before they were born, and because they believe slavery cannot be instantly abolished. We are confident that a large portion of our brethren at the South would rejoice to see any practicable scheme devised for relieving the country from slavery.

We have the best evidence that our slaveholding brethren are Christians, sincere followers of the Lord Jesus. In every other part of their conduct, they adorn the doctrine of God our Savior. We cannot, therefore, feel that it is right to use language or adopt measures which might tend to break the ties that unite them to us in our General Convention, and in numerous other benevolent societies; and to array brother against brother, church against church, and association against association in a contest about slavery.

We have presented these considerations, dear brethren, as among the reasons which compel us to believe that it is not the duty of the Baptist General Convention, or of the Board of Missions, to interfere with the subject of slavery. It ought, indeed, to be discussed at all proper times and in all suitable modes. We believe that the progress of public opinion in reference to slavery is very rapid; and we are quite sure that it cannot be accelerated by any interference which our Southern brethren would regard as an invasion of their political rights, or as an impeachment of their Christian character.

Most earnestly praying that the Father of Lights will illumine our path, and guide us to the adoption of such measures as shall advance His glory, and secure the temporal and eternal happiness of all men,

We are, dear brethren,

Your affectionate fellow-servants,

Lucius Bolles, Cor. Sec'y.

(From the *Baptist Magazine* [London], January, 1835, p. 11. Quoted in Foss-Mathews, *op. cit.*, pp. 20-23.)

b. *From abolitionists*

LETTER
TO ENGLAND FROM A BAPTIST CONVENTION HELD IN BOSTON, MAY 26 and 27, 1835. MORE THAN ONE HUNDRED AND EIGHTY SIGNATURES WERE OBTAINED TO IT.

To the Members of the Board of Baptist Ministers in and near London:

Respected and Dear Brethren:—The undersigned are Pastors and Ministers of the Baptist denomination in the United States of America. Your letter addressed to us in common with our brethren throughout our country, dated London, Dec. 31, 1833, and signed in your behalf by W. H. Murch, Chairman, Theological Tutor, Stepney College, has but recently reached us, or we should have given you an earlier reply. Indeed the fact that your letter had been received in America, was not known by most of us, until the month of February of this year. We sincerely regret that we and our churches, and the denomination at large, did not earlier receive the light which your excellent letter sheds on our duty, as Christians, and to feel the sacred influence it is so happily adapted to exert on our hearts.

We do not attempt to exonerate the nation as such from the charge of upholding slavery. This cannot be done so long as the laws of the nation hold, or allow to be held, in bondage a single slave; and the number

of persons now so held in the District of Columbia and the territories, which sections of country are under the exclusive jurisdiction of Congress, is about twenty-six thousand, whose posterity, if the present state of things should continue a half century longer, will amount to several times that number. Emigration to those territories is so rapid from the slave States, that, during the period named, the slave population may reasonably be expected to increase to a million or more. Neither can the free States be exonerated from the charge of upholding slavery so long as they aid in the restoration of the slaves who escape from their masters. We are verily a guilty nation before God, touching the inalienable rights of many of our fellowmen.

. . . .

We doubt not, you will sympathize and co-operate with us, and that you will be much in prayer for us and for those, both *slaves and masters,* for whose good it is our purpose to labor in the use of weapons not carnal but mighty through God to the overthrow of this as well as every other work of wickedness.

(From the *Free Missionary* [Boston], August, 1845. Quoted in Foss-Mathews, *op. cit.*, pp. 25-29.)

(3) Increasing American abolitionist sentiment

Baron Stow, an important officer of the American Baptist Board for Foreign Missions, reveals his abolitionist views.

From Baron Stow, A. M., of Boston, To Eld. W. H. Murch.

Boston, Jan. 11, 1839.

Dear Sir:—The communication of the Committee of the Baptist Union, which accompanies yours of Feb. 1, was immediately inserted in the Christian Watchman, and from that transferred to other religious journals which favor the cause of emancipation. Be assured, no effort shall be wanting on my part to get such appeals before our churches. Conceived and expressed in the kindest fraternal spirit, they cannot be turned aside without expressing a most unchristian and unmanly prejudice. That such prejudice exists, and is often developed, I admit; but I am happy to believe that it is wearing away before the light of truth, and the influence of judicious Christian effort.

Our friends in England must have patience with us, and not think us tardy in accomplishing an object which we, as well as they, are anxious for humanity's sake, and for Christ's sake, to see *immediately* effected. We have obstacles to overcome of which they are not at all aware, or which they do not, and cannot fully appreciate. Among these obstacles, I might name the inhuman prejudice against color, as the badge of servitude and debasement; the peculiar organization of our government, reserving to the State the entire control of slavery within their own limits; the opposition of Christians in all the slaveholding States to abolition, and in the free States to all agitation of the subject.

It would not be difficult to show that the influence of the American church, is, at present, the main pillar of American slavery.

But, my dear brother, God is on our side and the cause will prevail. Every day it is gaining friends, and though less rapidly than we could wish, yet steadily and surely advancing towards the desired consummation. Still help us by your prayers and remonstrances, and anticipate with us the joyful day when Republican America shall be purified of this foul and deadly leprosy.

In the kingdom and patience, &c.,

Your brother affectionately,

BARON STOW.

(From Foss-Mathews, *op. cit.*, pp. 40-41.)

2. *American Baptist Anti-Slavery Convention*

American Baptist abolitionists met on May 11, 1839, and formed the American Baptist Anti-Slavery Convention. The group issued two addresses—one to Baptists in the North and one to Baptists in the South.

The latter address stirred up much discussion. Subsequently, the abolitionists withdrew from the missionary societies to form their own organization.

(1) *Organization of the Anti-Slavery Convention*

To Baptist Conventions, Associations, Ministers, Churches, and congregations in the United States of America, Friends of the poor slave, and advocates of immediate emancipation.

Dear Beloved in the Lord:

We, the undersigned, address you as baptized believers, in the name of the Great Head of the church, and of His suffering poor. In the opinion of a meeting of Baptist abolitionists, held this day in the city of New York, and whose representatives we are, the period has arrived when some judicious measures should be taken to call a National Baptist Convention, to prepare the way for organizing an *American Baptist Anti-Slavery Society*.

The Providence of God seems to have caused a necessity for such an organization. And while we do not aim to array ourselves against any well managed societies already in existence, we think it obvious that as Baptists, we can accomplish more by laboring on our own platform, than any other way.

We, therefore, whose names are annexed, cordially address to you this Circular. You will oblige us by sending your names as soon as convenient, should you approve the object contemplated, to either of the following brethren:—Editors Eastern Baptist, Brunswick, Me.; editor Baptist Register, Concord, N. H.; editor Telegraph, Brandon, Vt.; editor Christian Reflector, Worcester, Mass.; Rev. Elon Galusha, Perry, Genesee Co., Western N. Y.; Rev. Nathaniel Colver, Greenwich, Washington Co., N. Y.; Rev. R. Turnbull, Hartford, Conn.; Rev. L. Fletcher, Spread Eagle, Chester Co., Pa.; Rev. Samuel Aaron, Burlington, N. J.; editor Philanthropist, Cincinnati, Ohio; all of whom, and any other who may receive names, will please transmit them to Rev. Duncan Dunbar, or to either member of the central corresponding committee, located for the purpose in the city of New York. At the proper time the committee will then be assembled, when the names which have been received will be appended to the call, the time and place of holding the Convention fixed, and both the call and address be circulated throughout our land.

Finally, brethren, let us exhort one another to increased diligence and more fervent prayer in this holy cause. Let us be up and doing: "and so much the more as we see the day approaching."

Signed:

CYRUS P. GROSVENOR, Chairman
CHARLES W. DENNISON, Secretary.

(From *The Emancipator* [New York], June 13, 1839.)

(2) *Address to the South*

ADDRESS TO SOUTHERN BAPTISTS.

The American Baptist Anti-Slavery Convention, holding its first session in the City of New York, on the 28th, 29th, and 30th of April, 1840—

To the Baptist Slaveholders
of the Southern States:

Fathers and Brethren,—

We have assembled, to the number of one hundred persons, at the written call of seven hundred Baptists from thirteen of the United States. Of this number, about four hundred are accredited ministers of Jesus Christ.

A conviction of duty, which, we humbly conceive, is based upon the fear of God, and the love of our fellow-men,—whether bond or free, oppressors or oppressed,—constrains us to submit a few thoughts for your special and candid consideration. In doing so, we appeal with the firmest confidence, to the Omniscient God, for the rectitude of our intentions. We solemnly profess a prayerful and submissive reverence for the principles of his recorded will. We feelingly avow a tender sympathy, not only for the *slave*, but also for you, upon many of whom slavery is entailed by heritage, and enforced by law; while inexorable habits, formed in the passive state of infancy, as well as universal usage, impose bonds upon yourselves scarcely less stronger or less oppressive than the fetters of the slave.

Hear us, then, with patience and kindness. It is our firm conviction that the whole system of American slavery, in theory and practice, is a violation of the instincts of nature,—a perversion of the first principles of justice,—and a positive transgression of the revealed will of God. *For*, man instinctively seeks happiness and repels outrage; while slavery compels him to forego the former and endure the latter, for himself and his posterity, until the end of time. Justice, in its very nature, assumes the existence of free moral agents, mutually bound by established principles, and acting towards each other with perfect reciprocity. We do not speak of justice towards each other with perfect reciprocity. We do not speak of justice towards a "chattel personal," a horse, or a swine. But the statutes of the South pronounce a slave "a chattel personal to all intents and purposes whatsoever;" and thus set him beyond the pale of justice, as utterly disqualified to assert a right and to redress a wrong.

Divine revelation as committed to Moses and expounded by our Lord, teaches, that pious self-love is the only proper measure of our love towards others. Does slavery, especially its laws which quench or smother in the slave the light of the mind, which tear from his agonized bosom the dearest objects of his natural affection—conform to that rule of Holy Writ?

We believe that God only has the right to take away the health, the wife, the children, or the life of men guilty of no social crime. When man, single or associated, uses his power for such ends, he appears to us to arrogate to himself the prerogative of the Almighty, and to assume a responsibility under which an archangel would stagger.

God, it is true, made use of the Jews to exterminate certain heathen tribes, and to inflict upon others a mild servitude, carefully defined and restricted. To employ this mode of punishment, or any other that He chose, was His unquestionable right. But where is the Scripture warrant to apply this special license of Jehovah for the extirpation of the human race at large, or the enslavement of any nation in particular? This specific direction to His oracular people is but *an exception* that confirms the general rule of His Son. "Thou shalt love thy neighbor as thyself." The heart of the blessed Jesus was, indeed, an overflowing fountain of the tenderest sympathy for human woe. Food, health, and life were his boon, never withheld, when solicited; and the gospel preached to the poor was the peculiar and characteristic proof of his being the Son of God and the Savior of the world. No evidence exists that He ever witnessed a scene of slavery. It is not shown that Hebrews of that day trafficked in human flesh. The chained coffle,—the naked gang of the cotton field,—the exposed female reeking under the lash,—the child torn forever from its mother's breaking heart,—these, and worse acts of slavery's tragedy, were not performed, so far as history speaks, before the face of Jesus. But His warmest, almost His only burst of indignation, is against those who devoured the helpless widow's substance, and, for a pretense, made long prayers and liberal contributions to the cause of God.

His itinerant, inspired followers were too busy in draining off the universal deluge of idolatry, explaining the nature of the one living God, and establishing the claims of Jesus as the true Messiah, to define, or to condemn, in form, every species and variety of crime, in every age, that hell, fruitful of inventions, might suggest, and fallen human nature perpetrate. Hence, horse-racing, gambling, piracy, the rum-traffick, and the African and American slave-trade, remain ungraduated in the scripture scale of human sins. Paul, however, exhorts the servants of *heathen* masters to respectfulness and patience, for the reason that the name of God be not blasphemed; and ad-

vises them, while patient under bondage, to prefer freedom. He enjoins *Christian* masters to give their servants what is just and equal. Do the slaves of American Baptists obtain justice and equity? He implores his brother Philemon to receive again the converted fugitive, not, as he probably had been, the heathen vassal of a heathen lord, but as a beloved brother in Jesus Christ. Thus *we* behold, in all the scriptures a virtual and total condemnation of American slavery.

Besides, American Calvinistic Baptists, as a whole denomination, have been hitherto regarded by the Christian world, *as responsible for the sins of Baptist Slaveholders, and the sufferings of one hundred thousand Baptist slaves*. And if we fail, as many do, to testify our abhorrence of a system that allows a fellow-Christian to sell his brother, or his brother's wife or child, or to dissolve the marriage tie at pleasure, we see not how to escape the merited contempt of mankind, the reproaches of conscience, or the displeasure of God. For, the followers of Jesus are ordained the light of the world, and *His witnesses of the truth* until the end of time.

Further, in the exhaustion of your once teeming soil,—the non-increase, and, in some parts, diminution of your white population,—the depreciation of your staple products, and the competition of British enterprise in India,—the jubilee shout of West Indian emancipation, rousing the dormant spirit of your slaves to assert the rights of man,—your intrinsic incapacity of self-defense in case of foreign aggression,—your constant exposure to servile insurrection and massacre,—and ir the general reprobation of republican slavery throughout the rest of the civilized and Christian world,—we behold indications that God attests, by earthly signs, the precept of his heavenly oracles, to "let the oppressed go free."

Again, if you have thus far heard us with candor, you may perhaps inquire, "What would you have us do?" We answer, —at once confess before heaven and earth the sinfulness of holding slaves; admit it to be not only a misfortune, but a crime; remonstrate against laws that bind the system on you; petition for the guaranty, to all, of "national and inalienable rights." If your remonstrances and prayers to man are disregarded, cast yourselves on the God of providence and justice; forsake, like Abraham, your father-land, and carry your children and your households to the vast asylum of our prairies and our wilderness, where our Father in heaven has bidden our mother earth to open her exuberant breast for the nourishment of many sons.

Finally,—if you should, (which Heaven avert!) remain deaf to the voice of warning and entreaty,—if you still cling to the power-maintained privilege of living on unpaid toil, and of claiming as property the image of God, which Jesus bought with His precious blood,—we solemnly declare, as we fear the Lord, that we cannot and we dare not recognize you as consistent brethren in Christ; we cannot join in partial, selfish prayers, that the groans of the slave may be unheard; we cannot hear preaching which makes God the author and approver of human misery and vassalage; and we cannot, at the Lord's table, cordially take that as a brother's hand, which plies the scourge on woman's naked flesh,— which thrusts a gag into the mouth of a man,—which rivets fetters on the innocent, —and which shuts up the Bible from human eyes. We deplore your condition; we pray for your deliverance; and God forbid that we should ever sin against Him by ceasing so to pray.

ELON GALUSHA, President.

O. S. MURRAY, Secretary.

(From *Christian Watchman* [New York], June 19, 1840.)

(3) Separation of abolitionists from the benevolent societies

CONSTITUTION AND BY-LAWS
of the American Baptist Free Mission
Society

Whereas, on the 4th day of May, in the year of our Lord one thousand eight hundred and forty-three, a Convention of Baptist ministers and members was held in the Tremont Chapel, Boston, in the State of Massachusetts, of the United States of North America, who adopted and signed the following pledge, to wit:

"We whose names are undersigned, solemnly pledge ourselves to God and one another, to unite in the support of a Baptist Missionary Society, with a Constitution yet to be adopted, that shall be distinctly and thoroughly separated from all connection with the known avails of slavery in the support of any of its benevolent purposes;" and this Society, shall be called The American Baptist Free Mission Society, and we hereby separate ourselves now and forever from all connection with religious societies that are supported in common with slaveholders:—

Therefore, under a deep sense of our responsibilities to God and our obligation to give the gospel in its purity to a perishing world; and looking towards Heaven for grace to strengthen us in the prosecution of this great work, and for success in an enterprise so important to the destinies of our fallen race, we, as a society, adopt the following articles, which, with this preamble as part thereof, shall be the Constitution of this Society.

1. The object of this society shall be to carry out the commission of our blessed Lord and Savior Jesus Christ, "Go ye into all the world and preach the gospel to every creature," and to employ, in order to effect this, all necessary measures and agencies at home and abroad.

2. This Society shall be composed of Baptists of acknowledged Christian character, who appear as delegates from churches or auxiliary societies, or in their own name, who are not slaveholders, but believe that slavery, under all circumstances, is sin, and treat it accordingly.

3. It shall be the duty of the Board of Trustees to receive and transmit to their proper destination, such sums as may be contributed according to the principles of the Preamble of this Constitution, by

Churches, either singly or acting together in Associations, for the support of Missionaries appointed by such churches or associations; provided that such Missionaries are members in good standing, of Baptist churches, and not slaveholders, or advocates of Slavery.

4. This Society shall meet at such time and place as the Society itself, or the Trustees, *under peculiar necessity* shall designate.

5. The Society being called to order at its annual meeting, the first business after singing and prayer, shall be the enrolment of members and the election of officers and a Board of Trustees.

6. The Society shall elect by ballot a President, Vice Presidents, a Corresponding Secretary, a Recording Secretary, Treasurer, and two Auditors.

7. The Society shall elect by ballot eleven Trustees who with the President, Vice Presidents, the Corresponding and Recording Secretaries, and the Treasurer, shall constitute the Board of Trustees of this Society, with full power to use all means necessary to secure the object of the Society, and who shall present a written report of their proceedings at each annual meeting.

8. At the meetings of the Board of Trustees for ordinary business, four members shall constitute a quorum, provided due notice be given of the same; but it shall require six members of the Board to be present for the selection of a Missionary station, for the appointment of Missionaries, or for any thing involving new and important responsibilities.

9. The Board of Trustees shall have power to fill all vacancies occasioned by death or otherwise.

10. Any amendment of this Constitution may be made at an annual meeting of the Society, provided such amendments do not affect the principles of the original plan, as set forth in the preamble, and the proposition be made known at least one session previous to its adoption.

(From Foss-Mathews, *op. cit.*, p. 398.)

3. Crisis in Home Mission Society

(1) Neutrality circular

The South demanded that the benevolent bodies adhere strictly to the constitution of each body. The Home Mission Society declared its neutrality.

CIRCULAR

Of the Executive Committee of the American Baptist Home Mission Society.

It is with reluctance and anxiety that the Executive Committee of the American Baptist Home Mission Society address themselves, at this time, to the churches. They yield to the stress of circumstances in speaking, when they would gladly keep silence. Hitherto enjoying, as they trust, the confidence and the prayers of the churches, they found in their appropriate work, enough to take their utmost strength, without allowing them either the time or the inclination to diverge to other objects.

. . . .

It scarce needs to be said that as a denomination, we have gloried in knowing no legislator in the church, but our Lord Jesus Christ, in whose written ordinances and pledged presence is all our trust. Our churches recognize no power, in the mass of the disciples even, to make laws. Our only book of canons was compiled in the days of plenary inspiration. The New Testament is the only book either of statutes or of precedents, whose authority we allow. We have contended with the utmost jealousy that the power of discipline rests in the individual church, and that such church forms the court of the last appeal—short of the bar of the Last Judgment. Our Associations and occasional Councils, are but advisory bodies, and though by usage respected and consulted, never were clothed with the power to legislate, or to exercise discipline, and have, therefore, no resemblance whatever to the Synods recognized by other denominations of Christians. The voluntary Societies in which we are united, composed as they are, in part, at least, of the unconverted world, have still less the right to enact ordinances and to administer government. The Scriptures give them no such powers, and the churches are neither inclined nor authorized to confer on them such power directly or indirectly. Were they to assume it, it might justly be resisted, in bodies whose terms of membership, and whose constitutional restrictions, and whose want of an equal representation from all the churches entirely disqualify them for its exercise. We make these remarks, not as if the principles thus stated were unknown or had been disputed, but because in the excitement of great questions, it is always safe to state and to review, even at the hazard of repetition and tediousness, the first elements of our peculiar polity.

A question has of late been most earnestly agitated, that awakens naturally the deepest feelings, especially at the South. We need not say we allude to the action of the Anti-Slavery Societies formed at the North. Our brethren at the South, with great unanimity, deprecate the discussion as unwarranted, the measures pursued as fatal to their safety, and complain of the language occasionally employed as cruel and slanderous. The brethren at the North are found divided in sentiment. Some are earnest and decided in believing it their duty to urge upon the South, with great plainness, the consideration of this question. Another portion incline to some of their views, but distrust the rightfulness and wisdom of their measures. But still another division feel, that to the churches of the South alone belong the examination and decision of this matter. In the South there is but one party, therefore; in the North there are several. Now should it be wished to procure the action of the denomination upon this question, we see no body at this time in existence, that is competent to commence the examination, out of the individual churches. The only general body that would be authorized to examine the question, must be composed of representatives from individual churches, delegated for that express purpose; and these could bind only the churches that sent them—

nor even them could they bind by any new laws. A general convention of our churches throughout the country, with general powers, we have not, and it would be dangerous to create such a body, wielding, as it necessarily would, a power of uncertain advantage, and of certain and lasting injury.

The wish has been manifested, on either side, that voluntary societies, our own among the number, should act upon this question, either by disapproving the civil institutions of the South, or censuring the course of those at the North who impugn these institutions. The Executive Committee believe that voluntary societies have no such right. It would be traveling out of the record to allow the introduction of the question, or admit it even as a subject of conference in the Society. We must, in doing so, act uncommissioned, and trample upon the ruins of our Constitution, to arrive at the question. It would be again a violation of our first principles as Baptists, recognizing no disciplinary power beyond the individual church, and no legislation out of the lids of the New Testament. And it would be the creation, in the most objectionable form, of a synod, one of that class of institutions whose usurpations laid the basis of the Romish apostasy. It was, as ecclesiastical history proves, not so much the acts of individual bishops in the first instance, as the collective acts of synods, and those too springing up in republican Greece, and acting on republican models, which laid smooth, broad and firm the highway over which came the Man of Sin traveling in the greatness of his strength. As Christians we dare not disregard the warning furnished by the past history of the church. As Baptists we must not forsake what our churches have regarded as the primitive way.

.   .   .   .

If any officer or agent has, through inadvertence, held different language, it has not been with the authority of this Committee. Against the disposition of some beloved brethren to withdraw from that union so dear to the Society, and, as we humbly trust, to God, we protest affectionately, respectfully and with earnest vehemence. We need union as a denomination. And, as patriots, we must cherish religious union as one among the strongest, although not the most prominent, of the bands that hold together the Union of these States. And, in a day when the infidel and the Romanist play each into the other's hands, forgetting all minor differences for a common end; amid scenes daily exhibiting the power of combination to obtain success for the worst objects, and the efficacy of dissension, to make shipwreck of the best; it is surely not when bad men league, that good men should strive.

. . . .

By order of the Executive Committee,
SPENCER H. CONE, Chairman.
BENJ. M. HILL, Cor. Sec. A. B. H. M. S.
February 16, 1841.

(From *Christian Reflector* [Worcester, Mass.], March 10, 1841.)

(2) Richard Fuller's resolution

Whereas, the question has been proposed—whether the Board would or would not employ slave-holders as missionaries of this Society; and whereas, it is important that this question should receive a full and unequivocal answer, therefore

Resolved, That as the Constitution of the Home Mission Society clearly defines its object to be promotion of the Gospel in North America, and as it is provided by such Constitution that any auxiliary society may designate the object to which the funds contributed by it shall be applied, and may also claim a missionary or missionaries, according to such funds, and select the field where the missionary or missionaries shall reside,

Therefore, 1st: That to introduce the subjects of slavery or anti-slavery into this body, is in direct contravention of the whole letter and purpose of the said Constitution, and is, moreover, a most unnecessary agitation of topics with which this Society has no concern, over which it has

no control, and as to which its operations should not be fettered, nor its deliberations disturbed,

2: That the Home Mission Society being only an agency to disburse the funds confided to it, according to the wishes of the contributors, therefore, our co-operation in this body does not imply any sympathy either with slavery or anti-slavery, as to which societies and individuals are left as free and uncommitted as if there were no such co-operation.

(From Home Mission Society *Minutes*, 1844, pp. 5-6.)

(3) Plan for amicable division in home missions

After years of protracted and sometimes acrimonious debate, it was generally agreed that separation would be better than the constant turmoil. In 1844 a committee was appointed to make plans for an amicable separation. Its report in 1845 is given.

Eld. Maginnis, of New York, offered the following substitute providing for an amicable dissolution of the Society:

Whereas, the American Baptist Home Missionary Society, is composed of contributors, residing in slaveholding and non-slaveholding States; and *whereas* the constitution recognizes no distinction among the members of the Society as to eligibility to all the offices and appointments in the gift, both of the Society and of the Board; and *whereas* it has been found that the basis on which the Society was organized is one upon which all the members and friends of the Society are not now willing to act; therefore,

1. *Resolved,* That in our opinion it is expedient that the members now forming the Society, should hereafter act in separate organizations at the South and at the North in promoting the objects which were originally contemplated by the Society.

2. *Resolved,* That a Committee be appointed to report a plan by which the object contemplated in the preceding resolution may be accomplished in the best way,

and at the earliest period of time, consistently with the preservation of the constitutional rights of all the members, and with the least possible interruption of the Missionary work of the Society.

. . . .

Eld. Maginnis, Chairman of the Committee on the proposed division, reported as follows:

The Committee appointed in relation to a note of separate action and organization, submit the following report:

As the existing Society was planted in the North, has its Executive Board, and there received a Charter of Incorporation, which it seems desirable to preserve, and as a separation seems to many minds inevitable, owing to the strong views of churches and individuals against the appointment of slaveholders to serve the Society, and as such views prevail principally at the North, therefore, in view of such separation, we recommend the adoption of the following resolutions:

1. *Resolved*, Should such separation among the former friends and patrons of the Society be deemed necessary, that the existing organization be retained by the northern and other churches, which may be willing to act together upon the basis of restriction against the appointment of slaveholders.

2. *Resolved*, That the Executive Board be instructed, in such case, to adjust upon amicable, honorable, and liberal principles, whatever claims may be presented by brethren who shall feel upon the separation, unable farther to co-operate with the society, or disposed to form a separate organization at the South.

(From Home Mission Society *Minutes*, 1845, p. 6 ff.)

4. *Crisis in the General Missionary Convention*

The foreign mission body also issued a neutrality circular. As a result of the controversy, Francis Wayland for the North and Richard Fuller for the South engaged in a series of literary discussions on the subject, *with courtesy and fair-mindedness observed on each side.*

(1) *Neutrality circular of foreign mission body*

At a regular meeting of the Baptist Board of Foreign Missions, at the Missionary Rooms, Boston, November 2, 1840, at which were present *Daniel Sharp, Solomon Peck, Heman Lincoln, Levi Farwell, Irah Chase, Joel S. Bacon, Nathaniel W. Williams, John Wayland, Richard Fletcher, Baron Stow, William Hague,* and *Charles Train,* the following address was *unanimously* adopted, and ordered to be printed and circulated.

ADDRESS.

The Board of Managers of the Baptist General Convention for Foreign Missions have observed, with painful interest, indications of a tendency on the part of some of their beloved brethren and co-adjutors, to withdraw from the Missionary connection in which they have been happily associated for so many years. And they are constrained by their sense of duty to the interests entrusted to their care, by their love to the Redeemer and the souls for whom he died, and by their affectionate regard to all who, at any time, have extended their aid to the Foreign Missionary cause, to remind their brethren of the design of their Association and the principles on which it was formed and has been conducted.

The primary and exclusive object of the founders of the General Convention, as expressed in the preamble to the Constitution, was to "send the glad tidings of salvation to the heathen, and to nations destitute of Gospel light." For the prosecution of this one object, the Board of Managers was created, and empowered to act on their behalf; and to this alone, (with the exception of a temporary, authorized, divergence to Home Missions and Education,) have the Board down to the present moment been restricted. So deeply indeed have the Board been impressed with the vastness and importance of this object, and with their responsibility for its faithful prosecution, that they have strenuously withstood every influence that threatened to turn them aside from it, and have even refrained from what would have been deemed by some a justifiable expression of their sentiments on controverted subjects, lest an unfavorable re-action should result therefrom upon the interests of this endeared and sacred cause.

Corresponding with the oneness of this object for which the Convention was organized, is the simplicity of the terms on which co-operation for its accomplishment may be proffered or received. Our venerated fathers who constituted the original Convention, contemplating in the new organization the prosecution of the Foreign Missionary enterprise alone, and justly appreciating the vast extent of the work, and the demands which it would make upon the sympathies and resources of *all* benevolent hearts within the bounds of the community whom the Convention was designed to represent, were careful to lay no obstruction in the way of any individual who might be disposed to communicate to its funds, nor any restriction on the liberty of counsel or direction in its concerns, further than was judged indispensable to their efficient and safe administration. Their purpose, distinctly avowed in the preamble already alluded to, was the eliciting, combining and directing the energies of the whole denomination in one sacred effort. And it was with evident reference to this proposed universality of interest and effort, that they assumed the comprehensive designation, "The General Convention of the Baptist Denomination of the United States," etc. In accordance with this design of securing the widest possible co-operation, the provisions for the admission of members into the Convention were made exceedingly simple and few. By the Constitution as it now stands, and has always stood, the right to a seat or representation in the Convention is based only on two conditions: 1st, That the religious body or the individual be of the Baptist Denomination; and, 2d, That the same shall have contributed to the Treasury of the Convention a specified annual sum. For appointment to the Board, the individual, being a member of one of the religious bodies represented in the Convention, must also "be a member of some Baptist church." Beyond these specifications it was deemed inexpedient to go.

Such being the design of the organization of the Convention, and such the principles on which co-operation may be tendered and accepted, the Board are unable to discover any sufficient reason for the withdrawal of support on the part of any of their contributors, in view of facts or considerations wholly extrinsic and irrelevant. That the influences which at the present time are apparently set toward this result, *are* wholly irrelevant, and should be steadfastly withstood, is evident, not only in view of the object and principles of the Convention above stated, but from a just consideration of the relations and responsibilities of the Board. These relations and responsibilities have to some extent been misapprehended by brethren near and remote, and the consequence of the misapprehension has been to hold the Board accountable for things done and not done, *in relation to all of which alike the Board has done nothing, because it had nothing to do.* With respect to such things the Board has, so to speak, neither a name nor existence. Its vitality and power are wholly derived, and can by its present Constitution act only to one end. As to all other intents and purposes, the Board can have power, and will, only when first it shall have been endued with them by the Convention, from whom it emanates. The Board is the executive of the Convention; the Convention alone is legislative. It is the province of the Board simply to carry into effect the will of the Convention.

These principles, the principles on which the Convention and the Board are constituted, and according to which only they can rightfully in their separate capacities act, are clearly defined in the Constitution and laws which the Convention has framed. And by provision of the same Constitution, they can be modified or repealed by the will of the Convention only, duly expressed. The Board has, for instance, no discretionary or dispensing power as to the receipt of contributions. Their duty is distinctly prescribed, and it simply is, to receive all moneys contributed for Foreign Missions to their funds, from whatever source they come, and to disburse them with fidelity for the ends to which they are designated by the contributors. The same general remarks are in point as it respects the qualification for membership either in Convention or Board. What the qualifications are, as defined by the Constitution, we have stated. The Board cannot change them; nor can it set them at naught. It has, in truth, no capacity to act in regard to them, further than to supply its own vacancies. It has no power of excision. The Convention appoints its own Board, triennially, in view of the qualifications which itself prescribes; and appoints whom it pleases.

. . . .

The Board look forward to the approaching anniversary of the Convention with mingled solicitude and hope,—with *hope*, for we shall greet on that high day of our solemnities endeared brethren and friends, from the North, from the South, and from the West, with whom we have often taken sweet counsel, and of whose affections and confidence, we trust, no disastrous influence shall have despoiled us, as *none will have estranged them from ours*; with *solicitude*, lest by the unseasonable diversion of our thoughts to irrelevant subjects, the unity of the design of our confederation be infringed, and the harmony of our counsels disturbed. We devoutly commend the occasion and all that may pertain to it, to the disposal of Him who is "wonderful in counsel and excellent in working;" and we entreat our brethren of every place and name, contributors to our funds and fellow-helpers in Christ, "to strive together with us in their prayers to God," that he may

shed down upon all who shall be convened as their representatives on that eventful day the "spirit of love and of a sound mind."

DANIEL SHARP, *President.*
BARON STOW, *Rec. Sec'y.*

(From the *Christian Reflector* [Worcester, Mass.], Dec. 2, 1840.)

(2) Compromise Article

In 1841 a group of Northern and Southern Baptist leaders met preceding the triennial session of the General Convention at Baltimore. The adoption of the following statement probably delayed separation for a period.

COMPROMISE ARTICLE

Whereas, The Scriptures constitute the only rule of conduct for Christians and Christian churches; and, whereas, it is evident in the Scriptures that churches are independent bodies, having no head but Christ, and no law but his revealed will; and, whereas, they have no right or authority to censure or excommunicate any but their own members; and, whereas, the Constitution of the Baptist General Convention of the United States, of the American Baptist Home Mission Society, and the American and Foreign Bible Society, require that the officers and managers of those institutions, be "brethren in good standing of Baptist churches, in general union with the denomination;" and, whereas, a "disposition has been manifested, in this age of innovation, to introduce new tests of good standing and fellowship, unknown to the denomination generally;" and whereas, the announcement of disfellowship, on the basis of such *new tests*, is now causing embarrassments and alienation among those who have been united in bonds of fraternal love for many years, and hitherto have delightfully co-operated in the holy enterprise of disseminating the truth of God, through these organizations, —therefore,

Resolved, That the undersigned deem it their duty and privilege to record their full conviction that no new tests unauthorized by the Scriptures, and by the established usages of the great body of our churches, should be suffered to interfere with the harmonious operations of our benevolent associations, as originally constituted; and they embrace this fitting occasion to express their decided disapprobation of all such tests, believing them to have a direct tendency to part asunder those who have "one Lord, one faith, one baptism," and above all that they invade the prerogative of Jesus Christ, the one and only legislator of the churches of the saints, to whom be glory for ever, amen.

(From Foss-Mathews, *op. cit.*, pp. 75-76.)

(3) Wayland-Fuller debate

Wayland summarizes the gist of their arguments.

If now we look back over the course of these remarks, I think we may easily discover the manner in which, commencing so widely asunder, we have come at last so nearly to coincide. In the first place, excluding from your definition of slavery all right to interfere with the *intellectual, moral, social,* and *domestic* condition of man, and admitting that for such interference slavery furnishes neither excuse nor palliation, you limit the institution which you defend to the mere right to oblige another to labor for us without his contract or consent. In the second place, as it seems to me, falling within your own definition, and "materially retrenching" from it, you defend a condition which may be *voluntary, limited by contract,* and one *which the laborer would not consent to relinquish.* In the third place, you affirm that this condition, even thus modified, could not properly be perpetuated. In how much soever then we may differ in our course of reasoning, the practical conclusions to which we arrive are singularly coincident.

Where there is so substantial practical agreement, it might seem that farther examination of the argument was unnec-

essary. I find, moreover, that I am in danger of extending this letter to an unreasonable length. I will not, therefore, pretend to examine your argument from the Scriptures in detail, but shall merely remark very briefly upon some of the points on which, as I suppose, the controversy mainly hinges.

Your argument drawn from the Old Testament in favor of slavery, is, I think, two-fold. In the first place, you infer that slavery cannot be wrong, that is, cannot be a violation of the relations which God has established, because the holiest men, both in ancient and modern times, have both held slaves and also spoken in favor of slavery. This argument, I fear, will not bear generalization. I have already alluded to the case of Dr. Stiles. You also remember that John Newton, for some years after his conversion, was the captain of a slaveship, and was thus doing acts which now would condemn him to the gallows, without being aware that he was doing wrong. This surely by no means proves that the *slave-trade* is innocent.

Secondly, you infer that slavery cannot be a wrong because God gave the various precepts concerning it, which you quote from the laws of Moses.

To this I have replied, that he gave various precepts in the same laws respecting other practices manifestly wrong, and that, therefore, your inference is not legitimate.

Polygamy and divorce come under precisely the same class of moral wrongs as slavery. You describe them as acts "conflicting with the relations designed at first by God between the sexes." I consider slavery to be wrong precisely because "it conflicts with the relations designed at first by God between" man and man. The generic character of the two acts is, that they *"conflict with the relations designed at first by God;"* their *specific difference* is, that in the one case the conflict is with the relations designed by God between *the sexes;* in the other it is with the relations between *man and man.*

Yet God did not prohibit polygamy and divorce among the ancient Hebrews, but enacted laws to regulate them. These practices were nevertheless clearly wrong, and Christ condemned and forbade them. I thence infer that an act may be wrong, a violation of the relations which God has established, and yet, at a particular time, he may not prohibit it, and may even enact laws concerning it. You say Christ forbade these wrongs, but did not forbid slavery. Very true. But this, I think, does not affect the general fact above stated; nay, it rather confirms it. Christ's condemnation of these institutions clearly shows them to have been wrong, and wrong from the beginning; but this only demonstrates the truth, that it is not inconsistent with the dealings of God with men, to give precepts regulating a practice in itself wrong, but concerning which he has not seen fit, at present, explicitly to reveal his will.

It would be improper in this closing letter to examine at length your argument from the New Testament. I could not do so without introducing new matter into the discussion. I am as confident as I usually am in any of the conclusions of my understanding, that I have interpreted the teachings of our Saviour and his apostles correctly. I must content myself with referring you in general to what I have already stated. I shall here very briefly allude to the different principles on which our argument rests.

Your argument, I think, intends to establish the following points:

1. God could not consistently with his attributes, in making a revelation, be silent as to any course of action and also give precepts concerning it, and yet inculcate principles in the same revelation, intended to subvert and abolish it.

2. God has been thus silent and has thus given precepts respecting the institution of slavery, and

3. Therefore, God has inculcated no such principles. Hence, you consider that by the apostolic directions on this subject the character of God is committed to the

innocence of this institution; and to suppose him to deny himself. This argument you have enforced with great copiousness of learning, and with all the advantages of an eloquence which I admire, but which I have no power to imitate. It moves me strongly every time I read it, but I must say it does not convince me. Suffer me briefly to hint at the reasons of my dissent.

1. I do not believe that we are competent thus to decide upon the manner in which God can or may teach us. I am confident, first of all, that God is consistent with himself, and that the Bible is his own revelation, and that therefore I can best justify his ways by receiving in humility all that he has there made known to me. You very well ask, "When the Scriptures have been received as a revelation, and the inquiry is about their meaning, how does it sound to affirm authoritatively as to what they ought to teach;" and I may add, to affirm authoritatively in what *manner* they shall teach it? The adoption of this principle has always led to error. Reasoning thus, you know that Luther is said to have rejected the Epistle of James from the canon, because he supposed that the views of faith taught by this apostle, could not have been dictated by the same spirit which indited the Epistle to the Galatians. I take a different view of this subject. I suppose the Most High to deal with us, as with beings endowed with an intelligent and moral nature; and, therefore, that he frequently makes known to us his will by teaching us the relations in which we stand, and the obligations thence resulting, without specifying to us the particular acts which he intends thereby to forbid. Whatever our reason clearly perceives to be contradictory to a relation which he has established, is thus forbidden. In this manner I suppose God to have made known his will concerning slavery. Again, on the other hand, I find in the Bible the precepts concerning masters and slaves which we have both quoted. I receive both of these as a revelation from God; and I hence conclude that it is consistent with the at-

tributes of God to teach us in this manner.

I ask myself, did he ever before teach in this manner? I find that he frequently did so under the old dispensation. I ask again, is it in analogy with his teaching in the New Testament that he should teach rather by principle than by precept? I find upon inquiry that this is there his ordinary mode of teaching. I ask again, is there any special reason why this mode of teaching should be adopted in this particular case? I find that this mode is specially adapted to the removal of a social evil, and that no other could, on the principles of human nature, be reasonably employed. Hence, I conclude that slavery is by the word of God forbidden, but that the word of God intends to remove it, not by immediate proclamation, as must be the case if it were treated preceptively, but by applying the principles of the gospel to the consciences of men, and thus, by changing the sentiments of the society, gradually and kindly work its entire extermination.

In the use which you have made of the saying of Lord Eldon, I think you have not taken notice of the point which I intended to illustrate. The question is not whether, if Lord Eldon had violated plainly a plain law, he would have been punished. This would have depended on the firmness of the judge, and the honesty of the jury. The question is, whether, the law being as it is, he could not have taught another man how to violate the whole intention of the law, and yet escape conviction, and thus make it necessary that the law should be amended. Nor is this really the question at issue. It is, in fact, this. Suppose a law forbidding forgery had been made by a Roman emperor in the time of Christ, and the law, from the constitution of things, could neither be altered nor amended; would Lord Eldon, or any other man, find the slightest difficulty in doing with impunity the very acts which the law intended to forbid? You think that my views of interpretation lead to laxity of morals. To me, their tendency seems exactly the reverse. In my view, a principle

is like the flaming sword, which, turning every way, guards on every side the tree of life; while a precept, made only for one age, and looking only in one direction, leaves the approach in every other direction unguarded and defenceless.

While, however, there seems to be this wide theoretical difference between us, I again perceive that, practically, we very nearly agree. While you hold that slavery is permitted, nay, sanctioned by God; and that, hence, to have taught any thing at variance with this permission would have been to deny himself; you still express your views of this institution in such language as the following: "If you had asserted the great danger of confiding such irresponsible power in the hands of *any man*, I should at once have assented. There is quite enough abuse of this authority to make me regret its *general existence.*" Again, "you must already have perceived that, speaking abstractly of slavery, I do not consider its perpetuation *proper, even if it were possible.* Nor let any one ask, why not perpetuate it if it be not a sin? The *Bible informs us what man is,* and among *such beings, irresponsible power is a trust too easily and too frequently abused.*" It may not be proper for me to ask how these assertions are to be reconciled with the views to which I have above referred. I cannot, however, but observe, that you *regret* the general existence of an institution, of which the general existence is, as you affirm, both *sanctioned* and *permitted* by God himself; and you declare that its perpetuation would be both *impossible* and *improper.* These opinions you must have derived, certainly, from *principles,* for there is, as we both grant, no direct *prohibition* on the subject. Nay more, you inform us that these principles are *derived from the Bible,* and that they result from what the Bible *teaches us of the character of man.* Now this looks to me marvellously like *controlling a permission by a principle.* In fact, I do not perceive that the ground which it covers is not precisely that which is covered by my illustration of the case of a young man and his parent, which you have considered so strangely unfortunate.

Before leaving this subject, suffer me, my dear brother, to ask you whether there be not reason to apprehend that your views on this whole subject will be misunderstood? I very much fear that when slavery is spoken of at the South, it is spoken of, not as you define it, but as it actually exists; and I perceive that it is boldly upheld as a thing desirable, and right—an institution both to be *perpetuated,* and even at all hazards to be *extended.* I ask, is there not reason to fear that, on your authority, the attributes of God will be appealed to, to sanction, *not the abstract idea of it,* which you believe to be in harmony with the word of God, *but the whole system, just as it exists?* Is it not important that you should express your views explicitly on this subject, so that the word of God may not, on your authority, be used to support what you believe it explicitly to condemn?

And now, to sum up the whole, let us briefly enumerate the points of agreement between us. In the first place, we both affirm that to hold slaves is not of necessity a guilt, and under peculiar circumstances it may not be a wrong; it is, therefore, *in itself,* no scripture ground for ecclesiastical excommunication. In the second place, you affirm that a slave is entitled to the same privileges, intellectual, moral, and domestic, as any other man; and, of course, that all that part of the system which interferes with those privileges, is wrong, and ought to be abolished. In the effort to effect this abolition, we can both co-operate. In the third place, you give us, in your own case, an example of what you believe to be the duty of masters. You teach your servants to read, you instruct them in the gospel of Christ, and by every means in your power are laboring to improve their intellectual, moral, social, and domestic condition. I do not here allude to your care of their physical comforts, for you could never be a selfish

or unkind man. We can both unite in the effort to render all slave-holders in this country just such masters as you. Thirdly, you believe it neither *possible* nor *proper* to perpetuate this institution. It must, then, in your view, cease. In my judgment, it would be a great calamity were it to terminate by violence, or without previous moral and social preparation. In the effort to prepare both the masters and slaves for this event, we can cordially co-operate. I neither ask you, nor any other man, to do any more. In the effort to accomplish these results, I pledge you my services to any extent that you are willing to accept of them.

In the doing of all this, I am well aware that great difficulties are to be encountered. I believe that the first labor must be the labor of preparation; but I think it must be a labor *directed specifically to this end.* I fear, with you, that the emancipation of the slaves in the West Indies is not accomplishing what was expected. I say *I fear;* for the reports are so absolutely contradictory, that I am unable to come to a decided opinion. But, aside from this cause, all history informs us that absolute liberty is too violent a stimulant to be safely administered to a race who have long been bred in slavery. They must be taught and become accustomed to the responsibilities which it involves, before they can use it aright. All this requires caution, boldness, philanthropy, and humble but earnest trust in God. "Prayers and pains," said Elliot, "with the blessing of God can do any thing." I do not pretend to dictate as to the *manner* in which this is to be done. This I leave to you, who are so much better able to judge. All I ask is, that the views which you entertain, so far as I understand them, be carried out into practice; and, in doing this, I here promise to give you my poor aid to any extent that I am able to render it.

Here I close this long and I fear, wearisome letter. This is the first time in my life—I hope it may be the last—in which it has fallen to my lot to engage in controversy. Be assured, my dear brother, that it has given me pain whenever I have been obliged to differ from one for whom I cherish so affectionate a regard. For that Christian urbanity with which you treated whatever I have written, from my heart I thank you. If I have in any manner been able to avoid the errors into which many have fallen who have treated on this subject, I ascribe it mainly to the influence of your example, and to the unfeigned esteem which I entertain for your character, as a gentleman and a scholar, a clergyman and a Christian. Or rather, if we have been enabled without bitterness to express our views to each other on a subject which is so liable to arouse the worst passions of our fallen nature, let us ascribe it all to that love of God shed abroad in our hearts, which teaches us to treat as a brother every disciple of our common Lord, though he may embrace opinions in many respects differing from our own. God grant that we may both meet in that world where neither of us shall any more see through a glass darkly, but where we shall see as we are seen, and know as we are known.

I am, my dear brother, yours with every sentiment of affection,

The Author of the Moral Science.

(From Fuller and Wayland, *Domestic Slavery Considered As a Scriptural Institution* [New York, 1845], pp. 244-45.)

Section Four

Prelude to Separation

The Reeve case (1844)

Georgia Baptists were not satisfied with the neutrality assurances of the Home Mission Society, particularly since leaders of the Society were constantly engaged in abolitionist activities. As a test case, Georgia sent the name of James E. Reeve, a slaveholder, to be appointed by the Society as missionary in the South. The answer to this application brought Georgia Baptists to the edge of separation.

1. Letter of Society to Georgia Baptists on the Reeve case

American Baptist Home Mission Rooms, New York, Oct. 7, 1844.

The Executive Board of the American Baptist Home Mission Society, having examined the application of the Executive Committee of the Georgia Baptist Convention for the appointment of Eld. James E. Reeve, feel it their duty to state that, in addition to the information required of applicants, this communication contains a statement that Mr. Reeve is a slaveholder, and that fact is offered as a reason for his appointment, in the following terms: "We wish his appointment so much the more, as it will stop the mouths of gainsayers. I will explain. There are good brethren among us, who, notwithstanding the transactions of your Society at Philadelphia, are hard to believe that you will appoint a slaveholder as a Missionary, even when the funds are supplied by those who wish such an appointment." The application, therefore, is an unusual one.

At the last anniversary of this, the following preamble and resolution were passed, viz:

"Whereas, the question has been proposed, whether the Board would or would not employ slaveholders as Missionaries of this Society; and whereas, it is important that this question should receive a full and unequivocal answer, therefore,

"Resolved, That as the Constitution of the Home Mission Society clearly defines its object to be the promotion of the gospel in North America, and as it provides by such Constitution that any auxiliary Society may designate the object to which the funds contributed by it shall be applied, and may also claim a Missionary or Missionaries, according to such funds; and select the field where such Missionary or Missionaries should reside,

"Therefore, 1st. That to introduce the subjects of slavery or anti-slavery into this body is a direct contravention of the whole letter and purpose of the said Constitution and is moreover, a most unnecessary agitation of topics with which the Society has no concern, over which it has no control, and as to which its operations should not be fettered, nor its deliberations disturbed.

"2nd. That the Home Mission Society being only an agency to disburse the funds confided to it, according to the wishes of the contributors, therefore our co-operation in this body does not imply any sympathy either with slavery or anti-slavery, as to which, societies and individuals are left as free and uncommitted as if there were no such co-operation."

We disclaim attributing to our Georgia brethren a design to *disturb the deliberations of the Board* by introducing the subject of slavery through the medium of their application, but such, evidently, is its tendency. In the opinion of several members of the Board, the application seeks the appointment, not in the usual manner, merely of a Missionary, but of a slaveholder, and is designed as a test whether the Board will appoint a slaveholder as a Missionary, and this (in the language of the Society's resolution) "in direct contravention of the whole letter and spirit of the Constitution" introduces the subject of slavery. They, moreover, believe that if the application were entertained by them it would, consequently, introduce a discussion on the admissibility of a Missionary of the Society being a slaveholder; from which they are restricted by the vote of the Society which declares it to be a topic *"over which it has no control, and as to which its operations should not be fettered, nor its deliberations disturbed."* To such an alternative they should not be driven. The Constitution, the "Circular" of the Board published in 1841, the resolution of the Society at its last anniversary, and the harmony of the Board all forbid it.

The appointment of Missionaries, constitutionally eligible, and recommended according to our established rules, without the introduction of extraneous considerations calculated to disturb our delibera-

tions, this Board are during the period of their appointment, sacredly bound in equity and justice, to make, to the extent of their pecuniary ability—keeping in view a fair distribution throughout the field, of the funds, committed to their trust. But when an application is made for the appointment of a slaveholder, or an abolitionist, or an anti-slavery man, *as such,* or for appropriations to fields where the design of the applicant is apparently to test the action of the Board in respect to the subjects of slavery or anti-slavery, their official obligation either to act on the appointment or to entertain the application, ceases. Therefore,

Resolved, That in view of the preceding considerations it is not expedient to introduce the subjects of slavery or anti-slavery into our deliberations, nor to entertain applications in which they are introduced.

Resolved, That taking into consideration all the circumstances of the case, we deem ourselves not at liberty to entertain the application for the appointment of Rev. James E. Reeve.

Resolved, That the Corresponding Secretary transmit a copy of the foregoing views and resolutions to the Chairman of the Executive Committee of the Georgia Convention.

By order of the Executive Board.
BENJAMIN M. HILL, Cor. Sec'y.

(From *Minutes of the Meetings of the American Baptist Home Mission Society and of its Executive Committee* [New York], Book 2, page 303, for October 7, 1844.)

The Alabama Resolutions (1844)

Alabama Baptists, aroused by the Reeve case and other events, demanded a specific avowal from the foreign mission body that slaveholders would be treated the same as any other members of the Society. The response provided the breaking point between Northern and Southern Baptists.

1. The text

Marion, Perry Co., Alabama, Nov. 25, 1844.

Eld. Daniel Sharp, President of the Board of Managers of the Baptist General Convention.

Dear Brother:—Agreeably to the appointment of "The Baptist State Convention of Alabama," we transmit to you the following preamble and resolutions, and request you to lay them before the Board. We shall wait your reply.

Preamble and Resolutions

Whereas, The holding property in African negro slaves has for some years excited discussion, as a question of morals, between different portions of the Baptist denomination united in benevolent enterprise; and by a large portion of our brethren, is now imputed to the slaveholders in these Southern and South-western States, as a sin, at once grievous, palpable, and disqualifying:—

1. *Resolved,* By the Convention of the Baptist denomination in the State of Alabama, that when one party to a voluntary compact among Christian brethren is not willing to acknowledge the entire social equality with the other, as to all the privileges and benefits of the union, nor even to refrain from impeachment and annoyance, united efforts between such parties, even in the sacred cause of Christian benevolence, cease to be agreeable, useful, or proper.

2. *Resolved,* That our duty at this crisis requires us to demand from the proper authorities in all those bodies to whose funds we have contributed, or with whom we have in any way been connected, the distinct, explicit, avowal that slaveholders are eligible, and entitled, equally with non-slaveholders, to all the privileges and immunities of their several unions; and especially to receive any agency, mission, or other appointment, which may run within the scope of their operation or duties.

3. *Resolved,* That to prevent a gradual departure from the principles of church independence, and the assumption, by Societies, Boards or Committees, of the inalienable rights of the churches, as well as

to prevent the recurrence of difficulties in future, this Convention do hold, that in all those Conventions, Societies or Boards, of which we may be a constituent part, whenever the competency or fitness of an individual to receive an appointment is under discussion, if any question arises affecting his morals, or his standing in fellowship as a Christian, such question should not be disposed of to the grief of the party, without ultimate appeal to the particular church of which such individual is a member,—as being the only body on earth authorized by the Scriptures, or competent to consider and decide this class of cases.

4. *Resolved,* That the President and Secretary of this body be a committee to transmit copies of this preamble and these resolutions to those bodies for whose treasuries any of the funds, now in hand, or hereafter to be received, may be designed, and to call their attention expressly to our *second resolution;* that, should any responses be received, the President of this Convention shall call together the officers and directors thereof, by a notice in the Alabama Baptist, inserted at least thirty days previous to the time of meeting; that a majority of these persons, or eight in number, shall be a quorum for business: and the quorum assembled, or a majority of them, shall decide whether the said moneys, or any portion of them, shall be forwarded to the bodies for whom they were designed, or be held until the next meeting of this body, subject to be reclaimed or re-appropriated by the donors severally.

5. *Resolved,* also, That the Treasurer of this body be, and he is hereby instructed, not to pay any money intended to be applied without the limits of this State, except at the written order of the President of this Convention, with the concurrence of the Board of officers before mentioned; and this body, profoundly sensible of the vast issues dependent on the principles herein advanced, will await, in prayerful expectation, the responses of our non-slaveholding brethren.

6. *Resolved*, That the Secretary of this Convention, as far as practicable, transmit at least one copy of these minutes, when published, to the presiding officers of each Baptist State Convention or General Association in the slaveholding States.

JESSE HARTWELL,
President of the Alabama Baptist State
Convention.

M. P. JEWETT, Recording Sec.

(From *The Baptist Missionary Magazine*, August, 1845, Vol. XXV, 220 ff. Original resolutions found in Alabama State Convention *Minutes*, p. 8.)

2. *Reply of the Acting Board*

Boston, Dec. 17, 1844.

Dear Sir:—We have received from you a copy of a Preamble and Resolutions which were passed by the "Baptist State Convention of Alabama." And as there is a "demand" for distinct and explicit answers from our Board to the inquiries and propositions which you have been pleased to make, we have given to them our deliberate and candid attention.

Before proceeding to answer them, allow us to express our profound regret that they were addressed to us. They were not necessary. We have never, as a Board, either done, or omitted to do, any thing which requires the explanations and avowals that your resolutions "demanded." They also place us in the new and trying position of being compelled to answer hypothetical questions, and to discuss principles, or of seeming to be evasive and timid, and not daring to give you the information and satisfaction which you desire. If, therefore, in answering with entire frankness your inquiries and demands, we should express opinions which may be unsatisfactory or displeasing to you, our plea must be, that a necessity was laid upon us. We had no other alternative, without being wanting, apparently, in that manly openness which ought to characterize the correspondence of Christian brethren.

In your first Resolution, you say, "that

when one party to a voluntary compact between Christian brethren is not willing to acknowledge the entire social equality with the other, as to all the privileges and benefits of the union, nor even to refrain from impeachment and annoyance, united efforts between such parties, even in the sacred cause of Christian benevolence, cease to be agreeable, useful or proper." In these sentiments we entirely coincide. As a Board, we have the high consciousness that it has always been our aim to act in accordance therewith. We have never called in question your social equality as to all the privileges and benefits of the Foreign Missionary Union. Nor have we ever employed our official influence in impeaching you. Should we ever do this "our united efforts," as you justly say, "would cease to be agreeable, useful or proper."

In your second Resolution, you, "demand the distinct and explicit avowal that slaveholders are eligible and entitled to all the privileges and immunities of their several unions, and especially to receive any agency, mission, or other appointment which may fall within the scope of their operations and duties."

We need not say that slaveholders, as well as non-slaveholders, are unquestionably entitled to all the privileges and immunities which the Constitution of the Baptist General Convention permits and grants to its members. We would not deprive either of any of the immunities of the mutual contract. In regard, however, to any agency, mission, or other appointment, no slaveholder or non-slaveholder, however large his subscription to Foreign Missions, or those of the church with which he is connected, is on that account entitled to be appointed to an agency or a mission. The appointing power, for wise and good reasons, has been confided to the "Acting Board," they holding themselves accountable to the Convention for the discreet and faithful discharge of this trust.

Should you say, "The above remarks are not sufficiently explicit, we wish distinctly to know whether the Board would or would not appoint a slaveholder as a Missionary;"—before directly replying, we would say, that in the thirty years in which the Board has existed no slaveholder, to our knowledge, has applied to be a Missionary. And as we send out no domestics or servants, such an event as a Missionary taking slaves with him, were it morally right, could not, in accordance with all our past arrangements or present plans possibly occur. If, however, any one should offer himself as a Missionary, having slaves, and should insist on retaining them as his property, we could not appoint him. One thing is certain; we can never be a party to any arrangement which would imply approbation of slavery.

In your third Resolution you say, that "whenever the competency or fitness of an individual to receive an appointment is under discussion, if any question arises affecting his morals, or his standing in fellowship as a Christian, such question should not be disposed of to the grief of the party, without ultimate appeal to the particular church of which such an individual is a member, as being the only body on earth authorized by the Scriptures, or competent to consider and decide this class of cases."

In regard to our Board, there is no point on which we are more unanimously agreed than that of the independence of churches. We disclaim all and every pretension to interfere with the discipline of any church. We disfellowship no one. Nevertheless, were a person to offer himself as a candidate for Missionary service, although commended by his church as in good standing, we should feel it our duty to open our eyes on any facts to the disadvantage of his moral and religious character, which might come under our observation. And while we should not feel that it was our province to excommunicate or discipline a candidate of doubtful character, yet we should be unworthy of our trust, if we did not, although he were a member of a church, reject his application. It is for the Board to determine on the prudential, moral, religious and theological

fitness of each one who offers himself as a Missionary. It is for the church of which such an one is a member, to decide whether he be a fit person to belong to their body.

The other Resolutions which were passed in your recent Convention, regard more your own action than ours. They therefore call for no remarks from us. We should have been gratified in the present impoverished and embarrassed state of our treasury, if the brethren in Alabama confiding in the integrity and discretion of the Acting Board, could unhesitatingly have transmitted to us their funds. We have sent out Missionaries, and enlarged our operations, in the expectation that, so long as we acted in conformity with the rules and spirit under which we were appointed, we should be sustained both by the East and the West, the North and the South. If in this just expectation we are to be disappointed, we shall experience unutterable regret.

We have with all frankness, but with entire kindness and respect, defined our position. If our brethren in Alabama, with this exposition of our principles and feelings, can co-operate with us, we shall be happy to receive their aid. If they can not, painful to us as will be their withdrawal, yet we shall submit to it as neither sought nor caused by us.

There are sentiments avowed in this communication, which, although held temperately and kindly, and with all due esteem and Christian regard for the brethren addressed, are nevertheless dearer to us than any pecuniary aid whatever.

We remain yours truly,
In behalf of the Board,
DANIEL SHARP, President,
BARON STOW, Rec. Sec.

REV. JESSE HARTWELL, President of Alabama Baptist State Convention.

(Ibid.)

Virginia's call for a consultative convention

To the Baptist Churches in Virginia:
Dear Brethren:—Accompanying this com-

munication you will find a letter addressed by the Board of the Baptist Triennial Convention to the Rev. Jesse Hartwell, President of the Alabama State Convention, in reply to a preamble and resolutions recently adopted by this body. Of the expediency of pressing the Board to an expression of their views on the subject of slavery, under the exciting and embarrassing circumstances under which they were placed, we forbear to express an opinion. For ourselves, feeling an ardent desire for the conversion of the heathen, and sincerely deprecating disunion in the denomination, we were willing to co-operate with the Board, until, in the regular course of action, some decision should be made adverse to our rights. Confiding fully in their wisdom, moderation, and integrity, we did not believe that such a decision would be made. These so far as we are informed, are the views entertained by the brethren whom we represent. But the letter of the Board has dissipated all misconception of this subject. From it we learn that no slaveholder, under any circumstances, would be appointed by the Board as a Missionary, or even as an agent, (this is plainly implied) to collect funds from slaveholding churches. Concerning this unexpected resolution of the Board, we wish to speak with candor and courtesy, but we must also speak with frankness and firmness. It is an outrage on our rights. This will clearly appear from the following considerations:

1. The decision of the Board is *unconstitutional*. The Triennial Convention was formed, and, from its organization, it has been sustained by slaveholders and non-slaveholders. They have met and acted in the Convention itself, and in its Board, on terms of perfect social and religious equality. No man, who is at all acquainted with the history of the Convention, can entertain any doubt that the southern Baptists would have indignantly refused to co-operate with it on any terms implying their inferiority. But the uniform action of the Convention has placed the matter beyond cavil. Slaveholders have presided over this body—have

been appointed as Vice Presidents, and as members of the Board—a slaveholder was elected as a delegate to represent the Convention at the meeting of the English Baptist Union—and in general, slaveholders have been held by the Convention itself as eligible to the highest offices and trusts within its gift. And are we now to be told by the Board, that if "any one should offer himself as a Missionary having slaves, and should insist on holding them as his property, we could not appoint him?"

"The appointing power for wise and good reasons," we are told, "has been confided to the Acting Board." Very true. But what is the Acting Board? An agent of the Convention. It was organized to carry out the views and plans of the Convention. It derives its whole power from the Convention, consisting partly of slaveholders and partly of non-slaveholders, a Convention distinctly recognizing the eligibility of slaveholders to the highest offices of trust. If a member of the Board should conscientiously decline retaining such power, we should respect his scruples, though we deem them erroneous. But for the "Acting Board," in violation of the Constitution and the spirit of the Missionary compact, and disregarding the precedents set by the Convention for their guidance, to employ their power according to their private views and scruples, is in our view a flagrant breach of trust—a breach not the less to be deplored or censured because they hold themselves accountable to the Convention for the discreet and faithful discharge of this trust.

2. The decision of the Board is a manifest violation of the *compromise resolution* adopted at the last meeting of the Convention. This is the resolution:

"*Resolved*, That, in co-operating together as members of this Convention in the work of Foreign Missions, we disclaim all sanction, either expressed or implied, whether of slavery or anti-slavery; but, as individuals, we are perfectly free, both to express and to promote, elsewhere, our own views on these subjects in a Christian manner and spirit."

The circumstances under which this resolution was adopted are well known. The Abolitionists were clamorous for a dismemberment of the body. The good, moderate, and discreet men, of the North and South, deprecating division, and desirous to avoid embarrassing the action of the Convention by the introduction of irrelevant subjects, in the spirit of fraternal kindness and compromise, adopted, with great unanimity, this resolution. It was designed to relieve the tender consciences of certain brethren who were apprehensive that by co-operating with the Convention they were sanctioning slavery. It was resolved that the co-operation did not sanction either slavery or anti-slavery; and that the members of the Convention were at liberty to promote their views on these subjects "elsewhere"—plainly implying that they had no such liberty in the Convention. During the recess of the Convention it is represented by the "Acting Board," and this agent has no authority to pass beyond the instructions of the appointing body, either expressed or implied. And now how stands the case? The Convention, the largest ever held, forebore to sanction "anti-slavery"—but so does not its Board, or agent. This body makes a marked difference between slavery and anti-slavery—slaveholders and non-slaveholders. The members of the Convention bound themselves, by obvious implication, to abstain from "their own views on these subjects" in the Convention; the members of the "Acting Board," as representatives of the Convention, employ the whole weight of their official influence and authority to promote their "own views on these subjects." The Convention resolved that the views entertained of slavery or of anti-slavery should be no bar to harmonious effort; and the Board has reversed the judgment.

3. The decision of the Board is *inconsistent with admissions* made in the letter under consideration.

The Alabama Convention say, "when one party to a voluntary compact between Christian brethren is not willing to acknowl-edge the entire social equality with the other, as to all the privileges and benefits of the union, united efforts between such parties, even in the sacred cause of Christian benevolence cease to be agreeable, useful, or proper." "In these sentiments," say the Board, "we entirely coincide. We have never called in question your social equality as to all the privileges and benefits of the Foreign Missionary Union." What are these privileges and benefits? Is not eligibility to offices of trust included among them? Suppose the Board were situated in Richmond, instead of Boston, and choosing to promote their "own views," they should decide that no man not admitting that the Scriptures countenance slavery should be appointed as a Missionary. Would this be acting on the principle that our northern brethren, who do not admit this proposition, are entitled to all the benefits and privileges of the Missionary Union? They would not think so. The Board have strange ideas of equality. They approve equally of burdens, and monopoly of privileges. Transmit us your funds, they say, and we will see to it that no one holding slaves shall be appointed a Missionary.

4. The decision of the Board is *unjust* to the southern supporters of the Convention.

From the organization of the Convention to the present time, the Baptists of the South have contributed cheerfully, and in some cases liberally to its treasury. But, can any man believe they would have made these contributions, had they known or even suspected, that the Board would have refused to appoint a slaveholder, under any circumstances, as a Missionary or agent? Of our views and purposes in relation to this matter, there has been no concealment. For thirty years, the Board have received no application to appoint a slaveholder as a Missionary; but we are left to infer that had such application been made, it would at any time have been rejected. If this be so, the southern Baptists have been contributing under a delusion which a small measure of candor . . . would have dispelled.

5. The decision of the Board, supposing it not intended to produce division, is as *unwise* as it is unjust.

A slaveholder would not be likely to apply for an appointment as a Missionary to the East—and certainly he would not think of carrying slaves with him on such a mission. But suppose a slaveholder should desire an appointment as a Missionary among the Indians,—he might be eminently qualified for the office; intelligent, pious, humane to his slaves, held in high estimation by his brethren; such a minister, in a word, as has heretofore been cheerfully admitted into northern pulpits; his slaves might earnestly desire to accompany him, and there might be no law to prevent it, and no prejudice against slavery in the proposed field of his labor to diminish his usefulness; and yet, under the decision of the Board, he would be ineligible to the appointment.

The Board do not affirm, but it may be fairly inferred from their reasoning, that they could not appoint an agent, who holds slaves, to collect money from slaveholding churches. If the appointment of a slaveholding Missionary implies a sanction of slavery, then the appointment of a slaveholding agent equally implies it.

This is high ground. If the object of the Board was to sever their connection with the southern Baptists, they acted with good policy in occupying it; but if this was not their design, their course, to say the least was unwise.

In view, brethren, of these considerations, we feel that we have been injured by the decision of the Board. For their conscientious opinions on the subject of slavery, we censure them not. If they are unwilling to co-operate with slaveholding Christians in the Missionary enterprise, we have no right to complain. We have cherished a sincere sympathy with them in their delicate and embarrassing situation. We have vindicated their conduct and their motives. We have cherished no unfavorable suspicion against them. But we are disappointed and pained at their decision—a decision which tramples alike on

the Constitution, and the rights of southern members.

And now, brethren, in this exigency, what shall we do? To remain united with the Board is impossible. Self-respect forbids it. All hope that the Board will revoke their decision is vain. They have acted, so we learn from the Christian Reflector, deliberately and unanimously. They have examined the ground, and taken their position.

The Convention will not meet for two years, and even from that, redress cannot be expected. To abandon the Foreign Missionary enterprise, we cannot. It has a strong hold on our affections. Far from diminishing, let us augment our contributions to the object; and let us increase the fervency of our prayers for the conversion of the world.

Towards our northern brethren, let us cultivate feelings of kindness. We shall be in great danger of indulging an unchristian spirit of hostility against them; and this spirit we should repress with diligence, remembering who hath said, "Let all bitterness, and wrath, and anger, and clamor, and evil speaking, be put away from you, with all malice."

In view of the considerations above presented, the Board of the Virginia Foreign Mission Society have adopted the following resolutions:

1. *Resolved,* That this Board have seen with sincere pain the decision of the Board of the Baptist Triennial Convention, contained in a recent letter addressed to Rev. Jesse Hartwell, of Alabama, and that we deem the decision unconstitutional, and in violation of the rights of the southern members of the Convention; and that all farther connection with the Board, on the part of such members is inexpedient and improper.

2. *Resolved,* That the treasurer of this Board be required to deposit in one of the Savings Banks of the city, any funds which may be in his hands, or may come into them, to be disposed of as the Society, at its annual meeting, may direct.

3. *Resolved,* That this Board are of

opinion, that in the present exigency, it is important that those brethren who are aggrieved by the recent decision of the Board in Boston, should hold a Convention, to confer on the best means of promoting the Foreign Mission cause, and other interests of the Baptist denomination in the South.

4. *Resolved*, That in the judgment of this Board, Augusta, Ga., is a suitable place for holding such a Convention; and the Thursday before the second Lord's day in May next is a suitable time.

5. *Resolved*, That while we are willing to meet our southern brethren in Augusta, or any other place which may be selected, we should heartily welcome them in the city of Richmond—and should it be deemed proper to hold it in this city, the Thursday before the fourth Lord's day in June next will be a suitable time.

On motion,

Resolved, That the churches and Associations of the State be recommended to appoint delegates to the proposed Convention.

Resolved, That the proceedings of this meeting be published under the direction of brethren Taylor, Jeter, Walker, and Smith.

J. B. TAYLOR, Pres't. Board.
C. WALTHALL, Sec.

(From *Religious Herald* [Virginia], April 10, 1845, p. 2, cols. 3-4.)

Part Four
Separation and War
1845-1865

Section One

Antecedents to
Southern Baptist Organization

Suggestions about kind of
organization to be formed

*The first general organizations of Ameri-
can Baptists for foreign missions, home missions, and tract distribution were developed
as societies (one organization for each
benevolence with membership based on a
financial contribution). Southern Baptists
faced the question in 1845 of whether to
organize under this plan or follow some
other.*

1. William Bullein Johnson's proposal

*Johnson, pastor of the Edgefield (S.C.)
Baptist Church and president of the Baptist State Convention of South Carolina,
called a special meeting of the state body
at Edgefield on May 3, 1845, for the purpose of appointing representatives to the
consultative meeting to take place at Augusta, Georgia, the following week. Johnson addressed the meeting at length, during the course of which he discussed the
kind of organization to be formed by Southern Baptists.*

In view of a new organization for benevolent objects for the Denomination in the
Southern and South Western portions of
the United States, I invite your attention
to the consideration of two plans:—The one
is that which has been adopted for years
past, viz: Separate and independent bodies
for the prosecution of each object. Your
familiarity with this plan, renders any re-

marks upon it unnecessary. The other proposes one Convention, embodying the
whole Denomination, together with separate and distinct Boards, for each object
of benevolent enterprise, located at different places, and all amenable to the Convention.

Judicious concentration is of the first
moment in all combinations of men for important enterprises. The plan, just suggested, proposes such combination. In its
successful operation, the whole Denomination will be united in one body for the purpose of well-doing, with perfect liberty secured to each contributor of specifying the
object or objects, to which his amount shall
be applied, as he please, whilst he or his
Delegation may share in the deliberations
and control of all the objects, promoted
by the Convention. The Minutes of the
Convention will contain, not only a statement of its own doings, but also a statement of the doings of *each* Board.—Such
a document would comprise a body of valuable information, and form a volume of
respectable size, worthy of being bound,
and carefully preserved. Such a volume
might be sold at a small advance upon the
cost, and thus contribute to the funds of
the body, whilst it diffused abroad interesting intelligence of all the Missionary
and other benevolent efforts of the whole
Denomination.

(From *Edgefield Advertiser* [South
Carolina], May 7, 1845.)

*2. Excerpt from Johnson's suggested con-
stitution for the new body*

*Because Dr. Johnson was chairman of the
committee that recommended the constitu-*

tion at the consultative meeting at Augusta on May 10, his suggested constitution in his address on May 3 is significant. A comparison of his suggested Article 4, which would determine the character of the new convention, with Article V, adopted at Augusta, shows that Johnson's view was accepted.

CONSTITUTION

Art. 1. This body shall be styled, the Convention of the Baptist Denomination in the Southern and South Western portions of the United States of America for Missionary and other benevolent objects.

Art. 2. This Convention shall be composed of Delegates from Mission Societies, State Conventions, Associations, Churches, Religious Bodies, and Individuals, that shall each pay, for entrance into the membership of the Convention, the sum of ―――dollars, and thereafter annually the like sum of ――― dollars. But no member of the Convention shall be entitled to more votes than one. The Convention shall hold its meetings triennially, but extra meetings may be called by the President with the approbation of either of the Boards of Managers. A majority of the attending delegates shall form a quorum for the transaction of business.

Art. 3. The officers of this Convention shall be a President, Vice President, and Secretaries, who shall be elected at each triennial meeting, and hold their offices until a new election.

Art. 4. The Convention shall elect at each triennial meeting, as many Boards of Managers, as, in its judgment, will be necessary, for carrying out the benevolent objects, it may determine to promote; all which Boards shall continue in office until a new election. Each Board shall consist of a President, Vice President, Secretaries, Treasurer, Auditor, and ――― other members, ――― of whom, including one or more of the officers, shall form a quorum for the transaction of business. To each Board shall be committed, during the recess of the Convention, the entire management of all the affairs relating to the object, with whose interest it shall be charged; all which management shall be in strict accordance with the Constitutional provisions adopted by the Convention, and such other instructions, as may be given from time to time. Each Board shall be in strict accordance with the Constitutional provisions adopted by the Convention, and such other instructions, as may be given from time to time. Each Board shall have power to make such compensation to its Secretaries, and Treasurer, as it may think right; fill the vacancies occurring in its own body, appoint its own by-laws; have an annual meeting at any place it may appoint; and other meetings at such times and places as it may think best; keep a record of its proceedings, and present a report of them to the Convention at each Triennial Meeting.

Art. 5. The Treasurer of each Board shall faithfully account for all moneys received by him; keep a regular entry of all receipts and disbursements, and make report of them to the Convention, when ever it shall be in session, and to his Board as often as required. He shall also, on entering upon the duties of his office, give competent security to the President of his Board, for all the stock and funds, committed to his care. His books shall be open, at all times, to the inspection of any member of the Convention and of his Board. No moneys shall be paid out of any of the treasuries of the Boards, but by an order from that Board, from whose treasury the money is to be drawn, which order shall be signed by its presiding officer.

Art. 6. The Corresponding Secretaries of the several Boards, shall maintain intercourse by letter, with such individuals or public bodies, as the interests of their respective bodies may require. Copies of all such communications, with their answers, if any, shall be kept by them on file.

Art. 7. The Recording Secretaries of the several Boards, shall keep a fair record of their proceedings, and of such other documents, as may be committed to them for the purpose.

Art. 8. All the Officers, Boards, Missionaries and Agents appointed by the Convention, or by any of its Boards, shall be members of some regular Church in union with the churches composing this Convention.

Art. 9. Missionaries appointed by any of the Boards of this Convention, must, previous to their appointment, furnish evidence of genuine piety, fervent zeal in their Master's cause, and talents, which fit them for the service for which they offer themselves.

Art. 10. The Bodies and Individuals, composing this Convention, shall have the right to specify the object, or objects, to which their contributions shall be applied. But where no such specification is made, the Convention will make the appropriation at its own discretion.

Art. 11. Any alterations, which experience shall dictate, may be made in these Articles, by a vote of two thirds of the members present at any triennial meeting of the Convention.

In this plan, provision is made for an indefinite number of Boards, according to the number of the objects adopted by the Convention. Each Board will be independent of the others, and will receive the contributions made for that object, with the management of whose interests it shall be charged. An act of incorporation for each Board, in the state of its location, will give legal security to the funds contributed. All these Boards will report at each triennial meeting of the Convention, and they will each receive the instructions of that Body.

(Ibid.)

Section Two

Organization of the Southern Baptist Convention

Francis Wayland's advice concerning separation

The break between Baptists North and South was felt to be wise by practically all of the important leaders in the two sections. There was no anticipation of rivalry and

tension between the older societies and the new organization. Typical of many comments is Wayland's, an influential leader.

"You will separate of course. I could not ask otherwise. Your rights have been infringed. I will take the liberty of offering one or two suggestions. We have shown how Christians ought not to act, it remains for you to show us how they ought to act. Put away all violence, act with dignity and firmness and the world will approve your course."

(From *Daily Chronicle & Sentinel* [Augusta, Ga.], May 10, 1845.)

Preamble and Constitution of the new body

Following the suggestion of Dr. Johnson, the new body adopted a plan to provide for "judicious concentration" in order to elicit, combine, and direct the energies of the whole denomination. A foreign mission board was established at Richmond, Virginia; Marion, Alabama, was the headquarters for a domestic mission board. Article V anticipated that other benevolences would be fostered by the body, which resembled the old associational philosophy of benevolent work rather than the society plan. However, the financial basis of representation still prevailed.

Preamble and Constitution
of the
Southern Baptist Convention

We, the delegates from Missionary Societies, Churches, and other religious bodies of the Baptist Denomination, in various parts of the United States, met in Convention, in the city of Augusta, Georgia, for the purpose of carrying into effect the benevolent intentions of our constituents, by organizing a plan for eliciting, combining and directing the energies of the whole denomination in one sacred effort, for the propagation of the Gospel, agree to the following rules, or fundamental principles:

ARTICLE I. This body shall be styled the Southern Baptist Convention.

ARTICLE II. It shall be the design of this Convention to promote Foreign and Domestic Missions, and other important objects connected with the Redeemer's kingdom, and to combine for this purpose, such portions of the Baptist denomination in the United States, as may desire a general organization for Christian benevolence, which shall fully respect the independence and equal rights of the Churches.

ARTICLE III. A triennial Convention shall consist of members who contribute funds, or are delegated by religious bodies contributing funds, and the system of representation and terms of membership shall be as follows, viz: An annual contribution of one hundred dollars for three years next preceding the meeting, or the contribution of three hundred dollars at any time within said three years, shall entitle the contributor to one representative; an annual contribution of two hundred dollars, as aforesaid, shall entitle the contributor to two representatives; and so, for each additional one hundred dollars, an additional representative shall be allowed. Provided, however, that when application shall be made for the first time by bodies, or individuals, to be admitted into the Convention, one delegate shall be allowed for each one hundred dollars. And provided, also, that in case of great collateral Societies, composed of representatives, receiving contributions from different parts of the country, the ratio of representation shall be one delegate for every thousand dollars, annually contributed for three years, as aforesaid; but the number of representatives shall never exceed five.

ARTICLE IV. The officers of this Convention shall be a President, four Vice Presidents, a Treasurer, and two Secretaries, who shall be elected at each triennial meeting and hold their offices until a new election; and the officers of the Convention shall be, *each by virtue of his office*, members of the several Boards.

ARTICLE V. The Convention shall elect at each triennial meeting as many Boards of Managers, as in its judgment will be necessary for carrying out the benevolent objects it may determine to promote, all which Boards shall continue in office until a new election. Each Board shall consist of a President, Vice Presidents, Secretaries, Treasurer, Auditor, and fifteen other members, seven of whom, including one or more of the officers, shall form a quorum for the transaction of business. To each Board shall be committed, during the recess of the Convention, the entire management of all the affairs relating to the object with whose interest it shall be charged, all which management shall be in strict accordance with the constitutional provisions adopted by this Convention, and such other instructions as may be given from time to time. Each Board shall have power to make such compensation to its Secretaries and Treasurer, as it may think right; fill the vacancies occuring in its own body; enact its own by-laws; have an annual meeting at any place it may appoint, and other meetings at such times and places as it may think best; keep a record of its proceedings and present a report of them to the Convention at each triennial meeting.

ARTICLE VI. The Treasurer of each Board shall faithfully account for all monies received by him, keep a regular entry of all receipts and disbursements, and make report of them to the Convention, whenever it shall be in session, and to his Board as often as required. He shall also, on entering upon the duties of his office, give competent security to the President of his Board, for all the stock and funds committed to his care. His books shall be open at all times, to the inspection of any member of the Convention and of his Board. No monies shall be paid out of any of the Treasuries of the Boards, but by an order from that Board, from whose Treasury the money is to be drawn, which order shall be signed by its presiding officer.

ARTICLE VII. The Corresponding Secretaries of the several Boards shall maintain intercourse by letter, with such individuals or public bodies, as the interests of their respective bodies may require. Copies of all such communications, with their answers, if any, shall be kept by them on file.

ARTICLE VIII. The Recording Secretaries of the several Boards, shall keep a fair record of their proceedings, and of such other documents as may be committed to them for the purpose.

ARTICLE IX. All the Officers, Boards, Missionaries and Agents, appointed by the Convention, or by any of its Boards, shall be members of some regular Church, in union with the Churches composing this Convention.

ARTICLE X. Missionaries appointed by any of the Boards of this Convention, must, previous to their appointment, furnish evidence of genuine piety, fervent zeal in their Master's cause, and talents which fit them for the service for which they offer themselves.

ARTICLE XI. The bodies and individuals, composing this Convention, shall have the right to specify the object, or objects, to which their contributions shall be applied. But when no such specification is made, the Convention will make the appropriation at its own discretion.

ARTICLE XII. The Convention shall hold its meetings triennially, but extra meetings may be called by the President, with the approbation of any one of the Boards of Managers. A majority of the attending delegates, shall form a quorum for the transaction of business.

ARTICLE XIII. Any alterations which experience shall dictate, may be made in these articles, by a vote of two-thirds of the members present, at any triennial meeting of the Convention.

(From *Annual* of the Southern Baptist Convention, 1845, pp. 3-5.)

Address to the public

It was a regular practice in 1845 to prepare an address to the public explaining the necessity and purpose of a new organization. The new Southern Baptist Convention followed this practice, and the speech was prepared by William B. Johnson.

THE SOUTHERN BAPTIST CONVENTION,

To the Brethren in the United States;
to the congregations connected with
the respective Churches; and
to all candid men.

———

A painful division has taken place in the missionary operations of the American Baptists. We would explain the origin, the principles and the objects of that division, or the peculiar circumstances in which the organization of the Southern Baptist Convention became necessary.

Let not the extent of this disunion be exaggerated. At the present time it involves only the Foreign and Domestic Missions of the denomination. Northern and Southern Baptists are still brethren. They differ in no article of the faith. They are guided by the same principles of gospel order. Fanatical attempts have indeed been made, in some quarters, to exclude us of the South from christian fellowship. We do not retort these attempts; and believe their extent to be comparatively limited. Our christian fellowship is not, as we feel, a matter to be obtruded on any one. We abide by that of our God, his dear Son, and all his baptized followers. The few ultra Northern brethren to whom we allude, must take what course they please. Their conduct has not influenced us in this movement. We do not regard the rupture as extending to foundation principles, nor can we think that the great body of our Northern brethren will so regard it. Disunion has proceeded, however, deplorably far. The first part of our duty is to show that its entire origin is with others. This is its history.

I. The General Convention of the Baptist denomination of the United States was composed of brethren from every part of the American Republic. Its Constitution knows no difference between slaveholders and non-slaveholders. Nor during the period of its existence, for the last thirty years, has it, in practice, known any thing of this distinction. Both parties have contributed steadily and largely (if never adequately) to those funds which are the basis of its constituency; both have yielded its office-bearers of all grades; its missionaries and translators of God's word; its men of toils many, and of prayers not unavailing, abroad and at home. The honored dead of both these classes have walked in closest sympathy with each other; anticipating in the Board-room and in the Monthly Concert, that higher, but not holier union now in their case consummated. Throughout the entire management of its early affairs, the whole struggle with its early difficulties, there was no breath of discord between them. Its Richard Furman and its Wm. Staughton, its Jesse Mercer and its Thomas Baldwin, led on the sacramental host shoulder to shoulder, and heart to heart. Their rivalry being only in earnest efforts for a common cause, their entire aversions and enmities were directed with all the strength of their souls, against the common foe. And to the last, did they not cherish the strong belief that they left no other enmities or aversions; no other rivalry to their successors?

In particular, a special rule of the Constitution defines *who* may be missionaries, viz: "Such persons only as are in full communion with some church in our denomination; and who furnish satisfactory evidence of genuine piety, good talents, and fervent zeal for the Redeemer's cause." Now, while under this rule the slaveholder has been, in his turn, employed as a missionary, it is not alledged that any other persons than those above described, have been appointed. Moreover, the important post of a superintendent of the education of native missionaries, has been assigned, with universal approbation, to the pastor of one of our largest slaveholding churches.

But an evil hour arrived. Even our humble efforts in the conquest of the world to God, excited the accuser of our brethren to cast discord among us; and in the last two Triennial Conventions, slavery and anti-slavery men began to draw off on different sides. How did the nobler spirits on each side endeavor to meet this? They proposed and carried almost unanimously, the following explicit resolution:

"Resolved, That in co-operating together, as members of this Convention, in the work of foreign missions, we disclaim all sanction, either expressed or implied, whether of slavery or anti-slavery; but as individuals, we are free to express and to promote, elsewhere, our views on these subjects, in a christian manner and spirit."

Our successors will find it difficult to believe that so important and plain a declaration had become, before the close of the first year of the triennial period, a perfect nullity. In December last, the acting Board of the Convention, at Boston, adopted a new qualification for missionaries, a new special rule, viz: that "If any one who shall offer himself for a missionary, having slaves, should insist on retaining them as his property, they could not appoint him." "One thing is certain," they continue, "we could never be a party to any arrangement which implies approbation of slavery."

We pray our brethren and all candid men to mark the date of this novel rule—the close of the first six months of their three years' power, a date at which the compromise resolution could scarcely have reached our remoter mission stations. If usurpation had been intended, could it have been more fitly timed? An usurpation of ecclesiastical power quite foreign to our polity. Such power was assumed at a period when the aggrieved "thousands of Israel" had, as it now appears, no practical remedy. Its obvious tendency was, either our final subjugation to that power, or a serious interruption of the flow of Southern benevolence. The latter was the far more probable evil; and the Boston Board knew this well. They were from various quarters apprised of it. We, on the other hand, did not move in the matter of a new organization until three liberal States had refused to send northward any more contributions. Our leaders had chosen new rules. Thus came war within our gates: while the means of war on the common enemy were daily diminishing.

By this decision, the Board had placed itself in direct opposition to the Constitution of the Convention. The only reason given for this extraordinary and unconstitutional dictum being—that "The appointing power for wise and good purposes, is confided to the acting Board." On such a slight show of authority, this Board undertook to declare that to be a disqualification in one who should offer himself for a missionary, which the Convention had said shall *not* be a disqualification. It had also expressly given its sanction to anti-slavery opinions, and impliedly fixed its condemnation on slavery, although the Convention had said that "neither" should be done. And further, it forbade those who shall apply for a missionary appointment, to "express and promote elsewhere" their views on the subject of slavery in a right "manner and spirit," when the Convention declared they "were free" to do so. These brethren, thus acted upon a sentiment they have failed to prove— That slavery is, in all circumstances, sinful. Whereas their own solemn resolution in the last Convention, (their's as much as our's) left us free to promote slavery. Was not this leaving us free, and "in a Christian spirit and manner" to promote that which in their hearts, and according to the present shewing of their conduct, they regard as a sin?

Enough, perhaps, has been said of the origin of this movement. Were we asked to characterize the conduct of our Northern brethren in one short phrase, we should adopt that of the Apostle. It was "FORBIDDING US to speak UNTO THE GENTILES." Did this deny us no privilege? Did it not obstruct us, lay a kind of Romish interdict upon us in the discharge of an imperative duty; a duty to which the church has been, after the lapse of ages, awakened universally and successfully; a duty the very object, and only object, of our long cherished connection and confederation?

And this would seem the place to state, that our Northern brethren were dealt with as brethren to the last moment. Several of our churches cherished the hope that

by means of remonstrance and expostulation, through the last Annual Meeting of the Board of Managers, at Providence, the Acting Board might be brought to feel the grievous wrong they had inflicted. The Managing Board was therefore affectionately and respectfully addressed on the subject, and was entreated to revise and reverse the obnoxious interdict. Alas! the results were—contemptuous silence as to the application made; and a deliberate resolve, expressing sympathy with the Acting Board, and a determination to sustain them.

II. THE PRINCIPLES of the Southern Baptist Convention, it remains then to be stated, are conservative; while they are also, as we trust, equitable and liberal. They propose to do the Lord's work in the way our fathers did it. Its title designates at once its origin, and the simple, firm abiding of the South on the ground from which it has been so unconstitutionally and unjustly attempted to eject us. We have but enquired for "the old paths" of missionary operations; "asked" for, and attempted to restore the practically "good way." The Constitution we adopt is precisely that of the original union; that in connection with which throughout his missionary life, Adoniram Judson has lived, and under which Ann Judson and Boardman have died. We recede from it no single step. We have constructed for our basis no new creed; acting in this matter upon a Baptist aversion for all creeds but the Bible. We use the very terms, as we uphold the true spirit and great object of the late "General Convention of the Baptist denomination of the United States." It is they who wrong us that have receded. We have receded neither from the Constitution nor from any part of the original ground on which we met them in this work, And if, we ask in parting, the original and broad Bible ground of confederation were not equitable, how came it so nobly and so long to be acted upon? If equitable, why depart from it?

We claim to have acted in the premises, with liberality towards our Northern brethren. Thrust from the common platform of equal rights, between the Northern and Southern churches, we have but reconstructed that platform. Content with it, we adhere to it, and reproduce it, as broad enough for us and for them. Have they thrust us off? We retain but one feeling in the case. *That we will not practically leave it on any account:* much less in obedience to such usurped authority, or in deference to such a manifest breach of trust as is here involved. A breach of covenant that looks various ways—heavenward and earthward. For we repeat, THEY WOULD FORBID US TO *speak unto* THE GENTILES. The Jerusalem church, then, must be regathered at the suspected Samaria, or at some new centre of operations, like Antioch. "One thing is certain"—We must go every where preaching the word.—"We can never be a party to any arrangement" for monopolizing the Gospel: any arrangement which like that of the Autocratical Interdict of the North, would first drive us from our beloved colored people, of whom they prove that they know nothing comparatively, and from the much-wronged Aborigines of the country;—and then cut us off from the whitening fields of the heathen harvest-labor; to which by cogent appeals and solemn prayers, they have so often protested that, without us, they were inadequate.

III. OUR OBJECTS, then, are the extension of the Messiah's kingdom, and the glory of our God. Not disunion with any of his people; not the upholding of any form of human policy, or civil rights; but God's glory, and Messiah's increasing reign; in the promotion of which, we find no necessity for relinquishing any of our civil rights. We will never interfere with *what is Caesar's.* We will not compromit what is God's.

These objects will appear in detail on the face of our Constitution, and in the proceedings, which accompany this address. They are distributed, at present, between two acting Boards for Foreign and Domestic Missions, having their respective seats at Richmond, Va., and Marion, Ala. We sympathise with the Macedonian cry from every part of the heathen world,—with the low moan, for spiritual aid, of the four millions of half stifled Red Men, our neighbors; with the sons of Ethiopia among us, stretching forth their hands of supplication for the gospel, to God and all his people,—and we have shaken ourselves from the night mare of a six years' "strife about words to *no* profit," for the profit of these poor, perishing and precious souls. Our language to all America, and to all christendom, if they will hear us, is *"come over,"* and for *these* objects, as ye love souls, and the divine Saviour of souls, *"help us."* We ask help at this juncture for nothing else. We have had more talk than work about these objects too long. We have waited quite too long for the more learned and gifted, and opulent, and worthy, to lead our way toward these objects; and we have shortened debate upon them to get to business. Our eyes and hearts are turned with feelings of parental fondness to Burmah and the Karens; with a zeal in which we are willing to be counselled by God and all considerate men, (but by none else,) to the continent of Africa, and her pernicious fountains of idolatry, oppression and blood; but yet more, with unutterable hope and thankfulness, to China and her providentially opened ports, and teeming thirsty millions. Among us, in the South, we have property, which we will offer to the Lord and his cause, in these channels—some prudence with which we would have our best wisdom to dwell; and professions of a piety which we seek to have increased and purified, like that of the first Baptist churches, when they had "rest; and walking in the fear of the Lord, and in the comfort of the Holy Ghost, were multiplied."

In parting with beloved brethren and old co-adjustors in this cause, we could weep, and have wept, for ourselves and for them; but the season, as well of weeping as of vain jangling, is, we are constrained to believe, just now past. For years the pressure of men's hands has been upon us far too heavily. Our brethren have pressed upon every inch of our privileges and our sacred rights—but this shall only urge our gushing souls to yield proportionately of their renewed efforts to the Lord, to the church universal, and to a dying world; even as water pressed from without rises but the more within. Above all, the mountain pressure of our obligations to God, even our own God; to Christ and to Him crucified; and to the personal and social blessings of the Holy Spirit and his influences, shall urge our little streams of the water of life to flow forth; until every wilderness and desolate place within our reach (and what extent of the world's wilderness wisely considered is not within our reach?) "shall be glad"—even at this passing calamity of division; and the deserts of unconverted human nature "rejoice and blossom as the rose."

By order of the Convention.

WILLIAM B. JOHNSON, D.D.

Augusta, Ga., 12th May, 1845.

(Ibid., pp. 17-20.)

The first charter

Act of Incorporation

Be it enacted by the Senate and House of Representatives of the State of Georgia, in General Assembly, met, and it is hereby enacted by the authority of the same, That William B. Johnson, Wilson Lumpkin, James B. Taylor, A. Dockery, R. B. C. Howell, and others, their associates and successors, be, and they are hereby, incorporated and made a body politic, by the name and style of the "Southern Baptist Convention," with authority to receive, hold, possess, retain and dispose of property, either real or personal, to sue and be sued, and to make all by-laws, rules and regulations necessary to the transaction of their business, not inconsistent with the laws of this State, or of the United States: Said corporation being created for the purpose of eliciting, combining and directing the energies of the Baptist denomination of christians, for the propagation of the gospel, any law, usage or custom to the contrary notwithstanding.

Approved, December 27th, 1845.

(From *Annual* of the Southern Baptist Convention, 1846, p. 37.)

Section Three

Foreign Missions

The first secretary of the Foreign Mission Board

Southern Baptists were most fortunate in their choice of Dr. James B. Taylor as first secretary of this Board. He resigned the pastorate of the Second Baptist Church in Richmond to accept the post, and for twenty-five critical years led superbly.

He had now reached the goal to which he had long looked forward. The meetinghouse done and nearly paid for, he might devote himself exclusively to the spiritual work of a pastor, which he so much loved, to study, and to the preaching of the gospel, both in the pulpit and from house to house. But it was not to be. His labors for the Foreign Mission Board had deepened the conviction upon their minds, as well as upon the minds of the denomination throughout the South, that he was the man for the secretaryship; and his own conviction so pointed it out to him as the post of duty that when it was again formally pressed upon him, this time by the Southern Baptist Convention, which met in Richmond in June, 1846, he was constrained to accept it, though it involved the surrender of cherished wishes and specially congenial employments, and the assumption of the most crushing labors and responsibilities. On the 21st of June, therefore, he resigned his care of the church, and on the 16th of August preached his farewell sermon. Never did a pastor leave a people more unwilling to give him up, though the church could not but recognize the hand of God in the matter.

(From George B. Taylor, *Life and Times of James B. Taylor* [Lynchburg, 1908], pp. 173-74.)

Agreement with Boston Board on fields and property

Transfer of Missions

In obedience to the direction of the Convention, a correspondence was immediately opened with the Boston Board, on the transfer of a portion of their missions. This subject was by them referred to a called meeting of the General Board, held in Philadelphia, Sept'r 24th, 1845. The Board decided, "that the contract between the Convention and their missionaries does not allow of any change in the relations of the parties without the full consent of the missionaries; and, that any authoritative action on this subject, is out of the power of the Board. At the same time, it is perfectly consistent with the obligations of the parties to each other, that the missionaries should have their choice of the associations with which they would be connected, and if any of them should prefer to change their relations from us to the Southern Board, they should, in the spirit of fraternal regard, be allowed every facility for doing so."

Mutual Claims

On the subject of claims, concerning which a correspondence was directed, the General Board, meeting in Philadelphia, adopted the following preamble and resolution:

"Inasmuch as brethren from the south have retired from the General Convention, and formed a new organization for themselves, the property and liabilities of the General Convention should remain with that body; and that no other mode of adjusting supposed claims in the case, would be more equitable in itself, or more likely to prove satisfactory. The circumstances under which the separation above named took place, are of themselves sufficiently painful, and it may well be a matter of solicitude with all the parties concerned, that no new questions which might lead to farther mis-understanding should, without the most urgent necessity, be started. Of such a tendency the question of claims is believed to be, which either party might make upon the other. In view of all these circumstances,

"Resolved, That it is inexpedient, either for the General Convention, or for those who may have retired from it, to make any claim, the one upon the other, respecting the property of the said General Convention on the one hand, or the payment of its present debts on the other."

(From *Annual* of the Southern Baptist Convention, 1846, pp. 21-22.)

First fields of service

In the early part of their labors, the Board turned their attention to the important question of fields of labor. In lifting up their eyes they were not at a loss to find whole nations of men involved in spiritual darkness, and needing the light of the Gospel. Their selection was to be made according to the facilities of diffusing that light. They soon determined that the indications of Providence were favorable to the occupancy of China as missionary ground. This nation, on account of its widely extended territory, its immense population and its comparatively civil and social improvement, may be regarded as the most interesting upon the face of the earth. What renders this a point of such vast importance to the christian missionary, is the sudden surprising change which has recently been wrought in the policy of the government towards other nations. This change must affect the whole spirit and character of the people. Their self-complacency will give way to the spirit of enquiry, and an irresistible flood of light will pour in upon them. Intercourse with christian nations must increase. Regular steamers for Great Britain and America will soon enter all her ports, and an opportunity will soon be furnished of sounding in the ears of her teeming millions, the gospel's joyful sound. This field, "white already to harvest," the Board have determined to occupy with all the force they can command. A score of men would not be too many at once to send, in addition to those already appointed. They could find immediate and profitable employment.

Another important position which the Board consider themselves as specially invited to occupy, is Africa. They are only waiting to secure men of suitable qualifications to enter the field. Africa is doubtless to be evangelized. Who can doubt that she will be claimed by him who has been authorized to ask for his possession, "the uttermost parts of the earth." Various considerations combine to urge upon our sympathies, her spiritual interests. Many of her sons are among us, and from them we may hope, in process of time, to select those who will become eminently qualified to preach to their countrymen "the unsearchable riches of Christ." The mission could be economically sustained. The preacher or teacher located in the vicinity of the colonies on the western coast, would find immediate access to several tribes, and might commence operations without the tedious process of acquiring a new language. From communications recently received, the most encouraging prospects of success urge the immediate occupancy of the field. The Convention, during its session, will doubtless take the subject into consideration. Their united wisdom may suggest some method of securing an immediate supply of the field.

(*Ibid.*, p. 24.)

Problems of the Civil War

The war of 1861 made it difficult to provide support for the foreign missionaries in China and Africa. Some of the missionaries secured secular work on their fields. A Provisional Board was established at Baltimore (in Union hands) to forward funds from Maryland, Washington, D. C., and friends in the North. The border states of Kentucky and Missouri responded nobly. Some funds were sent by purchasing cotton, which was shipped to England by running the Federal blockade of the South.

The receipts from the cotton were then sent directly to China and Africa.

The fiscal year commencing April 3rd, 1865, found the Treasurer with no available funds. The way was now open for the transmission of monies to our missionaries. With more distinctness we learned the hardships and trials to which they had been subjected, and their absolute need of assistance to prevent still more painful suffering. It became necessary to commence anew the work of collection. This, in most of the Southern States, was known to be an impossible thing, as the available currency of the country had not found circulation. The Board, however, did not suffer themselves to be discouraged, but with new energy, sought to overcome the difficulty. They were assured that God would open a plain path in which they might be able to walk. In the new exigencies of their condition, they were shut up to the necessity of appealing to their brethren of Baltimore and Kentucky, and to those portions of the South where the ravages of war had not been so terribly felt, for continued and extraordinary help. This appeal received a noble response. With generous promptitude, churches in Baltimore came to our relief. By request of the Board, our esteemed brother, Rev. J. W. M. Williams, visited the Baptist General Association of Kentucky in May last, and secured in cash and subscriptions nearly *two thousand dollars*. Since that time, the Corresponding Secretary has made two visits to Kentucky, and spent a few days in attendance at the General Association of Missouri. In both these States he received a cordial welcome, substantial evidence of their interest in our mission cause. From all sources, since the 3rd of April last, the sum of $6,630 56 has been paid into the hands of the Treasurer.

Of this amount, $6,619 65 have been expended, leaving a balance of $10 91. The sum of $381 83, the avails of a bale of cotton given by S. Root, of Geo., has also been sent to Africa. In addition to this, our committee in Baltimore transmitted to the missionaries, and otherwise expended since April last, the sum of $2,794 06. Our agent, I. T. Smith, of N. Y., expended also during the fiscal year $220, making a total of $10,026 48 received and disbursed during the last fiscal year.

(From *Annual* of the Southern Baptist Convention, 1866, p. 57.)

Section Four

Home Missions

Dreary prospects reported in 1846

In view of these and kindred considerations, the Board for Domestic Missions regret, that circumstances beyond their control, have greatly circumscribed their labors, and will render their report less interesting and encouraging.

Rev. B. Manly, D.D., President of the Board, by the appointment of the Convention, resigned the office tendered him. Distance of residence from the Board, and other reasons, rendered it inconsistent with his view of duty to retain it.

Professor Reynolds, of South Carolina, selected by the Convention as the Corresponding Secretary, sent his resignation to the Board, soon after the adjournment of the meeting in Augusta.

Some time elapsed before another could be secured. At length the Rev. D. P. Bestor, of Alabama, was induced to engage in the work. In November last, he presented to the Board a report of his labors, accompanied with the following note of resignation:

"And now, dear brethren, I resign the office which your partiality induced you to confer upon me. You remember, I doubted the propriety of accepting it. The short experience I have had satisfies me that it is my duty to resign.

"I have learned by visiting many, and by an extensive correspondence, that our brethren prefer carrying on their domestic missionary operations, through their Associations and State Conventions. They

approve, invariably, of our Southern organization; but I cannot persuade them to act efficiently in its support. Some one should be employed who can be more successful than I have been; who can induce the churches and Associations to unite with the Board, and to pour their funds into a common treasury."

On the reception of this, the present incumbent was elected to fill the vacancy; who entered upon the duties of his office on the first of December following.

Our Treasurer also resigned his office on removing from the seat of the Board.

These changes in the acting officers of the Board, almost paralyzed its efforts, and at one time threatened its overthrow.

An empty treasury was another obstacle in the way of the efficient action of the Board. Up to the first of December last, they did not receive sufficient funds to defray current expenses.

The difficulty in securing collecting agents was another hindrance to our success. We were unable to send an agent into the field until the first of January of the present year.

These are some of the embarrassing difficulties that crippled the energies of the Board during the first seven months of the Conventional year; yet, we trust our Annual Report will not be destitute of interest and encouragement.

While we state these unpleasant things in reference to the beginning of the year's labor now closed; it is with gratitude to the Great Head of the church, we can say, "Better is the end of a thing than the beginning thereof."

(From *Annual* of the Southern Baptist Convention, 1846, pp. 49-50.)

First fields

The field of labor, in the providence of God, assigned us, though not as large as previous to the separation, is vast in extent, important in its relations, and in many sections extremely destitute of the word of life. It embraces fourteen States, with an aggregate area of 955,664 square miles, and a population of about eight millions. To supply this vast multitude with the bread and water of life, we have, connected with our denomination, about 2,000 preachers, including the superannuated, and those of feeble and broken constitutions, together with those employed as teachers, farmers, merchants, mechanics, lawyers, &c., which reduces those wholly given "to prayer and preaching of the word" to a much smaller number. And this small number is very unequally distributed throughout the field,— some portions having much more than a needful supply,—others scantily furnished— others still, entirely destitute. It is painfully true, that there are many of our white population of mature age, in each State, embraced in our field of labor who have never heard the gospel. . . .

Add to this matter the wants of our colored population. Although vast numbers of them enjoy religious advantages far superior to multitudes of our poor white citizens, yet greater numbers are in a condition to require the special attention of this body. It is gratifying to see the increasing interest on this subject in our churches. The time is not far distant when a wise and prudent plan for the religious improvement of that class of our population will be generally approved and adopted.

(*Ibid.*, p. 34.)

Effect of the Civil War

Every phase of the work was either destroyed or impaired. More than 150 missionaries had been engaged before outbreak of hostilities, but their work was suspended. Army missions became the principal work. Southern Baptists were particularly displeased with the action of the American Baptist Home Mission Society in securing authorization to take possession of Baptist meetinghouses in the South. The Society explained that it was trying to preserve this property for Baptist use, but some flagrant abuses aroused much Southern Baptist indignation. Indignation brought results, as this letter indicates.

WAR DEPARTMENT, WASHINGTON
January 14, 1864

To the Generals commanding the Military Division of the Mississippi, and the Department of the Gulf, of the South, and of Virginia and North Carolina, and all the Generals and Officers Commanding Armies, Detachments and Posts, and All Officers in the Service of the United States, in the Above Mentioned Departments:

You are hereby directed to place at the disposal of the American Baptist Home Mission Society all houses of worship belonging to the Baptist Churches South, in which a loyal minister of said church does not now officiate. It is a matter of great importance to the Government, in its efforts to restore tranquility to the community and peace to the nation, that Christian ministers should, by example and precept, support and foster the loyal sentiment of the people. The American Baptist Home Mission Society enjoys the entire confidence of this Department, and no doubt is entertained that all ministers who may be appointed by it will be entirely loyal. You are expected to give it all the aid, countenance, and support practicable in the execution of its important mission.

You are also authorized and directed to furnish their executive officer, or agent, and his clerk, with transportation and subsistence, when it can be done without prejudice to the service, and will afford them courtesy, assistance and protection.

(From *Minutes* of the American Baptist Home Mission Society, 1864, p. 15.)

Section Five

Other Benevolent Activities

Southern Baptist Publication Society

There had been calls for the organization of a southern publication society even before the formation of the Southern Baptist Convention. At Augusta in 1845 a resolution to establish such a society was voted down, but approximately one hundred of the out-

standing leaders of the Southern Baptist Convention met at Savannah, Georgia, on May 13, 1847, and organized the Southern Baptist Publication Society. This had no official connection with the Convention. The Society rendered excellent service until late 1863 or 1864, when it became a casualty of the war. It prepared the way for the program of the first Sunday School Board.

PREAMBLE

Whereas, an invitation was given in the year 1846 by the Central Baptist Association of Georgia to the Baptist Denomination in the Southern and Southwestern States to meet by Delegates in Convention in the city of Savannah, at the time of the meeting of the Georgia Baptist State Convention in 1847, for the purpose of deliberating on the expediency of forming a Southern Baptist Publication Society.,

And, whereas, in answer to this invitation, Delegates from South Carolina, Georgia, Virginia and Alabama have assembled, Therefore

Resolved—That in consideration of the limited representation from the Denomination, the Convention thus assembled, deeply impressed with the importance of engaging at once in the work of circulating religious publications, do now enter upon the formation of a Southern Baptist Publication Society, as an incipient and provisional measure.

In pursuance of this resolution the delegates proceeded to form the Society, and adopted the following Constitution, which they commend to the consideration and acceptance of the Denomination in the Southern and Southwestern States. They also request the attendance of the Denomination by Delegates at the time and place of the next meeting of the Society in 1848, that the measure may be consummated by the concurrence of the whole Denomination in the South and Southwest of the United States.

CONSTITUTION.

Article 1. The name of the Society shall be "The Southern Baptist Publication Society." Its objects shall be, to publish and distribute such books as are needed by the Baptist denomination in the South.

Art. 2. Any person may become a member of this Society, by paying annually the sum of one dollar or more; a member for life by the payment at one time of ten dollars; and a manager for life, by the payment, at one time, of fifty dollars.

Art. 3. There shall be a public anniversary meeting of the Society, at such time and place as shall be appointed by the Board, when the following officers shall be chosen by ballot, viz:—A President, three Vice Presidents, a Corresponding Secretary, a Recording Secretary, a Treasurer, and fifteen other members, all of whom shall be members of Baptist Churches, in good standing, who shall be a Board of managers for the direction of all the concerns of the Society, of whom seven shall be a quorum. A majority of the Board shall be laymen.

Art. 4. The Board shall have power to fill any vacancy which may occur in its own body; to make its own By-laws; and to appoint such agents and committees as may be deemed necessary.

Art. 5. The managers shall superintend the publication and distribution of such books, tracts and periodicals, as they may approve—the establishment of depositories—and the formation of auxiliary Societies. They shall hold frequent meetings, under such regulations as they may adopt, in conformity with the general provisions of this Constitution. The managers and the Treasurer shall make an annual report of their proceedings.

Art. 6. Any Baptist Church or Society, contributing annually to the funds of this Society, shall be deemed auxiliary and entitled to one delegate.

Art. 7. The Corresponding Secretary shall conduct the correspondence of the Society; shall superintend its publications under the direction of the Board, and perform such other duties as pertain to his office.

Art. 8. The Recording Secretary shall keep a record of the proceedings of the

Society and of the Board of Managers.

Art. 9. The Treasurer shall give to the President for the time being, satisfactory security for the safe keeping of the funds committed to him.

Art. 10. The President shall call a meeting of the Society, at the request of the majority of the Board of Managers.

Art 11. Alterations of this Constitution may be made at the annual meeting, by the concurence of two-thirds of the members present.

(From *Baptist Banner and Western Pioneer* [Kentucky], June 10, 1847.)

The Bible Board

In 1836, in a controversy over the proper form of Bible translation, the American and Foreign Bible Society was organized by former members of the American Bible Society. The Southern Baptist Convention was friendly to the American and Foreign Bible Society, authorizing cooperation with that body in 1846 in distributing copies of the Scriptures. However, this Society became embroiled in a controversy over a revision of the King James Version, and a schism followed in 1850. Uncertain as to which side to support, Southern Baptists formed a Bible Board in 1851 and located it at Nashville, Tennessee. The new Board, however, was not supported by many Southern Baptists because it began to be controlled by the Landmark faction at Nashville. After Nashville was captured by Federal armies, the Convention in 1863 abolished the Bible Board.

1. Authorization of the Bible Board

The committee to whom was confided the task of devising an efficient plan for the circulation of the Scriptures, report:

That the Baptists of the South are contributing less to this important department of Christian usefulness, than their resources would justify and the wants of the world imperatively demand, is indisputable. That they are doing less in this noble enterprise than in former years, is attributable, we are of opinion, not to a diminution of their

means, or liberality, or interest in the work, but the want of some central and efficient organization for prosecuting the work, securing the confidence, combining the energies, and eliciting the liberality of the whole denomination. Experience has demonstrated that our Mission Boards, occupied in the cultivation of the foreign and domestic fields, cannot pay to this subject the attention which its importance and diversified bearings demand. The denomination, divided in their views and modes of operating, have been dispirited, and their diminished contributions, flowing in different channels, have presented a beggarly result. To your committee, the most likely method of remedying these evils appears to be the creation of a new Board, having full authority to appoint agents, collect funds, receive bequests and co-operate with state Boards, or other Bible or Mission Boards, as they may deem it expedient, in the circulation of the Scriptures, in the most faithful versions of our own and foreign languages. Your committee, therefore, respectfully recommend:

1. The organization of a Board, whose seat of operations shall be the city of Nashville, to be styled "The Bible Board of the Southern Baptist Convention."

2. That we earnestly request the Baptists, and the friends of the Bible in the South, who are willing to contribute to its circulation through this channel, to rally to a united and generous support of the Bible Board of this Convention.

3. That a committee be appointed to prepare and publish an address to the Baptists of the South in behalf of this plan, and that periodicals friendly to the object be respectfully requested to give it circulation.

All which is respectfully submitted.

J. B. JETER, Chairman.

(From *Annual* of the Southern Baptist Convention, 1851, p. 14.)

2. The Board abolished

The committee which was directed by the Convention of 1861, to inquire if it be possible to arrange a plan of union between the Bible Board and the Southern Baptist Publication Society,

REPORT:

That the inquiry thus directed involved much consultation with both parties, that before arrangements for this purpose could be made, the city of Nashville had fallen into the hands of the enemy, who have continued to hold it, and that no opportunity presenting itself to consult the Bible Board, the end proposed was unattainable, and no negotiations have consequently been held with the Southern Baptist Publication Society, over which, as no connection is sustained with it, this Convention has no control.

No injury thus will result however, to the Convention. The present position of the Bible Board has satisfied your committee that the best course of the Convention will be to abolish the Bible Board, and to commit its work to the other Boards. They would therefore recommend the following resolutions for the adoption of this body:

Resolved, That the Bible cause can be as effectually conducted under the direction of the other Boards of this Convention as by a separate organization.

Resolved, That the Bible Board of the Southern Baptist Convention be and the same is hereby abolished.

Resolved, That the Churches be requested to send contributions for Bible purposes in foreign countries to the Foreign Mission Board, and those for home purposes to the Domestic Mission Board, or to such other agencies as they may deem best.

Resolved, That the various Boards are authorized to use the funds contributed for general purposes in such Bible operations as are made necessary by their work.

JAMES P. BOYCE,
B. MANLY, SR.,
A. M. POINDEXTER
Com.

(From *Annual* of the Southern Baptist Convention, 1863, p. 51.)

Indian missions

The American Baptist Indian Mission Association was organized as a society in 1842 with headquarters at Louisville, Kentucky. In 1855 leaders of the Association proposed that the Southern Baptist Convention assume this work. The Convention of 1855 voted to do so with reluctance, not from lack of interest in Indian missions, but because the financial affairs of the Association were in bad condition.

Resolved, That the Convention accept the transfer tendered by the American Indian Mission Association.

Resolved, That the Domestic Mission Board at Marion, Ala., be charged with the conduct and management of all matters pertaining to Indian missions, and the continuance of the same, within the sphere of operation.

Resolved, That prior to the consummation of said transfer, the Board of the American Indian Mission Association, shall make a full exhibit of its condition to the Marion Board.

(From *Annual* of the Southern Baptist Convention, 1855, p. 13.)

First Sunday School Board

Sunday School work was carried on in the South in several ways during the first half of the nineteenth century. The interdenominational American Sunday School Union (organized in 1817) was active. Literature was provided for the schools by the American Baptist Publication Society after 1840. The Southern Baptist Publication Society, the Bible Board of the Southern Baptist Convention, and the Domestic Mission Board also did some work in this sphere. In 1857 a Southern Baptist Sunday School Union was organized under the aegis of the Landmark group, and for that reason was not generally supported. By 1863 little was being done for the Sunday Schools. The Bible Board was abolished in that year; the Southern Baptist Publication Society and the Sunday School Union were on their last legs. Basil Manly, Jr. was made *chairman of a committee to see what could be done to promote Sunday Schools. His report is the first apologetic for the Sunday School movement adopted by the Southern Baptist Convention.*

SUNDAY SCHOOLS.

The Committee appointed to inquire into the expediency of the Convention's attempting, in any direct way, the promotion of Sunday Schools, respectfully submit the following

REPORT:

It is needless to argue before this body, the importance of Sunday Schools, or the duty of promoting their establishment and increasing their efficency, in every legitimate way. All of us have felt that the Sunday School is the nursery of the Church, the camp of instruction for her young soldiers, the great missionary to the future. While our other benevolent agencies relate primarily to the present, this goes to meet and bless the generation that is coming, to win them from ignorance and sin, to train future laborers, when our place shall know us no more. All of us have seen how Sunday Schools tend to direct increasing attention to the Bible, to elevate the ministry, to train young ministers to build up Churches in destitute parts, to foster the missionary spirit, to increase both our capacity and willingness for every good work. And most of us, in some form or other, have labored for their advancement. The questions before us reduce themselves to these:—Whether it is expedient for the Convention to attempt any thing in this direction? Whether the present is a proper time; and in what way the effort should be made?

That the subject comes fairly within the range of the Constitution, and accords with the design of this Convention is unquestionable. All our State organizations embrace this, along with the methods of benevolent enterprize, and the very symmetry and completeness of our system of religious effort, seems in fact, to demand that this, as well as others, should be di-

rectly fostered by our general organization, and claim its share of attention, when our brethren come up from all sections of our land. Without such recognition, it is liable to be thrust out as an intruder, instead of being welcomed as a sister and admitted affectionately, though least and youngest, to a place in the family.

There seems to be no imperative reason restricting this work to State limits. The same plan and means which are effectual in one region will apply, if extended, to another. The books which suit Virginia Baptist Sunday Schools, will be useful to Alabama, and the agencies for stimulating interest in the subject in Georgia, can be applied with little increase of expenditure, and great increase of efficiency to the Carolinas. In fact, while aggregate expense slightly enlarged, the expense to each is greatly diminished, since many thousands can be supplied at much smaller individual cost than few—and if it has been found in other operations, that a general union is desirable, all the arguments apply, and some of them with increased force, to show that Sunday Schools, too, may be more efficiently promoted by similar united efforts.

It may be questioned, however, whether Baptists in the Confederacy, should act in this matter for themselves, or wait the cooperation of other denominations, in some Society like the American Sunday School Union. While all the valuable service formerly rendered by that organization is cheerfully acknowledged, your Committee believe that the time has come for us, as a denomination, to commence this work on our own account, with no unfriendliness or ungenerous feeling towards others, but under a simple sense of our solemn responsibility. We are more deeply interested than any others can be, in instituting a Sunday School in every Baptist Church; and we can do more, if we will, towards accomplishing it, than others can. Without therefore, dwelling upon the difference of views pertaining to the status of the children of Christians, and the method of religious nurture—a difference which our brethren can scarcely help obtruding upon us, when they seem desirous of avoiding it—it is sufficient to say, that the duty rests upon us to "provide for them of our own household." And if we enter upon this work, it will promote both the enlargement and economy of the enterprise, and at the same time, contribute to harmony and good understanding among ourselves, for us to labor in it together, in connection with this Convention.

But should any attempt be made now? It is evident that the need of Sunday Schools is as great as ever, is even greater with us than heretofore. There is less instruction in other ways. There are more orphans and destitute. There are more ignorant and neglected. These must grow up to vice and ruin—must poison the very fountains of our young Confederacy—must infect the moral atmosphere in which we and our children shall live, unless met by early and vigorous efforts. Who shall care for these helpless ones, if not the Churches of Christ?

Yet, at this time, less than usual is being done in this direction. If the causes of this deficiency were essential or irremediable, we might strive to bear it, though we could not become content with it. But though many of the accustomed and skillful laborers have been called from their homes, and though there is a lack of some of the usual facilities and incitements, there remain enough at home, too old or too young for the army, to carry on our Sunday Schools, especially with the aid of that never failing and invincible corps of reserves, the sisterhood, who ever ready for every good word and work, need only to have the way opened and pointed out to them.

There is now no general organization actively engaged in this work. Here is at once an open door, and an urgent claim, both opportunity and argument for activity.

The close of the war may be looked to as a more propitious season for organizing such an enterprise. But if the need is now pressing, and the opportunity is now open,

shall we defer any commencement until that uncertain period? Who knows when the war will end? Moreover, though the return of peace may be more favorable in some respects, in others, the reverse is true. The rush into new business, the many changes of occupation, the inevitable emigrations and removals, and the generally unsettled state of society, will present new reasons for postponement. It seems to your Committee, that though we cannot now do all we would wish, or as easily as we would desire, we shall not find in this an excuse that will satisfy Him, who consigned one to everlasting remembrance and honor, because she had "done what she could." It will be a thing worthy for our children to remember, that in the crisis of this great revolution, in the very blood of our birth as a Confederacy, we are careful to think of and provide for the religious nurture of the children that are growing up; and that while thousands from our Churches were swelling the army of independence, their children at home, and the fatherless and destitute, were not left neglected, but that a noble and generous plan had been set on foot, for taking our part fully in training in knowledge and piety, the future citizens of our land.

As to the best method of accomplishing the object, it is respectfully suggested that the details of the plan cannot be judiciously and minutely settled in advance. The question is not how much can be done. If but little can be accomplished, all the greater reason for attempting to do that little, and preparing to do more hereafter. In all its other enterprizes, the Convention has entrusted the management to a Board. There seems no reason for departing from this plan in the present instance. And the subject is sufficiently distinct and sufficiently important to claim the attention of a separate Board.

Actuated by these views, the Committee recommend for the adoption of the Convention, the following Resolutions:

1. *Resolved*, That a Board be established consisting of the usual number, to be

entitled the Board of Sunday Schools of the Southern Baptist Convention.

2. *Resolved,* That the Board be charged with the duty of taking all measures adapted to promote the establishment, enlargement, and higher efficiency of Sunday Schools throughout our land; provided that the Board shall not establish a printing house.

3. *Resolved,* That a Committee of one, from each State, be appointed to recommend a suitable location, and to nominate said Board.

All of which
is respectfully submitted,
B. MANLY, JR., *Chairman.*

(From *Annual* of the Southern Baptist Convention, 1863, pp. 45-47.)

Section Six

Theological Education

James P. Boyce, who received his college training in Brown University and theological training in Princeton Seminary, had a sense of vocation regarding theological education. While being ordained he was asked, "Do you expect to give your life to the pastorate?" and he replied, "Yes, if God does not call me to teach in a theological seminary." In 1855 he was elected professor of theology in Furman University. At that time Southern Baptists, under the leadership of Basil Manly, R. B. C. Howell, and others, were making plans to found a theological school. When Boyce delivered his inaugural address at Furman in 1856, he suggested the direction such a theological school might take. The principles he enunciated have become basic in Southern Baptist theological education.

Excerpt from Boyce's address

Gentlemen of the Board of Trustees
   of the Furman University:

I congratulate myself that I address tonight a body of men pledged to the interests of Theological Education, and that I do it in the existence of our present rela-

tions and in the discharge of the duty assigned me.

. . . .

It is on this account that in performing the duty assigned me, I find myself irresistibly forced from other subjects which might have been appropriate, and led to suggest to you THREE CHANGES IN THEOLOGICAL INSTITUTIONS, which would enable them to fulfil more adequately at least, if not completely, the hopes of their founders. These changes are intended to meet evils which, in one case by the many, in the others by the few, have been already experienced, and they are suggested as furnishing ample remedies for the existing evils.

The first evil to which I would apply a remedy, is one which has been universally experienced—which, more than anything else, has shaken the faith of many in the value of Theological Institutions, has originated the opposition which they have at any time awakened, and has caused the mourning and sorrow of those who, having laid their foundations, still continue to cluster around them. I refer to the failure of the Theological Institution to call forth an abundant Ministry for the Churches, and supply to it adequate instruction.

. . . .

Permit me to ask what has been the prominent idea at the basis of Theological Education in this country? To arrive at it we have only to notice the requistions necessary for entrance upon a course of study. Have they not been almost universally that the student should have passed through a regular College course, or made attainments equivalent thereto? and have not even the exceptional cases been rare instances in which the Faculty or Board have, under peculiar circumstances, assumed the responsibility of a deviation from the ordinary course.

The idea which is prominent as the basis of this action, is, that the work of the Ministry should be entrusted only to those who have been classically educated—an assumption which singularly enough is made for no other profession. It is in vain to say that such is not the theory or the practice of our denomination. It is the theory and the practice of by far the larger portion of those who have controlled our Institutions, and have succeeded in engrafting this idea upon them, contrary to the spirit which prevails among the Churches. They have done this without doubt in the exercise of their best judgment, but have failed because they neglected the better plan pointed out by the providence and word of God.

The practical operation of this theory has tended in two ways to diminish the ranks of our valuable Ministry. It has restrained many from entering upon the work, and has prevented the arrangement of such a course of study as would have enabled those who have entered upon it to fit themselves in a short time for valuable service. The consequences have been, that the number of those who have felt themselves called of God to the Ministry, has been disproportioned to the wants of the Churches; and of that number but a very small proportion have entered it with a proper preparation for even common usefulness. And only by energy and zeal, awakened by their devotion to the work, have they been able to succeed in their labors, and to do for themselves the work, the greater part of which the Theological school should have accomplished for them.

In His word and in His providence, God seems to have plainly indicated the principle upon which the instruction of the Ministry should be based. It is not that every man should be made a scholar, an adept in philology, an able interpreter of the Bible in its original languages, acquainted with all the sciences upon the various facts and theories of which God's word is attacked and must be defended, and versed in all the systems of true and false philosophy, which some must understand in order to encounter the enemies who attack the very foundations of religion, but that while the privilege of becoming such shall be freely offered to all, and every student shall be encouraged to obtain all the advantages that education can afford, the opportunity should be given to those who cannot or will not make thorough scholastic preparation to obtain that adequate knowledge of the truths of the Scriptures systematically arranged, and of the laws which govern the interpretation of the text in the English version, which constitutes all that is actually necessary to enable them to preach the Gospel, to build up the Churches on their most holy faith, and to instruct them in the practice of the duties incumbent upon them.

The Scriptural qualifications for the Ministry do, indeed, involve the idea of knowledge, but that knowledge is not of the sciences, nor of philosophy, nor of the languages, but of God and His plan of salvation. He who has not this knowledge, though he be learned in all the learning of the schools, is incapable of preaching the word of God. But he who knows it, not superficially, not merely in those plain and simple declarations known to every believing reader, but in its power, as revealed in its precious and sanctifying doctrines, is fitted to bring forth out of his treasury things new and old, and is a workman that needeth not to be ashamed, although he may speak to his hearers in uncouth words or in manifest ignorance of all the sciences. The one belongs to the class of educated Ministers, the other to the Ministry of educated men, and the two things are essentially different.

The one may be a Bunyan, unlearned withal, and in many respects ignorant, rough and rugged of speech, with none of the graces of the orator or the refinement of the rhetorician, but so filled with the grace abounding to the chief of sinners, so learned in the Scriptures quoted at every point for the support of the truth he speaks, and discoursing such sweet and godly doctrine, that he is manifest as one taught so truly in the Gospel that the most learned scholars may sit silently at his feet and learn the wonders of the word of God. The other may be a Parker, with all the grace and polish of the finished scholar, pouring forth the purest and most powerful English, able to illustrate and defend his cause by contributions from every storehouse of knowledge, presenting attractions in his oratory which induce his educated audience to receive or to overlook his blasphemous doctrines, yet so destitute of the knowledge of true Christianity, and of a genuine experience of the influences of the Holy Ghost, that he denies the plainest doctrines of the Bible, saps the very foundation of all revealed truth, and manifests so profound an ignorance of the book he undertakes to expound, and the religion of which he calls himself a Minister, that the humblest Christian among our very servants shall rise up in condemnation against him in the great day of accounts.

Who is the Minister here—the man of the schools, or the man of the Scriptures? Who bears the insignia of an ambassador for Christ? Whom does God own? Whom would the Church hear? In whose power would she put forth her strength? And yet these instances, though extreme, will serve to show what may be the Ministry of the educated man, and what that of the illiterate man, the educated Minister. The perfection of the Ministry, it is gladly admitted, would consist in the just combination of the two; but it is not the business of the Church to establish a perfect, but an adequate Ministry—and it is only of the latter that we may hope for an abundant supply. The qualification God lays down is the only one He permits us to demand, and the instruction of our Theological schools must be based upon such a plan as shall afford this amount of education to those who actually constitute the mass of our Ministry, and who cannot obtain more.

. . . .

Let such a change be made in the Theological Department as shall provide an English course of study for those who have only been able to attain a plain English education. Let that course comprise the Evidences of Christianity, Systematic and Polemic Theology, the Rules of Interpretation applied to the English version; some

knowledge of the principles of Rhetoric, extensive practice in the development from texts of subjects and skeletons of Sermons, whatever amount of Composition may be expedient, and full instruction in the nature of Pastoral duties—let the studies of this course be so pursued as to train the mind to habits of reflection and analysis, to awaken it to conceptions of the truths of Scripture, to fill it with arguments from the word of God in support of its doctrines, and to give it facility in constructing and presenting such arguments—and the work will be accomplished.

. . . .

I proceed now to speak more briefly of a second change needed in our Theological Institutions, by which it is to be hoped they will be enabled to produce scholars adequate to the exigencies of our own denomination, and to the common cause of Christianity.

. . . .

It has been felt as a sore evil, that we have been dependent in great part upon the criticism of Germany for all the more learned investigations in Biblical Criticism and Exegesis, and that in the study of the development of the doctrine of the Church, as well as of its outward progress, we have been compelled to depend upon works in which much of error has been mingled with truth, owing to the defective standpoint occupied by their authors.

. . . .

But the question arises, how can we avoid it? The amplest course now afforded, gives to students but slight preparation for entrance upon such duties. Our Ministry receives no such support as warrants the purchase of more than moderate libraries. The labors of most of our Pastoral charges are sufficient fully to occupy the time of those upon whom they are devoted. And how shall we avoid it?

. . . .

It is scarcely necessary to remark, that any plan which can be devised, must be based upon the presence in the Institution of a good Theological library—one which shall not only be filled with the gathered lore of the past, but also endowed with the means of annual increase. Without this, no Institution can pursue extensive courses of study, or contribute anything directly to the advancement of learning. The Professor is cut off from valuable and necessary books, and the student hindered from making even the least important investigations in the course of study he is pursuing.

The plan I propose to you, supposes the possession of such a library; and this, even if it be such, is its only peculiar item of expense. Taking the idea from the provision made in some of our Institutions for the degree of Master of Arts, it has occurred to me that an additional course of study might be provided for those who may be graduates of Theological Institutions. This course might extend over one or two years, according to the amount of study the student may propose to accomplish. In it the study of the Oriental languages might be extended to the Arabic and the Syriac. The writing of exegetical theses would furnish subjects for investigation, and give a more ample acquaintance with the original text, and with the laws of its interpretation. The text-books or lectures studied in Systematic and Polemic Theology, could be compared with kindred books; the theories of opponents examined in their own writings, and notes taken for future use from rare and costly books. These and similar studies which should be laid down in a well-digested course would bestow accurate scholarship, train the student in the methods of original investigation, give him confidence in the results previously attained, and open to him resources from which he might draw extensively in interpreting the Scriptures, and in setting forth the truths they contain. The result would be, that a band of scholars would go forth from almost every one of whom we might expect valuable contributions to our Theological literature.

. . . .

The change which I would in the last place propose, is not intended to meet an evil existing in our Theological Institutions so much as one which is found in the denomination at large, and which may at some future time injuriously affect this educational interest. It is the adoption of a declaration of doctrine to be required of those who assume the various professorships.

The most superficial observer must perceive that in our day the sound doctrine of our Churches is much imperilled. Campbellism, though checked in every direction in which it attempted to develop itself, has left no little of its leaven among us, and exerts no inconsiderable influence. The distinctive principles of Arminianism have also been engrafted upon many of our Churches; and even some of our Ministry have not hesitated publicly to avow them. That sentiment, the invariable precursor, or accompaniment of all heresy—that the doctrines of Theology are mere matters of speculation, and its distinctions only logomachies and technicalities, has obtained at least a limited prevalence. And the doctrinal sentiments of a large portion of the Ministry and membership of the Churches, are seen to be either very much unsettled, or radically wrong.

. . . .

Peculiar obligations rest, however, upon those to whom are entrusted the education of the Rising Ministry. God in His mercy preserve the instructors from the crime of teaching a single error, however unimportant, and grant unto all our Boards the grace necessary for faithfulness to the trusts devolved upon them, that false doctrine, however trifling, may receive no countenance.

It is with a single man that error usually commences, and when such a man has influence, or position, it is impossible to estimate the evil that will attend it. Ecclesiastical history is full of warning upon this subject. Scarcely a single heresy has ever blighted the Church, which has not owed its existence or its development, to that one man of power and ability, whose name has always been associated with its doctrines. And yet seldom has an opinion been thus advanced, which has not subsequently had its advocate in every age, and which in some ages has not extensively prevailed.

The history of our own denomination in this country, furnishes an illustration. Playing upon the prejudices of the weak and ignorant among our people, decrying creeds as an infringement upon the rights of conscience, making a deep impression by his extensive learning and great abilities, Alexander Campbell threatened at one time the total destruction of our faith. Had he occupied a chair in one of our Theological Institutions, that destruction might have been completed. There would have been time to disseminate widely, and fix deeply, his principles, before it became necessary to avow them publicly; and when this necessity arrived, it would have been attended by the support of the vast majority of our best educated Ministers. Who can estimate the evil which would then have ensued!

. . . .

By the Baptists of all ages, creeds have been almost universally used, and invariably in this two-fold way. To some of other denominations, it has seemed that we have been without them, because the principle of liberty of conscience which we have at the same time maintained, has forbidden the laying of civil disabilities upon those who have differed from us. We have appeared to them, therefore, to put them forth only as declarative of our principles. It is to be regretted that many Baptists in our own day have given countenance to this opinion by misstatements of our practice. And it would, therefore, have been to me to-night a pleasant labor to pass over the history of our denomination in the past, in proof of the position we have undoubtedly occupied. But I could not have done this without sacrificing a stronger desire to present to your consideration questions of greater practical utility. Suffice it to state, that we have simply maintained that civil disabilities are not the means of punishing the offending members of the Church of Christ. We have looked to the Scriptures for the rule to govern us in such matters,

and we have adopted the truly Apostolic plan by which we have accomplished all at which they aimed. The truth of God, which we have held, has been plainly declared. A confession of faith in Christ and in at least the prominent doctrines of Christianity, has been required of the candidate for baptism. By the principles thus set forth, we have judged the heretical among us, and wherever they agreed not with us, have excommunicated them from our Churches and our fellowship. The ideas which we have held of the spiritual nature of the kingdom of Christ, have developed the principle of liberty of conscience, and debarred us from the infliction of bodily punishment, or the subjection to any civil disability. But the same views of the spirituality of the Church, have impressed upon us the necessity of excluding those who have violated the simplicity which is in Christ.

It is, therefore, gentlemen, in perfect consistency with the position of Baptists, as well as of Bible Christians, that the test of doctrine I have suggested to you, should be adopted. It is based upon principles and practices sanctioned by the authority of Scripture, and by the usage of our people. In so doing, you will be acting simply in accordance with propriety and righteousness. You will infringe the rights of no man, and you will secure the rights of those who have established here an instrumentality for the production of a sound Ministry. It is no hardship to those who teach here, to be called upon to sign the declaration of their principles, for there are fields of usefulness open elsewhere to every man, and none need accept your call who cannot conscientiously sign your formulary. And while all this is true, you will receive by this an assurance that the trust committed to you by the founders is fulfilling in accordance with their wishes, that the Ministry that go forth have here learned to distinguish truth from error and to embrace the former, and that the same precious truths of the Bible which were so dear to the hearts of its founders, and which I trust are equally dear to yours, will be propagated in our Churches, giving to them vigor and strength, and causing them to flourish by the godly sentiments and emotions they will awaken within them. May God impress you deeply with the responsibility under which you must act in reference to it!

(From James P. Boyce, *An Inaugural Address* [Furman University, Greenville, S. C.], 1856.)

Wayland's opinion of Boyce's suggestions

President Francis Wayland of Brown University was the leading American Baptist educator at this time. His remarks on the ideas of Boyce are significant since they illustrate the amorphous situation regarding theological education.

Providence, January 26, 1857
My dear Professor Boyce.—I have read with great interest your Inaugural Address. It is the first common sense discourse on theological education I have yet seen. I like it for several reasons. In the first place, it does not take it for granted that the Theological Seminary is a stereotyped institution from which nothing is to be taken and to which nothing is to be added in all coming time; in the next place, it takes it for granted that a seminary is made for the church and not that the church was created by Christ for the seminary and especially for the professors; and then it recognizes the fact that there *is a* Baptist church now existing, as a matter distinct from other churches, which has been in fact almost ignored, that Baptists are capable of understanding what they want and of devising the means for supplying it; and again, that educating the Baptist ministry does not mean educating a little band who shall form a clique separate from their brethren, of whom they may speak in public as almost interlopers; and finally, that that is not the best education for us which by its own necessity reduces the number of those who receive advantages to the lowest possible number.

Whether seminaries and theological schools are the proper places to educate the ministry, I know not. It is a matter of experiment in our day, and time alone can decide it. Their tendency is to raise intellectual above spiritual qualifications, and such it has thus far proven. Of old, they have I think proved to be, after a generation or two, schools of heresy. In this country, from the errors I have intimated, they have not had a fair chance. Your plan is the only plan I have seen which gives them a fair opportunity of doing well. You embrace the whole ministry, you mingle them all together and treat them all as brethren equally honored and honorable if God has called them to the ministry, and you give them an opportunity to learn something of the pastoral duties before they enter upon them.

I wish you every success. I hope you will be well sustained, and that Baptists, as they have done before, may show other Christians how the church of Christ is to be built up by following more closely in the steps of the Master. I am yours truly,

F. WAYLAND

REVEREND J. P. BOYCE.

(From *Religious Herald* [Virginia], January 11, 1872.)

Founding of the first Southern Baptist seminary

Pursuant to the suggestions of Boyce, an Abstract of Principles was adopted by the seminary, which opened in Greenville, South Carolina, in 1859. This Abstract was criticized by some because it was a "creed," and by others because it did not detail ecclesiastical practices of Baptists. Boyce defended the Abstract, and said that by design no reference was made to those practices upon which Baptists differed. The twenty articles presented deal with beliefs which Baptists held in common.

1. *Abstract of Principles*

ABSTRACT OF PRINCIPLES
I. The Scriptures.

The Scriptures of the Old and New Testaments were given by inspiration of God, and are the only sufficient, certain and authoritative rule of all saving knowledge, faith and obedience.

II. God.

There is but one God, the Maker, Preserver and Ruler of all things, having in and of himself, all perfections, and being infinite in them all; and to Him all creatures owe the highest love, reverence and obedience.

III. The Trinity.

God is revealed to us as Father, Son, and Holy Spirit each with distinct personal attributes, but without division of nature, essence or being.

IV. Providence.

God from eternity, decrees or permits all things that come to pass, and perpetually upholds, directs and governs all creatures and all events; yet so as not in any wise to be the author or approver of sin nor to destroy the free will and responsibility of intelligent creatures.

V. Election.

Election is God's eternal choice of some persons unto everlasting life—not because of foreseen merit in them, but of His mere mercy in Christ—in consequence of which choice they are called, justified and glorified.

VI. The Fall of Man.

God originally created man in His own image, and free from sin; but, through the temptation of Satan, he transgressed the command of God, and fell from his original holiness and righteousness; whereby his posterity inherit a nature corrupt and wholly opposed to God and His law, are under condemnation, and as soon as they are capable of formal action, become actual transgressors.

VII. The Mediator.

Jesus Christ, the only begotten Son of God, is the divinely appointed mediator between God and man. Having taken upon Himself human nature, yet without sin, He perfectly fulfilled the law, suffered and died upon the cross for the salvation of sinners. He was buried, and rose again the third day, and ascended to His Father, at whose right hand He ever liveth to make intercession for His people. He is the only Mediator, the Prophet, Priest and King of the Church, and Sovereign of the Universe.

VIII. Regeneration.

Regeneration is a change of heart, wrought by the Holy Spirit, who quickeneth the dead in trespasses and sins enlightening their minds spiritually and savingly to understand the Word of God, and renewing their whole nature, so that they love and practice holiness. It is a work of God's free and special grace alone.

IX. Repentance.

Repentance is an evangelical grace, wherein a person being, by the Holy Spirit, made sensible of the manifold evil of his sin, humbleth himself for it, with godly sorrow, detestation of it, and self-abhorrence, with a purpose and endeavor to walk before God so as to please Him in all things.

X. Faith.

Saving faith is the belief, on God's authority, of whatsoever is revealed in His Word concerning Christ; accepting and resting upon Him alone for justification and eternal life. It is wrought in the heart by the Holy Spirit, and is accompanied by all other saving graces, and leads to a life of holiness.

XI. Justification.

Justification is God's gracious and full acquittal of sinners, who believe in Christ, from all sin, through the satisfaction that Christ has made; not for anything wrought in them or done by them; but on account of the obedience and satisfaction of Christ, they receiving and resting on Him and His righteousness by faith.

XII. Sanctification.

Those who have been regenerated are also sanctified, by God's word and Spirit dwelling in them. This sanctification is progressive through the supply of Divine strength, which all saints seek to obtain, pressing after a heavenly life in cordial obedience to all Christ's commands.

XIII. Perseverance of the Saints.

Those whom God hath accepted in the Beloved and sanctified by His Spirit, will never totally nor finally fall away from the state of grace, but shall certainly persevere to the end; and though they may fall, through neglect and temptation, into sin, whereby they grieve the Spirit, impair their graces and comforts, bring reproach on the Church, and temporal judgments on themselves, yet they shall be renewed again unto repentance, and be kept by the power of God through faith unto salvation.

XIV. The Church.

The Lord Jesus is the Head of the Church, which is composed of all his true disciples, and in Him is invested supremely all power for its government. According to his commandment, Christians are to associate themselves into particular societies or churches; and to each of these churches he hath given needful authority for administering that order, discipline and worship which he hath appointed. The regular officers of a Church are Bishops or Elders, and Deacons.

XV. Baptism.

Baptism is an ordinance of the Lord Jesus, obligatory upon every believer, wherein he is immersed in water in the name of the Father, and of the Son, and of the Holy Spirit, as a sign of his fellowship with the death and resurrection of Christ, of remission of sins, and of his giving himself up to God, to live and walk in newness of life. It is prerequisite to church fellowship, and to participation in the Lord's Supper.

XVI. The Lord's Supper.

The Lord's Supper is an ordinance of Jesus Christ, to be administered with the elements of bread and wine, and to be observed by His churches till the end of the world. It is in no sense a sacrifice, but is designed to commemorate his death, to confirm the faith and other graces of Christians, and to be a bond, pledge and renewal of their communion with him, and of their church fellowship.

XVII. The Lord's Day.

The Lord's day is a Christian institution for regular observance, and should be employed in exercises of worship and spiritual devotion, both public and private, resting from worldly employments and amusements, works of necessity and mercy only excepted.

XVIII. Liberty of Conscience.

God alone is Lord of the conscience; and He hath left it free from the doctrines and commandments of men, which are in anything contrary to His word, or not contained in it. Civil magistrates being ordained of God, subjection in all lawful things commanded by them ought to be yielded by us in the Lord, not only for wrath, but also for conscience sake.

XIX. The Resurrection.

The bodies of men after death return to dust, but their spirits return immediately to God—the righteous to rest with Him; the wicked, to be reserved under darkness to the judgment. At the last day, the bodies of all the dead, both just and unjust, will be raised.

XX. The Judgment.

God hath appointed a day, wherein he will judge the world by Jesus Christ, when every one shall receive according to his deeds; the wicked shall go into everlasting punishment; the righteous, into everlasting life.

(From *Annual* of the Southern Baptist Convention, 1954, pp. 38-39.)

2. Boyce's defense of the Abstract of Principles

It was with great difficulty, at first, that some of the members of the Convention were led to vote for what they called a Creed. But it was manifest that some such provision ought to exist. Yet is this Seminary, I believe, the only one among the Baptists in the whole country which throws this safeguard, as to the future teachings of the professors, around the endowments which have been raised for it. Lest there should be some misconception, it may be proper to state this abstract of principles has nothing to do with the students. No one is understood as subscribing to it except a professor.

But, after the decision had been reached to have this abstract established, the question still arose, What shall it be? That was the region in which the old Philadelphia Confession, or to speak more properly the Century Confession, had had its influence. If the Convention had been acting only for its own members, I believe that that confession might have been adopted. But they realized that there was a large part of the denomination, particularly at the West, which object to many of the features of that confession. The New Hampshire Confession would have been acceptable to some, but not to all. The Convention therefore made its own articles. The committee to whom work was entrusted took all the Baptist confessions which could be obtained and elaborated, article by article, a platform for the Seminary. The Convention then spent the greater portion of its time in revising and perfecting what the committee suggested.

Both in the Committee and the Convention there were three principles which underlay all this work. The abstract of principles must be: 1. A complete exhibition of the fundamental doctrines of grace, so that in no essential particular should they speak dubiously; 2. They should speak out clearly and distinctly as to the practices universally prevalent among us; 3. Upon no point, upon which the denomination is divided, should the Convention, and through it, the Seminary, take any position.

Had not these principles guided the Convention, the Seminary could not have been established. There were brethren there—and I admit that I was one of them—who would then and there have abandoned our object, rather than aid in raising an institution whose funds and endowment were not secured to the maintenance of the principles and practices then prevalent, and still prevailing, in our Southern Zion. The doctrines of grace are therefore distinctly brought out in the abstract of principles. No less true is this of Baptist practices. . . .

While, however, it was deemed essential to avow distinctly and unreservedly the sentiments universally prevalent among us, both as to doctrine and practice, it was equally important that upon these questions upon which there was still a difference of opinion among Southern Baptists, the Seminary articles should not bind the institution. It must be remembered that at that time one-half the amount then thought necessary for the permanent endowment had been raised. If the members of that Convention had adopted one set of views, rather than another, on those mooted points, and had forced the acceptance of these upon the professors, all those who differ from the majority of those present would have been cut off from that endowment which was then the common heritage of the whole denomination of the South. The members present were mostly from the East. In the West chiefly there had lately arisen peculiar views known as Landmarkism. Had those present chosen, they might have inserted an article which would forever have prevented any one holding such views from even being a professor in the Seminary. The whole influence of the institution would thus perpetually have been cast against those views. Would that have been just? So also as to any other question upon which there was division of opinion. And it was especially true of this subject of alien immersions at the time the Seminary was established, that great and wide-spread differences of opinion existed.

. . . .

It will be seen, therefore, that the wise course of the Convention was to carry out this third principle, by which they refrained from binding the Seminary upon any point which the denomination is not agreed. It is hoped that the time will come when all Baptists shall see eye to eye upon all points. But this is to be accomplished by mutual forbearance and instruction. Let us all pray for that guidance of God's Spirit by which alone that end can be attained.

(From *Western Recorder* [Kentucky], June 20, 1874.)

3. *The founders of the South Carolina seminary*

The old Baptist house of worship had been divided by partitions into two lecture-rooms and a library. The theological portion of the library of Furman University had been turned over, amounting to some two thousand volumes, and the following summer, at the suggestion of Dr. G. W. Samson, the Columbian College of Washington City presented nearly two hundred volumes, including several sets of complete works of the highest value. The now large private library of Dr. Boyce was a treasure to his colleagues in pursuing the studies connected with their several schools. The four professors were all young, and full of enthusiasm for their new undertaking, while none of them was without considerable experience in preaching and instruction. The Baptist Colleges of the South had amiably recognized their destitution of all titles of dignity, and at the Commencements of May and June had made each of them a D.D. Surely all was now ready.

The preparation of James P. Boyce for this position appears from all that we have seen of his history and character. Recall his thorough general education at the College of Charleston and at Brown University, his useful experience as editor in Charleston and full theological course at Princeton, his four years as pastor in Columbia, and now four years as theological professor in Furman University, two of them spent in laborious teaching there, and two in agency work for the proposed institution. He presented a remarkable combination of business talent, with thorough education and wide reading, and with experience as a preacher and professor, and was singularly adapted to be at once the Chairman of the Faculty and Treasurer of the Seminary, and its Professor of Systematic and of Polemic Theology.

We have seen that Basil Manly, Jr., now thirty-three years old, had been graduated at the State University of Alabama, and had taken a full theological course at Newton and Princeton. After a rich pastoral experience, including four years in the famous First Baptist Church of Richmond, Va., he had now been for five years the principal of the Richmond Female Institute, taking a large part in the higher instruction. He was already well known to be a man of great versatility and varied attainments, as strong in will as he was gentle in spirit, and sure to be warmly loved by his associates and pupils.

William Williams was now thirty-eight years old, a native of Georgia, and a graduate of the University of Georgia. He practised several years as a lawyer, having been graduated in the Law School of Harvard University. From 1851 he was a pastor in Alabama and Georgia, and since 1856 had been Professor of Theology in Mercer University, then located at Penfield, Ga. His legal studies and practice had disciplined his great mental acuteness. He had extraordinary power in the clear and terse statement of truth, and when kindled in preaching or lecturing he spoke with such intensity as is rarely equalled. He was also a man of great purity of character, certain to command the profoundest respect.

John A. Broadus was thirty-two years old, being a few days younger than Boyce. A native of Virginia, and from early youth a school-teacher by inheritance, he had been graduated in 1850 as M. A. of the University of Virginia. After another year of teaching he was pastor of the Baptist Church at Charlottesville, the seat of the University, from 1851 to 1859. During the first two years of this period he was also assistant-instructor in Latin and Greek, under the revered guidance of the famous Dr. Gessner Harrison. For the two years for 1855 to 1857 he again resided in the University as chaplain, his place in the Charlottesville church being filled by Rev. A. E. Dickinson. Then two remaining years in Charlottesville, and he went to the Seminary.

(From John A. Broadus, *Memoir of James P. Boyce* [New York, 1893], pp. 167-69.)

Section Seven
Beginnings of Landmarkism

In the fifth decade of the nineteenth century the movement known as Landmarkism began to take shape. Evidently sparked by the practical question of accepting pedobaptist immersion, it gradually developed into a full-blown system of theological interpretation and ecclesiastical practice. The leaders of the early thrust were J. R. Graves, J. M. Pendleton, and A. C. Dayton. Pendleton later turned away from most of the Landmark conclusions.

Cotton Grove Resolutions

The early thinking of J. R. Graves, principal leader of the movement, is reflected in the series of resolutions he presented at a mass meeting convened at Cotton Grove, Hardeman County, Tennessee, on June 24, 1851.

Rev. J. R. Graves then proceeded to offer the following queries, which he wished to be considered at this meeting, and referred to some adjourning meeting.

1st. Can Baptists consistently, with their principles or the scriptures, recognize those societies, not organized according to the pattern of the Jerusalem Church, but possessing a *government,* different *officers,* a different *class of membership,* different *ordinances, doctrines* and *practices,* as the Church of Christ?

2d. Ought they to be called Gospel Churches or Churches in a religious sense?

3d. Can we consistently recognize the ministers of such irregular and unscriptural bodies, as gospel ministers in their official capacity?

4th. Is it not virtually recognizing them as official ministers to invite them into our pulpits, or by any other act that would or could be construed into such a recognition?

5th. Can we consistently address as brethren, those *professing* christianity, who not only have not the doctrines of Christ, and walk not according to his commandments, but are arrayed in direct and bitter

opposition to them?

After considerable discussion, which showed an unanimous feeling and sentiment,

On motion and second, the above queries were referred to a subsequent meeting.

(From *Tennessee Baptist,* June 19, 1851.)

Old Landmarkism: What Is It?

The most definitive work of Graves on the nature of this movement is found in this little book by him.

1. Purpose of writing the book

Now the work I have undertaken to accomplish by this "little book" is *threefold:*

1. To establish the fact in the minds of all, who will give me an impartial hearing, that Baptist churches are the churches of Christ, and that they *alone* hold, and have alone ever held, and preserved the doctrine of the gospel in all ages since the ascension of Christ.

2. To establish clearly what are the "Old Landmarks," the characteristic principles and policy, of true Baptists in all these ages.

3. To demonstrate, by invincible argument, that treating the ministers of other denominations as the accredited ministers of the gospel, and receiving any of their official acts—*preaching* or *immersion*—as scriptural, we do proclaim, louder than we can by words, that their societies are evangelical churches, and their teachings and practices orthodox as our own; and that by so doing we do encourage our own families and the world to enter their societies in preference to Baptist churches, because, with them, the offense of "the cross hath ceased."

(From J. R. Graves, *Old Landmarkism: What Is It?* [Memphis, 1880], pp. 25-26.)

2. Landmark beliefs

Landmark Baptists very generally believe that for the Word of the Living God to stand, and for the veracity of Jesus Christ to vindicate itself, the kingdom which he set up "in the days of John the Baptist," has had an unbroken continuity until now. I say kingdom, instead of succession of churches, for the sake of perspicacity. Those who oppose "church succession" confuse the unthinking, by representing our position to be, that the identical organization which Christ established—the First Church of Judea—has had a continued existence until to-day; or, that the identical churches, planted by the apostles, or, at least, *some one* of them, has continued until now, and that Baptist ministers are successors of the apostles; in a word, that our position is the old Romish and Episcopal doctrine of apostolic success. I have, for full a quarter of a century, by pen and voice, vehemently protested against *these* misrepresentations, as Baptists have, for twice as many more, against the charge of teaching that no one can be saved without immersion, and quite as vainly; for those who oppose us seem determined to misrepresent, and will not be corrected. We repudiate the doctrine of apostolic succession; we do not believe *they* ever had a successor, and therefore, no one to-day is preaching under the apostolic commission any more than under that which Christ first gave to John the Baptist. They are our opposers who, in fact, hold to apostolic succession; for the majority do believe that, if ministers, they are preaching by the authority contained in that commission! So much for this charge.

Nor have I, or any Landmarker known to me, ever advocated the succession of any particular church or churches; but my position is that Christ, in the very "days of John the Baptist," did establish a visible kingdom on earth, and that this *kingdom* has never yet been "broken in pieces," or given to another class of subjects—has never for a day "been moved," or ceased from the earth, and never will until Christ returns personally to reign over it; that the organization he first set up, which John called "the Bride," and which Christ called his church, constituted that visible kingdom, and to-day all his *true* churches on earth constitute it; and, therefore, if his *kingdom* has stood unchanged, and will to the end, he must always have had true and uncorrupted churches, since his kingdom can not exist without true churches.

The sense in which any existing Baptist church is the successor of the First Church of Judea—the model and pattern of all—is the same as that existing between any regular Masonic Lodge and the first Lodge that was ever instituted. Ten thousand local Lodges may have existed and passed away, but this fact in nowise affects the continuity of Masonry. From the day it was organized as symbolic Masonry, it has stood; and, though it may have decayed in some places, it has flourished in others, and never has had but *one beginning.* Thus it has been with that institution called the Kingdom of Christ; it has had a continuous existence, or the words of Christ have failed; and, therefore, there has been no need of originating it, *de novo,* and no unbaptized man ever had any authority to originate baptism, or a church, *de novo.* I understand that Christ's declaration (Matt. 16:18), and Paul's statement (Heb. 12:28), are emphatic commentaries upon the prophecy of Daniel (2:44).

We do not admit that it devolves upon us more than upon every other lover of Jesus to prove, by incontestible historical facts, that this kingdom of the Messiah has stood from the day it was set up by him, unbroken and unmoved; to question it, is to doubt his sure word of promise. To deny it, is to impeach his veracity, and leave the world without a Bible or a Christ. We dare not do this. We believe that his kingdom has stood unchanged, as firmly as we believe in the divinity of the Son of God, and, when we are forced to surrender the one faith, we can easily give up the other. If Christ has not kept his promise concerning his *church* to keep it, how can I trust him concerning *my salvation?* If he has not the power to save his *church,* he certainly has not the power to save me. For Christians to admit that Christ has not preserved his kingdom unbroken, unmoved, unchanged, and uncorrupted, is to surrender the whole ground to infidelity. I deny that a man is a believer in the Bible who denies this.

Nor do we admit the claims of the "Liberals" upon us, to prove the continuous existence of the church, of which we are a member, or which baptized us, in order to prove our doctrine of church succession, and that we have been scripturally baptized or ordained. As well might the Infidel call upon me to prove every link of my descent from Adam, before I am allowed to claim an interest in the redemptive work of Christ, which was confined to the family of Adam! We point to the Word of God, and, until the Infidel can destroy *its* authenticity, our hope is unshaken. In like manner, we point the "Liberal" Baptist to the words of Christ, and will he say *they are not sufficient?* When the Infidel can prove, by incontestible historical facts, that *his* kingdom has been broken and removed one year, one day, or one *hour* from the earth, then we surrender our Bible with our position.

(From J. R. Graves, *op. cit.*, pp. 121-125.)

3. Answer to false charges

Landmark Baptists are continually charged by all who oppose their characteristic principles and policy—Baptists who know better, not excepted—with many and grievous offenses, in order to make us obnoxious to our own brethren, and detested by all others. It seems proper, therefore, at this point. to refute all these, by stating, first, what Old Landmarkism is not, before making a summary of what it is. Then—

1. Old Landmarkism is not the denial of spiritual regeneration to those with whom we decline to associate ministerially or ecclesiastically.

. . . .

2. Landmarkism is not the denial of the honesty and conscientiousness of Pedobaptists and Campbellites.

. . . .

3. Landmarkism is not a proof of our uncharitableness.

. . . .

4. Landmarkism is not the denial to others the civil right, or the most perfect liberty to exist as professed churches, or to their ministers to preach their views, as is falsely asserted.

(*Ibid.*, pp. 131-35.)

4. The full-rounded "Old Landmark"

1. As Baptists, we are to stand for the supreme authority of the New Testament as our only and sufficient rule of faith and practice. The New Testament, and that alone, as opposed to all human tradition in matters, both of faith and practice, we must claim as containing *the* distinguishing doctrine of our denomination—a doctrine for which we are called earnestly to contend.

2. As Baptists, we are to stand for the ordinances of Christ *as* he enjoined them upon his followers, the same in *number,* in *mode,* in *order,* and in *symbolic meaning,* unchanged and unchangeable till he come.

3. As Baptists, we are to stand for a spiritual and regenerated church, and that none shall be received into Christ's church, or be welcomed to its ordinances, without confessing a personal faith in Christ, and giving credible evidence of piety.

The motto on our banner is:
CHRIST BEFORE THE CHURCH, BLOOD BEFORE WATER.

4. To protest, and to use all our influence against the recognition, on the part of Baptists, of human societies as scriptural churches, by affiliation, ministerial or ecclesiastical, or any alliance or co-operation that is susceptible of being apparently or logically construed by our members, or theirs, or the world, into a recognition of their ecclesiastical or ministerial equality with Baptist churches.

5. To preserve and perpetuate the doctrine of the divine origin and sanctity of the churches of Christ, and the unbroken continuity of Christ's kingdom, "from the days of John the Baptist until now," according to the express words of Christ.

6. To preserve and perpetuate the *divine, inalienable,* and *sole* prerogatives of a Christian church—1, To preach the gospel of the Son of God; 2, To select and ordain her own officers; 3, To control absolutely her own ordinances.

7. To preserve and perpetuate the

scriptural design of baptism, and its validity and recognition only when scripturally administered by a gospel church.

8. To preserve and perpetuate the true design and symbolism of the Lord's Supper, as a local church ordinance, and for but *one* purpose—the commemoration of the sacrificial death of Christ—and not as a denominational ordinance, or as an act expressive of our Christian or personal fellowship, and much less of *courtesy* toward others.

9. To preserve and perpetuate the doctrine of a divinely called and scripturally qualified and ordained ministry, to proclaim the gospel, and to administer the ordinances, not upon their own responsibility, but for, and under the direction of, local churches alone.

10. To preserve and perpetuate that primitive fealty and faithfulness to the truth, that shunned not to declare the whole counsel of God, and to teach men to observe all things whatsoever Christ commanded to be believed and obeyed.

Not the belief and advocacy of one or two of these principles, as the marks of the divinely patterned church, but the cordial reception and advocacy of all of them, constitute a full "Old Landmark Baptist."

(Ibid., pp. 139-41.)

Challenge to Southern Baptist Convention in 1859

J. R. Graves went to the Southern Baptist Convention of 1859 determined to oust his personal enemy, R. B. C. Howell, from the presidency of the body, and to challenge the "Board" system of foreign missions. Howell was reelected president but immediately resigned as a gesture of peace. The Convention disarmed Graves by offering their aid in transmitting funds for any churches which might wish to carry on a foreign mission program apart from the Foreign Mission Board. This move neutralized the Landmark attack on foreign mission methods until the Gospel Mission

controversy, in which Landmarkers were once more vocal.

REPORT OF THE COMMITTEE OF INQUIRY AS TO THE IMPROVEMENT OF THE SYSTEM OF MISSIONS AND MISSIONARY OPERATIONS.

The committee to whom was referred the resolution of the Convention, directing them to inquire whether any and what improvements can be made upon the present system of missions and missionary operations, have had the same under consideration, and have instructed me to report as follows:

Upon such consideration as your committee have been enabled to bestow upon the subject referred to them, no plan has been suggested, and none occurs to the committee, contemplating a change in our present system of missions or missionary operations not subject to objection. Through the blessing of God upon the past labors of the Convention, such progress has been made in the diffusion of gospel light, as calls for profound gratitude to the Father of Mercies; and, inasmuch as change is undesirable in itself, only as a means of accomplishing some greater good, therefore, we recommend the adoption of the following resolutions:

1. *Resolved,* That in the judgment of this Convention, it is inexpedient to make any change in the existing plans of missionary operation.

2. *Resolved,* That in case any churches, associations, or other bodies entitled to representation in this Convention, should prefer to appoint their own missionaries, and to assume the responsibility of defraying their salaries and entire expenses, that the respective Boards are authorized, under our present organization and fundamental rules, to become the disbursing agents of the bodies so appointing missionaries and appropriating funds, whether such contributions be intended for the civilization or the evangelization of the heathen; provided that such expenses of forwarding

the money, as have to be specially incurred, be borne by the contributors.

All which is fraternally submitted,

W. P. CHILTON, *Chairman.*

(From *Annual* of the Southern Baptist Convention, 1859, pp. 95-96.)

Part Five
Growth of Denominational Consciousness
1865-1917

Section One
Organizational Advance

Collapse of first Sunday School Board

Despite many difficulties, the Sunday School Board established in 1863 achieved a great deal. The postwar financial crisis was principally responsible for the decision of the Convention in 1873 to abolish this Board and assign its work to the Domestic or Home Mission Board.

Report of the Committee on the Future Plans and Prospects of the Sunday School Board.

Resolved, That the Sunday School Board of this Convention be consolidated with the Domestic and Indian Mission Board, with the understanding that the latter Board, if it deems best, employ an Assistant Secretary and make arrangements to secure the continued publication of the "Kind Words," and the stereotyped books of the Sunday School Board, in the interest of the denomination, but without pecuniary liability on the part of this Convention or its Boards for said publication.

Resolved, That the style of the consolidated Boards shall be "The Domestic and Indian Mission, and Sunday School Board of the Southern Baptist Convention."

(From *Annual* of the Southern Baptist Convention, 1873, p. 29.)

Establishment of the present Sunday School Board

1. *Effort to meet Southern publication needs*

I. T. Tichenor, secretary of the Home Mission Board, recognized the possibilities of the Kind Words *series of publications which had been transferred to the Board in 1873.*

(1) *Tichenor's vision of the publication work*

Acting under the instruction and led on by their Secretary the Home Mission Board issued the *Kind Words Series of Sunday School Periodicals* under a five-year contract with printers in Atlanta on a royalty basis. The Series consisted of *Kind Words, The Child's Gem, Kind Words Teacher* (a monthly magazine), and three quarterlies. We shall have more to say of these periodicals further on in our story. They are introduced now simply as a new enterprise in the Convention's life, and the immediate occasion of perhaps the most trying disturbance in the experience of our people. Dr. Tichenor believed in the movement profoundly, even unto conviction, and walked the heights in his vision of what these periodicals were worth for the onward movement of our cause.

I recall an incident concerning him. We had attended a State Mission Board meeting at Selma, Ala., where I was then pastor. Though after midnight we stood at the gate of his friend, Captain Hugh Haralson, with whom he was stopping, and talked for two hours. Rather he talked and I listened. I was sympathetic, but unable to follow his sweep of thought in outlining the future, showing what the Baptists of the South might accomplish, and the imperative need that a people make their own literature.

(From J. M. Frost, *Sunday School Board*

History and Work [Nashville, n.d.], pp. 10-11.)

(2) Authorization of an enlarged publication ministry

In his report to the Convention in 1885, Tichenor urged the messengers to consider the great opportunity involved in providing Sunday School publications in the South. As a result, a committee of the Convention suggested that the Board "mature some plan" for a graded series of publications to reach from the infant classes to the mature ages. Tichenor felt that this was all the authorization he needed to enter into a lease for five years for the printing of a graded series of Kind Words *on a royalty basis.*

Report on "Kind Words."

This cherished paper maintains its character most creditably as a sound, able publication. The Rev. S. Boykin has shown himself eminently qualified to do all that can be done within the scope contemplated by the original establishment of the paper, as throwing a broad influence among the young, instructing them in Bible truth and instilling mission principles into their minds, and leading them to Christ. But on the principle of division of labor, neither brother Boykin nor any other man can supply all the demands of the literature essential to efficient Sunday-school work. The very best writers of our denomination are needed to supply, in adequate measure, what is now needed. If, therefore, we expect to meet these varied demands, we must very materially increase the facilities for producing this literature. Multitudes of our churches are already ordering their publications from Northern and Western publishing houses, not only on account of their cheapness, but because of the ability with which they are prepared, as many of their ablest men are editing these publications. Whether we can, under present circumstances, compete with these houses in these respects, is a question to be determined. On some accounts it may be well to make the experiment. We only speak what we all feel when we say that no one man can supply the demands of this service. We must have something adapted to all stages of mental and moral development—a graded series reaching from our infant classes to mature age.

In view of the early expiration of the contract for the publication of *Kind Words,* we suggest to the Home Board to mature some plan by which these growing demands may be met. With Rev. Samuel Boykin as chief, supported by such talent as can be found in our midst, this paper would meet all the demands of the case, and none of our people would look either North or West for any Sabbath-school literature.

(From *Annual* of the Southern Baptist Convention, 1885, pp. 24-25.)

2. The Sunday-school Committee

As the expiration of the five-year contract for the Kind Words *series approached, a new leader arose to call for an enlarged publication ministry. J. M. Frost, pastor of Richmond, Virginia, introduced a resolution in 1890 at the Convention, proposing the formation of a Board of Publications. However, opposition within the committee considering this resolution led to a compromise—the forming of a standing committee to handle these matters and to make a recommendation in the following year concerning Sunday Schools.*

(1) Authorization of the Sunday-school Committee

The committee, to whom was referred the Resolutions on Board of Publications and other papers relating to *Kind Words* Series, beg leave to submit the following:

Whereas, The Sunday-school work within the bounds of the Southern Baptist Convention is in our judgment of sufficient magnitude and importance to deserve and require specific attention;

Whereas, The contract for publishing the Sunday-school literature of the Convention, now under the management of the Home Mission Board, will expire shortly after the meeting of the next Convention;

Whereas, The Home Mission Board is entrusted with other work sufficient to demand all its strength and energy, therefore be it resolved:

1. That a standing committee of nine be appointed to be known as the Sunday-school Committee of the Southern Baptist Convention.

2. That the location and nomination be hereafter determined. If this is adopted the committee wish to report place and names.

3. That said committee be entrusted with our Sunday-school interests and requested to gather statistical information as to the condition of our Sunday-schools, and to see what can be done toward increasing their number and efficiency, and by annual report to bring the whole Sunday-school work fully before the sessions of the Convention—always in co-operation, however, with existing Sunday-school or Colportage Boards.

4. That the committee be requested to canvass the whole subject of catechetical instruction in its relation to Sunday-schools and make some recommendations concerning it to the Convention in its session of 1891.

5. That said committee be entrusted with the management of our Sunday-school publications, now published in Atlanta as the *Kind Words* Series, and be authorized to do, what, in their judgment, may seem wise, to improve the series and increase its circulation, consistent with the present contract, and to this end the Home Board is instructed to transfer to the committee the said literature and contract under which it is now published.

6. That said committee be empowered to invite sealed bids from publishing houses for the printing of said literature after the expiration of the present contract, and to accept the one which seems best, subject to the ratification of the next Convention. The said contract in no case to entail financial responsibility upon the Convention, nor to extend over three years.

7. That any necessary expense in carrying out the above instructions be paid out of the royalty of $1,000 on account of the literature.

8. That we cordially commend this committee and its work to the churches within our bounds, respectfully asking their sympathy and prayers, and their patronage so far as may accord with their judgment.

(From *Annual* of the Southern Baptist Convention, 1890, pp. 23-24.)

(2) Report of the Sunday-school Committee in 1891

In 1891 at the Birmingham convention, a committee was appointed to study the report of the Sunday-school Committee which had functioned during the previous year, and to bring recommendations. J. M. Frost and J. B. Gambrell were appointed as a subcommittee to prepare the report, Frost favoring a separate Board for Southern publication work and Gambrell opposing it. After a day of conference and prayer, Gambrell agreed to let Frost write the report, provided Gambrell could add one paragraph; Frost agreed, provided Gambrell would allow him to add one last sentence.

REPORT OF THE SUNDAY-SCHOOL COMMITTEE.

Your committee, to whom was referred the report of the Sunday-school Committee, have given it very earnest consideration and beg leave to submit the following:

We desire to express our appreciation of the painstaking and conscientious manner in which they have discharged, with very limited powers, the duties imposed on them by this Convention.

1. From papers presented we find that the *Kind Word's* Series, on the basis of the present circulation can be issued at a cost of less than twenty (20) thousand dollars per annum, while the income is over thirty (30) thousand dollars. We therefore cannot recommend the ratification of the bid which the Sunday-school Committee has

presented with its report and which offers to the Convention one half of the profits. We think a better arrangement can be made as presently will be indicated.

2. We recommend the adoption of this suggestion to create a new Board, to be called the Sunday-school Board of the Southern Baptist Convention, to have a Corresponding Secretary, and to be nominated from year to year as the other two Boards are.

3. That said Board be entrusted with the Convention's Sunday-school series, and be authorized to use their best efforts to improve the series and to increase the circulation, but shall not engage in any other publication work, except as hereinafter provided.

4. That the Board be entrusted with the Sunday-school interests in our territory, and be requested to gather statistical information as to the condition of our Sunday-schools, to see what can be done toward increasing their number and efficiency, and by annual report to bring the whole Sunday-school work fully before the sessions of the Convention.

5. Thinking it best to discontinue the leasing system, so as to eliminate all personal interests from the business, we recommend that the Board be instructed to make the best arrangement possible for having the series brought out at the lowest cost under a printing contract.

6. That the Board continue the work begun by the Sunday-school Committee of making a list of such books as may be wisely recommended to the Sunday-schools.

7. We recommend that the Board carry out the following arrangement, as suggested by the Sunday-school Committee along with its report:

As to the matter of catechetical instruction referred to the committee, we found that Dr. John A. Broadus had been applied to by the American Baptist Publication Society to prepare such catechisms as were proposed, viz.: Advanced, Intermediate and Primary. He declined to do so unless the work could be done for the Society and for the committee jointly. Conferring with him and with the Society, it was agreed to suggest to the Convention that Dr. Broadus be employed to prepare an Intermediate catechism first, for the sum of $500, to be paid jointly by the committee and the Society, $250 each, the copyright belonging to both, and each to publish at a uniform price; and each, in publishing, should place its own imprint first.

It is further proposed that Dr. Broadus prepare the Primary catechism for $200 when called for, upon and under the same conditions. It was deemed best to make no arrangement for the Advanced catechism for the present.

8. The Board in its work will aid mission Sunday-schools by contributions of literature and money; doing this, however, through State organizations, and using for this purpose the net proceeds of the business, together with all contributions therefor, provided that, while the Secretary may, when necessary, raise funds for the promotion of the Sunday-school interests committed to the Board, no system of State or sub-agencies shall be organized.

9. That the Board be located at Nashville, Tennessee, and to be composed of fifteen brethren as named by the Committee on Nominations.

10. That the selection of a Corresponding Secretary be left to the Board.

11. That the Sunday-school Committee be instructed to perfect the necessary arrangement for the issue of the third quarter's series of the Sunday-school literature, and after making such arrangement, the committee be authorized to close its affairs by handing over to the Board, as provided for above, all its assets, books, papers, etc.

In conclusion your committee, in its long and earnest consideration of this whole matter in all its environments, have been compelled to take account of the well known fact, that there are widely divergent views held among us by brethren equally earnest, consecrated and devoted to the best interest of the Master's Kingdom. It is therefore, recommended that the fullest freedom of choice be accorded to every one as to what literature he will use or support, and that no brother be disparaged in the slightest degree on account of what he may do in the exercise of his right as Christ's freeman. But we would earnestly urge all brethren to give to this Board a fair consideration, and in no case to obstruct it in the great work assigned it by this Convention.

Signed by the Committee.

(From *Annual* of the Southern Baptist Convention, 1891, pp. 22-23.)

Woman's Missionary Union

1. Resolution to appoint official delegates from states

Baptist women of the South were organized into local societies for missions shortly after the turn of the nineteenth century. State organizations began to develop in the 1860s and 1870s. In 1887 a resolution was passed in a convention-wide meeting that looked to securing official representation from the various state organizations for the purpose of considering the formation of a convention-wide body.

In Louisville, Ky., May 1887, was held the 4th Annual Meeting of Woman's Missionary Societies, connected with the churches of the Southern Baptist Convention.

It was not a body composed of delegates with authority to act for others. Learning from experience, the transient effect of such a gathering, and from history, the permanent benefit of an organization whose elected officers should continue the work during the interim of the meetings, a series of resolutions was passed, as follows:

"Whereas, the Baptist ladies assembled at Louisville, in connection and sympathy with the Southern Baptist Convention, are deeply impressed with the importance of thorough and efficient organization among the ladies of the South, to aid in the support of missions now conducted by Southern

Baptists; therefore,

"1. *Resolved,* That a committee be appointed to request Central Committees of the several States, each to appoint three lady delegates, to meet during the next session of the Southern Baptist Convention, to decide upon the advisability of organizing a general committee; and if advisable, to provide for the appointment, location and duties thereof.

"2. *Resolved,* That the above is not to be construed as a desire, upon the part of the ladies, to interfere with the management of the existing Boards of the Convention, either in the appointment of missionaries, or the direction of mission work; but is a desire, on their part, to be more efficient in collecting money and disseminating information on mission subjects.

"3. *Resolved,* That in order to provide for our next meeting, a committe, composed of the Secretaries of Central Committees of the various States, be appointed to confer with the Central Committees of the State in which the Convention shall be held (Virginia,) to select a presiding officer and secretary, and to arrange a programme."

A copy of the resolutions was forwarded to Secretaries of State Central Committees, requesting a delegation of three from each State "to decide upon the advisability of organizing a general committee; and, if found advisable, to provide for the appointment, location and duties thereof."

At Richmond, May, 1888, the Woman's Meeting was convened, composed on roll call of 32 delegates from 12 States; West Virginia, North Carolina and Alabama unrepresented by delegates. In accordance with the resolutions, the delegates came prepared to vote by instructions from their States. Ten States most cordially endorsed the movement as an advance upon other methods, and as an aid to progress in mission work. Two States, Virginia and Mississippi, while expressing a deep interest in Woman's Work, preferred to delay action in reference to the general organization till further instructed by their States.

(From *Sketch and Constitution of the*

Woman's Missionary Societies, [Auxiliary to S.B.C.], May, 1887, to May, 1888, pp. 3-4.)

2. *Preamble and Constitution of Woman's Missionary Union*

In 1888, by the vote of delegates from ten states, the Woman's Missionary Union, Auxiliary to the Southern Baptist Convention, was formed and a constitution adopted.

CONSTITUTION.

PREAMBLE.

We, the Women of the churches connected with the Southern Baptist Convention, desirous of stimulating the missionary spirit and the grace of giving, among the women and children of the churches, and aiding in collecting funds for missionary purposes, to be disbursed by the Boards of the Southern Baptist Convention, and disclaiming all intention of independent action, organize and adopt the following:

CONSTITUTION.

ARTICLE 1.—*Name.*

This organization shall be known as the Executive Committee of the Woman's Mission Societies—(auxiliary to the Southern Baptist Convention).

ARTICLE II.—*Object.*

The two-fold object of this Executive Committee shall be:

1st. To distribute missionary information and stimulate effort, through the State Central Committees, where they exist; and where they do not, to encourage the organization of new societies.

2nd. To secure the earnest systematic co-operation of women and children in collecting and raising money for missions.

ARTICLE III.—*Officers.*

The officers shall be a President, a Vice-President from each State, a Corresponding Secretary, a Recording Secretary, and a Treasurer, with a local committee of nine managers, who shall reside in or not remote from the place appointed at the annual meeting. These shall constitute the Executive Committee, five of whom shall be a quorum for the transaction of business.

ARTICLE IV.—*Annual Meeting.*

The annual meeting for the election of officers and transaction of business shall be held each year at such time and place as may be determined at previous annual meeting or by the Executive Committee.

ARTICLE V.—
Representation at the Annual Meeting.

The officers of the committee and three delegates from each State shall be entitled to vote. Only such delegates as are personally present and duly accredited by the Central Committee or State societies they represent shall be entitled to vote.

ARTICLE VI.—*Conduct of Meetings.*

Every session of the Executive Committee shall be opened and closed with religious exercises.

ARTICLE VII.—*Amendments.*

The Constitution may be altered or amended by a two-thirds majority vote, at any annual meeting, three months previous notice having been sent through the State secretary to the Executive Committee. The corresponding secretary shall notify each vice-president of proposed amendment.

(From *Sketch and Constitution of the Woman's Missionary Societies* [Auxiliary to S.B.C.], from May, 1887, to May, 1888, pp. 5-6.)

Baptist World Alliance

In 1904, J. N. Prestridge introduced a resolution at the Southern Baptist Convention calling for a committee to cooperate with other Baptist bodies in a plan for a "Pan-Baptist Conference."

1. *Antecedents to the first gathering*

The desire for a world gathering of Baptists has been expressed by several influential men within the last five years, but it was left to Dr. J. N. Prestridge of Louisville, Kentucky, to give the necessary driving force to the suggestion. In an editorial in his paper, *The Baptist Argus,* two years ago, he pleaded for a meeting of the leading officers of the various Baptist Unions with a view to a Congress. Later, he appealed to Dr. Clifford and myself [J. H. Shakespeare]. We favoured the holding of the Congress itself at an early date. Dr. Prestridge obtained opinions from Baptists in different parts of the world, published them in his paper, and when it was found that the project would meet with universal acceptance, a resolution of invitation was adopted by the Baptist Union, assembled at Bristol, October, 1904, for the Congress to be held in London in July, 1905. A strong Baptist Union Committee was elected, representatives were added from the Committee of the Baptist Missionary Society, and the work of preparation began. Special Committees were formed to deal with the different sections of this great undertaking.

(From *Baptist World Alliance*, First Congress [London, 1905], p. v.)

2. *Constitution of the Baptist World Alliance*

CONSTITUTION OF THE BAPTIST WORLD ALLIANCE.

Preamble.

Whereas, in the providence of God, the time has come when it seems fitting more fully to manifest the essential oneness in the Lord Jesus Christ, as their God and Saviour, of the churches of the Baptist order and faith throughout the world, and to promote the spirit of fellowship, service, and co-operation among them, while recognizing the independence of each particular church and not assuming the functions of any existing organization, it is agreed to form a Baptist Alliance, extending over every part of the world.

Articles.

I. *Designation.*—This Alliance shall be known as "The Baptist World Alliance."

II. *Membership.*—Any general Union, Convention, or Association of Baptist churches shall be eligible for membership in the Alliance.

III. *Officers.*—The officers of the Alliance shall be: A President, a Vice-President from each country represented in the Alliance, a Treasurer, a British Secretary, and an American Secretary.

IV. *The Executive Committee.*—The Executive Committee shall consist of the President, Treasurer, Secretaries, and twenty-one other members, all of whom, together with the officers, shall be elected at each General Meeting of the Alliance and enter upon office at the close of such meeting. Of the twenty-one elected members:—

Five shall be from Great Britain, seven shall be from the United States of America, two shall be from Canada, and the remaining seven shall be from the rest of the world.

Five members shall constitute a quorum for a meeting of the Executive, but absent members shall have the right of voting by proxy, through any other member of the Executive who shall produce a written authorisation. A majority of those voting in person or by proxy shall be sufficient for the transaction of business. Three months' notice shall be given to every member of the Executive of all business to be brought before the next meeting, which is other than routine business. The President shall appoint at a general meeting of the Alliance a Committee of nine members to submit the names of the officers and of the Executive Committee for the approval of the General Meeting.

V. *Advisory Committee.*—At a date not later than one year preceding a General Meeting of the Alliance, the Executive Committee shall have authority to appoint an Advisory Committee of not more than three hundred members of the Alliance, to confer with the Executive Committee on any matter pertaining to the objects of the Alliance. The Executive shall, however, have power to appoint an Advisory Committee not exceeding three hundred members at such other times as it may consider necessary.

VI. *Powers of the Executive.*—The Executive Committee shall have the power of filling vacancies which may occur among the officers and the Executive when the

Assembly is not in Session. It shall be the first business of the Executive Committee, after its appointment, and the forming of this Alliance, to frame the by-laws for the administration of business.

VII. *General Meeting.*—The Alliance shall meet in general assembly ordinarily once in five years, unless otherwise determined by the Executive Committee, the specific date and place to be determined by the Executive Committee, which shall have power to make all necessary arrangements therefor.

VIII. *Representation for General Meeting.*—Each constituent body of the Alliance may appoint messengers to the General Meeting from its own resident members on a basis to be determined by the Executive Committee.

Amendment.—No change shall be made in this Constitution except by a two-thirds majority at a General Meeting of the Alliance after at least two days' notice of the proposed action, such vote not to be taken on the last day of the meeting.

Amendments to the Constitution
Made at Philadelphia.

All articles not here reproduced [marked by italics] remain unchanged:

2. Membership: Any General Union, Convention, or Association of Baptist churches, *or Conference of Native churches and missionaries or general Foreign Missionary Society,* shall be eligible for membership in the Alliance.

3. Officers: The officers of the Alliance shall be: A President, *a Deputy President,* a Vice-President from each country represented in the Alliance, a *European Treasurer, an American Treasurer,* a European Secretary, and an American Secretary. *The European Secretary shall deal with everything outside of America.*

4. The Executive Committee: The Executive Committee shall consist of the President, *the Deputy President,* the Treasurer, the Secretaries, and twenty-*two* other members, all of whom, together with the officers, shall be elected at each general meeting of the Alliance, and enter on office at the

close of each meeting. *The Deputy President shall be appointed by the President on the nomination of the Executive Committee, and shall be chosen from the hemisphere in which the President does not reside.* Of the twenty-*two* elected members, five shall be from Great Britain, seven shall be from the United States of America, two shall be from Canada, and the remaining eight shall be from the rest of the world.

Meetings of the Executive shall be summoned by both Secretaries. Five members shall constitute a quorum, etc. (For last sentence substitute.) *At the meeting of the Alliance, it shall be the first business of the Executive to select a committee for the nomination of officers, which committee shall be appointed by the President in open meeting.*

By-Laws.

2 (a) That the Program for each World Alliance shall be printed at least two years in advance, on the initiative of the *Secretary for the hemisphere in which the Congress is being held* in consultation with the members of the Baptist World Alliance Executive resident in the *same hemisphere.*

4. (Substitute *hemisphere* for country)

8. That the clerical *and other* expenses incurred by each Union or Convention in the transaction of Alliance business shall be borne by itself.

(From *Record of Proceedings,* The Baptist World Alliance [Philadelphia, 1911], pp. xiii-xiv.)

Negro seminary

In 1913 a committee was appointed to consider the establishment of a Negro theological school. The report in 1914 was adopted but a delay was caused by division in the Negro convention. Additional developments took place in the next period.

1. Southern Baptist Convention action

Your Committee begs leave to report that, in accordance with the instructions of the Convention, a joint meeting was held with the Committee of the National Baptist Convention of Negroes and full discussion of the proposed Theological Seminary was had.

We are rejoiced to report that we found a most fraternal spirit on the part of our negro brethren, and they very gladly welcomed an offer of coöperation on the part of the Convention in the establishment of a Negro Theological Seminary. The joint conference adopted unanimously the following as an expression of the views of those present regarding the establishment of the Theological Seminary:

"Whereas, The National Baptist Convention has decided to establish a general seminary for the training of the negro preachers of the gospel; and,

"Whereas, the Southern Baptist Convention has expressed its sympathy with the movement, and has shown its interest by the appointment of a Committee of Conference, to meet a like Committee from the National Baptist Convention;

"Therefore, be it resolved by the Joint Committee in session, that we recommend:

"1. That it is exceedingly desirable and expedient that such a seminary be established.

"2. That the institution be under the government of and be controlled by the National Baptist Convention.

"3. That the National Baptist Convention invite and welcome the practical and financial coöperation of other organizations of Baptists who may indicate a desire to share in this important work.

"4. We strongly recommend that the government and control of the seminary be retained by the National Baptist Convention, whatever assistance may be rendered by other Baptist organizations.

LOCATION.

"Then the question of location was taken up for consideration. The following was adopted as the unanimous sentiment of the Joint Committee:

"Resolved, that the question of the location of the seminary be for the present deferred, but that we express the conviction that it should be located in one of the following cities: Memphis, Tenn.; Nashville, Tenn.; Birmingham, Ala.; Atlanta, Ga., or Louisville, Ky., provided proper inducements are offered for its location.

"Resolved, further, that the matter of the location be brought to the notice of the proper authorities in these cities by the Corresponding Secretary of the Educational Board of the National Baptist Convention, with a view to ascertaining what inducements, financial and otherwise, they may be ready to offer.

"Resolved further, that the seminary be located where it will do the greatest good to the greatest number.

FINANCIAL ASSISTANCE.

"Upon motion it was decided to recommend that the Southern Baptist Convention be requested to raise fifty thousand dollars ($50,000) toward the establishment of said seminary, provided that the National Baptist Convention supply the necessary grounds and additional equipment to warrant the expectation of a successful school, adapted to the ends in view.

"This is not to be so construed as to mean that the S. B. C. will not render further additional aid. But it is distinctly understood that should the school ever cease to perform the services herein contemplated, the amount of money that has been supplied by the Southern Baptist Convention, whatever that amount may be, shall be returned by the National Baptist Convention to the Southern Baptist Convention."

In accordance with the above, your Committee recommend that the matter of finding a location for the proposed school be referred back to a Committee from this Convention and a Committee from the Negro Baptist Convention.

We also recommend that the matter of devising a plan for raising the above sum of money be referred to a Committee of this Convention, with the authority to work out all details necessary in the employment of an agent or agents for raising the money and of payment of their salaries out of funds raised for the purpose. Your Committee wishes to express the judgment that there should be one or more white men on the faculty of the proposed seminary.

The suggestion has been made that a Committee be appointed by the Southern Baptist Convention to consider in general the status of the negro industrially, economically and religiously in the South, and that such information be secured and reported to the Convention on this subject as may tend to promote a better understanding between the white and colored races and which may tend to the welfare of the negro race.

(From *Annual* of the Southern Baptist Convention, 1914, pp. 25-26.)

2. *National Baptist Convention resolution*

The preamble and resolution adopted by the National Baptist Convention at Nashville, Tenn., September, 1913, relative to the founding of a National Baptist Theological Seminary:

"Whereas, The Southern Baptist Convention, in its recent session at St. Louis, Mo., passed resolutions, offered by Dr. E. Y. Mullins, President of the Southern Baptist Theological Seminary at Louisville, Ky., proposing to coöperate with the National Baptist Convention in the founding and operation of a general Theological Seminary for the education of the negro ministers; and, whereas, they appointed a Committee of nine of their number to confer with a like number from our body

"Therefore, be it resolved, that we most cordially and thankfully receive this proffered hand and enter upon the suggested coöperation with faith in our white brethren, and thanks to God for the coming of this timely help.

"Be it resolved, that the President of this Convention be sent to the coming session of the Southern Baptist Convention to more fully convey our thanks."

(*Ibid.*)

Relations with Home Missions Council

In 1909 the Home Mission Board asked the Convention's advice about affiliating with the new interdenominational Home Missions Council composed of representatives from the various home missions organizations in the United States. This document is the reply of the Convention. The Home Mission Board did not choose to align themselves with the body since they felt themselves to be unique as a denomination, and since they would not have wished their liberty to be circumscribed.

Our Home Mission Board having appealed to this Convention to define the relation which it shall bear to the Home Missions Council located in New York City, and representing many of the Christian denominations of this country, respectfully recommend that this Convention shall make the following deliverance for the guidance of the Board:

1. That we rejoice heartily in the courtesy and fraternity which has always marked the relations between our Board with kindred organizations in the past, and most sincerely desire that this spirit of neighborship and kindliness shall always continue.

2. We desire also that our Board shall have ample liberty for conference and for such concert of action with other Home Mission Boards, so far as it may deem proper for the maintenance of kindly relations and good understanding as to the vast and unspeakably important work of Home evangelization.

3. We feel it to be of the utmost importance, however, to remind our Board that the people who make the Convention, hold doctrines set forth in the Scriptures, which are held only in part or not at all by many of our brethren of other denominations, who are engaged in Home Mission work. These doctrines we hold only as we find them in the Scriptures, and they constitute, very largely, the reason for our denominational existence, and we can not look with approval upon any alliances on the part of our Board that could possibly imperil these doctrines.

4. We deem it necessary to say further

to our Board, that we cannot justify its entrance into any relations with other Boards which can possibly circumscribe our independence or liberty as to the fields which we are to occupy, or the methods which we are to adopt in carrying forward the work which we feel that the Lord has committed to us. Our churches, which make up this body, are independent of each other so far as their internal government is concerned, and therefore, cannot be lined up in any sort of federation that can subject them to any external authority, or commit them to any special line of policy.

5. It is to us a matter of honest regret that our honored brethren of other denominations seem unable to get our own point of view as to our attitude and spirit as a denomination. We do not mention this in any mood of critical or censorious complaint against any, for we love all, but we deem it essential to say to our Board that we can do none other than to maintain our position in such a manner as will leave to us the broadest freedom in proclaiming our distinctive doctrines and establishing churches of our faith wherever we can. We feel that it is our duty to lead the people, so far as possible, in accepting Christ, to adopt those doctrines which we believe to be of the gravest importance, though often overlooked by many brethren whom we love and honor. We believe in charity, but we believe the highest type of charity is that which sweetly, graciously and courageously seeks to present to the people the whole counsel of God.

6. We do, therefore, with the utmost earnestness and yet with the most cordial goodwill and brotherly kindness to all, say to our Home Mission Board that we deem it inadvisable to form any relations with the Home Missions Council which can in any way abridge its freedom, warp its policy or embarrass its action in the future.

The report was discussed by the Chairman of the Committee, and it was adopted by a rising vote.

(From *Annual* of the Southern Baptist Convention, 1909, pp. 27-28.)

Section Two

Securing the Home Field

Between 1865 and 1917 the Southern Baptist Convention won its own field in the areas of home missions and publications. Several adversaries vigorously competed with the Convention in an effort to meet the needs of the South.

Home missions

One of the adversaries of the Convention in the South during this period was the American Baptist Home Mission Society of New York. This Society had carried on work in the South during the united period (1832-1845). Their missionaries had never withdrawn entirely, and during the Civil War an extensive program was developed to meet the needs of Negroes and whites. By 1894 this Society operated 32 schools in the South for Negroes and Indians, employing 177 teachers with 5,357 pupils. It also employed 112 missionaries in 18 southern states by 1894, working with all races, and assisted many southern white, Negro, and Indian churches in erecting edifices for worship. It had asserted a policy of cultivating the entire southern field as its own.

1. The beginning of Northern-Southern Baptist tension

The controversy erupted in 1867. The Society had already sent a number of missionaries into the South, and in that year the Southern Baptist Convention stated its official position relative to the work of the Society in the South.

Your Committee to whom was referred the religious instruction of the colored population, beg leave to submit the following resolutions:

Resolved, That this body cherishes a deep and lively interest in the moral and religious improvement of the colored people of the land.

Resolved, That our ministers and

Churches should more than ever realize the great importance of active, constant and vigorous effort for the evangelization and enlightenment of this class of our population; that they should continue as heretofore to preach to them on all suitable occasions, and endeavor to establish and maintain Sunday Schools, encourage day schools among them, and by every practical means seek to promote their temporal and eternal happiness.

Resolved, That the Domestic Mission Board of this Convention be directed, as opportunity may offer, to encourage and establish Missions for their special benefit.

Resolved, That this Convention having learned, though informally and unofficially, that the American Baptist Home Mission Society is desirous of laboring in the religious instruction of this class of our population, the Domestic Mission Board be directed to make known to that Society our willingness to cooperate in this work, by appropriations made to the Boards of this Convention.

(From *Annual* of the Southern Baptist Convention, 1867, p. 79.)

2. *The controversy of 1879*

The resources and zeal of the Society, contrasted with the postwar poverty and hardships of the South, almost destroyed the Home Mission Board. With receipts dwindling year by year and future prospects poor, there was talk of abolishing the Board. In 1879 a resolution was introduced by I. T. Tichenor which some persons wrongly thought was designed to dissolve the Convention.

(1) *Resolution of Tichenor in 1879*

Whereas, the time has come when all who believe in Jesus should work mightily for the deliverance of the nation from the bondage of sin; when the voice of Divine Providence calls us to greater sacrifices and nobler efforts to secure the triumphant coming of His kingdom; and,

Whereas, the cordial co-operation of the Baptists of the United States would tend greatly to promote their efficiency in this grand work; and,

Whereas, the love of Jesus and the wants of dying men demand that, allowing "the dead past to bury its dead," we, leaving the things which are behind, should press forward to deliver the kindreds of the earth from ignorance and vice, and bring them into the liberty wherewith Christ is able to set them free: therefore,

Resolved, That five brethren be appointed by this Convention to bear to our Baptist brethren of the Northern States, at their approaching anniversaries, expressions of our fraternal regard and assurances of our readiness to co-operate cordially with them in promoting the cause of Christ in our own and all foreign lands.

Resolved, That we respectfully suggest to them the propriety of holding, at some convenient time and place, a meeting of representative men from all sections of our common country, to devise and propose such plans of co-operation between this Convention and other Baptist bodies of the United States as may best contribute to the more efficient working of the Baptist brotherhood, to the good of all men, and to the glory of our Redeemer.

(From *Annual* of the Southern Baptist Convention, 1879, p. 14.)

(2) *A substitute resolution adopted*

The Tichenor resolution brought immediate controversy at the Convention. After long and exhausting debate, the Convention adopted a substitute introduced by John A. Broadus.

The Committee, to whom were referred the resolutions on co-operation with our Northern brethren, have had the same under consideration, and instruct me to report the following resolution:

Resolved, That five brethren be appointed by this Convention to bear to our Baptist brethren of the Northern States, at their approaching anniversaries, expressions of our fraternal regard, and assurances that, while firmly holding to the wisdom and policy of preserving our separate organizations, we are ready, as in the past, to co-operate cordially with them in promoting the cause of Christ in our own and foreign lands.

(*Ibid.*, p. 26.)

(3) Tichenor's explanation of his resolution

When W. H. Whitsitt delivered the historical address in 1895, he interpreted Tichenor's resolution as a move to dissolve the convention. Tichenor rose to a point of order and explained what he had had in mind.

70. I. T. Tichenor, Georgia, as a matter of privilege, introduced the following paper, which was ordered to be printed in the proceedings:

We, the undersigned members of the committee to whom was referred the resolutions at Atlanta, in 1879, in reference to co-operation with our Northern brethren, desire to put on record this simple statement: The very able historical address of our honored brother, Dr. W. H. Whitsitt (usually so accurate in any statement he makes), is at fault in representing those resolutions, or the report on them, as in any way designed or tending to the dissolution of our Convention.

On the contrary, they were intended to strengthen the Convention by fixing definitely its territorial limits, and securing the co-operation of our Northern brethren in certain lines of work.

It was, in purpose, the same proposition as that adopted by the Convention last year, and which resulted in the "Fortress Monroe Conference," and plans that have grown out of it.

I. T. TICHENOR,
J. WM. JONES,
GEO. A. LOFTON,
J. H. KILPATRICK.

(From *Annual* of the Southern Baptist Convention, 1895, p. 41.)

3. The removal of the Home Mission Board to Atlanta, Georgia

In 1882, because of a continuing decrease in receipts of the Board, the Convention moved it to Atlanta, Georgia. A new secretary, I. T. Tichenor, was secured.

Condition of the Home Board.

Your Committtee to whom was referred the consideration of the present condition, prospects and enlargement of the Home Mission work of this Convention, beg leave to report that we find a want of enthusiasm on the part of the denomination in the work of this Board, and since from the experience of a series of years, it seems impossible to arouse this enthusiasm without making material changes, your Committee feel constrained, as on the whole promising the best results, to recommend the following resolutions, viz;

1st. That the Home Mission Board be removed from Marion, Alabama, to Atlanta, Georgia, as soon after the adjournment of this Convention as such transfer can be made.

2nd. That the Board be instructed to employ a Corresponding Secretary, and in addition thereto, one or more district Secretaries, if found best for the efficient prosecution of its work.

3d. That the Committee on Nomination of new Boards be instructed to render their report in accordance with the foregoing resolutions.

Your Committee desire, in presenting the above recommendations, to state distinctly and emphatically, that in all their inquiries, they have heard no word of complaint against any of the brethren composing the present Board, but, on the contrary, only words of commendation and praise for their faithful attention to the work committed to their trust, and they cannot close this report without recommending the adoption of the following resolution, viz:

"That the earnest and sincere thanks of this Convention be and are hereby tendered to the Home Mission Board, at Marion, Alabama, and to its Corresponding Secretary, and to each member thereof, for long and faithful services rendered so willingly and gratuitously."

(From *Annual* of the Southern Baptist Convention, 1882, p. 29.)

4. The remarkable victory of the Board in securing its field

Tichenor worked effectively for a decade to win the southern field to the support of the Board. His summary in 1892 is quite significant.

Ten years ago the Convention then in session at Greensville, S. C., resolved to remove the Board from Marion, Ala., to Atlanta. The condition of the Board at that time excited the gravest apprehensions. Its total receipts for the year were about $28,000. It had but forty missionaries. Except those in the Indian Territory it had few west of the Mississippi river. The Baptist Convention in Arkansas was in cooperation with the Home Mission Society of New York. Nothing had been attempted in Missouri for years, and that State seemed lost to the Board forever. Texas was divided into five missionary organizations, four of which were receiving aid from the Home Mission Society, and the fifth was paralyzed by its own dissensions. Thus the entire terrtiory west of the Mississippi river had passed out of the hands of the Board.

East of the river, Mississippi was in alliance with the Publication Society, Georgia was co-operating with the Society in New York in work among the negroes, while Florida was hesitating between remaining with the Board, or forming alliance with the same Society. The State Boards had grown vigorously, and from several of the States the Home Mission Board was excluded by action of their State Conventions. It is not to be wondered that the Convention at Greenville pondered the question whether removal or abandonment was the wiser policy. When it was decided to remove it to Atlanta, and the present Board was put in charge of its affairs, the outlook was by no means assuring. A survey of the field indicated a great defeat and a lost cause.

Impressed with the conviction that the existence of this Convention depended upon the resuscitation of its fortunes, the new Board threw itself into the arduous work before it with the determination to use every proper effort to reclaim its lost territory, and make itself a support to the Convention. This could not be done without money, and our impoverished and disheartened people could not be expected to give a speedy or a liberal response to its demands. But such were the earnestness of its efforts and the happy results of its policy, that in five years there was not a missionary to the white people of the South who did not bear a commission from either the Home Mission Board of the Southern Baptist Convention, or one of our State Boards in alliance with it. Its territory had been reclaimed.

(From *Annual* of the Southern Baptist Convention, 1892, pp. x-xi.)

5. Comity agreements regarding the home field

Between 1894 and 1912 Northern and Southern Baptists had three principal conferences relative to problems of the home field.

(1) The Fortress Monroe Conference

On September 12, 1894, at the request of the Southern Baptist Convention, a conference between leaders of the Northern Baptist Societies and the Southern Convention was held at Fortress Monroe, Virginia. In an atmosphere of friendly, courteous discussion, the following document was prepared. Subsequently, all three items were approved by both Conventions.

Your Committee, appointed at the last annual meeting of the Society, met in New York City, at the Home Mission Rooms, July 12, 1894, and organized, by the election of James L. Howard, Chairman, and Nathan E. Wood, Secretary. It was found that the Executive Board had thought it wise to enlarge the committee, by adding four new names. This enlarged committee met with the committee appointed by the Southern Baptist Convention at Fortress

Monroe, Virginia, September 12, 1894. The sessions were held through parts of two days. There were present from the Southern Baptist Convention, T. T. Eaton, H. H. Harris, I. T. Tichenor, J. B. Gambrell, T. P. Bell, Noah K. Davis, O. F. Gregory. There were present from your committee, James L. Howard, T. J. Morgan, H. L. Morehouse, J. B. Thomas, E. H. Johnson, A. S. Hobart, Nathan E. Wood, and, by invitation, M. MacVicar. The Joint Committee chose James L. Howard, Chairman, and O. F. Gregory and Nathan E. Wood, Secretaries.

The spirit of God was manifest in the meeting from the beginning. A most earnest desire for concord was exhibited by every member. The discussions were full, frank, and always brotherly. All the matters entrusted to us by the Society were carefully considered, and we are profoundly grateful to God to report to you that an agreement was reached on all the questions at issue, with entire and hearty unanimity. Never was meeting held by men of equally pronounced convictions, from North and South, where there was profounder exhibition of the fact that "we are brethren in Christ Jesus." The Joint Committee, as the result of its deliberations, unanimously adopted the following:

UNANIMOUS ACTION OF THE JOINT COMMITTEE.

I. *As to Schools among the Colored People.* 1. That the Home Board of the Southern Baptist Convention appoint a local Advisory Committee at each point where a school controlled by the American Baptist Home Mission Society is, or shall be located, and that this committee shall exercise such authority as shall be conferred upon it, from time to time, by the American Baptist Home Mission Society. 2. That the control of the schools shall remain in the hands of the American Baptist Home Mission Society, but these local Advisory Committees shall recommend to the American Baptist Home Mission Society any changes in the conduct or in the teaching force of these schools, including the filling of vacancies, with the reasons for

their recommendations. 3. That the Southern Baptist Convention, through its Home Mission Board, shall appeal to Baptists of the South for moral and financial support of these schools, and that these local committees shall encourage promising young colored people to attend these institutions. 4. That the Joint Committee recommend to the respective bodies appointing them the adoption of the foregoing section as unanimously expressing their views as to the work in the schools among the colored people.

II. *As to Mission Work among the Colored People.* It is unanimously voted by the Joint Committee to recommend to our respective bodies that the American Baptist Home Mission Society and the Home Mission Board of the Southern Baptist Convention co-operate in the mission work among the colored people of the South, in connection with the Baptist State bodies, white and colored, in the joint appointment of general missionaries, in holding Ministers' and Deacons' Institutes, and in the better organization of the missionary work of the colored Baptists. The details of the plan are to be left to be agreed upon by the bodies above named.

III. *As to Territorial Limits.* I. The committee of the American Baptist Home Mission Society not being instructed to consider any subject except co-operation in labor for the colored race, respectfully refers to the Board of the American Baptist Home Mission Society the proposition of the Committee of the Southern Baptist Convention on the subject of Territorial Limits, and ask for its favorable consideration. The following is the text of the proposition referred to: "We believe that, for the promotion of fraternal feeling and of the best interests of the Redeemer's kingdom, it is inexpedient for two different organizations of Baptists to solicit contributions, or to establish missions in the same localities, and for this reason we recommend to the Home Mission Board of the Southern Baptist Convention and to the American Baptist Home Mission Society, that in the prosecution of their work already begun on contiguous fields, or on the same field, that all antagonisms be avoided, and that their officers and employees be instructed to co-operate in all practical ways in the spirit of Christ. That we further recommend to these bodies and their agents, in opening new work, to direct their efforts to localities not already occupied by the other."

We are also glad to report the hearty concurrence of the Southern Baptist Convention in the agreements reached by the Joint Committee, and the equally hearty adoption of them by the Executive Board of New York. We are able, at last, to say that the day of unity, peace, and loving co-operation for Northern and Southern Baptists in the varied service of the kingdom of our Divine Lord has come. Your Committee was greatly impressed with the manifest guiding of the spirit of God during their deliberations and in the conclusions reached.

They desire to place on record their devout thanksgiving to the glorified Lord and Head of the Church.

(Signed)
JESSSE B. THOMAS,
NATHAN E. WOOD,
E. H. JOHNSON,
ALVAH S. HOBART,
      JAMES L. HOWARD,
      HENRY K. PORTER,
      HENRY L. MOREHOUSE,
      LEVI K. FULLER,
      T. J. MORGAN.

(From *Home Mission Monthly* [American Baptist Home Mission Society], July, 1895.)

(2) The Washington Conference

A disagreement over work in New Mexico led to a second conference between Northern and Southern Baptists at Washington, D. C., on April 15, 1909. The following document was adopted. However, because the Southern Convention adopted an amendment to the effect that nothing in this agreement would limit any Baptist

church, association, or other body in its freedom, the Society was unwilling to confirm the action of its committee.

The Washington Conference.

For several years our Board has been importuned to help churches in New Mexico. We have not done so chiefly because of our limited financial ability. These calls for help have during the past two years been more frequent and urgent than ever before. In view of the rapidly increasing wealth of our Southern people and of a growing conviction that the territory west of the Mississippi river is not equally divided between Northern and Southern Baptists, your Board has been favorably disposed toward entering New Mexico. On learning this the American Baptist Home Mission Society through their Corresponding Secretary, Dr. H. L. Morehouse, protested against our entering that territory, claiming that it was pre-empted by them, and invoked the Fortress Monroe Conference of 1894 in support of their protest. Whereupon the Home Mission Board asked for a Conference between representatives of our Board and the Home Mission Society touching the matter in question. The request for a Conference was acceded to by the Home Mission Society and the Conference was held in a lecture room of the Calvary Baptist church, Washington, D. C., April 15, 1909. Representing the Home Mission Society were Rev. A. S. Hobart, Rev. H. L. Morehouse, Rev. L. C. Barnes, Rev. T. J. Villers, and Mr. D. G. Garabrant, while the Home Mission Board was represented by Rev. J. E. Briggs, Mr. Sam D. Jones, Gov. J. M. Terrell, Rev. B. D. Gray and Rev. J. F. Love. After thorough and fraternal discussion during the morning, afternoon and evening, the following paper was adopted:

In view of the increasing numerical and financial strength of Southern Baptists,

RESOLVED, That we recommend that the Home Mission Board upon the consent of the New Mexico Convention relieve entirely the American Baptist Home Mission

Society of further responsibility for mission work, in that territory, on the understanding that the Home Mission Board give assurance that they will put into the work in New Mexico next year an amount equal to that expended by the Home Mission Society this year and will take over the Navahoe mission property at its cost to the Home Mission Society.

RESOLVED, Further, that we recommend that the question of territorial adjustment on the part of both Boards be considered settled for a period of at least five years.

RESOLVED, Further, that in case of the approval of this arrangement by the Southern Baptist Convention and the American Baptist Home Mission Society, a joint communication be addressed to the New Mexico Baptist churches to this effect, expressing the hope that they will regard this arrangement with favor.

H. L. MOREHOUSE, Chairman.
JOHN E. BRIGGS, Secretary.

(From *Annual* of the Southern Baptist Convention, 1909, pp. 206-207.)

(3) The Old Point Comfort-Hot Springs Conference

On September 27-28, 1911, in Virginia (and subsequently in another meeting in Arkansas, January 24-25, 1912), a joint committee met to discuss both the New Mexico problem and the possibility of adopting principles of comity agreeable to both sections. The following document enunciates the principles which have been agreed to, North and South, as constituting the continuing comity understanding between the sections.

Statement of Principles Adopted by the Committees of Conference of the Northern and Southern Baptist Conventions.

At a meeting of the committees of conference of the Northern and Southern Baptist Conventions held at Old Point Comfort, Va., September 27 and 28, 1911, after mutual correspondence and conference, the following statement of principles

and their application was unanimously adopted:

Since the ultimate purposes of the two Conventions are the same and the aims of the two committees, co-laboring as one, are the same, the fresh recognition of some of the simple and fundamental principles for which Baptists stand should help us to eliminate misunderstandings between the constituencies of the two Conventions and more effectively promote their happy coöperation for "the world-wide spread of the gospel and the world-wide sway of Baptist principles."

It is unnecessary to review the last half century of denominational history. The possibility of errors in judgment on the part of individuals or of missionary organizations is freely conceded. We must look to the future to correct the errors and failings of the past.

We recognize the following as fundamental Baptist principles:

Fundamental Principles.

1. The independence of the local Baptist church.

2. The moral interdependence and the coöperation of Baptist churches in promoting the interests of the kingdom of God.

3. The purely advisory nature of all denominational organizations in their relation to Baptist churches.

Organizing Principles.

The voluntary principle should rule in all general organizations among Baptists.

Contiguous Baptists churches should unite in district associations and in State conventions for the promotion of the kingdom of God and their common denominational interests. The ideal organization is one association in a given territory and one convention in a given State. There may be local conditions, however, which make impracticable the immediate attainment of this ideal.

Concerning Comity.

1. Financial aid given to churches by a general denominational body should create gratitude to God and promote Christian

fraternity in service, but should not impair in any way the freedom or autonomy of the church or churches receiving such aid.

2. Denominational organizations of every kind should "jealously regard the rights of all sister organizations, and of the churches, being always careful to promote unity and harmony, and to maintain inviolate the highest principles, thus exemplifying the noblest function of liberty, to wit: a proper respect for the liberties of others."

3. No Baptist body should use its influence to disintegrate or injure the work of any other Baptist bodies. Every Baptist organization should be an integrating and constructive force.

Application of the Foregoing Principles.

Because the kingdom of God and its interests are greater than the interests of any organization, whatever its constituency, and because "associations, societies, conventions and boards are expedients and agencies to be created and used by the churches," and because the kingdom of God can be promoted only when its work is conducted and its agencies and personal workers conduct themselves in the spirit of our Lord Jesus Christ, the Northern and Southern Baptist Conventions, putting aside all unholy competitions and realizing their unity in our Lord Jesus Christ, should "work together in the most agreeable and loving manner," each "promising to contribute to our common welfare, assuring one another of the full and abiding desire to work in fullest accord." Coöperative relations should not be only in fraternal feeling and Christian respect for one another's work in territory now exclusively occupied by either Convention, but by both Conventions, which have churches affiliated with them in the same State, should strive to effect the best possible working union of our forces in that State. While this statement sets forth our right attitude in such States, the ideal condition is that in which the entire body of the membership follows the majority in its coöperation

with any general body. These principles should be applied as follows:

1. When a State body is in coöperation with a general denominational organization, any proposed modification of their relation should be the subject of mutual consideration by and between the two bodies concerned, which should recognize the right of either to terminate coöperation whenever in its judgment the conditions justify. It is inexpedient for any outside denominational body, State or general, to interfere with or to disturb in any manner the free action of the State organization through official visitation, literature, or other form of influence. No advisory relation with a State organization should be undertaken by an outside body, except upon the invitation of the State organization itself.

2. In case churches in a State are affiliated with different general organizations, and the ideal of unity which we have presented cannot be realized at once, such churches should associate themselves in district associations, and so far as practicable in one State organization. All appropriations and the method in which they are made should be left to the administrative agencies themselves, State and general. All agents of State conventions, thus dependent upon outside financial aid, should scrupulously abstain from anything that will influence the churches of the State in their affiliation or create sectional feeling. Contributions of individual churches in such a State should be applied as each may designate, and all undesignated contributions should be applied to the work represented by the two general Conventions in such proportion as may be agreed upon by all parties concerned.

3. The fraternal relation between the American Baptist Home Mission Society and the Foreign Mission Board of the Southern Baptist Convention in their work in Mexico is a matter for rejoicing. The proposals of the National Baptist Convention of Mexico, in September, 1910, for the establishment of one theological school and

one publishing house, to be managed and
maintained by the three bodies, should be
approved, and there should be a clearer
division of territory in the republic between
the Home Mission Society and the Foreign
Mission Board of the Southern Baptist
Convention.

4. The happy coöperative arrangements
between the American Foreign Mission Society and the Foreign Mission Board of the
Southern Baptist Convention in educational
enterprises in their mission fields in the
Orient is also a matter for rejoicing. There
should be an extension of such coöperation
by the foreign mission agencies of both
Conventions.

(From *Annual* of the Southern Baptist
Convention, 1912, pp. 49-51.)

Publications

*As previously sketched, the Sunday
School needs of Baptists in the South had
been met in various ways before 1845. The
Convention established the first Sunday
School Board in 1863, but it was abolished
in 1873 and the work committed to the
Home Mission Board. In 1891 the present
Sunday School Board was established. It
did not provide the Sunday School literature for the southern field immediately,
however. The American Baptist Publication Society, which had long served the
southern Sunday Schools, was not willing
to withdraw. In a series of events between
March 18, 1896, and the meeting of the
Convention in 1910, the Sunday School
Board fully secured its home field.*

*1. Proposition by the American Baptist
Publication Society*

*The tension between the relatively new
Sunday School Board and the older Publication Society came to a climax in 1896
when the Society proposed to unite operations with the Southern Board.*

March 18, 1896

Dear Brethren:

We are informed by those whom we believe to be acquainted with the facts that
there is an earnest desire on the part of
many of our brethren in the South that our
Society should make overtures to your
Board looking to a greater harmony in the
publication of Sunday School literature.
Influenced by this, and also by a desire to
enter into a closer relation with our
Southern brethren we present the following proposition for your earnest consideration:

1. We propose that from July 1896 to
the end of this year, or six months longer
if necessary, we print the Sunday School
publications as now issued by your Board;
this literature to bear the imprint and to
be sent out in the name of the Sunday
School Board of the Southern Baptist
Convention; we agreeing to pay the net
profit of such publications during the period named to the Treasurer of your Board.

2. We propose that not later than July
1, 1897 such portions of the literature of
the Sunday School Board as are now essentially duplicated, for example the Teacher
and the Quarterlies, be incorporated with
similar issues of our publications; the remaining numbers of the series now issued
by the Sunday School Board should be
continued as far as may be desired, the
whole to be combined in a series to be
called the "Southern Series."

3. We propose and will agree that our
Society use its influence to have the
"Southern Series" taken throughout the
territory covered by the Southern Baptist
Convention and not to push the circulation
of any other Sunday School periodicals
upon that field.

4. We propose and will agree to pay to
the Sunday School Board one half the net
profits of the "Southern Series" to be issued
by the Sunday School Board at its discretion in Sunday School work in the South.
We agree also to co-operate in the employment of Sunday School missionaries, and
other agencies in such work.

5. We propose the annual appointment
by the Sunday School Board, said appointment to be subject to the approval of our
Society, of an editor who shall have sole

charge of that portion of the series which shall be continued without change, and shall co-operate with our editor of periodicals in the production of the other issues of the Series, said editor to reside at Nashville or Philadelphia as may be deemed best.

Requesting your early consideration of the propositions, we remain

Very truly yours,

Executive Committee of the

American Baptist Publication Society

A. J. ROWLAND, General Secretary

(From the correspondence of J. M. Frost and the American Baptist Publication Society.)

2. Reply by J. M. Frost

J. M. Frost, pioneer of the Board, knew that the Society had many supporters in the South and that a refusal by his Board would bring a spirited controversy, but he wrote plainly what he thought.

April 1, 1896

Dear Brethren:

Your communication of March 18, embodying certain propositions submitted to us, came to hand by due course of mail. At a called meeting of our Board today, the earliest date convenient for our coming together, your communication was laid before the Board by our Secretary as had been previously done with the correspondence between him and Dr. Rowland. After due consideration of your proposition, we are unanimous and hearty in our decision and submit the following answer:

1. As clearly set forth in the correspondence with Dr. Rowland, we cannot accept your proposition, deeming such alliance neither desirable or feasible.

2. We have no thought whatever of surrendering the work entrusted to us by the Southern Baptist Convention. Under the blessing of God our work has had in these five years a success almost phenomenal and altogether without precedent in Baptist circles. Every day the Board is growing in power for usefulness and in its ability to

meet the great ends for which the Convention brought it into existence.

3. Your proposition does not commend itself to us as a business proposition. It offers nothing in the way of sufficient inducement, is impracticable, not to say impossible, of execution, involves not only the integrity and efficiency of the Board but its very existence, and contemplates the destruction of our own Sunday school periodicals. We contend not simply for a "Southern Series," but a Series owned and operated by the Southern Baptist Convention; a series with distinctive features, and a great factor in the work of the Convention, being an immense power in the execution of the Convention's purpose as set forth in its Constitution of "eliciting, combining, and directing the energies and benevolence of our churches."

4. Your proposition moreover involves questions which have been repeatedly passed upon by the Southern Baptist Convention with uniform result and each time in a more pronounced way. We must be excused from being in any sense a party to their reopening and agitation. It cannot be otherwise than exceedingly distasteful, not to use a stronger term, to the great majority of our brethren as well as to the rank and file of our great Baptist brotherhood in the South. It will bring harm and nothing but harm to the good of the general cause; it will surely awaken in more intense form the strife and bitterness which we all regretted and which this Board has diligently sought these five years to allay.

5. We agree with you as to a desire for "greater harmony in the publication of Sunday School literature," indeed as a Board we have always desired and wished for this. Every policy we have adopted in the conduct of our affairs has contemplated the allaying of ill-feeling and the promotion of a spirit of fraternity becoming our great brotherhood, a spirit before which even business friction would be either entirely removed or at least reduced to a minimum.

In conclusion we venture to express the conviction that it is possible for you and us to mark out a plan of co-operation, in which we could conduct each his respective work in a way that would render no injustice to either and be helpful to both. We have always held ourselves ready for this, and we are willing to make any concession toward it, provided always the Board itself be not marred as to its integrity, or weakened in its efficiency for meeting the great responsibilities which God has opened to us here in the South.

Praying that God may guide us in the conduct of these great affairs to the glory of his name and the bringing in of the kingdom of his Son, we remain,

> Sincerely yours,
> Sunday School Board of the
> Southern Baptist Convention
> J. M. FROST, Secretary

(Ibid.)

3. Frost's account of the ensuing controversy

The American Baptist Publication Society of Philadelphia was still in the field after Birmingham, and announced its purpose to continue its policy as hitherto. It had already branch houses in Atlanta and St. Louis, and almost immediately established a third at Dallas.

It was strongly entrenched in the South through its business and benevolence, had a host of friends who were sympathetic, sincere and earnest in its support. It claimed to be Southern in itself, to be equal with the Sunday School Board in rank and relation to our organized work. It was accorded place on the program and platform of State Conventions, sometimes of the Southern Baptist Convention—sometimes along with the new Secretary, sometimes in advance of him. It several times reduced the prices of its periodicals, once very seriously, and every year announced increase of its business in its Southern territory and received the plaudit of its host of friends.

At times the situation was very acute, more frequently in State Conventions and in denominational papers; but sometimes even in the Southern Baptist Convention, for example, Chattanooga, 1896, and Wilmington, 1897. Prior to Chattanooga the Society had first proposed to the Sunday School Board to absorb its life and business, and when this was declined, it then circularized the Baptists of the South to make the offer effective through the approaching session of the Convention. I had just returned to the secretaryship to encounter this new phase of the opposition, but it failed to get any public consideration, though the situation was painful in private circles.

At Wilmington, however, a year later the opposition got into the open and produced a scene well-nigh dramatic. It was commonly reported that the Society had seventeen officials and employees in attendance. One of them made an open attack from the platform on the Sunday School Board, especially on its Bible work in a lengthy and elaborate speech. Governor Northen, of Georgia, with an able committee, had presented his report and followed with a few remarks of kindly commendation when the attack came. It created a stir of resentment in the audience as could be easily seen. At its close many men made an effort to get the floor. I never saw so many heavy guns unlimber so quickly and get ready for action. Dr. William E. Hatcher, of Virginia, got the floor, and in twenty-five minutes made a speech that was a marvel even for him. All of his powers with an audience came into play in that short time. He told how he had not favored making the Board at first; how it had won its place in the denomination; how the Baptists of the South had set it out as their policy; now with humor that convulsed the audience; now with pungent statement that shot like an arrow from a master's hand; now with pathos that swept like fire in a prairie; now again as he came to the close like thunder in the gathering storm. Can anyone who was present ever forget how he stirred and swept the people as he turned with a mighty sweep in the declaration: "I have been a life-long friend of the Publication Society, but it must not come here to interfere with our work. We have our way of doing things, and woe betide the man who crosses our path." He ended, and there was no need for anything further. The case was disposed of, and a calm followed the storm.

(From J. M. Frost, *Sunday School Board History and Work*, pp. 81-83.)

4. Resolution of 1910 to enlarge the ministry of the Sunday School Board

WHEREAS, The removal of the branch houses of the American Baptist Publication Society from the South has left open a great field for the preparation and dissemination of Christian literature of many sorts, especially of the Baptist type; and,

WHEREAS, Somebody is going to occupy this field, more or less, to the advantage of our Baptist interests; and,

WHEREAS, There is no agency, individual or other, so well qualified to occupy it to the satisfaction and profit of our people as is our own Sunday School Board, which has means, experience, business touch with all our churches, Sunday schools, and pastors, knows well the needs of our people and enjoys their confidence and affection; therefore be it resolved:

1. The Board be authorized and urged to enter, at as early date as possible, on the work of supplying the brethren of our churches with books, tracts, hymn and song books, and indeed all supplies for churches, Sunday schools, missionary societies, Young People's Unions, such as are suitable and desirable.

2. That in the prosecution of this work it enter into the closest possible coöperation, consistent with wise business management, with Baptist book houses in the various States, especially those under control of organized Baptist bodies.

3. That the Board be authorized to seek from the churches, Sunday schools, and other organizations coöperating with this Convention, gifts for its distinctively missionary operations in the matter of colportage, tract distribution, etc.

(From *Annual* of the Southern Baptist Convention, 1910, p. 50.)

Section Three
Theological Education

The Toy case

Crawford Howell Toy was a brilliant young Virginian appointed to Japan by the Foreign Mission Board, when the Civil War disrupted these plans. After the war he studied in Germany and returned to teach Old Testament in Southern Seminary. Toy's views on inspiration were criticized, so in 1879 he prepared a paper setting forth his understanding of that doctrine and submitted it, along with his resignation in case his position was not satisfactory, to the Board of Trustees. His resignation was accepted with two dissenting votes.

To the Board of Trustees of the Southern Baptist Theological Seminary:

Dear Brethren,—It having lately become apparent to me that my views of Inspiration differ considerably from those of the body of my brethren, I ask leave to lay my opinions on that subject before you, and submit them to your judgment.

At the outset I may say that I fully accept the first article of the Fundamental Principles of the Seminary; "the scriptures of the Old and New Testament were given by inspiration of God, and are the only sufficient, certain and authoritative rule of all saving knowledge and obedience," and that I have always taught, and do now teach in accordance with, and not contrary to it.

It is in the details of the subject that my divergence from the prevailing views in the denomination occurs. The divergence has gradually increased in connection with my studies, from year to year, till it has become perceptible to myself and others.

In looking for light on Inspiration, my resort has been, and is, to the scriptures themselves alone, and I rest myself wholly on their testimony. It seems to me that, while they declare the fact of Divine Inspiration, they say nothing of the manner of its action. We are told that men spake from God, borne along by the Holy Ghost, and that all scripture is given by Inspiration of God, and is profitable for doctrine, for reproof, for correction, for instruction in righteousness, that the man of God may be complete, thoroughly furnished for every good work. The object of the scripture is here said to be an ethical, spiritual one. They were given man for his guidance and edification in religion, as our Lord also says: "Sanctify them in the truth; thy word is truth."

As nothing is said of the mode of operation of the Divine Spirit, of the manner in which the divine saving truth is impressed on the mind, of the relation of the divine influence to the ordinary workings of the human intellect, we must, as to these points, consult the books of the Bible themselves and examine the facts. Against facts no theory can stand, and I prefer, therefore, to have no theory, but submit myself to the guidance of the actual words of Holy scripture.

As the result of my examination, I believe that the Bible is wholly divine and wholly human; the scripture is the truth of God communicated by him to the human soul. To undertake to say what must be the outward forms of God's revelation of himself to man, seems to me presumptuous. If rationalism be the decision of religious questions by human reason, then it appears to me rationalistic to say that a Divine revelation must conform to certain outward conditions; to insist, for example, that it must be written in a certain style, or that it must teach certain things in geography, or astronomy, or similar matters.

I hold all *a priori* reasoning here to be out of place, and all theories based on it to be worthless. Such procedure seems to me to be out of keeping with the simple, reverent spirit appropriate to him who comes to search into the truth of God. For

this reason I am forced to discard the theories of some pious men, as Fichte and Wordsworth, who have proceeded in this *a priori* way, and to keep myself to the facts given in the Bible itself.

These facts make on me the impression that the scripture writers are men who have received messages from God and utter them under purely free, human conditions. The inspired man speaks his own language, not another man's, and writes under the conditions of his own age, not under those of some other age. His personality, his individuality has the freest play, all under the control of the guiding Divine spirit. In illustration of what I mean I refer to I Cor. 1:14, 15, where Paul first says he had baptized nobody at Corinth but Crispus and Caius; then, a while later, remembering himself, adds that he had baptized also the household of Stephanas; and finally coming to doubt his memory, declares that he doesn't know whether he had baptized any other person. Here, if we indulge in arithmetical criticism, is a flat contradiction, but if we see simply the free play of the writer's mind under the ordinary conditions of human thought, there is no difficulty. If any one asks me how this perfectly free thought consists with Divine guidance, I answer that I cannot tell no more than how supernatural Divine power co-exists with free action of the soul in conversion, or how I exist at all, or how, in general, the finite and the infinite can co-exist.

I find that the geography, astronomy and other physical science of the sacred writers was that of their times. It is not that of our times, it is not that which seems to us correct, but it has nothing to do with their message of religious truth from God. I do not feel authorized to impose on Divine revelation the condition that it shall accord with modern geography and geology, nor to say that I will not accept it except on this condition. It seems to me that geography has nothing to do with religion. The message is not less Divine to me because it is given in Hebrew and not in English, or because it is set in the framework of a primitive and incorrect geology. When the Psalmist says (Ps. CXXI, 6): "The sun shall not smite thee by day, nor the moon by night," it does not matter to me whether the moon is injurious or not at night, for the obvious religious thought is independent of this outward form; or when discrepancies and inaccuracies occur in the historical narrative, this does not even invalidate the documents as historical records, much less does it affect them as expressions of religious truths. I am slow to admit discrepancies or inaccuracies, but if they show themselves I refer them to the human conditions of the writer, believing that his merely intellectual status, the mere amount of information possessed by him, does not affect his spiritual truth. If our heavenly Father sends a message by the stammering tongue of a man, I will not reject the message because of the stammering.

My position is the same when I find that political details have not fallen out in accordance with the form in which the prophets clothe their religious exhortations. If Hosea looked for a captivity of Ephraim in Egypt (Hos. IX, 3), or Isaiah for political friendship between Assyria, Egypt and Israel (Isaiah XIX, 23-25), that is the mere clothing of their real thought. The prophets uttered everlasting truths which are embodied and fulfilled in Jesus Christ, and with which the geographical and political details have no essential connection. To them Israel was the centre and hope of the world, and prospective possessor of all prosperity, and the spiritual gist of their teachings has been perpetuated in Christ, while the merely outward has passed away.

The prophets and priests were not only preachers of religion, but writers of religious history. The early history of Israel was for a long time not committed to writing, but handed down by oral tradition, under which process it was subject to a more or less free expansion. In this expanded form it was received at a compara-

tively late time by the prophets and priests who put it into shape, and made it the vehicle of religious truth. The idea of scientific history did not then exist—it was all pragmatic, that is, written for the purpose of inculcating a truth. The traditional history is treated by the pious of Israel in the spirit of profound trust in God and regard for his law. I can no more demand historical science in the scriptures than geological science. I regard them both as being outside of the domain of religion.

The same thing I hold in respect to the Levitical law, which grew up, as it seems to me, from generation to generation on a Mosaic basis, and could thus be called Mosaic.

In one word, I regard the Old Testament as the record of the whole circle of the experiences of Israel, the people whom God chose to be the depository of his truth, all whose life he so guided as to bring out of it lessons of instruction which he then caused to be written down for preservation. The nation lived out its life in a free human way, yet under divine guidance, and its Prophets, Priests and Psalmist recorded the spiritual, religious history under the condition of their time. The divine truth is presented in a framework of relatively unessential things, as Christ in his Parables introduced accessories merely for the purpose of bringing out a principle, so that the Parable of the Ten Virgins, for example, may properly be said to be the framework or vehicle of religious truth. As a whole the Parable may in a sense be called a religious teaching—but speaking more precisely we should say that a part of it is such teaching, or that the teaching is contained in it.

What I have said of the outward form of the Old Testament applies, as I think, to the outward form of the New Testament. I will not lightly see a historical or other inaccuracy in the Gospels or the Acts, but if I find such, they do not for me affect the divine teachings of these books. The centre of the New Testament is Christ himself, salvation is in him, and a historcal error cannot affect the fact of his existence and his teachings. The apostles wrote out of their personal convictions of the reality of the truth of Christ. If Paul makes a slip of memory, as in the case above cited, that cannot affect his spiritual relation to Christ and to the Father, nor detract from his power as an inspired man. If his numerical statements do not always agree with those of the Old Testament (as in Gal. III, 17, compared with Exodus XII, 40), that seems to be a matter of no consequence. If the New Testament writers sometimes quote the Old Testament in the Greek version, which does not correctly render the Hebrew (as in Heb. X, 5, quoted from Psa. XI, 6), that does not affect the main thought or the religious teaching. And it may be that in some cases my principles of exegesis lead me to a different interpretation of an Old Testament passage from which I find given by some New Testament writer, as in Psa. XI, 6, above mentioned; this again I look on as an incidental thing, of which the true religious teaching is independent. I should add that in the majority of cases I hold that the New Testament quotations correctly represent the sense of the Old Testament, and there is always a true spiritual feeling controlling them. I think that Peter's discourse, in Acts II, gives the true spiritual sense of the passage in Joel, and so, many references of Old Testament passages to Christ throughout the New Testament. It ought also to be noticed that the ancient ideas of quotations were different from ours; ancient writers cite in a general way from memory for illustration, and permit themselves without remark such alterations as a modern writer would think it necessary to call attention to. This is to be regarded as a difference of habit arising from a difference of the times. The freedom of quotation in the scripture-writers does not, for example, affect their honesty and truthfulness, nor their spiritual train of thought, nor their spiritual authority. It is only a human condition of the divine truth they utter. In these men the spirit of God dwelt,

and out of their writings comes a divine power. Recognizing in them a divine element, I cannot reject it because of what seems to me outward or non-spiritual limitations. I do not condition Divine action, but accept it in the form in which I find it.

As to criticism (question of date and authorship) and exegesis, these stand by themselves and have nothing to do with Inspiration. The prophecy in Isa. XL–LXVI is not less inspired if it be assigned to the period of the Babylonian Exile, and the "servant of Jehovah" be regarded as referring primarily to Israel. These are questions of interpretation and historical research, in which, as it seems to me, the largest liberty must be allowed. If some of the Psalms should be put in the Maccabean period (B.C. 160), this is no reason for doubting their inspiration; God could as easily act on men in the year B.C. 160 as B.C. 400, or B.C. 700.

It is proper to add that the above statement of my views on Inspiration is the fullest that I have ever expressed. Some things I have not thought it expedient to state to my classes in the Seminary. At the same time I regard these views as helpful for Bible study. If at first they seem strange, I am convinced that they will appear more natural with further strict study of the text.

I beg leave to repeat that I am guided wholly by what seems to me the correct interpretation of the scriptures themselves. If an error in my interpretation is pointed out, I shall straightway give it up. I cannot accept a priori reasoning, but I stake everything on the words of the Bible, and this course I believe to be for the furtherance of the truth of God.

And now, in conclusion, I wish to say distinctly and strongly that I consider the view above given to be not only lawful for me to teach as Professor in the Seminary, but one that will bring aid and firm standing-ground to many a perplexed mind and establish the truth of God on a firm foundation.

But that I may relieve the Board of all embarrassment in the matter, I tender my resignation as Professor in the Southern Baptist Theological Seminary.

Respectfully submitted
C. H. TOY

May, 1879.

(From the *Baptist Courier* [South Carolina] for Nov. 27, 1879. Also found in the *Religious Herald* [Virginia] for Dec. 11, 1879, and the *Western Recorder* [Kentucky] for Jan. 1, 1880.)

The Whitsitt case

William Heth Whitsitt became professor of church history in Southern seminary in 1872 and its president in 1895. His views on the adoption of immersion by English Baptists were presented in an encyclopedia and in four articles in a periodical, and in 1896 those views brought a storm of protest. In 1897 he read a conciliatory statement to the Board of Trustees at Wilmington, but the attacks continued. He resigned as professor and president in 1899.

1. Whitsitt's statement of the controversy

The question does not relate to the origin of immersion. Immersion as a religious rite was practiced by John the Baptist about the year 30 of our era, and was solemnly enjoined by our Savior upon all his ministers to the end of time. No other observance was in use for baptism in New Testament times. The practice, though sometimes greatly perverted, has yet been continued from the Apostolic age down to our own. As I understand the Scriptures immersion is essential to Christian baptism. The question as to the origin and essential character of immersion is, therefore, not in issue. That is a closed question; it does not admit of being opened among Baptist people.

The issue before us is far different, namely: Whether the immersion of adult believers was practiced in England by the Anabaptists before the year 1641? Whether these English people first adopted immer-

sion for baptism and thus became Baptists in or about the year 1641?

This is purely a question of modern historical research. It does not affect any items of Baptist principle or practice. These are all established upon the Bible. Our watchword for generations has been, "The Bible, the Bible alone, the religion of Baptists!" It is now too late in the day to alter our views and set forth any new battle cry. Baptists have always maintained that "the Scriptures of the Old and New Testaments were given by inspiration of God, and are the only sufficient, certain and authoritative rule of all saving knowledge, faith and obedience." Other foundation can no man lay. Whoever attempts it must inevitably fall into error. Let us stand by the old landmarks; let us walk in the old paths.

(From William H. Whitsitt, *A Question in Baptist History* [Louisville, 1896], pp. 5-6.)

2. Whitsitt's statement at Wilmington

The Trustees of the Southern Baptist Theological Seminary, assembled in their annual meeting at Wilmington, N. C., May the 6th, 1897, desire to submit to the Baptists of the South the following statement, in regard to the institution whose interests have been committed to their care and management:

1. That we account this a fitting occasion to reaffirm our cordial and thorough adherence to the fundamental articles adopted at the time when the Seminary was established, and to assure those on whose behalf we hold in trust and administer the affairs of this institution, of our steadfast purpose to require hereafter, as we have in the past, that the fundamental laws and scriptural doctrines embodied in those articles shall be faithfully upheld by those occupying chairs as teachers.

2. That we cannot undertake to sit in judgment on questions in Baptist history which do not imperil any of these principles, concerning which all Baptists are agreed, but concerning which serious, conscientious and scholarly students are not

agreed. We can, however, confidently leave to continued research and discussion, the satisfactory solution of these questions.

3. That believing the Seminary to hold an important relation to the prosperity and usefulness of Southern Baptists, we consider it our duty, while demanding of those in charge of the departments of instruction the utmost patience in research and the greatest discretion in utterance, to foster, rather than repress, the spirit of earnest and reverent investigation.

4. That being fully assured that the tender affection which we cherish for this institution, founded by our fathers and bequeathed by them to us, is shared by the Baptists of the South, we can safely trust them as we ask them to trust us, to guard its honor, promote its usefulness and pray for its prosperity.

Upon the adoption of the foregoing statement, the Trustees appointed a committee to notify Dr. Whitsitt of this action, and to invite him to meet with them and to make any voluntary statements he might desire. Whereupon Dr. Whitsitt appeared before the Board and read the following paper:

Wilmington, N. C., May 7, 1897.

To the Board of Trustees of the Southern Baptist Theological Seminary:

Dear Brethren:—I beg leave to return sincerest and heartiest thanks for the noble and generous treatment that you have bestowed upon me. I have only words of affection for every member of the Board. After consulting with the committee I have the following to say:

1. That in regard to the articles written as editorials for the *Independent,* I have long felt that it was a mistake, and the generous action of the Board of Trustees renders it easy for me to make this statement. What I wrote was from a Pedobaptist standpoint with a view to stimulating historical research, with no thought that it would injure the Baptists, and with no intention to disparage Baptist doctrines or practices.

2. That the article in *Johnson's Encyclopedia* has probably passed beyond my control; but it will be very pleasing to me if I can honorably procure the elimination from it of whatsoever is offensive to any of my brethren.

3. Regarding the charge that I expressed a conviction that a kinswoman of mine ought to follow her husband into a Pedobaptist church, that it was never my intention to indicate a belief that the family outranked the Church of God. I believe that obedience to God's commands is above every other human duty, and that people in every relation of life ought to obey God rather than man.

4. That on the historical questions involved in the discussion I find myself out of agreement with some honored historians; but what I have written is the outcome of patient and honest research, and I can do no otherwise than to re-affirm my convictions and maintain my position. But if in the future it shall ever be made to appear that I have erred in my conclusions, I would promptly and cheerfully say so. I am a searcher after truth, and will gladly hail every helper in my work.

5. That I cannot more strongly assure the brethren that I am a Baptist than by what I have recently declared with regard to the abstract of principles set forth in the Fundamental Laws of the Seminary. I am heartily in accord with my Baptist brethren in every distinctive principle that they hold. My heart and life are bound up with the Baptists, and I have no higher thought on earth than to spend my days in their fellowship and service, in the name of the Lord Jesus Christ.

Respectfully submitted,

WM. H. WHITSITT.

At the conclusion of the reading of the foregoing paper the trustees joined in singing

"How firm a foundation, ye saints of the Lord,

Is laid for your faith in his excellent Word,"

during which, amid flowing tears and many

expressions of satisfaction and joy, the members of the Board pressed forward and gave Dr. Whitsitt the hand of fellowship and confidence. The trustees then instructed B. H. Carroll of Texas, and W. E. Hatcher of Virginia, to communicate to the Southern Baptist Convention this action, and also to give it to the public press. Please bear in mind that this statement is made to the Convention for information and not for action.

(From *Annual* of the Southern Baptist Convention, 1897, pp. 14-16.)

Section Four

Controversies

Landmarkism

1. Memorial from Arkansas Landmark Baptists

In 1905 a memorial from representatives of fifty-two Baptist churches in Arkansas holding Landmark views was presented to the Convention. It demanded that a church basis of representation be substituted for the financial basis.

Dear Brethren.—We, the Committee appointed by the preliminary meeting of the General Association of Baptists of the United States of America, to memorialize the Southern Baptist Convention concerning the things to which objections have been made by many churches and individuals, beg your respectful attention and careful consideration of the matters hereinafter mentioned.

We were appointed by the messengers of fifty-two Baptist churches who met in Texarkana, Ark., March 22, and we feel certain that thousands of churches are in sympathy with what we have done. But if only one church should come with a memorial of this sort, it should be heard and its requests given careful and prayerful attention.

Our sincere desire is for peace and harmony among Baptists, but we want this peace and harmony to be on Bible principles and methods. We love peace, but we love principle better. First pure and then peaceable. Besides, we do not think we are guilty of causing the division which has been troubling our Zion. We have protested against what we honestly believe to be unscriptural principles and methods of work, and we think those who have persistently clung to those objectionable principles and methods are the cause of the division. He that drives the wedge is guilty of splitting the log.

We do not desire that any part of the work of evangelizing the world should stop, but on the other hand want to help in all Scriptural ways in this great work, and we honestly desire to work with the brethren composing the Southern Baptist Convention, and will do so if you will at this session of the Convention make the following change in your Constitution:

First, we want the money and the associational basis of representation eliminated from the Constitution and a purely church basis substituted instead. We believe in the churches to whom the Lord gave the commission, and that a church which is willing to co-operate should be entitled to a seat in this Convention by messenger, whether it be large or small, rich or poor, without any specified sum of money being fixed as the basis of co-operation. There is other and greater work to do than the handling of cash, and the money basis is the lowest and most unscriptural that is possible to ask Baptists to co-operate on. We can never agree to it and would rather suffer division than submit to it. The numerical basis is objectionable because such a basis carries with it the idea that the commission was given to the individual as such and not to the churches as such. Nothing short of exclusive church representation will satisfy us. We ask that you eliminate all other basis and adopt the church basis of representation.

We object to the power put into the hands of the Boards by the Convention to appoint and remove missionaries at pleasure without giving them the right to appeal to the Convention, as has been seen in some cases; we ask that this power be taken away from the Boards of the Convention.

Third, we object to the Boards being influenced or controlled by what is known as denominational comity. We think that our commission is to go into all the world, no matter who may occupy the field. We therefore object to the way in which I. N. Yohanon and Said M. Jureidini have been set aside. These men are well qualified for their work and no objection has ever been raised to their going to their fields, so far as we can learn, except a letter of protest from a Presbyterian Secretary, and after that for some reason Yohanon was set aside. We cannot agree to that sort of a thing, and we would rather suffer division than to do it. But since denominational comity is not necessary to Baptist success, the Convention can easily right that wrong. If the Foreign Mission Board has not been guilty of this thing it can be made unmistakably plain by that Board being instructed to open mission work in Persia and Syria, and by its obeying its instructions.

Fourth, some of us object to many other matters of detail concerning the methods of the Convention and its Boards, but we are willing for the sake of peace and harmony among Baptists to waive these objections; we are willing to meet you half way, yea, more than half way for the sake of peace and harmony among the Baptist host. Will you do as much? We are not asking that any part of the work stop, but instead we are asking you to so arrange matters that more workers can be induced to enter the work that better work may be done.

Fifth, we attach hereto a copy of our statement of principles and methods of work. We do not ask that you adopt these in full, but send it with this communication so that you may see that we, while we ask you to concede two or three points for the sake of harmony and peace, are really conceding more than we ask you to concede. We are not asking you to make all the concessions; we are willing to meet

you as brethren on half-way ground. At the same time we are stating the least we can ask of you. If you reject this at this session we shall consider that we have done our duty and shall trouble you no more.

We bid you God speed in every good work, and ask you to prayerfully consider our request.

> B. M. BOGARD,
> J. B. SELLMAN,
> J. K. P. WILLIAMS,
> J. T. TUCKER,
> A. J. ROBINS,
> J. H. KUYKENDALL,
> J. Y. FREEMAN.

(From *Annual* of the Southern Baptist Convention, 1905, pp. 43-45.)

2. Reply of the Convention

The following reply to this memorial resulted in the excision of a number of Arkansas churches from Convention fellowship and the formation of a separate general body.

Texarkana Convention Memorial.

Your Committee, to whom was referred the Texarkana Memorial, beg respectfully to submit the following report:

1. That we have sought to give to this memorial a patient and fraternal consideration, and we feel that the Convention ought to make reply to its petitions in the spirit of brotherly kindness.

2. We beg to report to the Convention that our study of the subject-matter of this memorial forces us to the conclusion that it would not be for the best interests of the work which the Convention is seeking to do, to accede to the petitions contained in this memorial. These petitions call for action so entirely out of harmony with the principles of our organization, and the methods upon which our work is conducted, that we feel constrained to ask that they shall be denied. We feel the strongest assurance that the principles upon which the work of our Convention is organized and conducted are in accord with the teachings of God's Word, and in harmony

with Baptist history, Baptist usage, and Baptist doctrine.

. . . .

4. We beg to assure those from whom this memorial has come that we would look upon any possibility of their separation from our organized work with unfeigned regret, and trust that no such unhappy event shall ever occur. We are sure that our Baptist churches throughout the South are cordially united in their doctrinal beliefs, and in their love of our common Lord and Master, and we greatly desire, and earnestly pray, that we may all be one in purpose and one in a movement for advancing the kingdom of our Redeemer.

(*Ibid.*, pp. 42-43.)

Gospel Missionism

The leader in the movement known as Gospel Missionism was T. P. Crawford, veteran missionary of the Foreign Mission Board in China. Deeply affected by some abuses in the use of mission funds he found on the field, he became convinced that radical changes should be made in the operation of the mission program. He developed the view that the local church, not a Board, should be the agency by which missionary work should be done. Missionaries should be self-supporting; "subsidy money," "native employees," and other "worrying adjuncts" should be eliminated.

1. The beginning of the controversy with the Foreign Mission Board

In our last June number it was mentioned that Dr. T. P. Crawford, of Tung Chow, China, had returned to this country "to confer with the Boards in Richmond and Boston regarding the future direction of our Foreign Mission Work." Efforts were made to have him meet our Board in June, and again in July, but communications by letter and by telegraph failed to reach him in time. During August and September many members of the Board were out of town, and so it was not till the 12th of October that the Doctor presented his views to the Board, and requested the ap-

pointment of a committee who should hear him more fully, and report. This special committee was made to consist of the chairmen of the Standing Committees on Chinese, African, European, Mexican, and Brazilian Missions, and after a full hearing of the matter entered into an arrangement, by which another meeting of the Board was held October 27th, and brethren David, of Africa, and Taylor, of Rome, along with Dr. Crawford, were invited to present their views candidly and fully. Dr. Taylor was detained by sickness, but presented his views in writing. The other two were present, and spoke at some length. The questions at issue, together with a mass of letters and documents, were then referred back to the special committee, who, after mature deliberation, presented the following report. It was adopted November 6th, and ordered to be published in the JOURNAL.

We prefix this sketch of the origin of the report, both to explain its verbiage, and to show that it embodies the results of long and patient consideration. It is proper to add, that besides the honored brethren, whose names have been mentioned, several other missionaries communicated their views by letter. We trust that the conclusions reached will be generally acceptable, and that all who have been so deeply interested in the issues will join in earnest work for a practical realization of the common end. All may not be able to work on the same line, but all can press toward the same end.

REPORT

Your committee have heard with interest the views of our veteran missionary, Dr. T. P. Crawford, on self-support, or the policy of confining appropriations strictly to work done by our missionaries, and leaving native laborers to support themselves, or be supported by their fellow converts.

We clearly recognize self-support, as the consummation towards which all missionary operations should tend. Without such an aim missions are, and must be, a failure.

We believe that the principle of self-support should be put into practice as soon as possible in every mission field, and that wherever it cannot be adopted in whole, but might be in part, there it should be adopted just to the extent to which its adoption is practicable. These are our convictions of the rightfulness and necessity of self-support as an end to be kept in view; and we do not doubt that they are shared by all the missionaries under our appointment.

. . . .

An entirely different question is presented when we consider whether we will incorporate this principle into a rule which would, in the future, forbid all appropriations for work done by native Christians, at least in the fields of missionaries that may be appointed hereafter. Should self-support assume the shape of inflexible law? We are constrained to think not.

1. It would introduce confusion into our missionary operations. If we applied the rule to missionaries now in the field, they might find occasion to complain that we had imposed conditions upon them that did not enter into the original agreement; and if we restricted the application to new missionaries, a difference would be made between the old and the new which might become a source of discontent and friction.

2. An inflexible rule would seem to assume what we think the facts would not sustain. It would assume that circumstances and conditions are the same everywhere; that missionary labor has like environment under every sky, and among every people and tribe; that one method is equally suited to the plodding Chinaman and to the restless Mexican, to the jungles of Africa and to the classic shores of Italy; that in dealing with men no account need be taken of race distinctions, of different social customs, and different degrees of enlightenment.

3. It would seem to imply a distrust of the effects of God's grace in mission fields. We would seem to say we fear the gospel cannot lift the Chinaman or African above the corrupting influences of money.

To the foregoing views your committee append two resolutions, recommending their adoption by the Board.

Resolved 1, That while the principle of self-support in our mission work is essential to healthy progress and ultimate success, we believe its practice is to be established not by formal rule, but as the result of growth and development.

Resolved 2, That we urge upon our missionaries the duty of holding constantly in view self-support as an object to be attained, and of training their converts and churches in this direction with all possible diligence.

Two other subjects were brought to our attention by Dr. Crawford: the plan of making exactly the same appropriation to each missionary, and the abolition or modification of the system technically called "missions." But as these questions properly belong to your Committee on Revision of Rules we have not felt it our duty to give special consideration to them.

(From *Foreign Mission Journal* [Richmond, Va.], December, 1885.)

2. Crawford's attack on the Board method of missions

In 1892 Crawford published a little book entitled, Churches, To the Front! *in which he openly attacked the Board system. He was joined by many who held Landmark views. As a result of this attack, Crawford was dropped from the roll of missionaries. He had a private income and had been rather independent of the Board for several years. His wife resigned on July 25, 1892. Several other missionaries in China under the Board resigned during this controversy.*

On reading a recent letter from a Baptist pastor in one of our American country towns, saying that his Church had resolved to support a missionary in China, I felt like exclaiming, Is this the beginning of a new era among our Baptist Churches? Are they, at last, about to rise in their individual capacity and do their own work? About to carry out the commission of Christ in harmony with the independent, self-acting principles of their time-honored constitution? What a glorious movement this! How it will revive their waning sense of responsibility, deepen their devotion, develop their energies and clothe them with salvation as with a garment! It will also effectually counteract that dangerous tendency of our times towards centralization by closing the door against those "outside organizations" which encourage it through taking control of their work, their workers and their contributions. To take control of these, or any part of them, is so far to take control of the Churches, so far to overthrow their independence and self-respect, so far to reduce them to the position of mere "tributary appendages."

These organizations, beginning in 1814 with foreign missions alone, have gone steadily on enlarging the sphere of their operations until they have now come to embrace almost every kind of religious work. Not content with this, they have added many enterprises of a secular character and also placed them upon the Churches for support, in direct violation of our time-honored principles. According to these principles, Baptist Churches are self-acting religious bodies, constituted for religious purposes only; each one being directly responsible to Christ for the faithful execution of its sacred trust. Hence it can never abdicate nor transfer any part of its work to the control of an outside body. Neither can it permit any encroachment upon its appropriate sphere or any extension of it into the secular realm. Moreover, it can never sanction the formation of any central power within itself or within the denomination to which it belongs; but must, as a body, hold control of its ministerial gifts, contributions and missionary work. Besides, it must preserve its autonomy and equality in all its co-operative relations with sister Churches, the only bodies with which it can properly or safely have such relations. As Churches are the only religious organizations recognized in the New Testament, intruders are necessarily excluded. If Churches, as bodies, cannot properly or safely co-operate with such, how can their members, as individuals, do so? But this does by no means preclude individuals from co-operating with those organizations which do not intrude upon the appropriate sphere of the Churches.

This "organization craze" has gone to great extremes, and the time has come for our people "to call a halt." Say what you may, its tendency is to break our spiritual moorings and drive us upon the lee shore of secularization and ring-government. We have had enough of General Conventions, National Societies, Central Boards, Executive Committees and other like agencies "for doing Church work"—or rather, for preventing it; "for pushing our principles" —or rather, for overthrowing them; "for promoting union among brethren"—or rather, for keeping up rivalries among themselves. They promise one thing and, by the law of their own gravitation, accomplish another. They occupy a false position in our economy and cannot be made to run in harmony with it. Their meetings are too large and their operations too complicated to be either manageable or efficient for good. A revolution towards simplicity or local action and responsibility in mission matters, is imperatively demanded. Any co-operation of Baptist Churches in work requiring the employment of man and money, to be efficient, must necessarily be limited in its range and definite in its aim.

. . . .

Baptists are a Gospel-loving, Gospel-preaching people, and it will be well for them to adhere to their calling. It is their mission to maintain spirituality, soul-liberty, and religious simplicity. They cannot safely follow the lead or the methods of other denominations, as many seem too much inclined to do. Ours is a different type of Christianity; not a manufactured form, but a living, self-acting and self-propagating principle. Centralization and ring-government may suit the policy of other denominations. They do not suit ours, but are deadly hostile to it. Yet, strange to say, this dangerous element was first introduced among us with the first session of the Old Triennial Convention in 1814; and, stranger, still, the Northern Baptist Union and the Southern Baptist Convention have continued it down to the present day. Their Boards are located permanently in leading cities, are legally chartered corporations, and, so far as the Churches are concerned, self-perpetuating, irresponsible central bodies with unlimited permission to grow in power by absorbing the prerogatives and resources of our Churches, as the old Roman hierarchy grew by absorbing those in the early ages of Christianity. These permanant Boards, by taking in hand the missionary work of our Churches and mixing it up with various enterprises of a popular kind, have now come to control a vast amount of labor, money, property, credit and patronage, all professedly in the name of the Baptist denomination, as if it were an actual entity capable of doing work by employing men and means like the consolidated denominations around us! Add to the above sources of power the ready use of the pulpit, the press, the mails, the telegraphs and other means of creating, manipulating and directing public sentiment in their favor, and you will at once see that they are the actual masters of the situation—the powers to whom pastors, editors, and missionaries must bow or perish—not by fire and sword as in the olden times, for these are out of fashion now; but by ostracism, suppression, refrigeration and other like pious modes of destruction.

If ever our Churches, North and South, had cause for protecting their freedom against encroachments, they have it now. This they may readily do by casting off this incongruous system with all its expensive adjuncts at home and abroad and, taking up their evangelistic work, singly or in groups, after the simple manner above

suggested. By so doing, they will be able not only to preserve their autonomy and spirituality, but also to save on foreign missions alone forty to sixty cents in the dollar, and, without increasing their present contributions, be able to send from their midst more than double as many missionaries into foreign fields. In my opinion, $650 per individual, or $1400 per family, is amply sufficient to cover, on an average, all necessary expenses, including passage, children, work—everything. Many missionaries will doubtless require much less.

Please do not misunderstand the origin of these views. They do not spring from any personal grievance or sudden impulse, but from many years of observation in connection with mission operations, and from deep-seated Baptist convictions; convictions which cannot be bound by a money consideration or the fear of consequences to myself, as my friends well know. For several years past, I have preferred to support myself from a small private income rather than seem, by taking a salary, to sanction either the principles or the practices of the system. Right or wrong, it seems to me not only to undermine the independence and spirituality of our Churches at home, but also to parasite our work abroad. Hence I long to see a thorough revolution, both in the spirit and in the methods of our missions affairs.

Again, I am not opposed to the existence of Conventions, Societies, Boards or Committees of the proper kind, in the proper place, and for the proper purpose; but I am deeply opposed to all those which intrude themselves and their enterprises upon the Churches—to all those which take any part of their work, their workers, or their funds away from their control. To this class—without mentioning others here—clearly belong the Northern Baptist Union, the Southern Baptist Convention and their Boards. These Boards, though not subject to the Churches, both *originate* and carry on such enterprises as they think proper—whether religious or secular, wise or otherwise—at the expense of the Churches. They are, therefore, unlawful bodies within the Baptist fold and should disband. Good men, by adopting a wrong system, are the ones who lead the public astray and prepare the way for those of a different type.

While opposing all intruding bodies, I could readily sanction General and State Conventions for mutual acquaintance, for interchange of views on matters of common concern, for gathering information regarding the condition and work of the various Churches, for stimulating religious zeal and Christian fellowship, and for keeping the unity of the faith in the bonds of Gospel love, purity and peace. But these Conventions should collect no funds, employ no men, hold no property and exercise no authority over the government or the work of the Churches.

CHURCHES, AS SUCH, TO THE FRONT!

(From T. P. Crawford, *Churches, To the Front!* [China, 1892]. Copy in Treasury Room, Fleming Library, Southwestern Baptist Theological Seminary, Fort Worth, Texas.)

Haydenism

In the 1890s Texas was the scene of a bitter feud between S. A. Hayden and many of the leaders of the state convention. Apart from the personal animosities involved, an important principle was enunciated in this controversy. Hayden asserted that a convention is composed of churches, while convention leaders held that a convention is made up of individuals only, who are not "delegates" or "official representatives" of churches.

1. The view of S. A. Hayden

The Church Party believe that the commission was given to the Churches, and in them resides all the Divine authority there is in the world to evangelize the race; and that no body of men calling themselves a Committee, a Board, a Convention, or anything else, has the authority to employ missionaries and locate their labors, and fix their salaries; unless said body derives its authority directly from the Churches, and itself acting as an instrumentality for them. The Churches, having the work to do and the authority to do it, only employing a Convention as an instrument or medium to better dispatch a common labor.

B. The Board Party believe that our Conventions are not representative bodies at all, but that they are "independent of the Churches" and "Sovereign in their spheres." Their "spheres" being the several states they occupy, as to territory, and the evangelization of the world as to their work.

The Church Party believe that our Associations and Conventions are representative bodies, and that like other representative bodies, their membership is made up according to a Constitution previously adopted by the bodies represented.

C. The Board Party believes that every deliberative body has a right to determine who its members shall be, and hence they have a right to reject whom they choose in the organization, or to exclude whom they will after the organization is completed.

The Church Party believes that all representative bodies are to be governed by a Constitution previously arranged by the primary bodies they represent, and that only violations of this Constitution may furnish grounds for rejection or expulsion, and hence no representative body has a right to say who its members shall be, that matter being fixed before the body can convene in the very nature of the case.

(From the *Texas Baptist-Herald* [Dallas, Texas], February 9, 1900 [Vol. 50, No. 21], p. 7.)

Part Six
The Modern Period
1917-1966

Section One
Organizational Development

Executive Committee

In the second decade of the twentieth century Southern Baptist leaders recognized that the rapidly expanding work of the Convention imperatively demanded some type of continuing administrative body to function between sessions of the body. In 1913 a Committee on Efficiency was appointed to study the organization, plans, and methods of the Convention. After considerable discussion, in 1917 the Convention established a small Executive Committee.

1. The formation of the Executive Committee

The committee appointed at the last Convention to consider and report on a resolution to revise Articles 5 to 10 of the Constitution so as to create one strong executive board which should direct all the work and enterprises fostered and promoted by this Convention, beg leave to report that, obeying the instructions of the Convention, a majority and minority of the committee put forth, through the denominational press, last January tentative statements making certain suggestions covering the matter submitted to the committee. Having further considered the whole question, the committee respectfully submits as their completed report the following recommendations:

First: In view of the diversity of opinions concerning the best method of conducting our work, and the distressing conditions in our country, resulting from the world-war, we recommend that the Boards of the Convention remain separate as at present.

Second: Recognizing, however, that there is a strong sentiment in favor of greater unity in the general direction of the Convention's affairs, and believing that some improvement in the methods of conducting the work would be attained by the creation of a standing committee of the Convention to act for the body between its sessions in ways hereinafter set forth, we recommend that an executive committee of seven, representing the different parts of the territory of the Convention, be elected annually by the Convention as are its standing committees. No officer or member of any of the Boards of the Convention shall be eligible to membership on the executive committee. The duties of the committee shall be to have oversight of the arrangements for the meetings of the Convention with power to change both the time and place of meeting in case an emergency arises making such change necessary; that this committee shall act for the Convention ad interim on such matters as may arise pertaining to the general business of the Convention and not otherwise provided for in its plans of work; that this committee shall also be empowered to act in an advisory way on all questions submitted to it on matters arising between the Boards of this Convention, but only on request of one or more of the Boards concerned; that this committee shall have no further duties except as other things may be specifically committed to it by the Convention itself at its annual meeting; that the committee shall hold meetings at such time and places as it may select and its necessary expenses shall be a charge equally divided among the three Boards of this Convention.

(From *Annual* of the Southern Baptist Convention, 1917, pp. 33-34.)

2. The enlargement of the Committee

By 1927 the worth of the Committee was recognized. The membership and functions were enlarged, an executive secretary was secured, and the present body was developed.

After the most earnest consideration, we are convinced that the Convention should have some agency keeping in close touch with all the work of the Convention and its agencies. The affairs of the Convention and its agencies are too varied and too great to be handled effectively without it. It is evident to us that the affairs of the Convention have suffered greatly in the past from lack of such agency. The logical agency to do this is the Executive Committee of the Convention. Under the head of recommendations, we make specific recommendation for the enlargement of the functions of the Executive Committee.

. . . .

I. An Operating Budget

We recommend that the Convention, at this time, commit itself to the policy of having an Operating Budget as a financial working basis for the Convention and its agencies.

II. The Executive Committee

We recommend that Article 11 of the By-Laws of the Convention be changed to read as follows:

The Executive Committee of the Convention shall consist of the president and senior secretary of the Convention, and one member from each co-operating state and the District of Columbia and nine members at large. Nine members shall constitute a quorum for the transaction of business. No salaried official of the Southern Baptist Convention or of any of its agencies, or salaried official of any state convention, or a salaried official of any state agency, may be a member of the Executive Committee. This rule shall not apply in the case of the president or of the senior secretary of the Convention. No member of any board, or board of trustees, or commission of the Southern Baptist Convention, may be a member of the Executive Committee. This shall not apply in the case of the president or senior secretary of the Convention.

For next year the Executive Committee (excluding the president and secretary of the Convention) shall be divided into three equal groups—one group to serve for one year, a second group for two years, and the third group for three years. After that, one-third of the members of the committee shall be appointed for a term of three years. Any member appointed to fill a vacancy in a group shall serve for the unexpired term of that group.

The Executive Committee shall elect a president, recording secretary, treasurer, executive secretary, who shall be the executive officer of the committee, and such other officers and employes as it may deem necessary for the efficient conduct of its work and business. The compensation of its officers and employes shall be fixed by the committee. But no salaried officer or employe of the committee may be a member thereof. The Executive Committee shall have the books of its treasurer audited annually by a Certified Public Accountant. The Executive Committee shall establish and maintain suitable offices or headquarters in some central city within the bounds of the Southern Baptist Convention.

The duties and functions of the Executive Committee shall be as follows:

1. To act for the Convention ad interim in matters not otherwise provided for in its plans of work.

2. To have oversight of arrangements for meetings of the Convention with authority to change, if necessary, the time and place of meeting.

3. To act in an advisory way on matters of policy and co-operation arising between

the agencies of the Convention, or between agencies of the Convention and co-operating state agencies.

4. To represent the Southern Baptist Convention in all negotiations with state conventions, and state boards, and other co-operating bodies in matters of common interest. The Executive Committee shall be the authorized agency of the Southern Baptist Convention to conclude all agreements with co-operating state agencies for the conduct of necessary arrangements as to handling of Southwide funds raised in the various states, and all other related matters.

5. To recommend to the Convention an Operating Budget for the Convention year, and to recommend the percentages of Southwide funds to be allocated to each cause or agency. The Operating Budget shall include all agencies of the Southern Baptist Convention.

6. To present to the Convention a consolidated financial statement of all the agencies of the Convention. The statement shall show the assets, liabilities, and the debts of the agencies.

7. The Executive Committee shall notify the agencies of the Convention of all actions or instructions of the Convention relating to the work or other matters of the agency or agencies involved, and shall report to the Convention whether such agency or agencies have carried out the wishes of the Convention.

8. To hold meetings at such times as may be necessary or advisable for the transaction of the business committed to it by the Convention.

9. To make reports of its proceedings to the Convention at each annual session, and to make any recommendations it may desire concerning the affairs of the Convention, or concerning the affairs of the agencies of the Convention.

The Executive Committee shall have no authority to control or direct any agency of the Convention. But the Executive Committee shall have full authority to study the affairs of the agencies of the Convention, and to make suggestions, when deemed advisable, to the agencies, and to report its findings to the Convention, and to make recommendations to the Convention concerning any matters whatsoever.

The expenses of the Executive Committee shall be borne by the Sunday School Board. The Sunday School Board shall advance to the Executive Committee, from time to time, funds sufficient for the Committee to discharge its duties without financial embarrassment.

. . . .

1. We recommend that all the work now done by the Co-operative Program Commission be taken over by the Executive Committee.

2. That for the purpose of raising the funds sought by the budget adopted each year by this Convention, that the secretaries of the Boards of the Convention, the presidents of our Southwide Seminaries, the president and corresponding secretary of the W.M.U. Auxiliary to the Southern Baptist Convention, the secretary of the Baptist Brotherhood of the South, the secretaries of the state boards and the editors of the state Baptist papers be joined with the Executive Committee as constituting the Promotional Agency of the Convention in the work of projecting the campaign to this end.

. . . .

We recommend that the Executive Committee be the Fiduciary Agency of the Southern Baptist Convention; that it receive, hold and administer all funds and legacies given directly to the Southern Baptist Convention; that all funds, and property, both real and personal, owned by the Convention and now in the hands of the treasurer of the Convention be turned over to the Executive Committee as soon as the Executive Committee is legally qualified to receive them; and that the Executive Committee present to the next Convention detailed plans for establishing a Southern Baptist Foundation.

(From *Annual* of the Southern Baptist Convention, 1927, pp. 67-71.)

Annuity Board

The last of the four Boards of the Convention was formed in 1918. This document is its authorization by the Convention.

We, your committee to whom was referred the report of the Commission on Ministerial Relief and Annuities, beg leave to report as follows:

1. That we recommend the adoption of the report of the Commission as printed, except as to the location of the Board.

2. That this Board be located in the city of Dallas, Texas.

. . . .

The Commission makes the following recommendations to the Convention:

1. That the Convention create the Board of Ministerial Relief and Annuities. This Board to be constituted and appointed as are the other Boards of the Convention, and that said Board be instructed to secure a charter.

2. We recommend that Birmingham, Alabama, shall be the location for the Board of Ministerial Relief and Annuities.

3. We recommend that the plan herein submitted be adopted as the basis on which the Board of Ministerial Relief and Annuities shall operate.

4. We recommend that the Convention ask the several states to raise one hundred and fifty thousand dollars during the coming year for Ministerial Relief, and that the Apportionment Committee shall apportion the same among the states.

5. We recommend that the work of this Board both as to apportionment of beneficiaries and the collection and distribution of funds be done in the closest cooperation and harmony with the present state organization.

6. The Commission recommends that as soon as the Board of Ministerial Relief and Annuities is organized and properly chartered the Sunday School Board be in-

structed to transfer to said Board of Ministerial Relief and Annuities the funds which it now holds in custody for the purpose of ministerial relief under the instructions of the Convention.

7. The Commission further recommends that the Board shall endeavor to secure the requisite number of names with which to begin the operation of the annuity side of the plan, and as many others as wish to join.

(From *Annual* of the Southern Baptist Convention, 1918, pp. 80, 453.)

Cooperative Program

In 1939 the Executive Committee described the Cooperative Program as "the greatest step forward in Kingdom finance Southern Baptists have ever taken." It grew out of the programing and budgeting emphasis of the 75 Million Campaign, and represents a capstone of the convention-type of organizational structure.

Recommendations

First. That a simultaneous every-member canvass of every Baptist church in the South be conducted from November 30th to December 7th, 1924, for subscriptions to cover denominational needs for the calendar year 1925, ever keeping before our people the ideal of an annual increase over each year's gifts.

Second. That in this, and future campaigns, chief emphasis shall be placed upon the need for permanency in our financial plans through the Bible principles of Stewardship and Tithing.

Third. That we recognize the right of individuals and churches to designate their gifts, but it is earnestly hoped that contributions will be made to the whole program. It is urged that pastors, denominational representatives and all others of our workers shall present the whole program and press upon the people the importance of unity in its support. If, notwithstanding, there be individuals who of their own accord wish their gifts to go to special objects and who indicate the same when the gift is made, this gift shall not be charged against the sums allocated to the object to which it was given. Any solicitation of such gifts through this Every-Member Canvass will be regarded as a breach of comity and opposed to the spirit of the campaign. All designated gifts of individuals and churches made subsequent to and above the campaign pledge shall go to the causes for which they are designated without being charged against the percentage which those causes are due to receive from the general fund, but these designated gifts shall not be considered as counting on the amounts already pledged by churches or on the total amount of the pledges of the members of the church. Bequests shall be considered as "subsequent" gifts.

Fourth. Participating South-wide Causes shall, after the simultaneous campaign, have the right of approach to individuals in soliciting large gifts, provided such solicitation be approved by the state organizations of the states in which this is to be done.

An emergency now existing in the Building Program of the Southern Baptist Theological Seminary, we recommend that the Seminary be given the right of approach to individuals, after the simultaneous campaign, for large gifts to the Building Fund, payable within one year.

Fifth. We recommend that there be a General Committee, with headquarters in Nashville, for the promotion of this program, consisting of the General Secretaries, State Secretaries, Secretary of Laymen's Movement, President and Secretary of the W.M.U., Presidents of the three South-wide Institutions and ten others, three of whom shall be women and the remainder Pastors and Laymen. The expenses of the meetings of the Committee to be borne by the several States, Boards and Institutions represented, except for the ten members at large, whose expenses shall be charged to general expenses. We favor the election by the Committee of a competent General Director, who shall be under the direction of the Committee. The Committee to em-

ploy such other help as may seem advisable.

Sixth. We recommend that we undertake to raise for South-wide objects during 1925 the sum of $7,500,000.00, the same to be allocated as follows:

Foreign Missions 47%
Home Missions 20%
Christian Education 20%
Ministers' Relief and Annuities .. 10%
New Orleans Hospital 3%

Total 100%

The percentages recommended for Home and Foreign Missions have been arranged for the purpose of restoring to those Boards the funds heretofore loaned to the two Seminaries and the Baptist Bible Institute.

The 20% allocated to Christian Education to be apportioned as follows:

Southern Baptist Seminary 10%
W. M. U. Training School 1%
Southwestern Baptist Seminary .. 4%
S. W. Training School .... ½%
Bible Institute 3%
Education Board 1%
Negro Seminary .... ½%

Total 20%

Seventh. That hereafter the General Committee of the Convention shall ask from the various South-wide interests, prior to the meeting of the Southern Baptist Convention, a detailed written statement of their needs for the coming year and that, with these statements before them, the General Committee shall make a South-wide budget which shall be reported to the Convention at its annual session in a ratio of distribution based on this annual budget.

Eighth. That this Convention requests the states in the interest of exercising the spirit of co-operation, the interest of a unified program and in the interest of all our Convention causes, to leave the percentages of distribution of South-wide funds to this Convention or its General Committee. That the General Committee be instructed to confer with the several states for the adjustment of this matter.

Ninth. That monthly remittances shall be insisted upon from all Treasurers of all funds for South-wide objects on such percentage of total collections as shall be agreed upon at the outset of the campaign.

Tenth. That State Treasurers be asked to take out of the total receipts all expenses before they divide and remit to the various objects the amounts due them according to the percentages of collections.

Eleventh. That the Special Days in the Sunday Schools, as heretofore provided for by the Southern Baptist Convention and the several State Boards, shall continue to be a part of this Campaign.

In making these recommendations, your Committee is keenly sensible to the fact that all of this proposed machinery shall be but sounding brass and clanging cymbal unless it be infilled and vitalized by the Spirit of God. We, therefore, call all our people everywhere to constant and persistent intercession in behalf of all our great causes which Christ has committed to our trust.

We believe that Southern Baptists should go forward, and forward together, year by year, in high and holy endeavor until His Kingdom shall stretch from shore to shore and His name shall be known from the river to the ends of the earth.

(From *Annual* of the Southern Baptist Convention, 1924, pp. 68-69.)

Negro seminary

On October 1, 1924, the American Baptist Theological Seminary for Negro theological training was opened in Nashville, Tennessee.

1. The initial agreement of 1922

(1) There shall be two governing bodies, one to hold and control the property; the other to organize and conduct the affairs of the Seminary. Each of these two bodies shall be incorporated according to the laws of Tennessee, and the first named, or "holding body," shall for a nominal sum, lease the property to the second, or "governing body," which latter body shall then have complete direction of the "American Baptist Theological Seminary, U. S. A."

(2) The Board to hold the property shall consist of twelve (12) members, eight (8) to be elected by the Southern Baptist Convention, and four (4) to be elected by the National Baptist Convention, U. S. A.

(3) The number of the members of the Board to direct the affairs of the Seminary shall be determined by the National Baptist Convention, and shall be in the proportion of two (2) to one (1), to be elected by the National Baptist Convention, U. S. A. and the Southern Baptist Convention, respectively.

(4) Each Board shall elect its own officers. The president of the "governing body" shall be a member of the National Baptist Convention, U. S. A. and the secretary of that body shall be a member of the Southern Baptist Convention and a paid officer.

(5) The president of the Seminary shall be a member of the National Baptist Convention, U. S. A.

(From *Annual* of the Southern Baptist Convention, 1922, pp. 72-73.)

2. The revised basis of cooperation in 1964

Whereas in the life of American Baptist Theological Seminary, it has now become necessary—the continued welfare of the Seminary demanding it—that there be a more definite and mutually satisfactory basis of co-operation in the operation of the Seminary, the following agreement is entered into between the National Baptist Convention, U.S.A., Inc., and the Southern Baptist Convention.

1. There shall be one governing body to hold the property and to conduct the affairs of the Seminary. This body, to be known as the American Baptist Theological Seminary Board of Directors, shall consist of 32 members, equally divided between the two conventions. Twelve of the directors, also equally divided between the two conventions and elected from the Nashville

area, shall comprise the local board or executive committee of the Seminary. Terms shall be for three years, with the privilege of re-election for a second term. One year must elapse before being eligible for election. The treasurer of the Southern Baptist Commission on the American Baptist Theological Seminary of the Southern Baptist Convention also shall serve as an ex-officio member of the Board but without vote if not one of the 16.

2. Both conventions, utilizing their own ways and means, will give financial support to the Seminary. In the case of the Southern Baptist Convention, support shall come through the Southern Baptist Commission on the American Baptist Theological Seminary.

3. The Southern Baptist Commission on the American Baptist Theological Seminary shall consist of the 16 SBC members of the Board of Directors, six of whom shall live in the vicinity of Nashville and shall be members of the local board of the Board of Directors. This Commission shall receive and transmit Southern Baptist Convention funds for the operation of the Seminary. In event buildings are to be constructed with Southern Baptist Convention funds, the Commission shall supervise such construction, working in close co-operation with the Board of Directors. In event the Board of Directors does not carry sufficient insurance or conduct proper maintenance, responsibility for these items may be cared for by the Southern Baptist Commission on the American Baptist Theological Seminary.

4. All new buildings and equipment for the buildings must have the approval of the Board of Directors. Furnishings will be provided by the National Baptist Convention, U.S.A., Inc.

5. Ownership of the main campus of the Seminary will be vested in the Board of Directors with a reversionary clause in the deed providing that the buildings and grounds will revert to the Southern Baptist Convention if the school's purpose to provide theological education is changed.

Townsend Hall, owned by the National Baptist Convention, U.S.A., Inc., will be deeded to the Seminary Directors with a like reversionary provision.

6. The Board of Directors and the administration of the Seminary shall abide by the business and financial plans of both conventions. Any conflict or overlapping will be resolved through conferences, in consultation with the Executive Committee of the Southern Baptist Convention and the office of president of the National Baptist Convention, U.S.A., Inc.

7. The American Baptist Theological Seminary Board of Directors, through the president, shall submit a budget request to the executive boards of both conventions by December 1 for the fiscal year beginning the following August 1 for the operation of the Seminary. This budget request is to be approved by the Board of Directors and/or its local board of the Seminary, and by the executive boards of the two conventions in whatever way they care for such matters. The budget shall include all operating expenses, teachers and administration salaries; promotion; boarding department and grill, adequate insurance, repairs and maintenance of buildings, and such other operating expenses as may be agreed upon. It is understood that the reserve fund cannot be spent for any items not definitely listed in the budget. It can be used only when income for regular budget items is not received.

8. Income and expenditures through the budget shall be subject to monthly review of the local board. Semiannual reports shall be made to the Board of Directors. The Board of Directors and the president of the Seminary shall abide by the financial plans of both National Baptist Convention, U.S.A., Inc., and Southern Baptist Convention. Conflicts between these plans will be resolved in co-operation with the executive officers of the two conventions.

9. The charter of the Holding Board shall be surrendered. Until such time as this can be accomplished legally, the mem-

bership of the Holding Board shall consist of the six SBC local board members, two other SBC board members, and four National Baptist Convention, U.S.A., Inc., Seminary Board of Trustees members.

10. The president of the Seminary to be from either the National Baptist Convention, U.S.A., Inc., or from the Southern Baptist Convention.

11. This agreement, upon approval of the Southern Baptist Convention and the National Baptist Convention, U.S.A., Inc., to become effective at the beginning of the fiscal year of the Southern Baptist Commission on the Seminary, January 1, 1966.

(From *Annual* of the Southern Baptist Convention, 1964, pp. 63-64.)

Constitutional changes

Many relatively minor changes have been made in the Convention's constitution through the years. Two major changes have been made since the opening of this period.

1. The cooperating constituency relationship of states

The important place held by the Boards, Commissions, and permanent committees of the Convention has been recognized by the development of a structure to allow representation on a state basis under specified conditions. The recognition appears first in the By-Laws in 1931, and has been modified somewhat through 1965.

(1) The 1931 statement on representation on Boards

17. Any state desiring representation on any Board or the Executive Committee of this Convention shall make formal application for the representation desired, stating the number of Baptists in the state who are co-operating with this Convention and the total amount of money given to the Convention objects the preceding year. The Convention shall then make such investigation as it may desire and shall upon the basis of the information obtained vote on the question of representation on each Board and the Executive Committee upon which representation is sought and the question shall be decided by a majority vote.

(From *Annual* of the Southern Baptist Convention, 1931, p. 13.)

(2) The 1965 By-Law providing such representation

18. Representation from New States and Territories: When the co-operating Baptist churches in a state or territory have 25,000 members, they may file application for representation on the Executive Committee, boards, commissions, standing committees, and special committees as provided by the By-Laws of the Convention. This application shall be filed with the secretary before the annual meeting of the Convention, stating the number of members in the churches, the amount of money given to the work of the Convention during the preceding year, and other relevant information. The application shall be referred to the Executive Committee who shall investigate all matters pertaining to the request and make report to the next annual session of the Convention for its action.

(From *Annual* of the Southern Baptist Convention, 1965, p. 40.)

2. Basis for messenger representation at the Convention

A very significant change was made in the Constitution in 1931 which affected the basis of representation. At that time the strictly financial basis for messenger representation was eliminated in favor of the election of messengers by churches. This, of course, also terminated associational and state representation that had stemmed from the financial basis.

(1) The revision of 1931

Art. III. The Convention shall consist of messengers who are members of missionary Baptist churches co-operating with the Southern Baptist Convention on the basis of one messenger for every church contributing to the work of the Convention and one additional messenger for every $250 actually paid to the work of the Convention during the calendar year preceding the annual meeting of the Convention, such messengers to be appointed to the Convention by the churches and certified by the churches to the Convention, provided no church shall be entitled to more than three messengers.

(From *Annual* of the Southern Baptist Convention, 1931, p. 9.)

(2) The 1965 statement
Several historical factors modified the details of the 1931 revision, and these can be glimpsed from a comparison with the 1965 statement.

Article III. Membership: The Convention shall consist of messengers who are members of missionary Baptist churches co-operating with the Convention as follows:

1. One messenger for each regular Baptist church which is in friendly co-operation with this Convention and sympathetic with its purposes and work and has during the fiscal year preceding been a bona fide contributor to the Convention's work.
2. One additional messenger for each such church for every 250 members; or for each $250.00 paid to the work of the Convention during the fiscal year preceding the annual meeting.
3. The messengers shall be appointed and certified by the churches to the Convention, but no church may appoint more than ten (10).

(From *Annual* of the Southern Baptist Convention, 1965, p. 32.)

Section Two

Expansion of the Home Field

The California decision
Despite the fact that Southern Baptists *had extended the ministry of their Home Mission and Sunday School Boards into the fringe areas for various reasons, it seems likely that the significant decision of the Convention to follow its original constitution and make all of the United States and its territories its home field can be dated from 1942, when the Convention voted to recognize Southern Baptist work in California. The form of the motion was not correct (since California Baptists should not have been admitted as a body), but the action was decisive. This step having been taken, the Convention gradually moved into additional areas.*

After a careful study of the situation and in consideration of the provisions of the Constitution and By-Laws of this Convention, we recommend that the Southern Baptist General Convention of the state of California be admitted to membership in the Southern Baptist Convention.

They have thirty-one cooperating churches with an approximate membership of 3,000, fifteen of these churches having been organized during the past twelve months. They have sent $560.23 during the past twelve months to the Southwide causes. They give 20% of all co-operative program receipts to the Southwide causes.

They will be admitted to representation on only three Boards of this Convention by the provisions of the Constitution till they attain a membership of ten thousand within their state.

(From *Annual* of the Southern Baptist Convention, 1942, p. 50.)

Principles of pioneer work
As the Home Mission Board enlarged its field to include northern areas under the name of "Pioneer Missions," it developed basic principles of operation that gave guidance to the work.

Western and Pioneer Missions
The work of Western and Pioneer Missions has been one of the most rapidly expanding phases of co-operative missions.

At present the Home Mission Board co-operates with the following state conventions in this western and pioneer work: New Mexico, Arizona, California, Oregon-Washington, Kansas, Illinois, Kentucky, Arkansas, and Ohio. This work now covers all of the fifteen states west of Texas and Oklahoma in which there are churches co-operating with one of the five western state conventions. The Home Mission Board co-operates with Illinois, Arkansas, Kentucky, Maryland, Ohio, and Missouri in promotion of work in Iowa, Wisconsin, Northern Illinois, Michigan, Indiana, Delaware, Pennsylvania, and Ohio.

There are many requests that come from other areas for our co-operation, but the Home Board can only reach them through the state conventions with which they may become affiliated.

The policies adopted by the Home Mission Board and the state mission boards in this western and pioneer field are as follows:

1. In the work directly committed to this Board by the Southern Baptist Convention, or historically a part of the home mission program, it is the responsibility of this Board to develop co-operatively various programs and act as a clearinghouse for the exchange of information as to methods of use and application of programs so developed.

2. State conventions which are financially able and administratively prepared are encouraged to engage in a co-operative program of home missions within their own territory without financial aid from the Home Board so far as practical.

3. Where state conventions are not able financially to carry on a co-operative program of home missions, grants-in-aid of money should be made by this Board to the state convention for use in such programs under the administrative supervision of the state convention.

4. In western and new areas the work of this Board is co-operatively done through the state mission board nearest to the field or the convention with which the existing Southern Baptist churches are affiliated. (1) The Home Mission Board acts only upon request of the state board, and the work and workers are elected and directed by the state boards. The Home Mission Board aids only in providing funds and counsel for the work and approves the mission workers. The Home Board does not pay salaries directly to these missionaries or mission pastors but makes allocations to the state conventions for such salaries. (2) The Home and state mission boards do not solicit or invite Baptist churches already affiliated with some other convention to join our associations or conventions. In fact, we prefer that they not do so. (3) The Home Mission Board, in co-operation with the state boards, seeks to establish new churches in communities and in areas of larger communities where there is no other Baptist church. The Home Board requires a survey to be made of any community where a new church is to be located and this survey filed with the Home and state board offices. (4) The Home Board makes allocations through the state mission boards to aid mission pastors' salaries for new work. This is done only when satisfactory application has been received from prospective mission pastors and approved by both the Home and state boards. Allocations are made for periods of from three to six months, with the hope that the new work may become a self-supporting church within that period of time.

These policies have been followed carefully in the promotion of our work. Conferences have already been held with the secretaries of the American Baptist Convention in some of these states, and the plan is to hold such conferences with others during 1955. Southern Baptists in these fields will find many opportunities to plant new churches and to win the lost without going into the fields already occupied by any other Baptist group, and this is our policy.

(From *Annual* of the Southern Baptist Convention, 1955, p. 210.)

Canadian cooperation

The Baptist General Convention of Oregon-Washington, by its proximity to the Canadian field, has recognized the challenge of providing assistance to that area. Southern Baptists have differed about what form that assistance should take: whether to alter the Constitution and treat the Canadian work as though it were in one of the United States or its territories, or to assist in the development of an indigenous denominational program in Canada.

1. Petition of Oregon-Washington to assist Canadian Baptist churches

First, in offering this petition we wish to express our gratitude to the Southern Baptist Convention and to our Lord Jesus Christ for the blessings which have been ours since our petition for recognition and aid was granted at Oklahoma City in 1949.

In these five years we have grown from 21 churches to 87, plus 20 missions, and from 3,000 to 9,000 members. Last fall we had 10,000 enrolled and it seems now that we will reach our goal to add 5,000 to our Sunday School enrolment this year.

But at this time we wish to petition the Convention on behalf of Western Canada. Churches in British Columbia and the prairie provinces have asked for affiliation in our state convention, and are supporting the Cooperative Program of Southern Baptists. These churches are composed of Canadian members who have expressed the conviction that Canada desperately needs the program which Southern Baptists alone can give.

They call attention to the fact that in British Columbia and Alberta there is only one Baptist to 158 in the population. The population is 2,169,501, Baptist churches of all groups number 115, and total Baptist membership is 13,700. (In the whole of Canada the population is counted 50 per cent Catholic.)

The Baptist General Convention of Oregon-Washington is at this time aiding churches in Canada affiliated with us in opening up new fields in great un-churched areas out of funds given for our work by a great Southern Baptist church. Our needs are great but the needs of our Canadian brethren are greater.

We call attention to the fact that through its Home Mission Board the Southern Baptist Convention aids such other countries as Cuba and Panama even though there is a language barrier to overcome. Here there is no language barrier and it is our conviction that in the great Northwest, what was once "the Oregon Country" could again be united in a common cause—this time under the banner of Christ to make strong the spiritual foundations of sister nations. Our Southern Baptist Boards are now aiding Alaska on one side and the Northwestern States on the other.

Our plea is that the Home Mission Board, the Sunday School Board and other Southern Baptist agencies be permitted to aid us in this work in Canada in and through churches affiliated with our state convention.

(From *Annual* of the Southern Baptist Convention, 1954, p. 53.)

2. The policy of the Southern Baptist Convention in Canada

We recommend that the policy adopted by the Home Mission Board and the Sunday School Board as authorized by the Southern Baptist Convention be recognized as the Southern Baptist Convention policy regarding Canada, as follows:

(1) That the Home Mission Board and the Sunday School Board shall recognize that Baptist brethren as individuals, local churches, associations, and state conventions are each autonomous bodies with the right to determine their own affiliation and co-operation with other Baptist bodies. Therefore, we would not question their own rights for mutual co-operation and promotion.

(2) We recommend that the Home Mission Board and the Sunday School Board as agencies of the Southern Baptist Convention may accept invitations from any Baptist church or group of churches in

Canada to help them in the promotion of their programs of education, stewardship, missions, and evangelism for the development of their own members.

(3) That no worker of the Home Mission Board or the Sunday School Board whose salary is paid in part or in full shall seek to align existing churches or new churches with our Southern Baptist work. This statement is to be understood as our policy in dealing with all missionary personnel employed in part or in full by the Home Mission Board.

(4) That, in accord with our generally accepted policy, it shall be the hope of the Home Mission Board and the Sunday School Board to render all assistance possible in helping the Baptist forces in Canada to develop an indigenous denominational program that will win Canada for Christ.

(From *Annual* of the Southern Baptist Convention, 1958, p. 72.)

Section Three

Special Emphases of the Convention

The 75 Million Campaign

After World War I many factors combined to cause Southern Baptists to adopt with enthusiasm a program to raise $75,000,-000 in five years for the organized work of Southern Baptists. Total subscriptions amounted to $92,630,923, but the deterioration of the economic situation in the South during the next five years resulted in collections of $58,591,713.69. The consequent heavy indebtedness, coming as it did just before a general economic collapse, severely tried the mettle of the Southern Baptist people. However, the positive results of this campaign far outweighed the debt, for during this period many accepted the call to a religious vocation, giving was accelerated, better methods of raising and disbursing funds were developed, the Cooperative Program probably evolved from the campaign, and the Executive Committee was strengthened and enlarged at least partly

by it. This document is the final report and summary of the movement.

FINAL REPORT
OF CONSERVATION COMMISSION
OF THE 75 MILLION CAMPAIGN

The Conservation Commission make this final report to the Southern Baptist Convention.

At the Convention in Atlanta, May, 1919, the 75 Million Campaign was projected. The Convention appointed a Campaign Commission. This Commission elected L. R. Scarborough General Director, and set up headquarters at Nashville, Tennessee. The Commission, under the leadership of the General Director, in June and July of 1919, set up the organization and made plans for putting on the 75 Million Campaign. In Victory Week, November 30 to December 7, 1919, pledges and covenants were secured to the amount of more than ninety-two million dollars to be paid in five years. At the Washington Convention in 1920 the Commission reported its work done. This Commission was succeeded by the appointment by the Convention of a Conservation Commission, which Commission has been reappointed from year to year. The duty of this Commission was to cooperate and lead in the collection of the pledges and the conservation of the causes involved in the 75 Million Campaign. The work of this Commission ended January 1, 1925. At a meeting of this Commission in January, 1925, a final report was made. At this time it was not possible to get all of the final returns and figures and record of achievements. So the Commission now makes its final report.

Collection by States

All of us were disappointed in that these collections were not greater. The Conservation Commission is gratified in that it feels that it did the best it could under existing conditions. We are grateful that this sum represents a far greater sum of money raised than was ever raised during any similar period by our people for the kingdom of God.

Since the responsibility of distributing these funds was not on the Commission, we can only report in general terms, as follows, the distribution of these funds. The full report of this distribution is in the records of the State Secretaries and the General Secretaries of this Convention, and will be found in the minutes of this Convention and the State Conventions. We submit herein a general summary of achievements in the different phases of the work these marvelous five years. We are grateful that God has so wonderfully and marvelously blessed our people and all the causes, institutions and movements in connection with the work of Southern Baptists in the homeland and around the world.

FINANCIAL STATEMENT ON THE 75 MILLION CAMPAIGN

Final returns upon the 75 Million Campaign as reported to the general headquarters office shows total cash collections in the sum of $58,591,713.69. While the Campaign did not attain its total financial goal, it came more nearly doing so than almost any other forward movement conducted by any of the large denominations during the period immediately following the war.

Of a special interest to our constituency will be the fact that an exceptionally low expense account was maintained throughout the inauguration and conduct of this forward movement. The expenses of the general headquarters in Nashville, both in the inauguration of the Campaign in 1919 and the conduct of that movement during the five and one-half years that followed was $427,878.11, or less than three-fourths of one per cent of the total amount of money raised. The total expenses for both the general headquarters office and the seventeen State offices in the projection and conduct of the Campaign throughout its entire period amounted to less than 4 per cent of the total cash sum collected. The expenses of the headquarters office since the last report to this Convention amounted to $26,892.26.

The final report on the collections as made to the general headquarters office by the various State offices is shown as follows:

Alabama	$ 2,717,464.62
Arkansas	2,319,654.72
District of Columbia	301,848.81
Florida	1,009,416.89
Georgia	5,282,493.24
Illinois	691,245.89
Kentucky	6,414,159.87
Louisiana	1,681,438.52
Maryland	729,440.82
Mississippi	3,107,040.36
Missouri	2,438,561.24
New Mexico	708,124.80
North Carolina	5,174,865.61
Oklahoma	1,462,030.34
South Carolina	4,773,889.11
Tennessee	3,950,655.49
Texas	8,720,161.50
Virginia	6,657,778.86
Foreign Board Specials	86,103.00
Contributed to Foreign Churches	350,000.00
Home Board Specials	15,340.00
Total	**$58,591,713.69**

This sum was distributed among the various co-operating objects in the Campaign as follows:

Foreign Missions	$11,615,327.91
Home Missions	6,622,725.55
State and Associated Missions	9,900,785.93
Christian Education	16,087,942.07
Orphanages	5,134,522.10
Hospitals	2,975,380.07
Ministerial Relief	1,786,676.30
Expenses not otherwise absorbed	2,164,776.38
Famine Relief	70,442.21
Credits claimed by churches on money sent direct and miscellaneous items	$ 2,163,454.57
Undistributed balance	69,689.60

Total $58,591,713.69

(From *Annual* of the Southern Baptist Convention, 1925, pp. 22-23.)

The Hundred Thousand Club

As a plan to help retire the large indebtedness of the Convention's agencies, an effort was made to enlist one hundred thousand persons who would give $1.00 a month over and above their regular subscriptions through their churches. The program, called "The Baptist Hundred Thousand Club," was very successful.

At a meeting of the Executive Committee, April 13, the following action was taken:

"We approve the organization of the Baptist Hundred Thousand Club method of systematically reducing the indebtedness of the institutions, boards and agencies of the Convention.

"We further recommend that the Executive Committee appoint a special committee of three to work out the details of such a plan and present them to the Promotion Committee."

Your committee, after giving the matter careful consideration, makes the following recommendations:

1. That the name of the organization be THE BAPTIST HUNDRED THOUSAND CLUB.

2. That the object of the club be the liquidation of the present debts of all the agencies of the Southern Baptist Convention.

3. That the membership of the Hundred Thousand Club consist of persons paying One Dollar ($1.00) per month over and above their regular subscriptions through the churches.

4. That the payments by the members shall be made through the churches in envelopes provided for that purpose.

5. That church treasurers be requested to remit on the first of each month to the treasurers of the respective states all funds accruing from membership payments, stating the purpose for which they are intended, the state treasurers to remit the same to the Executive Committee of the Southern Baptist Convention.

6. That the treasurer of the Executive Committee of the Southern Baptist Convention be instructed to transmit promptly all funds to the several agencies of the Convention, according to percentages determined by the Executive Committee, in ratio to the debt needs of the several agencies. Nothing in the foregoing shall interfere with the right of the donor to designate if he so desires.

7. That the plan of the organization be as follows:

That the promotional agency of the Southern Baptist Convention set up and direct the organization and the promotion of the club on the following general plan:

(a) A general leader who may be the executive secretary of the Convention's promotional agency, or a pastor serving without salary.

(b) A state leader in each state cooperating with the Convention.

(c) An associational leader in each association.

(d) A leader in each church. All state, associational and church directors to serve without pay.

8. The following plan of operation, with such changes as may be found necessary, is recommended:

(a) A membership card.

(b) A membership button reading, "Baptist Hundred Thousand Club."

(c) A certificate of membership bearing the names of the general director and the executives of all the Southwide agencies.

(d) Special Hundred Thousand Club envelopes.

(e) A suitable pamphlet setting forth the general purpose and plans of the club.

9. Since the organization and promotion of the Baptist Hundred Thousand Club is to be done by the Convention's promotional agency and such volunteer help as may be necessary, it is recommended that the expense of printing, stationery, postage, and

so forth, be provided for out of the funds of the promotional agency.

10. That further details of organization and promotion be left to the general leader and the promotional agency.

(From *Annual* of the Southern Baptist Convention, 1933, pp. 65-66.)

The Jubilee Advance

Looking forward to the one hundred fiftieth anniversary of the founding of the first Baptist general body in the United States, the Convention joined other Baptist groups in naming the period from 1959 to 1964 as "The Baptist Jubilee Advance." The document is the authorization of this program by the Convention.

(1) We recommend that the period from 1959 to 1964 be designated as "The Baptist Jubilee Advance."

(2) We recommend that the annual emphases be as follows: Evangelism through co-operative witness (in reference to the simultaneous revival movement), 1959; evangelism through Bible teaching and training, 1960; evangelism through stewardship and enlistment, 1961; evangelism through church extension, 1962; evangelism through world missions, 1963; and the Third Jubilee Celebration, 1964.

(3) We recommend that the agencies and institutions of the Southern Baptist Convention plan their five-year program from 1959 to 1964 within the framework of these emphases where possible.

(4) We recommend the adoption of the following as the purpose for the Baptist Jubilee Advance:

At the 1955 Southern Baptist Convention in Miami, it was voted "to confer with representatives of other Baptist conventions in North America, looking toward a five-year program of advance which will culminate in 1964, the date of the one hundred fiftieth anniversary of the organization of Baptist work on a national level in the United States and North America."

At the meeting of the American Baptist Convention, it was voted: "That we heartily

welcome the proposal of the Southern Baptist Convention and request that the Department of Evangelism of the Home Mission Society consider the implementation of American Baptist Convention participating in the Evangelistic Crusade and urge that the long-range objectives leading to the Sesquicentennial be referred with our cordial endorsement to the appropriate committee of the General Council for further development."

The National Baptist Convention of the U.S.A., Inc., took action in its September, 1955, meeting, endorsing the movement. At the organization meeting in Chicago on December 8, 1955, called by Dr. C. C. Warren, representatives were present from the Southern Baptist Convention, the American Baptist Convention, the National Baptist Convention, U.S.A., Inc. the National Convention of America, the North American Baptist General Conference, and the Baptist General Conference of America. Canadian Baptists have since expressed a desire to participate.

The resulting movement, called the Baptist Jubilee Advance, has as its purpose the dramatization and deepening of the Baptist witness to the world. It is to begin with a concerted evangelistic effort by all participating Baptist bodies in 1959, followed by appropriate co-ordinated emphasis in 1960, 1961, 1962, and 1963, and culminating in 1964 in the celebration of the Third Jubilee. Specifically:

(1) It is an attempt to quicken, in professed believers in Christ, a sense of responsibility for carrying out all phases of the Great Commission with zeal and fervor.

(2) It is an attempt, on the part of Baptists in the United States and Canada, to "see togther" the gigantic task before us. It is not, however either a movement toward organic union or a program to emphasize, rehearse, or even consider, past or present differences.

(3) It is a program focusing the efforts of Baptists on common goals and

objectives, which each participating body can achieve within the framework of its own organization. It is not a stereotyped program to be handed down by a central committee to the participating bodies.

(4) It is an effort to bring about, in the Third Jubilee year of 1964, the greatest achievements of any single year in Baptist history, to give to the world a dramatic presentation of what Baptists stand for and what they have done, and to gain a mighty impetus for even greater achievements for God's glory in the years ahead.

(From *Annual* of the Southern Baptist Convention, 1956, pp. 40-41.)

Study of the Southern Baptist Convention Program

In 1956 the Convention entered into an intensive self-study of its organization and work. From the program described in this document many important developments have taken place.

Whereas it is our conviction that a study of our total Southern Baptist program, if wisely conducted, would prove of great value in this effort toward strengthening and expanding our Christian ministry:

We therefore recommend the appointment of a committee by this Convention to make such study, and we further recommend that this committee consists of one member from each co-operating state, as defined in Bylaw 17 of the Convention, and three members at large, to be appointed by the president, the first and second vice-presidents, and the senior secretary of the Convention. It being understood that no employed personnel of the Convention shall be appointed to the committee.

It shall be the purpose of this committee to study the functions of the agencies and boards of the Southern Baptist Convention, and their relationship with the churches; with the state conventions, and with other agencies and boards of the Con-

vention, with a view of finding the most effective way of promoting the Kingdom through the Southern Baptist Convention. The committee shall be authorized to employ such professional assistance as it may deem wise in making this study with the understanding that the total expenditure for the year shall not exceed $25,000. This committee can make such recommendations as it may deem wise to the Southern Baptist Convention at its meeting in Chicago in 1957, and any recommendations contained in the committee's report shall be made available to the Baptist Press at least two months prior to the next meeting of the Convention, in order that our Baptist constituency may have ample time to study them.

(Ibid., p. 44.)

Section Four

Controversies

The Norris movement

During the first half of the twentieth century, J. Frank Norris of Fort Worth, Texas, a prominent pastor who had been excluded from the association, harassed Texas Baptists and the Southern Baptist Convention with incessant attacks through his church newspaper, sermons, and various other media. He claimed to be a champion of English Bible orthodoxy, church autonomy, and the pure gospel. It was his activity that led the Convention to adopt the words "in friendly co-operation with this Convention and sympathetic with its purposes and work" in Article III of the Constitution. The document is a tract written by President L. R. Scarborough of Southwestern seminary, evidently in the 1930s.

FOREWORD

This tract is a discussion of some of the fruits of an old cult under a new name. The following are some of the characteristics of this cult—Norrisism:

1. It is toward true religion what social-

ism and bolshevism are to politics and industry; wholly destructive in spirit and methods.

2. It is anti-missionary and anti-institutional. It gives nothing to associational, state or home missions and only enough to foreign missions to get representation in the convention. It spends most of its money on itself—some times in court trials for perjury, arson and murder, and in sending out free literature seeking to destroy the causes other people try to build.

3. It thrives on sensationalism, misrepresentation and false accusations of good men and true causes. It masquerades under the cloak of anti-evolutionism, anti-modernism, anti-catholicism in order to ride into public favor and cast poisonous suspicion on the leadership of the causes of constructive Christianity.

4. In its chief leadership it is the embodiment of autocratic ecclesiasticism. All the privileges and rights of the church heading up in the pastor.

5. It uses the pulpit, the press, and the radio to create suspicion, to foment class prejudices and to vent its hatred against innocent personalities and institutions.

6. It divides and splits families, churches, associations and strikes its poisonous fangs at the brotherhood of Christianity.

7. It lowers the standards of right conduct, individual righteousness, ministerial ethics, personal integrity, and gives to the world a false conception of the character, spirit and methods of Christianity.

8. The only people or causes it praises are those who bow down to its dictum or fail in any wise to cross its path.

9. The individual, the preacher or church who joins in sympathy with this cult will sooner or later cease to co-operate with the mission, educational or benevolent enterprises fostered by God's people.

10. It has some noble names upon the escutcheon of its false accusations and public misrepresentation; Carroll, Gambrell, McDaniel, McConnell, Mullins, C. V. Edwards, Brooks, Sampey, Groner, Ray, Robertson, Forrest Smith, Cullen Thomas, Truett and others—multitudes of false accusations, such as: infidelity, graft, heresy, theft and such like, and groundless insinuations have gone out against these good men for years. This tract deals with only a few of these false and slanderous charges against these brethren. These are but samples—there are many others which are as groundless as these.

(From L. R. Scarborough, *The Fruits of Norrisism* [Fort Worth, Texas, n.d.].)

Secular court decisions

One of the most critical problems facing all organizations of Baptists stems from the threat to the autonomy of churches by judicial decisions involved in litigation over church property. The state courts formerly followed one of two positions: (1) The majority of a Baptist congregation may do anything it wishes, even to alteration of accepted and traditional Baptist doctrine and practice; (2) if the majority leaves the accepted Baptist doctrine, tradition, and practice which had obtained before schism took place, then the minority constitutes the "true church" and should be awarded the property.

Either of these positions can be justified in Baptist polity and history. The classical example of this has been the North Rocky Mount Missionary Baptist Church of North Carolina. The majority withdrew from all affiliation with Southern Baptist bodies and looked toward affiliation with another Baptist denomination. The Superior and Supreme Courts held that this did not materially affect the problem of who should retain the property. However, the property was awarded to the minority because they, apart from any general denominational relationships, continued in the doctrines, traditions, and practice which had obtained before the schism, while the majority had departed from these.

1. Decision of the Supreme Court of North Carolina

In the instant case there is no allegation

in the complaint that the North Rocky Mount Missionary Baptist Church has been at all times governed and conducted by the rules, customs and practices of Missionary Baptist Churches in general, nor have the defendants made any such admission. The Record before us discloses that the North Rocky Mount Missionary Baptist Church from the beginning has been a pure democracy and independent of any external control. It is known to all that from the beginning Baptist Churches have retained, and refused to give up their independence.

The proper conclusion of law in this case is that the true congregation of the North Rocky Mount Missionary Baptist Church consists of those members of its congregation who adhere to the characteristic doctrines, usages, customs and practices of that particular church, recognized and accepted by both factions before the dissension between them arose.

The Trial Judge made elaborate findings of fact as to the organizational and operational structure of Missionary Baptist Churches generally in this State and nation. All of these findings of fact are irrelevant and immaterial. The question for decision before the Trial Court was the same as that presented to us for decision, which question we have stated heretofore in this opinion.

. . . .

The defendants, and those united in interest with them, by resolving that the North Rocky Mount Missionary Baptist Church shall continue its ministry in the community as an Independent Missionary Baptist Church, and by doing the things found as facts by the Trial Judge, as set forth in this opinion, and by being in possession of and using the church property for those purposes and plans have, as against the plaintiffs, and those united in interest with them, who are a faithful minority, diverted the property of the North Rocky Mount Missionary Baptist Church to the support of usages, customs, doctrines and practices radically and fundamentally

opposed to the characteristic usages, customs, doctrines and practices recognized and accepted by both factions of the congregation of this particular church before the dissension between them arose.

. . . .

The lower court ordered, adjudged and decreed: "That the plaintiffs and all other members of said church who adhere and submit to the regular order of the church, local and general, are the true congregation." That part of the judgment will be modified to read as follows: "That the true congregation of the North Rocky Mount Missionary Baptist Church consists of the plaintiffs and all other members of the congregation who adhere and submit to the characteristic doctrines, usages, customs and practices of this particular church, recognized and accepted by both factions of the congregation before the dissension between them arose."

(From *Advance Sheets of Cases* argued and determined in the Supreme Court of North Carolina at Raleigh, Fall Term, 1954, pp. 212-15.)

2. Critical decision by the Supreme Court of Kansas

In a case involving the First Baptist Church, Wichita, Kansas, the lower court held for the majority but the Supreme Court awarded the property to a small minority simply because the majority withdrew from the American Baptist Convention. There was no indication that the doctrines, traditions, and practices of the undivided church had been changed. This suggests that every general body has a vital interest in the church property of every Baptist church affiliating with it.

Of course, what we have said above is fortified by what this court has said in former cases. In *Hughes v. Grossman*, 166 Kan. 325, 201 P. 2d 670, the fifth paragraph of the syllabus spoke of a rather small Baptist church and not of the largest church of the denomination in the state. But in that case the court said:

"The record is an injunction action involving the custody, management and control of property belonging to a Baptist church is examined, and it is held, that under the facts and circumstances as fully set forth in the opinion, repudiation by the defendants of the national, state and local associations maintained by the churches of the Baptist faith constituted a departure from the original principles, rules and practices of church government recognized by the united body prior to the occurrence of any schism therein and entitled the plaintiffs to injunctive relief perpetually restraining and enjoining the defendants from occupying or possessing the church property and from interfering with the plaintiffs in the management, control, possession or custody of the church, its property or its business affairs." (Syl. parag. 5)

The case of *Whipple v. Fehsenfeld*, 173 Kan. 427, 249 P. 2d 638, follows *Hughes v. Grossman*, supra, perhaps on even a clearer set of facts.

However, we believe the rule of those two cases applies to the case at bar. We hold that not even in an autonomous Baptist church may the denomination of the church be changed by a mere majority vote.

In concluding this opinion it is evident from what has been said that the judgment of the trial court must be reversed. Therefore, the judgment appealed from is reversed and the trial court is directed to issue an injunction as prayed for by the plaintiffs. It is so ordered.

(From Supreme Court of Kansas, *Huber v. Thorn*, 371 P2d 143 [1962].)

Midwestern Seminary

The publication of a book by a professor in Midwestern Baptist Theological Seminary which some Southern Baptists felt was not true to the historic position of Southern Baptists relative to the Scriptures brought a controversy in 1962-63. Along with the doctrinal question was the issue of just how immediately the Convention controlled the institutions which it had entrusted into the hands of elected trustees.

The document is the report of the president of the Seminary to the 1963 Convention.

STATEMENT REGARDING MIDWESTERN SEMINARY

I come in the capacity as president of the board of trustees of Midwestern Baptist Theological Seminary. There were references made this morning to the institution where 30 of us serve as trustees, 10 of whom are from Missouri, the Midwestern Baptist Theological Seminary.

Your trustees have been and are now conscious of the action of this Convention taken last year in San Francisco. We have earnestly and diligently worked that Midwestern Seminary may be true to the historic position of Southern Baptists.

The board of trustees is representative of the diversity that exists among Southern Baptists. We have met four times as a full board and several times as subcommittees since the last meeting of this Convention. We have periodically released reports to the Baptist Press.

The trustees have set out nine principles of academic procedure to which the faculty has committed themselves:

I.

1. The particular method in using the Historical-Critical approach is recognized as a valid approach to Old Testament studies.

2. Differences of opinion on interpretations of biblical passages is recognized. Each student, with the guidance of the Holy Spirit, must seek understanding of the Bible. As long as the professor is on the faculty of the seminary, he is obligated to teach within the framework of the fundamentals of the Baptist faith.

3. It is affirmed that the seminary teacher is to approach his work from the viewpoint of a firm belief in the Bible as God's Word. The Bible does not depend for its trustworthiness upon verification from the fields of science, history, archaeology, and related fields.

4. We affirm our belief in the inspiration

of the Bible and all parts thereof. The method of inspiration is not to be thought of as a test for Baptist fellowship.

5. The task of the teacher is not to proclaim what he doesn't know about the Bible or to seek by "shock methods" to startle students by a negative approach to the Bible as the Word of God. His task is to strengthen the faith of the student and help him to prepare to present its message.

6. The Bible contains accounts of the miraculous and supernatural. The fact of miracles does not depend upon the human ability to understand or explain.

7. In presenting interpretations of passages and events in the Bible, various views should be presented.

8. We reject any theory that regards the Bible as a book of folklore and mythology.

9. The Bible is to be taught, and it is the task of the teacher to lead students in their teaching and preaching to go out and make known their faith and belief.

(From *Annual* of the Southern Baptist Convention, 1963, p. 68.)

Section Five

Confessions of Faith

The Southern Baptist Convention has twice adopted confessions of faith. These are of such significance that the major part of them, along with the introductory statements by the committees which prepared them, are included here.

The Memphis Articles of 1925

REPORT OF COMMITTEE ON
BAPTIST FAITH AND MESSAGE

Your committee beg leave to report as follows:

Your committee recognize that they were appointed "to consider the advisability of issuing another statement of the Baptist Faith and Message, and to report at the next Convention."

In pursuance of the instructions of the Convention, and in consideration of the general denominational situation, your committee have decided to recommend the New Hampshire Confession of Faith, revised at certain points, and with some additional articles growing out of present needs, for approval by the Convention, in the event a statement of the Baptist faith and message is deemed necessary at this time.

The present occasion for a reaffirmation of Christian fundamentals is the prevalence of naturalism in the modern teaching and preaching of religion. Christianity is supernatural in its origin and history. We repudiate every theory of religion which denies the supernatural elements in our faith.

As introductory to the doctrinal articles, we recommend the adoption by the Convention of the following statement of the historic Baptist conception of the nature and function of confessions of faith in our religious and denominational life, believing that some such statement will clarify the atmosphere and remove some causes of misunderstanding, friction, and apprehension. Baptists approve and circulate confessions of faith with the following understandings, namely:

(1) That they constitute a consensus of opinion of some Baptist body, large or small, for the general instruction and guidance of our own people and others concerning those articles of the Christian faith which are most surely held among us. They are not intended to add anything to the simple conditions of salvation revealed in the New Testament, viz., repentance towards God and faith in Jesus Christ as Saviour and Lord.

(2) That we do not regard them as complete statements of our faith, having any quality of finality or infallibility. As in the past so in the future Baptists should hold themselves free to revise their statements of faith as may seem to them wise and expedient at any time.

(3) That any group of Baptists, large or small, have the inherent right to draw up for themselves and publish to the world

a confession of their faith whenever they may think it advisable to do so.

(4) That the sole authority for faith and practice among Baptists is the Scriptures of the Old and New Testaments. Confessions are only guides in interpretation, having no authority over the conscience.

(5) That they are statements of religious convictions, drawn from the Scriptures, and are not to be used to hamper freedom of thought or investigation in other realms of life.

The Scriptures

1. We believe that the Holy Bible was written by men divinely inspired, and is a perfect treasure of heavenly instruction; that it has God for its author, salvation for its end, and truth, without any mixture of error, for its matter; that it reveals the principles by which God will judge us; and therefore is, and will remain to the end of the world, the true center of Christian union, and the supreme standard by which all human conduct, creeds and religious opinions should be tried.

God

2. There is one and only one living and true God, an intelligent, spiritual and personal Being, the Creator, Preserver and Ruler of the universe, infinite in holiness and all other perfections, to whom we owe the highest love, reverence and obedience. He is revealed to us as Father, Son and Holy Spirit, each with distinct personal attributes, but without division of nature, essence or being.

The Fall of Man

3. Man was created by the special act of God, as recorded in Genesis. "So God created man in his own image, in the image of God created he him; male and female created he them." (Gen. 1:27). "And the Lord God formed man of the dust of the ground, and breathed into his nostrils the breath of life; and man became a living soul." (Gen. 2:7.) He was created in a state of holiness under the law of his maker, but, through the temptation of Satan he transgressed the command of God and fell from his original holiness and righteousness; whereby his posterity inherit a nature corrupt and in bondage to sin, are under condemnation, and as soon as they are capable of moral action, become actual transgressors.

The Way of Salvation

4. The salvation of sinners is wholly of grace, through the mediatorial office of the Son of God, who by the Holy Spirit was born of the Virgin Mary and took upon him our nature, yet without sin; honored the divine law by his personal obedience, and made atonement for our sins by his death. Being risen from the dead, he is now enthroned in heaven, and, uniting in his person the tenderest sympathies with divine perfections, he is in every way qualified to be a compassionate and all-sufficient Saviour.

Justification

5. Justification is God's gracious and full acquittal upon principles of righteousness of all sinners who believe in Christ. This blessing is bestowed, not in consideration of any works of righteousness which we have done, but through the redemption that is and through Jesus Christ. It brings us into a state of most blessed peace and favor with God, and secures every other needed blessing.

The Freeness of Salvation

6. The blessings of salvation are made free to all by the Gospel. It is the duty of all to accept them by penitent and obedient faith. Nothing prevents the salvation of the greatest sinner except his own voluntary refusal to accept Jesus Christ as teacher, Saviour and Lord.

Regeneration

7. Regeneration or the new birth is a change of heart wrought by the Holy Spirit, whereby we become partakers of the divine nature and a holy disposition is given, leading to the love and practice of righteousness. It is a work of God's free grace conditioned upon faith in Christ and made manifest by the fruit which we bring forth to the glory of God.

Repentance of Faith

8. We believe that repentance and faith are sacred duties, and also inseparable graces, wrought in our souls by the regenerating Spirit of God; whereby being deeply convinced of our guilt, danger, and helplessness, and of the way of salvation by Christ, we turn to God with unfeigned contrition, confession, and supplication for mercy; at the same time heartily receiving the Lord Jesus Christ as our Prophet, Priest and King, and relying on him alone as the only and all-sufficient Saviour.

God's Purpose of Grace

9. Election is the gracious purpose of God, according to which he regenerates, sanctifies and saves sinners. It is perfectly consistent with the free agency of man, and comprehends all the means in connection with the end. It is a most glorious display of God's sovereign goodness, and is infinitely wise, holy and unchangeable. It excludes boasting and promotes humility. It encourages the use of means in the highest degree.

Sanctification

10. Sanctification is the process by which the regenerate gradually attain to moral and spiritual perfection through the presence and power of the Holy Spirit dwelling in their hearts. It continues throughout the earthly life, and is accomplished by the use of all the ordinary means of grace, and particularly by the Word of God.

Perseverance

11. All real believers endure to the end. Their continuance in well-doing is the mark which distinguishes them from mere professors. A special Providence cares for them, and they are kept by the power of God through faith unto salvation.

A Gospel Church

12. A church of Christ is a congregation of baptized believers, associated by covenant in the faith and fellowship of the gospel; observing the ordinances of Christ, governed by his law, and exercising the gifts, rights and privileges invested in them by his word, and seeking to extend the Gospel to the ends of the earth. Its Scriptural officers are bishops or elders and deacons.

Baptism and the Lord's Supper

13. Christian baptism is the immersion of a believer in water in the name of the Father, the Son and the Holy Spirit. The act is a symbol of our faith in a crucified, buried and risen Saviour. It is prerequisite to the privileges of a church relation and to the Lord's Supper, in which the members of the church, by the use of bread and wine, commemorate the dying love of Christ.

The Lord's Day

14. The first day of the week is the Lord's day. It is a Christian institution for regular observance. It commemorates the resurrection of Christ from the dead, and should be employed in exercises of worship and spiritual devotion, both public and private, and by refraining from worldly amusements, and resting from secular employments, works of necessity and mercy only excepted.

The Righteous and the Wicked

15. There is a radical and essential difference between the righteous and wicked. Those only who are justified through the name of the Lord Jesus Christ and sanctified by the Holy Spirit are truly righteous in his sight. Those who continue in impenitence and unbelief are in his sight wicked and are under condemnation. This distinction between the righteous and the wicked holds in and after death, and will be made manifest at the judgment when final and everlasting awards are made to all men.

The Resurrection

16. The Scriptures clearly teach that Jesus rose from the dead. His grave was emptied of its contents. He appeared to the disciples after his resurrection in many convincing manifestations. He now exists in his glorified body at God's right hand. There will be a resurrection of the righteous and the wicked. The bodies of the righteous will conform to the glorious spiritual body of Jesus.

The Return of the Lord

17. The New Testament teaches in many places the visible and personal return of Jesus to this earth. "This same Jesus which is taken up from you into Heaven, shall so come in like manner as ye have seen him go into Heaven." The time of his coming is not revealed. "Of that day and hour knoweth no one, no, not the angels in heaven, but my Father only." (Matt. 24:36.) It is the duty of all believers to live in readiness for his coming and by diligence in good works to make manifest to all men the reality and power of their hope in Christ.

Religious Liberty

18. God alone is Lord of the conscience, and he has left it free from the doctrines and commandments of men which are contrary to his word or not contained in it. Church and state should be separate. The state owes to the church protection and full freedom in the pursuit of its spiritual ends. In providing for such freedom no ecclesiastical group or denomination should be favored by the state more than others. Civil government being ordained of God, it is the duty of Christians to render loyal obedience thereto in all things not contrary to the revealed will of God. The church should not resort to the civil power to carry on its work. The Gospel of Christ contemplates spiritual means alone for the pursuit of its ends. The state has no right to impose penalties for religious opinions of any kind. The state has no right to impose taxes for the support of any form of religion. A free church in a free state is the Christian ideal, and this implies the right of free and unhindered access to God on the part of all men, and the right to form and propagate opinions in the sphere of religion without interference by the civil power.

Peace and War

19. It is the duty of Christians to seek peace with all men on principles of righteousness. In accordance with the spirit and teachings of Christ they should do all in their power to put an end to war.

The true remedy for the war spirit is the pure gospel of our Lord. The supreme need of the world is the acceptance of his teachings in all the affairs of men and nations, and the practical application of his law of love.

We urge Christian people throughout the world to pray for the reign of the Prince of Peace, and to oppose everything to provoke war.

Education

20. Christianity is the religion of enlightenment and intelligence. In Jesus Christ are hidden all the treasures of wisdom and knowledge. All sound learning is therefore a part of our Christian heritage. The new birth opens all human faculties and creates a thirst for knowledge. An adequate system of schools is necessary to a complete spiritual program for Christ's people. The cause of education in the Kingdom of Christ is co-ordinate with the causes of missions and general benevolence, and should receive along with these the liberal support of the churches.

Social Service

21. Every Christian is under obligation to seek to make the will of Christ regnant in his own life and in human society; to oppose in the spirit of Christ every form of greed, selfishness and vice; to provide for the orphaned, the aged, the helpless, and the sick; to seek to bring industry, government and society as a whole under the sway of the principles of righteousness, truth and brotherly love; to promote these ends Christians should be ready to work with all men of good will in any good cause, always being careful to act in the spirit of love without compromising their loyalty to Christ and his truth. All means and methods used in social service for the amelioration of society and the establishment of righteousness among men must finally depend on the regeneration of the individual by the saving grace of God in Christ Jesus.

Co-operation

22. Christ's people should, as occasion requires, organize such associations and

conventions as may best secure co-operation for the great objects of the Kingdom of God. Such organizations have no authority over each other or over the churches. They are voluntary and advisory bodies designed to elicit, combine and direct the energies of our people in the most effective manner. Individual members of New Testament churches should co-operate with each other, and the churches themselves should co-operate with each other, in carrying forward the missionary, educational and benevolent program for the extension of Christ's Kingdom. Christian unity in the New Testament sense is spiritual harmony and voluntary co-operation for common ends by various Christian denominations, when the end to be attained is itself justified, and when such co-operation involves no violation of conscience or compromise of loyalty to Christ and his Word as revealed in the New Testament.

Evangelism and Missions

23. It is the duty of every Christian man and woman, and the duty of every church of Christ, to seek to extend the gospel to the ends of the earth. The new birth of man's spirit by God's Holy Spirit means the birth of love for others. Missionary effort on the part of all rests thus upon a spiritual necessity of the regenerate life. It is also expressly and repeatedly commanded in the teachings of Christ. It is the duty of every child of God to seek constantly to win the lost to Christ by personal effort and by all other methods sanctioned by the Gospel of Christ.

Stewardship

24. God is the source of all blessings, temporal and spiritual; all that we have and are we owe to him. We have a spiritual debtorship to the whole world, a holy trusteeship in the Gospel, and a binding stewardship in our possessions. We are therefore under obligation to serve him with our time, talents and material possessions; and should recognize all these as entrusted to us to use for the glory of God and helping others. Christians should cheer-

fully, regularly, systematically, proportionately, and liberally contribute of their means to advancing the Redeemer's cause on earth.

The Kingdom

25. The Kingdom of God is the reign of God in the heart and life of the individual in every human relationship, and in every form and institution of organized human society. The chief means for promoting the Kingdom of God on earth are preaching the Gospel of Christ, and teaching the principles of righteousness contained therein. The Kingdom of God will be complete when every thought and will of man shall be brought into captivity to the will of Christ. And it is the duty of all Christ's people to pray and labor continually that his Kingdom may come and his will be done on earth as it is in heaven.

Since matters of science have no proper place in a religious confession of faith, and since it is desirable that our attitude towards science be clearly understood, your committee deem it proper to submit the following statement on the relation between science and religion, adopted in 1923 by this Convention at Kansas City, and request that it be published in the minutes of the Convention.

Science and Religion

1. We recognize the greatness and value of the service which modern science is rendering to the cause of truth in uncovering the facts of the natural and the Christian religion. We have no interest or desire in covering up any fact in any realm of research. But we do protest against certain unwarranted procedures on the part of some so-called scientists. First, in making discoveries, or alleged discoveries, in physical nature, a convenient weapon of attack upon the facts of religion; second, using the particular sciences, such as psychology, biology, geology, and various others, as if they necessarily contained knowledge pertaining to the realm of the Christian religion, setting aside the supernatural; third, teaching as facts what are

merely hypotheses. The evolution doctrine has long been a working hypothesis of science, and will probably continue to be, because of its apparent simplicity in explaining the universe. But its best exponents freely admit that the causes of the origin of species have not been traced, nor has any proof been forthcoming that man is not the direct creation of God as recorded in Genesis. We protest against the imposition of this theory upon the minds of our children in denominational, or public schools, as if it were a definite and established truth of science. We insist that this and all other theories be dealt with in a truly scientific way, that is, in careful conformity to established facts.

2. We record again our unwavering adherence to the supernatural elements in the Christian religion. The Bible is God's revelation of himself through men moved by the Holy Spirit, and is our sufficient, certain and authoritative guide in religion. Jesus Christ was born of the Virgin Mary, through the power of the Holy Spirit. He was the divine and eternal Son of God. He wrought miracles, healing the sick, casting out demons, raising the dead. He died as the vicarious, atoning Saviour of the world, and was buried. He arose again from the dead. The tomb was emptied of its contents. In his risen body he appeared many times to his disciples. He ascended to the right hand of the Father. He will come again in person, the same Jesus who ascended from the Mount of Olives.

3. We believe that adherence to the above truths and facts is a necessary condition of service for teachers in our Baptist schools. These facts of Christianity in no way conflict with any fact of science. We do not sit in judgment upon the scientific views of teachers of science. We grant them the same freedom of research in their realm that we claim for ourselves in the religious realm. But we do insist upon a positive content of faith in accordance with the preceding statement as a qualification for acceptable service in Baptist schools. The supreme issue today is between

naturalism and super-naturalism. We stand unalterably for the supernatural in Christianity. Teachers in our schools should be careful to free themselves from any suspicion of disloyalty on this point. In the present period of agitation and unrest they are obligated to make their position clear. We pledge our support to all schools and teachers who are thus loyal to the facts of Christianity as revealed in the Scriptures.

Signed by the Committee,
E. Y. MULLINS, Chairman;
S. M. BROWN,
W. J. McGLOTHLIN,
E. C. DARGAN,
L. R. SCARBOROUGH.

(From *Annual* of the Southern Baptist Convention, 1925, pp. 71-76.)

The Kansas City Confession of 1963

COMMITTEE ON BAPTIST FAITH AND MESSAGE

The 1962 session of the Southern Baptist Convention, meeting in San Francisco, California, adopted the following motion:

"Since the report of the Committee on Statement of Baptist Faith and Message was adopted in 1925, there have been various statements from time to time which have been made, but no overall statement which might be helpful at this time as suggested in Section 2 of that report, or introductory statement which might be used as an interpretation of the 1925 Statement.

"We recommend, therefore, that the president of this Convention be requested to call a meeting of the men now serving as presidents of the various state conventions that would qualify as a member of the Southern Baptist Convention committee under Bylaw 18 to present to the Convention in Kansas City some similar statement which shall serve as information to the churches, and which may serve as guidelines to the various agencies of the Southern Baptist Convention. It is understood that any group or individuals may approach this committee to be of service. The expenses of this committee shall be borne by the Convention Operating Budget."

Your committee thus constituted begs leave to present its report as follows:

Throughout its work your committee has been conscious of the contribution made by the statement of "The Baptist Faith and Message" adopted by the Southern Baptist Convention in 1925. It quotes with approval its affirmation that "Christianity is supernatural in its origin and history. We repudiate every theory of religion which denies the supernatural elements in our faith."

Furthermore, it concurs in the introductory "statement of the historic Baptist conception of the nature and function of confessions of faith in our religious and denominational life. . . ." It is, therefore, quoted in full as a part of this report to the Convention:

"(1) That they constitute a consensus of opinion of some Baptist body, large or small, for the general instruction and guidance of our own people and others concerning those articles of the Christian faith, which are most surely held among us. They are not intended to add anything to the simple conditions of salvation revealed in the New Testament, viz., repentance towards God and faith in Jesus Christ as Saviour and Lord.

"(2) That we do not regard them as complete statements of our faith, having any quality of finality or infallibility. As in the past so in the future, Baptists should hold themselves free to revise their statements of faith as may seem to them wise and expedient at any time.

"(3) That any group of Baptists, large or small, have the inherent right to draw up for themselves and publish to the world a confession of their faith whenever they may think it advisable to do so.

"(4) That the sole authority for faith and practice among Baptists is the Scriptures of the Old and New Testaments. Confessions are only guides in interpretation, having no authority over the conscience.

"(5) That they are statements of religious convictions, drawn from the Scriptures, and are not to be used to hamper freedom of thought or investigation in other realms of life."

The 1925 Statement recommended "the New Hampshire Confession of Faith, revised at certain points, and with some additional articles growing out of certain needs. . . ." Your present committee has adopted the same pattern. It has sought to build upon the structure of the 1925 Statement, keeping in mind the "certain needs" of our generation. At times it has reproduced sections of that Statement without change. In other instances it has substituted words for clarity or added sentences for emphasis. At certain points it has combined articles, with minor changes in wording, to endeavor to relate certain doctrines to each other. In still others—e.g., "God" and "Salvation"—it has sought to bring together certain truths contained throughout the 1925 Statement in order to relate them more clearly and concisely. In no case has it sought to delete from or to add to the basic contents of the 1925 Statement.

Baptists are a people who profess a living faith. This faith is rooted and grounded in Jesus Christ who is "the same yesterday, and to-day, and for ever." Therefore, the sole authority for faith and practice among Baptists is Jesus Christ whose will is revealed in the Holy Scriptures.

A living faith must experience a growing understanding of truth and must be continually interpreted and related to the needs of each new generation. Throughout their history Baptist bodies, both large and small, have issued statements of faith which comprise a consensus of their beliefs. Such statements have never been regarded as complete, infallible statements of faith, nor as official creeds carrying mandatory authority. Thus this generation of Southern Baptists is in historic succession of intent and purpose as it endeavors to state for its time and theological climate those articles of the Christian faith which are most surely held among us.

Baptists emphasize the soul's competency before God, freedom of religion, and the priesthood of the believer. However, this emphasis should not be interpreted to mean that there is an absence of certain definite doctrines that Baptists believe, cherish, and with which they have been and are now closely identified.

It is the purpose of this statement of faith and message to set forth certain teachings which we believe.

I. THE SCRIPTURES

The Holy Bible was written by men divinely inspired and is the record of God's revelation of Himself to man. It is a perfect treasure of divine instruction. It has God for its author, salvation for its end, and truth, without any mixture of error, for its matter. It reveals the principles by which God judges us; and therefore is, and will remain to the end of the world, the true center of Christian union, and the supreme standard by which all human conduct, creeds, and religious opinions should be tried. The criterion by which the Bible is to be interpreted is Jesus Christ.

. . . .

II. GOD

There is one and only one living and true God. He is an intelligent, spiritual, and personal Being, the Creator, Redeemer, Preserver, and Ruler of the universe. God is infinite in holiness and all other perfections. To him we owe the highest love, reverence, and obedience. The eternal God reveals Himself to us as Father, Son, and Holy Spirit, with distinct personal attributes, but without division of nature, essence, or being.

1. God the Father

God as Father reigns with providential care over His universe, His creatures, and

the flow of the stream of human history according to the purpose of His grace. He is all powerful, all loving, and all wise. God is Father in truth to those who become children of God through faith in Jesus Christ. He is fatherly in his attitude toward all men.

. . . .

2. God the Son

Christ is the eternal Son of God. In His incarnation as Jesus Christ He was conceived of the Holy Spirit and born of the virgin Mary. Jesus perfectly revealed and did the will of God, taking upon Himself the demands and necessities of human nature and identifying Himself completely with mankind yet without sin. He honored the divine law by His personal obedience, and in His death on the cross He made provision for the redemption of men from sin. He was raised from the dead with a glorified body and appeared to His disciples as the person who was with them before His crucifixion. He ascended into heaven and is now exalted at the right hand of God where He is the One Mediator, partaking of the nature of God and of man, and in whose Person is effected the reconciliation between God and man. He will return in power and glory to judge the world and to consummate His redemptive mission. He now dwells in all believers as the living and ever present Lord.

. . . .

3. God the Holy Spirit

The Holy Spirit is the Spirit of God. He inspired holy men of old to write the Scriptures. Through illumination He enables men to understand truth. He exalts Christ. He convicts of sin, of righteousness and of judgment. He calls men to the Saviour, and effects regeneration. He cultivates Christian character, comforts believers and bestows the spiritual gifts by which they serve God through His church. He seals the believer unto the day of final redemption. His presence in the Christian is the assurance of God to bring the believer into the fulness of the stature of Christ. He enlightens and empowers the believer and the church in worship, evangelism, and service.

. . . .

III. MAN

Man was created by the special act of God, in His own image, and is the crowning work of His creation. In the beginning man was innocent of sin and was endowed by His Creator with freedom of choice. By his free choice man sinned against God and brought sin into the human race. Through the temptation of Satan man transgressed the command of God, and fell from his original innocence; whereby his posterity inherit a nature and an environment inclined toward sin, and as they are capable of moral action become transgressors and are under condemnation. Only the grace of God can bring man into His holy fellowship and enable man to fulfil the creative purpose of God. The sacredness of human personality is evident in that God created man in His own image, and in that Christ died for man; therefore every man possesses dignity and is worthy of respect and Christian love.

. . . .

IV. SALVATION

Salvation involves the redemption of the whole man, and is offered freely to all who accept Jesus Christ as Lord and Saviour, who by His own blood obtained eternal redemption for the believer. In its broadest sense salvation includes regeneration, sanctification, and glorification.

1. Regeneration, or the new birth, is a work of God's grace whereby believers become new creatures in Christ Jesus. It is a change of heart wrought by the Holy Spirit through conviction of sin, to which the sinner responds in repentance toward God and faith in the Lord Jesus Christ.

Repentance and faith are inseparable experiences of grace. Repentance is a genuine turning from sin toward God. Faith is the acceptance of Jesus Christ and commitment of the entire personality to Him as Lord and Saviour. Justification is God's gracious and full acquittal upon principles of His righteousness of all sinners who repent and believe in Christ. Justification brings the believer into a relationship of peace and favor with God.

2. Sanctification is the experience, beginning in regeneration, by which the believer is set apart to God's purposes, and is enabled to progress toward moral and spiritual perfection through the presence and power of the Holy Spirit dwelling in him. Growth in grace should continue throughout the regenerate person's life.

3. Glorification is the culmination of salvation and is the final blessed and abiding state of the redeemed.

. . . .

V. GOD'S PURPOSE OF GRACE

Election is the gracious purpose of God, according to which He regenerates, sanctifies, and glorifies sinners. It is consistent with the free agency of man and comprehends all the means in connection with the end. It is a glorious display of God's sovereign goodness, and is infinitely wise, holy, and unchangeable. It excludes boasting and promotes humility.

All true believers endure to the end. Those whom God has accepted in Christ, and sanctified by His Spirit, will never fall away from the state of grace, but shall persevere to the end. Believers may fall into sin through neglect and temptation, whereby they grieve the Spirit, impair their graces and comforts, bring reproach on the cause of Christ, and temporal judgments on themselves, yet they shall be kept by the power of God through faith unto salvation.

. . . .

VI. THE CHURCH

A New Testament church of the Lord Jesus Christ is a local body of baptized believers who are associated by covenant in the faith and fellowship of the gospel, observing the two ordinances of Christ, committed to His teachings, exercising the gifts, rights, and privileges invested in them by His Word, and seeking to extend the gospel to the ends of the earth.

This church is an autonomous body, operating through democratic processes under the Lordship of Jesus Christ. In such a congregation, members are equally responsible. Its Scriptural officers are pastors and deacons.

The New Testament speaks also of the church as the body of Christ which includes all the redeemed of all the ages.

•   •   •   •   •   •   •   •   •   •   •

VII. BAPTISM AND THE LORD'S SUPPER

Christian baptism is the immersion of a believer in water in the name of the Father, the Son, and the Holy Spirit. It is an act of obedience symbolizing the believer's faith in a crucified, buried, and risen Saviour, the believer's death to sin, the burial of the old life, and the resurrection to walk in newness of life in Christ Jesus. It is a testimony to his faith in the final resurrection of the dead. Being a church ordinance, it is prerequisite to the privileges of church membership and to the Lord's Supper.

The Lord's Supper is a symbolic act of obedience whereby members of the church, through partaking of the bread and the fruit of the vine, memorialize the death of the Redeemer and anticipate His second coming.

•   •   •   •   •   •   •   •   •   •   •

VIII. THE LORD'S DAY

The first day of the week is the Lord's Day. It is a Christian institution for regular observance. It commemorates the resurrection of Christ from the dead and should be employed in exercises of worship and spiritual devotion, both public and private, and by refraining from worldly amusements, and resting from secular employments, work of necessity and mercy only being excepted.

•   •   •   •   •   •   •   •   •   •   •

IX. THE KINGDOM

The kingdom of God includes both His general sovereignty over the universe and His particular kingship over men who willfully acknowledge Him as King. Particular-

ly the kingdom is the realm of salvation into which men enter by trustful, childlike commitment to Jesus Christ. Christians ought to pray and to labor that the kingdom may come and God's will be done on earth. The full consummation of the kingdom awaits the return of Jesus Christ and the end of this age.

•   •   •   •   •   •   •   •   •   •   •

X. LAST THINGS

God, in His own time and in His own way, will bring the world to its appropriate end. According to His promise, Jesus Christ will return personally and visibly in glory to the earth; the dead will be raised; and Christ will judge all men in righteousness. The unrighteous will be consigned to hell, the place of everlasting punishment. The righteous in their resurrected and glorified bodies will receive their reward and will dwell forever in heaven with the Lord.

•   •   •   •   •   •   •   •   •   •   •

XI. EVANGELISM AND MISSIONS

It is the duty and privilege of every follower of Christ and of every church of the Lord Jesus Christ to endeavor to make disciples of all nations. The new birth of man's spirit by God's Holy Spirit means the birth of love for others. Missionary effort on the part of all rests thus upon a spiritual necessity of the regenerate life, and is expressly and repeatedly commanded in the teachings of Christ. It is the duty of every child of God to seek constantly to win the lost of God to Christ by personal effort and by all other methods in harmony with the gospel of Christ.

•   •   •   •   •   •   •   •   •   •   •

XII. EDUCATION

The cause of education in the kingdom of Christ is co-ordinate with the causes of missions and general benevolence and should receive along with these the liberal support of the churches. An adequate system of Christian schools is necessary to a complete spiritual program for Christ's people.

In Christian education there should be a proper balance between academic freedom and academic responsibility. Freedom in any orderly relationship of human life is always limited and never absolute. The freedom of a teacher in a Christian school, college, or seminary is limited by the pre-eminence of Jesus Christ, by the authoritative nature of the Scriptures, and by the distinct purpose for which the school exists.

. . . .

XIII. STEWARDSHIP

God is the source of all blessings, temporal and spiritual; all that we have and are we owe to Him. Christians have a spiritual debtorship to the whole world, a holy trusteeship in the gospel, and a binding stewardship in their possessions. They are therefore under obligation to serve Him with their time, talents, and material possessions; and should recognize all these as entrusted to them to use for the glory of God and for helping others. According to the Scriptures, Christians should contribute of their means cheerfully, regularly, systematically, proportionately, and liberally for the advancement of the Redeemer's cause on earth.

. . . .

XIV. CO-OPERATION

Christ's people should, as occasion requires, organize such associations and conventions as may best secure co-operation for the great objects of the kingdom of God. Such organizations have no authority over one another or over the churches. They are voluntary and advisory bodies designed to elicit, combine, and direct the energies of our people in the most effective manner. Members of New Testament churches should co-operate with one another in carrying forward the missionary, educational, and benevolent ministries for the extension of Christ's kingdom. Christian unity in the New Testament sense is spiritual harmony and voluntary co-operation for common ends by various groups of Christ's people. Co-operation is desirable between the various Christian denominations, when the end to be attained is itself justified, and when such co-operation in-

volves no violation of conscience or compromise of loyalty to Christ and his Word as revealed in the New Testament.

. . . .

XV. THE CHRISTIAN AND THE SOCIAL ORDER

Every Christian is under obligation to seek to make the will of Christ supreme in his own life and human society. Means and methods used for the improvement of society and the establishment of righteousness among men can be truly and permanently helpful only when they are rooted in the regeneration of the individual by the saving grace of God in Christ Jesus. The Christian should oppose in the spirit of Christ every form of greed, selfishness, and vice. He should work to provide for the orphaned, the needy, the aged, the helpless, and the sick. Every Christian should seek to bring industry, government, and society as a whole under the sway of the principles of righteousness, truth, and brotherly love. In order to promote these ends Christians should be ready to work with all men of good will in any good cause, always being careful to act in the spirit of love without compromising their loyalty to Christ and his truth.

. . . .

XVI. PEACE AND WAR

It is the duty of Christians to seek peace with all men on principles of righteousness. In accordance with the spirit and teachings of Christ they should do all in their power to put an end to war.

The true remedy for the war spirit is the gospel of our Lord. The supreme need of the world is the acceptance of His teachings in all the affairs of man and nations, and the practical application of His law of love.

. . . .

XVII. RELIGIOUS LIBERTY

God alone is Lord of the conscience, and He has left it free from the doctrines and commandments of men which are contrary to His Word or not contained in it. Church and state should be separate. The state owes to every church protection and full freedom in the pursuit of its spiritual ends. In providing for such freedom no ecclesiastical group or denomination should be favored by the state more than others. Civil government being ordained of God, it is the duty of Christians to render loyal obedience thereto in all things not contrary to the revealed will of God. The church should not resort to the civil power to carry on its work. The gospel of Christ contemplates spiritual means alone for the pursuit of its ends. The state has no right to impose penalties for religious opinions of any kind. The state has no right to impose taxes for the support of any form of religion. A free church in a free state is the Christian ideal, and this implies the right of free and unhindered access to God on the part of all men and the right to form and propagate opinions in the sphere of religion without interference by the civil power.

(From *Annual* of the Southern Baptist Convention, 1963, pp. 269-81.)

Section Six

Pronouncements of the Convention

Invitation by World Council of Churches

An invitation was extended to the Southern Baptist Convention in 1939 to join the World Council of Churches.

1. The report of the committee

To the World Council of Churches

Dear Brethren:

The invitation to the Southern Baptist Convention to accept membership in the World Council of Churches was received by the President of the Convention, and by him reported to the annual meeting of the Convention at Oklahoma City in May, 1939. A special committee of thirteen was appointed to consider the invitation and to make recommendations as to the answer that should be made by the Convention to your invitation.

First of all, we would express to you our sincere and grateful appreciation for the courtesy and Christian spirit expressed in your communication. Directly replying to your invitation, permit us to advise that the Southern Baptist Convention is a voluntary association of Baptists for the purpose of eliciting, combining and directing the energies of our denomination in missionary activity at home and abroad, and in educational and benevolent work throughout the world. Our Convention has no ecclesiological authority. It is in no sense the Southern Baptist Church. The thousands of churches to which our Convention looks for support of its missionary, benevolent and educational program, cherish their independence and would disapprove of any attempted exercise of ecclesiastical authority over them.

In a world which more and more seeks centralization of power in industry, in civil government, and in religion, we are sensible of the dangers of totalitarian trends which threaten the autonomy of all free churches. We wish to do nothing that will imperil the growing spirit of co-operating on the part of our churches in the work of giving the gospel of Christ, as we understand it, to all men everywhere. In the light of these considerations, we feel impelled to decline the invitation to membership in the World Council of Churches.

In conclusion, permit us to express the sincere desire of our hearts that the followers of Christ may all be one, not necessarily in name and in a world organization, but in spiritual fellowship with the Father and the Son. If Christ dwells in all our hearts by faith, we shall be brought into a spiritual unity that cannot be broken. We invoke the blessings of the triune God upon all who name the name of our Lord Jesus Christ.

GEORGE W. TRUETT, *Chairman.*

(From *Annual* of the Southern Baptist Convention, 1940, p. 99.)

2. A minority report

Ryland Knight, Georgia, offered the following request for rising vote:

The undersigned have the utmost respect for and confidence in the Committee which has just submitted its report. We believe however we represent a considerable number in our Convention who do not wish to precipitate a debate but who find themselves unable to agree to the report.

While we are fundamentally opposed to any step toward organic church union we are convinced that the basic spiritual unity of all believers should have a channel through which to give united expression to the mind and message of Christ in a world in which all Christian ideals are challenged.

In justice to our own consciences, and on behalf of those who hold with us, we wish to express our conviction that Southern Baptists, along with other Baptist groups, should associate ourselves with our brethren of other denominations "in a fellowship of churches which accept our Lord Jesus Christ as God and Saviour."

We request that a rising vote be taken on the report of the Committee in order that by standing we may register our conviction.

(Ibid., pp. 99-100.)

Relationship between the Convention and other Baptist bodies

According to instructions of the Convention, we submit the following statement of principles:

The relations between this Convention and other Baptist bodies can be understood in the light of a few basic New Testament principles, as follows:

The primary and fundamental principle is the direct relation of the individual soul to Jesus Christ as Saviour and Lord. To his own Master every Christian stands or falls.

All Christian relationships are free and voluntary. To become a Christian is not to be coerced into obedience to Christ, but to choose him voluntarily and freely. Christ's authority is accepted as final for the believer in all things when he is thus chosen freely as Lord and Saviour.

The relations of the believer with other Christians are also free and voluntary and subject only to the authority of Jesus Christ.

A church of Christ is a free and voluntary association of believers, in his name, in obedience to his command, and for the carrying out of his purposes.

It follows that each church is autonomous or self-determining in all matters pertaining to its own life and activities. . . .

All Baptist general bodies are voluntary organizations, established by individuals who wish to cooperate for some common end or ends in the kingdom of God. . . . Churches may seek to fulfill their obligation to exende Christ's kingdom by cooperating with these general organizations, but always on a purely voluntary basis, and without surrendering in any way or degree their right of self-determination. These associations, unions, or conventions vary greatly in form, in size, in purpose, in territorial extent and in conditions of membership. But they are all similar to churches in the fundamental principle of their organization and life in that each is independent of all others in its own work, free, fraternal, autonomous, or self-determining in its own sphere and activities.

The principle of cooperation between individuals and churches and general bodies in pursuit of great common ends is also a basic teaching of the gospel. . . .

The powers of Baptist general bodies are never legislative, but always advisory in their relations to churches, and to each other.

The cooperation of Baptist general bodies with each other may be desirable from time to time for the sake of greater economy and efficiency. But there are dangers connected with such cooperation due to misunderstanding, confusion of thinking, and sometimes to trespassing upon the rights of cooperating bodies by one or other of the parties to the arrangement.

One of the present danger points is the cooperative relations between the Southern Baptist Convention and the various state conventions. This Convention disclaims all authority over state convention, but wishes to define its own functions and activities in relation to state bodies. The following points should be stressed:

1. The cooperative relations between this Convention and state bodies as now established are limited to the one matter of collecting funds for Southwide and state objects in conjunction with a unified appeal for the objects. The state convention boards are at present recognized by this Convention as collecting agencies for Southwide as well as for state funds. This arrangement, however, is not an essential in Baptist organization, but is made simply as a matter of convenience and economy, and may be changed at any time.

2. The fact that the state bodies first handle the funds and are more directly related to the churches in the matter of collections does not alter the basic relations involved. For the practical ends in view this Convention cooperates in the unified appeal for funds through state agencies. But in principle it retains as inalienable and inherent the right to direct appeal to the churches. Furthermore, in all matters other than money raising it retains complete control of its own affairs, with the right to fix its own objectives and to determine the amounts of money allocated to its various objects.

3. The power of appointing the members of all committees and boards of this Convention resides in the Convention itself. When it is desirable that states, as such, or other territorial subdivisions of this Convention's area, be represented on the boards or committees of this Convention, this arrangement can easily be effected by consultation with the respective groups involved. But the power to appoint directly or to nominate the members of its own committees and boards must be retained.

4. The practice of careful discrimination and mutual respect as between the state

bodies and this Convention is called for. The main functions of this Convention and of state bodies remain inviolable. Neither body may impose its will upon the other in any manner or degree at any time. Conference and discussion between committees of the respective groups are always proper in regard to matters involved in joint effort and in so far as necessary to promote good will and mutual understanding. As the work is at present conducted such matters are the division of funds into state and Southwide, ways and means of promoting interest in the various causes, and the burden of cost of collections to be apportioned to state and Southwide funds. These are all matters involved in the one matter of joint effort; viz., the collection of money. In all other matters this Convention pursues its own objects in its own way. . . .

5. The observance of the above principles by this Convention and by state bodies is essential to the integrity and perpetuity of this Convention. . . .

6. It is important that the Executive Committee of this Convention receive instructions to conduct all negotiations with representatives of state or other bodies necessary to clarify relations and bring about a satisfactory adjustment, with a view to complete and hearty cooperation in all matters of common interest.

(From *Annual* of the Southern Baptist Convention, 1928, pp. 32-33.)

Statement on interdenominational relations

Last year the matter of making a reaffirmation of the Baptist position as held by Southern Baptists on interdenominational movements and relations was referred to a committee to report this year. This is our report:

1. We look with deep and sympathetic interest on the widespread desire and passion for Christian unity. We deplore all hurtful divisions existing among the disciples of Christ. We long for the union of all believers for which Christ prayed. We

shall pray and labor for it on a Scriptural basis; but we insist that it cannot and should not be obtained on any other basis.

2. We hold the immemorial position of Baptists, that all true believers in Christ as their personal Saviour, are saved, having been born again; and this, without the intervention of preacher, priest, ordinance, sacrament, or church. Therefore, we profoundly rejoice in our spiritual union with all who love the Lord Jesus in sincerity and truth. We hold them as brothers in the saving grace of Christ, and heirs with us of life and immortality. We love their fellowship, and maintain that the spiritual union of all believers is now and ever will be a blessed reality. This spiritual union does not depend on organizations, or forms. . . .

3. We here declare our unalterable belief in the universal, unchangeable, and undelegated sovereignty of Jesus Christ. . . .

4. Concerning the church, it seems to us that this is a divine institution; that it was not evolved from the changing conditions of society, but came from the mind of the Master; that it is an enduring institution, adapted as well to one time and one climate as another; that it is the custodian of the truth, to hold and teach it to the end of time and to all the peoples of the earth. It is a Scriptural body, with a divine constitution and mission, both of which are revealed in the New Testament. We believe that a church of Jesus Christ is a pure democracy, and cannot subject itself to any outside control, nor bend to a superior clergy. We also hold, with unshaken confidence, to the age-long contention of Baptists, that there must be absolute separation between church and state; and that the right of civil and religious liberty is, in the sight of God, the inalienable and indefeasible right of every human being. We maintain that the divine constitution of a church of Christ cannot be changed in order to effect organic, Christian union. . . .

5. We believe that intelligent, personal conviction in religion is essential to strength in Christian character and to success in any form of Christian work. It must be the working force in any Christian union. Our souls abhor the thought of any union inspired by convenience or by desire to save money. . . . To us it appears far more consistent and Christian, to appeal to the individual conscience to study the Word of God with openheartedness, and to follow the light that may therein be found. Any union founded on compromise and spurious appeals is a sham union, and will debilitate and retard the progress of Christianity the world over. Any such union must inevitably end in a wide apostasy, followed by inertia, indefiniteness, confusion and waste of spiritual force.

6. We would issue a fraternal warning to our brethren of every communion of the danger of a man-made union. It would constitute a powerful monopoly fraught with many possible perils for the world. . . .

7. Our message to our brethren of other communions is that since the present divided condition of Christendom is unquestionably the result of departures from the simple teaching of the Scriptures, the only possible road to organic union is back to the Scriptures, fairly interpreted. . . .

8. Pending the working out of the problem of union we are glad to say that we stand ready at all times to co-operate with all our fellow Christians and our fellow citizens, whether Protestant or Catholic, whether Jew or Gentile, in every worthy effort for the moral and social uplift of humanity, as well as for the equal civil and religious rights of all men in all lands. . . .

We beg to say this other word to our brethren of other communions. We cherish in our hearts a deep and abiding Christian love for all our fellow believers in Christ, whether in or out of other bodies, and gratefully rejoice in all that they are doing for the salvation of the lost of the earth. . . .

(From *Annual* of the Southern Baptist Convention, 1938, pp. 24-25.)

Index

FROM THE LIBRARY OF
ROBERT LORAN FORD